GROWING PAINS

Eric G. Flamholtz
with the assistance of
Yvonne Randle

GROWING PAINS

How to Make the Transition
from an
Entrepreneurship
to a
Professionally Managed Firm

Jossey-Bass Publishers

San Francisco   •   Oxford   •   1990

GROWING PAINS
How to Make the Transition from an Entrepreneurship to a
Professionally Managed Firm
  by Eric G. Flamholtz

Copyright © 1990 by: Jossey-Bass Inc., Publishers
                    350 Sansome Street
                    San Francisco, California 94104
                              &
                    Jossey-Bass Limited
                    Headington Hill Hall
                    Oxford OX3 0BW

Library of Congress Cataloging-in-Publication Data

Flamholtz, Eric G.
    Growing pains : how to make the transition from an
  entrepreneurship to a professionally managed firm / Eric G.
  Flamholtz : with the assistance of Yvonne Randle. — Rev. ed.
        p.   cm.—(The Jossey-Bass management series)
    Includes bibliographical references and index.
    ISBN 1-55542-272-1
    1. New business enterprises—Management. 2. Organizational
  change. I. Randle, Yvonne. II. Title. III. Series.
  HD62.5.F535   1990
  658.4′063—dc20   90-53088
                                                  CIP

Manufactured in the United States of America

The paper in this book meets the guidelines for
permanence and durability of the Committee on
Production Guidelines for Book Longevity of the
Council on Library Resources.

JACKET DESIGN BY FIFTH STREET DESIGN

REVISED EDITION

Code 9090

The Jossey-Bass Management Series

Contents

Tables, Figures, and Exhibits   xv

Preface   xix

Acknowledgments   xxxi

The Author   xxxv

Introduction: The Transitions Needed to Keep
a Growing Firm Successful   1

Custom Printing Corporation: An Entrepreneurial
Case Study • The Onset of "Growing Pains" •
Recognizing the Need for a Transition • Making
the Transition: Phase I • Making the Transition:
Phases II and III • Making the Transition: Phase
IV • Summary

**Part One: A Framework for Developing Successful
Organizations**   11

The First Challenge for Entrepreneurs • The
Second Challenge for Entrepreneurs • Making an
Organizational Transition

1. How to Build Successful Companies: The Pyramid of
Organizational Development   17

Six Key Organizational Development Tasks • The
Pyramid of Organizational Development •

Successfully Building the Pyramid: The Example of
IBM • Summary

2. Identifying and Surviving the First Four Stages
of Organizational Growth   32

Stages of Organizational Growth • Differences
Between Entrepreneurial and Professional
Management • Discrepancies Between Growth
and Organizational Development • Managing the
Transition Between Growth Stages • Managing
the Transition: Humana Versus Maxicare •
Summary

3. Recognizing Growing Pains and Assessing
the Need for Change   53

The Ten Most Common Organizational Growing
Pains • Measuring Organizational Growing
Pains • Organizational Growing Pains, Growth
Rates, and Infrastructure • Summary

**Part Two: Management Strategies for Each Stage of
Organizational Growth**   **71**

4. The New Venture and Expansion Stages   73

Developing Successful Stage I Organizations •
Keys to a Successful Stage I Firm • Developing
Successful Stage II Organizations • Keys to a
Successful Stage II Firm • Managing the New
Venture and Expansion Stages: A Comparison of
Osborne and Compaq • Summary

5. The Professionalizing Stage: Developing
Management Systems   90

Developing a Successful Stage III Organization •
Developing a Successful Stage III Organization: The
Case of Metro Realty • Other Examples of Success

with Professionalization • Keys to a Successful
Stage III Firm • Conclusion

6. The Consolidation Stage: Managing the
    Corporate Culture   119

    Developing Successful Stage IV Organizations •
    Tempo Products Unlimited: Background •
    Elements of TPU's Culture and Their Attenuation
    • Redefining a Culture • The New TPU Culture
    and Its Implementation • Keys to a Successful
    Stage IV Firm • Conclusion

    **Part Three: Mastering the Tools of
    Professional Management**   147

7. Strategic Planning   153

    The Nature of Strategic Planning • Strategic
    Issues • The Strategic Planning Process • Metro
    Realty: Development of a Strategic Plan • Ongoing
    Functions of Strategic Planning • Strategic
    Planning at Different Stages of Organizational
    Growth • A Final Note: Consultants and Strategic
    Planning Departments • Summary

8. Organizational Structure   184

    Nature of Organizational Structure • Alternative
    Forms of Organizational Structure • Criteria for
    Design and Evaluation of Organizational
    Structure • Organizational Structure Analysis
    • Case Studies of Organizational Structure •
    Organizational Structure at Different Stages of
    Growth • Summary

9. Management Development   212

    The Nature of Management Development •
    Functions of Management Development •
    Management Development Required at Different

Organizational Levels • Critical Dimensions of
Management Development • Knapp
Communications Corporation: Management
Development in the Transition to Professional
Management • Objectives of KCC's Management
Development Program • Nature of the Program
• Impact of the Program • Management
Development at Different Stages of Organizational
Growth • Investment in Management
Development • Summary

10. Organizational Control Systems   240

The Nature of Organizational Control • Tasks of
Control Systems • Design of Organizational
Control Systems • Superior Alarm Systems: Case
Study • Control Systems at Different Stages of
Organizational Growth • Conclusion

11. Effective Leadership   263

The Nature of Leadership • Styles of
Leadership • Factors Influencing Choice of
Leadership Style • Leadership Theories • Two
Sets of Effective Leadership Tasks • Key Tasks of
Strategic Leadership • Key Tasks of Operational
Leadership • Case Studies of Leadership •
Effective Leadership at Different Stages of
Organizational Growth • Summary

12. Corporate Culture Management   289

The Nature of Corporate Culture • The Impact of
Corporate Culture on Organizational Success • Real
Versus Nominal Corporate Culture •
Manifestations of Corporate Culture • How
Corporate Culture Changes • How to Manage
Your Corporate Culture • Corporate Culture at
Different Stages of Organizational Development •
Conclusion

Contents

**Part Four: Role of the Entrepreneur in a Growing
and Changing Company**   319

13. Managing the Advanced Stages of Growth:
A Preview of Future Challenges   321

    Nature of Problems Beyond Stage IV • The Stages
    of Growth Beyond Stage IV • Managing
    Transitions at Stages V through VII • The Special
    Challenge of Revitalization • Summary

14. The Transition CEOs Must Make to Survive
Beyond the Entrepreneurial Stage   343

    Personal Issues • Organizational Issues •
    Managing Organizational Transitions: A Capstone
    Case • Some Final Thoughts for the CEO •
    Some Thoughts for the Associates of a CEO •
    Summary

    Annotated References: Key Resources for
    Further Information   375

    Endnotes   391

    Index   397

Tables, Figures, and Exhibits

Chapter 1

Figure 1.1   Pyramid of Organizational
Development   19

Chapter 2

Table 2.1   Stages of Organizational Growth   33

Figure 2.1   Developmental Emphasis in a Stage I
Firm   36

Figure 2.2   Developmental Emphasis in a Stage II
Firm   39

Figure 2.3   Developmental Emphasis in a Stage III
Firm   41

Figure 2.4   Developmental Emphasis in a Stage IV
Firm   43

Table 2.2   Comparison of Professional
Management and Entrepreneurial
Management   45

Figure 2.5   Causes of Organizational Growing
Pains   48

Chapter 3

Exhibit 3.1   Organizational Growing Pains
Questionnaire   63

Table 3.1   Interpretation of Organizational
Growing Pains Questionnaire Scores   65

Table 3.2   Organizational Growing Pains by
             Company Size   66
Table 3.3   Organizational Growing Pains in
             Different Industries   66

                      Chapter 5

Table 5.1   Metro Realty Organizational
             Development Program: Contents and
             Schedule   100
Table 5.2   The "Old" and the "New" Metro   106

                      Part Three

Figure III.1 The Management System   150

                      Chapter 7

Figure 7.1   Flow Diagram of the Five Key Phases in
              the Strategic Planning Process   160
Table 7.1   Elements of the Business Plan   165
Figure 7.2   Flow Diagram of Steps in the Planning
              Process   170
Figure 7.3   Metro Realty: Alternative Concepts of
              Business   172
Table 7.2   Planning Steps and Related Questions   173
Exhibit 7.1   Action Plan for Metro Realty's
              Management Development Program   177

                      Chapter 8

Figure 8.1   Functional Organizational Structure   187
Figure 8.2   Prefunctional Organizational Structure:
              Plastic Molding Corporation   188
Figure 8.3   Divisional Organizational Structure:
              InfoEnterprises   191
Figure 8.4   Matrix Organizational Structure:
              Ultraspace Corporation   193

Figure 8.5   Organizational Hierarchy   195
Figure 8.6   Organizational Structure of Design
                Corporation (Managerial Strengths in
                Parentheses)   203

Chapter 9

Figure 9.1   Pyramid of Management Development
                Skills   221
Table 9.1   Critical Aspects of Management
                Development Transitions   226

Chapter 10

Figure 10.1   Model of Organizational Control
                Systems   246
Exhibit 10.1   Control Model's Application in
                Manufacturing Plant   250

Chapter 11

Figure 11.1   Continuum of Leadership Styles   265
Figure 11.2   Factors Affecting Choice of Leadership
                Style   272

Chapter 12

Table 12.1   Nominal Versus Real Culture: An
                Example   297
Table 12.2   Example of Entrepreneurial and
                Professional Cultures   306
Table 12.3   Stories and Their Elements   308

Chapter 13

Table 13.1   Advanced Stages of Organizational
                Growth   323

Chapter 14

Table 14.1   Management Systems at Different
                  Stages of Growth   350
Table 14.2   Organizational Characteristics During
                  Each Stage of Growth   351
Exhibit 14.1   Sample Questions for Organizational
                  Audit   354

Preface

This book is the result of the widespread growth of entrepreneur-ship throughout the United States as well as other nations. It deals not only with the establishment of new ventures but with what happens to companies after they have had an initial period (perhaps many years or even decades) of success. The term *entrepreneurship* can refer to an organizational type or to a process and we will treat it as both in this book

As entrepreneurship has increased throughout the economy during the past few years, a large number of remarkable entrepre-neurial successes have occurred. Companies in areas as diverse as pizza, computers, women's fashion, chocolate chip cookies, bioen-gineering, printing, publishing, distribution, and real estate, to cite just a few, have flourished. Some entrepreneurships—including Ap-ple Computer, Liz Claiborne, Mrs. Fields' Cookies, Federal Express, and Domino's Pizza—have become spectacular successes and house-hold names. Many more relatively unknown firms have also been very successful.

However, a significant number of entrepreneurial ventures have failed. Some firms, after a brilliant start, merely lose their luster. Others that exhibit initial meteoric success experience equally meteoric failure. Some entrepreneurial failures, such as Os-borne Computer and People Express, have been well publicized, but the majority are more private disappointments.

In many cases, despite the success or the failure of the overall enterprise, there has been a high degree of turnover among the founders of entrepreneurial companies. Some of the best-known cases of entrepreneurial founders who were later replaced include Steven Jobs and Jack Tramiel. Steven Jobs of Apple Computer gave way to John Sculley, who was brought in from Pepsico to help

professionalize the company. Jack Tramiel resigned from Commodore International, apparently responding to similar circumstances.
A company spokesman said that Tramiel and other people in the
organization wanted the company to have more discipline and
structure and that Tramiel felt this could happen only if he stepped
down.

Many founders have also faced problems in turning their
companies over to the next family generation. For example, Frederick Wang, son of An Wang, who was the founder of Wang Laboratories, resigned as president and chief operations officer in 1989
after the firm had experienced a number of years of declining profits
as well as deterioration of its overall market position. Frederick
Wang, then thirty-eight years old and a seventeen-year veteran at
Wang, was unable to repeat the initial success of his father.

A pattern emerges in what happened at Apple, Commodore,
Osborne, Wang, and many other entrepreneurial companies. In
brief, all these firms and their founders faced the need to make a
transition from an entrepreneurship to a more "professionally managed organization." All of them had reached a stage in their development that required a more sophisticated level of management and
organizational capabilities to continue to be successful. The management approach and support systems that had been appropriate
for the companies at the earlier stages of their development were
now a limitation rather than a strength. In other words, as we will
point out throughout this book, these companies as well as many
others had simply outgrown the very "management systems" that
had promoted their earlier success.

The new stage of development required that the company become a professionally managed firm. This meant making a transition
from a situation in which management and operational systems
could be accomplished informally to one in which management had
to receive significant attention and emphasis. In the early stages of
development, all that was required for initial success was a successful
product or service. As the company grew, however, its success required more planning, organization, systems, and, in essence, a different way of management. The earlier, informal new-venture-stage
approach was, quite simply, outgrown as a foundation for future
growth and development. Companies in this situation must make a

transition to a new system of management, one that is still entrepreneurially oriented but is more proactively managed—a professionally managed firm.

In a professionally managed firm, the founders do not necessarily have to step aside and bring in "professional managers," as Steven Jobs did with John Sculley at Apple. But the organization must now adopt some of the tools and strategies of professional management, while simultaneously retaining its entrepreneurial spirit.

Unfortunately, although all of the founders of the firms cited earlier had the skills and temperament to establish a successful entrepreneurship, not all of them possessed the very different skills, behavioral patterns, and will necessary to take the firm to the next stage of development. Adam Osborne, one of the most famous of entrepreneurs who experienced this phenomenon, seemed to understand it in retrospect. In reflecting on what had happened to Osborne Computer, Osborne said the firm "had existed only eighteen months in terms of operation—hardly time to get my feet wet; all of a sudden the job was a whole different order of magnitude. I realized it was no longer an entrepreneurial operation in any conceivable way."[1] The company had needed to change from what it had been during its initial period of rapid growth and success. Yet, the required transition had not been made and, consequently, the company ultimately failed.

Intended Audience

This book is addressed principally to the owners, managers, and employees of entrepreneurial companies; to investors, bankers, and venture capitalists; and to students and scholars of management who are interested in the success and failure of entrepreneurships. It focuses on the question of why, after successful or even brilliant beginnings, entrepreneurial companies often lose their way. More important, it explains what all companies—but especially those at the entrepreneurial stage—must do to be successful as they grow and describes the transitions they must make to survive. Case studies of entrepreneurial companies at different stages of growth, drawn from a wide variety of industries, are included to illustrate different aspects of the transitions that must be made. They also show how the framework provided in this book can be used as a conceptual map of what needs to be done by an organization at each developmental stage. In addition, the book specifies the adjustments the founder or chief executive officer of an entrepreneurial company needs to make so that he or she can grow with the organization and not be left behind, as Steven Jobs and Adam Osborne were.

The book is also addressed to those interested not only in entrepreneurships but in established companies as well. Although it has been positioned primarily to assist in helping managers and scholars understand the problems and processes related to managing the transition from an entrepreneurship to a professionally managed firm, the underlying framework and content are applicable to all organizations. Specifically, the book is based on two different but related conceptual frameworks: (1) an *organizational effectiveness model* and (2) an *organizational life cycle model*. The organizational effectiveness model, termed the *pyramid of organizational development* (discussed in Chapter One) explains the variables that must be managed by companies to give them the optimal (most likely) chance of long-term success. The life cycle model (discussed in Chapter Two and at greater length in Chapter Thirteen) identifies seven stages of growth from a new venture (corporate birth) to an established organization in decline and requiring revitalization. The book can, therefore, be viewed as providing a comprehensive framework for managing a company throughout its life-cycle but especially as focusing on the stages of growth after its inception and until it reaches maturity as a professionally managed firm.

The book is also appropriate for those companies that think of themselves as "professionally managed" but have begun to lose some of their momentum and may even have lost their entrepreneurial spirit. It can show them what has to be done to make the transition to a professionally managed firm rather than a bureaucracy. Accordingly, we will cite examples ranging from relatively small new ventures and medium-sized companies to very large organizations such as IBM.

Entrepreneurship Versus Professional Management

The basic theme of the book, as indicated by its title, is how to make the successful transition from an entrepreneurship to a professionally managed firm. Some people may conclude that because we suggest that entrepreneurships must make transitions and become something else we are negative about entrepreneurship, but this is hardly the case. We admire the entrepreneur, not only as an individual willing to bet his or her future on an idea but also as the critical element of our economy and the vanguard of the future. But we believe that at some stage "entrepreneurship" is not sufficient and that the nature of the organization must change, together with the people who run it.

The term *entrepreneurship* has, in current usage, taken on meanings that are somewhat different from its original meaning. In the classic sense, the entrepreneur is someone who creates a business, and an entrepreneurship is a business that has been created where none previously existed. In informal usage today, the term *entrepreneurship* seems to have the connotation of a certain way of managing a company. It appears to imply a very informal approach to management, or at a certain extreme the total lack of management of a firm. Since many initially successful entrepreneurships seem to be lacking in management, systems, or procedures, many people often incorrectly assume that these things are not required for successful organizations. Similarly, since many large established companies, such as AT&T, General Motors, and U.S. Steel, to cite just a few, have carried management, systems, and procedures to an extreme and become large bureaucracies, it is also assumed that management, far from a strength, is actually a weakness for organizations. Both of these viewpoints, while having undeniable attractiveness, are essentially simplistic.

Although it is true that management is often not a decisive factor in the early stages of a new venture success, it is essential if a firm is to continue to grow successfully and profitably throughout its life cycle. In addition, while it is true that many firms choke on their own bureaucracy, it is not management and systems that are at fault but the failure of the organization to have designed the proper management systems required for its continuing growth and vitality. Moreover, some firms, such as Compaq Computers and Federal Express, were actually professionally managed entrepreneurships from their inception (as discussed in Chapter Five), and this led to their spectacular success.

For some people the phrase *professional management* has negative connotations. They see it as synonymous with *bureaucracy*. The fact that a firm is professionally managed does not mean that the entrepreneurship must inevitably become bureaucratic. Management and management systems *are* required, but bureaucracy is a perversion of effective professional management, not a synonym for it. In my view, however, a professionally managed firm has achieved the best of both worlds. It is entrepreneurial without entrepreneurship being its only strength; it is well managed without becoming choked on its own systems and procedures. An analogy might be a great sports team that has an excellent offense as well as a superb defense. Entrepreneurship is the essence of an organization's offense, whereas effective management is the essence of its defense. Just as a great defense can create opportunities for the offense, so can the management systems initiated by professional managers create opportunities for entrepreneurship.

Background of the Book

This book is the outgrowth of more than fifteen years of research and consulting experience with many entrepreneurships as well as with large institutional organizations. My interest in this area began in 1976 when I was asked to assist the president of a small entrepreneurial firm in the health care industry in learning how to manage his business. This individual was a medical doctor who had started a business but knew relatively little about managing an organization. Since he was the president of a rapidly growing company, he did not have time to take two years off to get an M.B.A. degree. Nor was he interested in the M.B.A. "label"; he just wanted the knowledge base. Accordingly, I was asked to work with him as a tutor and provide him with a personalized on-the-job M.B.A.-type education. The challenge to me was to draw on the concepts and methods I had been teaching to students at universities such as

Columbia, Michigan, and the University of California at Los Angeles (UCLA), tailoring the material for an entrepreneur who was actually facing the day-to-day risks and pressures of building and running a business. I had to sift through such esoteric concepts as capital budgeting, responsibility accounting, MBO, Markov chains, Theory X and Y, sociotechnical systems, and a myriad of others to determine which were really useful in managing a business. It was a fascinating experience.

Within a few years other people had learned about the work I was doing with entrepreneurial organizations, and I found myself working with a number of companies of differing sizes in such varied industries as executive search, electronics manufacturing, residential real estate, industrial abrasive distribution, commercial banking, public accounting, garment manufacturing, advertising, mortgage banking, publishing, furniture manfacturing, public accounting, financial planning, motorcycle manufacturing, printing, law, restaurant management, and electronic components distribution. In almost every case, the president of the company would say to me something like, "The problems in my industry are unique." Initially, I believed this myth, but as a result of my research training I soon began to see common patterns in the problems and issues faced by a diverse set of companies, regardless of who the president was, irrespective of his or her personality or the nature of the industry.

Most, if not all, of the companies I was working with were successful firms. Their stories were quite similar: The entrepreneurs had been able to identify markets and develop suitable products or services that were geared to their markets' needs. Then they began to experience rapid growth. At some point in the growth process, a variety of problems surfaced in each organization: People were working harder and harder but were still unable to keep up with the load; people were spending too much time going from crisis to crisis; no one ever had time to do anything "right" the first time; there was too much duplication of effort; the entrepreneur was becoming a bottleneck; lots of people had the title of "manager" but there were relatively few good managers in the company; the organization's meetings were frustrating and were perceived as a waste of time; people had begun to grumble about their company's lack

of direction; some people began to feel insecure about their places
in the company and were spending too much time covering their
"vested interests." Many of the companies continued to grow in
revenues but not in profitability. In brief, I perceived that regardless
of the differences in personalities and industries, each of these companies as well as their founders and managers was facing the same
overarching problem: the need to make a transition from an entrepreneurship to a professionally managed firm. This transition required stepping back from the day-to-day activities of the enterprise
and understanding that the company's very success had created the
need for a different kind of organization and a different style of
management. The new challenge to senior management was to rethink the kind of organization that was needed in the new firm that
the enterprise had become. Most of these entrepreneurs were having
difficulty managing their organization's growth because they did
not have a "game plan" for developing their enterprise; rather, they
were too preoccupied with day-to-day issues.

My academic training had taught me to study the published
literature for research that might provide insights into the problems
these companies faced. Unfortunately, I found that most of the literature addressed the functions of management, such as planning,
organizing, and controlling, and the tools of business administration, such as statistics, accounting, and economics. The issues involved in organizational transitions were virtually ignored.

I may have been especially sensitive to those transition issues
because I was on the faculty at UCLA and am an ardent basketball
fan. I was well aware that John Wooden, who is widely regarded
as the greatest coach in the history of basketball, was a master of the
"transition game"—the change from offense to defense and back
again. I also understood that Wooden was, in essence, a manager
who had built a basketball dynasty because he was able to think
conceptually about the game as well as operationally; that is, he
could not only see his team and its competition as strategically
evolving wholes but could also focus on the day-to-day "nuts and
bolts" aspects of coaching.

With these ideas on the topic fusing and forming in my
mind, I began to do research on how and why some firms are successful in managing the stages of entrepreneurial growth while oth-

ers are not. I also wanted to see if it was feasible to develop a method or approach that organizations could use to successfully make the transition from one stage to the next. I used the real world of organizations as my laboratory, analyzing the data I had obtained from actual companies I had worked with as a consultant, researcher, and management development specialist with a number of large, successful, professionally managed firms that are among the Fortune 500. These include some of the most successful U.S. companies and range from such industrial enterprises as aerospace, business equipment manufacturing, petroleum refining and distribution, public utilities, and consumer goods manufacturing, as well as other high- and low-tech manufacturing businesses, to such service industries as public accounting, banking, insurance, residential and commercial real estate, and hotel management. From this experience, I was able to formulate ideas about what made companies successful. Out of this research evolved my theory of the pyramid of organizational development, described in Chapter One, which explains the key factors in developing a successful and profitable organization. I also developed a framework that identifies seven different stages of organizational growth and the key organizational development issues at each stage. This is the organizational life cycle model presented in Chapters Two and Thirteen. Moreover, from an analysis of the problems experienced by rapidly growing entrepreneurial organizations I identified a set of ten classic growing pains and developed a method of measuring these symptoms of organizational difficulty (described in Chapter Three). Using the Organizational Growing Pains Questionnaire, I began to collect a database on organizational growing pains experienced by organizations in different industries and at different stages of growth. My associates and I have used this database to conduct a variety of research studies, some of which are included in this book. Taken together, this research led to the ideas presented in Part One, "A Framework for Developing Successful Organizations."

Moreover, I was able to put this theory into practice with a number of companies that were faced with the need to move from one stage to the next. This "action research" was the basis of my ideas about how to successfully make the transition from an entrepreneurship to a professionally managed organization. It is described in the case studies that appear in Part Two, "Management Strategies for Each Stage of Organizational Growth."

My experience leads me to conclude that one of the key ingredients in successful organizational development is the leader's ability to think conceptually and strategically about the company, rather than merely in terms of products, people, and day-to-day operations. Some parts of this book require such conceptual and strategic thinking; that is, they require that we step back and view the organization in somewhat abstract terms. Entrepreneurs and their associates who master the framework provided here will be able to use it to understand where their organizations are in terms of current development and what their companies must do to continue to operate successfully.

Overview of the Contents

This book is divided into four related parts. Part One presents a conceptual framework for managers of entrepreneurial organizations to use in understanding what is happening to their firms and what they must do to achieve the next stage successfully. The framework includes the six key factors for developing an effective, profitable organization and descriptions of the successive stages of growth at which transitions must be made. Part One also describes the organizational growing pains that are common in rapidly growing firms and presents a method for assessing the extent to which an organization suffers from them.

Part Two presents a series of organizational case studies as a vehicle for examining what an organization must do to develop successfully from one stage to the next. Specifically, Part Two presents examples of companies at all the first four critical stages of growth, from new venture to organizational maturity. It describes the problems those companies faced and explains how such problems need to be dealt with as an organization grows.

Part Three presents a primer of the most significant managerial tools that entrepreneurial organizations must master if they are to grow and develop successfully and profitably: strategic planning, organizational structure, management development, organizational control, leadership, and corporate culture management. Part Four deals with the transitions facing the presidents or chief executive officers of entrepreneurial organizations; it is designed to help them make their firms grow successfully—and to help them grow personally along with their firms. It also presents a preview of the problems to be faced by companies as they grow beyond the early entrepreneurial stages to the more advanced stages of organizational growth.

The revised edition of this book differs from the first edition in several important respects. While the overall direction and thrust of the book have been retained, certain ideas and themes that were implicit have been more fully developed. These include a greater focus on the notion of striking a balance between an organization's size and its infrastructure throughout its life cycle, and the new challenges faced by companies once they achieve professional management. Three chapters have been added: Chapters Eight, Twelve and Thirteen, dealing with organizational structure, corporate culture management, and the advanced stages of growth (stages V–VII) in an organization's life cycle. Throughout the book, several new examples and/or "minicases" of companies dealing successfully and/or unsuccessfully with transitional issues have been included, and new conceptual material has also been added to most of the existing chapters. A number of cases (including Osborne Computer, IBM, Metro Realty, Apple Computer) are used throughout the book to provide a consistent frame of reference for the perspective being developed. Moreover, a number of examples are drawn from computer and other high-technology companies both because of their presence in our research database and their importance as representative of the types of firms we are dealing with in this book.

Entrepreneurship is a driving force in today's economy. Accordingly, entrepreneurial companies must be successful, not only for the good of the entrepreneurs and their employees but also because of the benefits to the general economy. Unfortunately, too many entrepreneurial companies flounder after promising or even brilliant beginnings. Companies such as People Express, Maxicare, Osborne Computer, and Victor Technologies were all once cited as great entrepreneurial successes; yet all have failed. Others such as Wang Laboratories, Apple Computer, and Mrs. Fields' Cookies all experienced significant difficulty and verged on failure. In the face of these failures and difficulties, some cynical observers have even begun to define an entrepreneur as someone, such as Adam Osborne or Robert Campeau, who can start and build a company to a given level and then watch it fail.

My experience in doing research and consulting with entrepreneurial companies has led me to write this book to help present and potential entrepreneurs as well as their employees, advisers, and venture capitalists understand the pitfalls typically faced by entrepreneurial organizations at different stages of growth and to explain how to make the successful transition from an entrepreneurship to a professionally managed firm. It is also intended to assist governmental policy makers in understanding the causes of the premature demise of entrepreneurial companies that are so vital to our economy. Although this book will not solve all the problems faced by entrepreneurial companies, my experience indicates that if the ideas and methods described in this book are applied, organizations will have a significantly improved likelihood of continued success. My hope for this book is that it will prove of practical utility to one of our most valuable resources—the entrepreneur.

Acknowledgments

Although a book may bear the name of an individual as an author, I doubt whether many manuscripts are ever completed without the assistance and significant contributions of a great many people. This is most certainly the case with the present volume, and I am indebted to several individuals for their support and assistance throughout the preparation of this book.

First, this work is a product of several years of consultation and action research with many different organizations. These range from new ventures to members of the Fortune 500. They were my research "laboratory." Simply stated, the most significant ideas that underlie this book were the products of observing, analyzing, and conceptualizing what actually happened in successful and unsuccessful organizations as they grew. The book could not have been written without my having had access to those companies of various sizes, in different industries, with different degrees of success. Accordingly, I am greatly indebted to the CEOs, presidents, senior managers, and others who invited me to serve as researcher, consultant, or adviser for their organizations. (Most of these companies will not be mentioned by name, to preserve their privacy. In some cases, fictitious names are used; in others, examples are cited without the company being named at all.) I am especially grateful to the two owners of the company disguised as "Tempo Products" in Chapter Six, who are referred to as "Ron" and "Cathy Forest Harrison," for their input concerning the chapter as well as their understanding of my desire to focus the chapter on those aspects of their company most relevant to this book.

Some other people also made significant contributions to the book. Special acknowledgment must be made to Yvonne Randle, Ph.D., who served as my research assistant at UCLA and as a consultant in my firm, Management Systems Consulting Corporation in Los Angeles. She assisted in the preparation of both the first and second editions of this book. In the first edition she prepared the case studies presented in Chapters Five and Six, under my direction. These cases were based on work that was done with different organizations that were clients of Management Systems Consulting Corporation. She also wrote the case study in the introduction, coauthored Chapter Three, and provided research and editorial assistance in the preparation of Chapter Eleven. In the second edition she has contributed Chapter Twelve, on corporate culture management, based on a framework we have jointly developed. Otherwise, she has reviewed the entire manuscript and made changes and suggestions for improvement throughout. In addition to these contributions, her insights, skill, motivation, enthusiasm, and ability to work under stress, as well as good humor, were invaluable and are gratefully acknowledged.

Chapter Nine, dealing with the role of management development in the transition from entrepreneurship to professional management, was coauthored in the first edition by H. Stephen Cranston, former president of Knapp Communications Corporation. I am also indebted to C. T. "Bud" Knapp, chairman, and Elizabeth Wood Knapp, then senior vice president, of Knapp Communications Corporation for their invitation to work on the management development program described in Chapter Nine. Moreover, I want to express my appreciation and respect for their encouraging me to present my own views of what happened at Knapp Communications Corporation, even when our opinions differed.

I am also indebted to Leslie Ray, Ph.D. candidate in UCLA's Anderson Graduate School of Management, for preparing summaries of a number of the new descriptions of companies that have been inserted throughout the book. These deal with such organizations as Compaq Computer, Mrs. Fields' Cookies, Federal Express, and Humana.

Quentin Fleming, a consultant in my firm, Management Systems Consulting Corporation, assisted with case studies that have been included in Chapter Eight on organizational structure.

I am indebted in several ways to the Anderson Graduate

School of Management at UCLA for various kinds of support in connection with this book. First, I wish to acknowledge J. Clayburn LaForce, dean of the Graduate School of Management, for his leadership in providing a supportive academic environment. The Price Institute for Entrepreneurial Studies, under the direction of Alfred Osborne, provided financial support for research assistance to prepare some of the case studies presented in this book. I used the manuscript for this book as a text in a special topics course entitled "Managing Entrepreneurial Organizations" as well as in a course on advanced management, both of which I developed in the Graduate School of Management at UCLA. I also used portions of the manuscript in a series of seminars titled, "How to Make the Successful Transition from an Entrepreneurship to a Professionally Managed Firm," which I developed and have offered in cooperation with the Office of Executive Education, under the direction of Victor Tabush, at UCLA.

The word processing and preparation of the manuscript for this book were done by Alice Clarke, my executive assistant at Management Systems Consulting Corporation. The data presented in Chapter Three are drawn from the organizational effectiveness database compiled by Management Systems Consulting Corporation. They are derived from a questionnaire that I developed. I am also indebted to Russell Coff, research project coordinator, and Joanne Cotter, then educational programs coordinator, of Management Systems Consulting Corporation; they assisted in preparation and interpretation of the data dealing with organizational growing pains (Chapter Three). Sigal Goland and Joseph Van Winkle assisted with the preparation of the annotated bibliography for the first edition.

I am indebted to the Jossey-Bass staff for the highly professional and competent way in which this project was handled. They were enthusiastic about this book from its inception and supportive throughout its execution. As with my previous book published by Jossey-Bass, it has been a genuine pleasure to work with them.

Acknowledgment of a different kind is appropriate for Diana Troik Flamholtz. As always, she provided personal and professional support throughout the development of this book. Although I acknowledge with gratitude the contributions of all those cited above, I remain responsible for the book and its imperfections.

Los Angeles   Eric G. Flamholtz
October 1990

The Author

Eric G. Flamholtz is a professor of management at the Anderson Graduate School of Management, University of California at Los Angeles, and assistant director of the Institute of Industrial Relations, University of California at Los Angeles, where he heads the Center for Research on Human Resource Management. His other administrative responsibilities have included vice-chairmanship of the Graduate School of Management and director of the Accounting-Information Systems Research Program. Dr. Flamholtz teaches courses in a variety of areas, including management, accounting-information systems, human resource management, planning and control systems, and managerial decision making. He is also the president of Management Systems Consulting Corporation, which he founded in 1978.

Flamholtz received his Ph.D. degree in 1969 from the University of Michigan, where he served on the staff of the Institute for Social Research under the direction of Rensis Likert. His doctoral dissertation, "The Theory and Measurement of an Individual's Value to an Organization," was co-winner of the McKinsey Foundation for Management Research Dissertation Award.

Flamholtz has also served on the faculties at Columbia University and the University of Michigan and has been a faculty fellow at Price Waterhouse & Co. He has broad interests in management and has done research on a variety of management topics, ranging from accounting and human resource management to organizational development and strategic planning. Dr. Flamholtz has conducted research projects for the National Science Foundation, the national Association of Accountants, and the U.S. Office of Naval Research.

The author of approximately 100 articles and chapters on a variety of management topics, Flamholtz published *Human Resource Accounting: Advances in Concepts, Methods, and Applications* (2nd ed., Jossey-Bass) in 1985. He also published *The Inner Game of Management,* coauthored with Yvonne Randle, in 1987. He has also published *Principles of Accounting* (coauthored) in 1986 and *Financial Accounting* (coauthored) in 1987.

As a consultant, Flamholtz has extensive experience with firms ranging from entrepreneurships to members of the New York Stock Exchange and the Fortune 500. He has also presented seminars and management development programs for organizations in Belgium, France, West Germany, Greece, Mexico, and the People's Republic of China, as well as throughout the United States.

GROWING PAINS

Introduction:
The Transitions Needed
to Keep a Growing Firm
Successful

This introduction presents a case study of an entrepreneurship that needed to make a transition to a new stage of growth. Although the case study selected is that of a printing company with approximately $10 million in annual revenues, the issues faced by the entrepreneur and the firm cited here are similar to those faced by managers in diverse organizations with revenue ranging from approximately $1 million to substantially more than $1 billion. In brief, it has been selected as a prototype of a widespread phenomenon, not one that is limited to companies or industry.

Custom Printing Corporation: An Entrepreneurial Case Study

Joe McBride began working at Custom Printing Corporation while he was still in high school. He worked hard to learn all that he could about the printing business, since he had decided he wanted a career in this industry. Two years after Joe's graduation from high school, when the original owner of the print shop retired, Joe borrowed money from his parents and bought Custom Printing for $10,000. At that time, the shop employed two persons besides Joe.

As is true in most entrepreneurial firms, the early years of Joe's ownership involved great struggle. Custom Printing had a high sales volume but operated without a profit. However, after about seven years of simply staying afloat, the business began to grow. This growth resulted, in part, from Joe's ability to seek a new market niche for his company and to acquire the resources to create products and services that fitted this niche. Joe's strategy was to make Custom Printing a "service printer." This meant that it would serve a small number of customers who had high demands for printing. This strategy proved successful, and in the decade between 1968 and 1978, the demand for Custom Printing's services grew so large that the company had to move to new facilities in order to accommodate it. In fact, during that decade, the company relocated its operations not once but twice.

After the final move in 1978, Joe decided to change his market niche by focusing a certain amount of effort on high-quality printing jobs such as limited edition prints and other artistic works. This helped Joe's customers begin to recognize that Custom Printing was more than just a "stationery printer." In 1980, the company's services expanded to include the production of annual reports for design companies. During this year, sales reached $10 million.

The Onset of "Growing Pains"

It was at about this time, in the early 1980s, that Custom Printing began to experience the typical symptoms of organizational growing pains. Some of these symptoms were more severe than others, but nearly all warranted attention. These symptoms will be discussed in order of severity, ranging from most to least severe.

People did not understand what their jobs were, what others' jobs were, or what the relationships were between their jobs and the jobs of others. This problem resulted, in part, from the company's tendency to add people without developing clear definitions of their roles and responsibilities. Custom Printing did not have a formal organization chart that clearly outlined roles, responsibilities, and relationships between positions and functions within the company.

Because of the lack of clearly defined roles and responsibilities, people did not know who they should report to, or what they could be held accountable for. For example, no one seemed to know who was responsible for shipping and receiving, which led to a situation in which packages often got "lost in the system." Furthermore, no one seemed to want to be held responsible for this and other activities. As a result, departments and individuals were constantly bickering over who should be held accountable when mistakes (such as lost packages) occurred.

Other problems that resulted from the lack of clearly defined roles and responsibilities were duplication of effort and loss of productivity. People and departments came to feel that "I need to do the job myself if I want it to get done," which often resulted in more than one person performing the same task. At the same time, individuals often assumed that "someone else will do it," so some tasks never got done at all. The overlap between the sales and production departments was particularly noticeable.

The lack of clearly defined linkages between organizational roles meant unnecessary isolation as well as unnecessary overlap. The production department, for example, often ignored the cost that the estimating department had suggested for a job and, instead, did it "their way." This sometimes resulted in unanticipated changes in costs, which were not communicated to the estimating department because there was no standard procedure for doing so. Even within departments, there was a lack of needed communication. For example, production coordinators, who were responsible for integrating the various stages of jobs, often were not notified about production problems until days after they occurred because other employees did not understand the coordinators' function. These organizational deficiencies resulted in unnecessary delays in completing jobs and led to customer frustration.

The company had a sales orientation rather than a profit orientation. Custom Printing, like many entrepreneurial firms, traditionally had been most concerned with increasing its sales. It had operated on the premise that if sales were increased, profit would also be increased. This belief affected all areas of the company's operations. At the organizational level, management emphasized "keeping the presses running," since this symbolized the fact that the company was generating business. At times, however, this practice led to decreasing rather than increasing profits.

At the individual employee level, the notion that "profit

would take care of itself if only sales were increased" was pervasive. The sales force held this belief very strongly. Salespeople believed that while the amount of sales was under their control, profit was not; as long as they were generating sales, profit would take care of itself.

As Custom Printing grew, its management began to realize that this sales orientation was adversely affecting the company. In order to continue to be successful, it needed to adopt a profit rather than a sales orientation. This became painfully evident when, in 1982, sales reached nearly $7 million but the company had an operating loss of $120,000.

Employees in some departments felt "overloaded." In sales, the lack of camaraderie between employees was blamed on a lack of time during which important relationships between people could be developed. Salespeople felt pressure to generate and maintain customers, a job that at times seemed to require twenty-four hours a day. In production, controllers said that they often felt overloaded because they were forced to work long hours in order to complete the high number of rush orders on time.

Many employees at Custom Printing said they felt as if they were constantly trying to "catch up"; no matter how hard they worked, there always seemed to be more to do. Joe McBride, the company's owner, suffered from this feeling probably more than anyone, for he sometimes devoted up to sixteen hours a day to his business. This constant time pressure put most employees at Custom Printing under a great deal of stress. It was suggested that the high turnover the company experienced during the early 1980s was due to too much stress.

Employees spent a lot of time resolving short-term problems that resulted from the lack of long-range planning. The production department seemed to suffer most from this problem. Because of both a lack of communication between departments and a lack of planning, production was often forced to complete orders on a rush basis. More often than not, these jobs had to be redone because of mistakes. This resulted in unanticipated delays for customers and unanticipated costs for Custom Printing.

Poor communication between the production and shipping departments contributed to other problems in completing orders.

For example, sometimes an order would be sent to shipping from production only to sit there for days either because shipping did not know what to do with it or because there was a backlog of other orders. When severe backlogs occurred, drivers had to be paid to work evenings and weekends, resulting in added costs for the company. At other times, when drivers weren't needed, they often simply sat around the plant doing nothing.

Lack of planning also resulted in short-term crises for the purchasing and marketing departments. Purchasing did not acquire new vendors until there was a "falling out" with an existing one. This meant that the organization was sometimes disrupted by having to wait for needed supplies until a new vendor could be located. In the marketing department, problems with reports were dealt with only when they became severe enough to be brought to the marketing manager's attention.

There were not enough good managers. Some managers at Custom Printing were described as "managers in title only." These people did not perform effectively in managerial roles. Some people suggested that this ineffectiveness existed because the company gave the managers responsibility but no authority. Others suggested that certain managers simply did not possess the training or skills necessary to be effective. For example, the best salesman in the company had been promoted to a management position. Unfortunately, his ability to manage people was much lower than his ability to complete sales, and this was reflected in his area's performance and subordinates' morale.

Custom Printing did not have an overall business plan, and when plans were made, there was no follow-up. Custom Printing had traditionally operated on an ad hoc basis; long-range planning was never a concern. As the firm grew, however, management began to realize it needed to make some sort of plan. Custom Printing was particularly concerned about setting and meeting financial goals related to sales and costs. Unfortunately, control systems to monitor performance on these and other goals had not been developed, so when goals were not met, there were no repercussions. Paperwork on sales, for example, was often not completed on time, yet no consistent action was taken to improve this situation.

Some employees felt that Custom Printing had no long-term

goals. This was articulated in statements like "Custom Printing lacks a presence" and "I don't know where the company is going." Such statements suggested that Custom Printing's management had failed to communicate its vision for the company to its employees. Employees were aware that changes were being made, but they did not know the ultimate goal toward which the changes were aimed. As a result, employees experienced a certain amount of anxiety and inability to focus on their work.

Some people and departments felt they needed to do every-thing themselves. Because of the lack of clearly defined roles and responsibilities and of coordination between people and departments, each department worked independently of the others. If something needed to be done, people either did it themselves or placed the blame for not accomplishing it on another area or person.

Some people complained that meetings were a waste of time. This was particularly true in the sales area, where time spent in meetings was time taken away from customers. Salespeople had yet to realize the value of meetings in coordinating activities, even though they often complained about the lack of established territories and coordination of sales efforts.

Some people felt insecure in their place at the firm. This was another problem that grew out of the large number of changes in the company, combined with the employees' lack of understanding of the company's long-range goals. The presence of high turnover suggested that some people may have left the firm because the anxiety of "living from day to day" and wondering what would happen next was too much to bear.

Recognizing the Need for a Transition

Joe McBride realized that despite his company's growth in sales, it was in trouble. He realized that he had to make changes in the way the company was operating as well as in his own style of running the business. He knew that both he and the firm had to make a transition from the present entrepreneurial style of operation to a more professional style of management.

Joe and his managers therefore began a four-step program to

allow Custom Printing Corporation to make the transition from an entrepreneurship to a more professionally managed firm. The specific steps in the program were as follows:

> PHASE I: Assess the company's current state of development as an organization and its future development needs.
>
> PHASE II: Design a program for the development of the organization as a whole.
>
> PHASE III: Implement the organizational development program.
>
> PHASE IV: Monitor the program and make changes as needed.

Making the Transition: Phase I

In order to assess the company's current state of development and future needs, an organizational audit was performed. The audit involved collecting information from the company's employees about their perceptions of Custom Printing and its operations. One tool used in this process was the "Organizational Growing Pains Questionnaire" described in Chapter Three. The score that was calculated from responses to this questionnaire revealed the severity of the company's organizational growing pains and indicated that it was time for the company to make some changes. Specifically, the audit revealed that the company needed to

- Define organizational roles and responsibilities and the linkages between roles;
- Become profit oriented rather than strictly sales oriented;
- Help employees plan and budget their time;
- Develop a business plan and a system for monitoring it;
- Increase the number of qualified present and potential managers;
- Identify the direction the company should take in the future;
- Reduce employee and departmental feelings that they always "need to do it themselves" if a job is going to get done;

• Reestablish the importance of meetings and make them more efficient.

Making the Transition: Phases II and III

Having identified its current needs, Custom Printing proceeded to the next step in its organizational development program: designing and implementing a program that would meet these needs and help the company prepare for its next stage of development. Management decided that the program should have three parts: (1) organization design, (2) strategic planning, and (3) management development.

Organization Design.   The first part of the program consisted of developing and communicating to all employees an organization chart and job descriptions that detailed each position's responsibilities and relationships to other positions. This aspect of the organizational development program was intended to help employees understand their own jobs, others' jobs, and the relationship between their job and others' jobs. It would help them begin to separate tasks they would be held accountable for from those that should be delegated to other individuals or departments. Such a division should reduce the number of employees who felt they needed to "do everything themselves."

Strategic Planning.   The strategic planning process involved determining "who the company was" (its business definition), "where it was going" (its goals and objectives), and "how it was going to get there" (action steps). A series of meetings at various levels of the organization was used to facilitate this process. Joe and other members of top management employed procedures such as use of agendas and establishment of a designated chair for each session to increase the effectiveness of the meetings.

The first step in the strategic planning process, that of establishing and formalizing the company's identity, helped employees begin to understand the direction the company was taking and their roles in its development. This clarification reduced some of the insecurity that employees had previously felt.

The second step in the strategic planning process involved designing procedures for setting, monitoring, and evaluating financial and nonfinancial goals. The emphasis in formulating financial goals was to be on planning both sales and expenses in order to increase profit. Procedures were developed to provide managers with monthly budgets and sales figures so that they could monitor performance in terms of progress toward goals and make changes as necessary. These procedures were intended to help the firm make the transition from a sales to a profit orientation.

Formalization of the strategic planning process was intended to help employees use their time more efficiently. This was accomplished by teaching employees how to set realistic financial and nonfinancial goals and how to develop contingency plans to be used in emergencies. Individuals were told that they would be held accountable for the accomplishment of only their own goals and helped to understand what their own and others' responsibilities were. The strategic planning process thus reduced the amount of time individuals needed to spend "putting out fires" or unnecessarily duplicating others' work.

Management Development. A third major goal of the organizational development program was to increase the effectiveness of current managers and develop a pool of qualified potential managers. To accomplish this goal, a formal management development program was created. This program consisted of lectures, exercises, and discussions designed to help participants develop the skills necessary to be effective leaders. These skills included the ability to delegate, make decisions effectively, and choose an effective leadership style.

Making the Transition: Phase IV

Joe McBride wanted to be sure that the changes brought about by the organizational development program would have a positive impact on his company's performance. He therefore established a system to monitor the program's progress in accomplishing its goals (phase IV). By monitoring the program, Joe was able to change it whenever he determined that it was no longer successful at meeting its goals or whenever employee resistance to the changes being implemented became too great.

Summary

In order to make the transition from an entrepreneurship to a professionally managed firm, a company must first recognize that such a change is needed and then design and implement a program that will facilitate the required transition.

Through the four-step program described in this introduction, Joe McBride was able to help his company begin to make a successful transition from an entrepreneurship to a professionally managed firm. The problems Joe encountered and the steps he took to overcome them were not unique to Custom Printing Corporation. In fact, Joe's experience is typical of many entrepreneurs who find that their firms have somehow "outgrown" their structure and operating systems. Joe was able to recognize these organizational growing pains and work to resolve them before it was too late.

As you will see in this book, such "organizational growing pains" occur in many entrepreneurships that reach a stage of development where a transition is needed. The methods that Joe's company used to resolve these problems have been used elsewhere and have proved quite successful.

This introductory case study has provided you with an overview of this book. In Part One we will begin to examine in detail the way to make the transition from an entrepreneurship to a professionally managed firm.

Part One

A Framework for Developing Successful Organizations

The First Challenge for Entrepreneurs

The first challenge entrepreneurs face is the challenge of establishing a successful new venture. The basic skills necessary to meet this challenge are the ability to recognize a market need and the ability to develop (or to hire other people to develop) a product or service appropriate to satisfy that need.

If these two fundamental things are done well, a fledgling enterprise is likely to experience rapid growth. At this point, whether the entrepreneur recognizes it or not, the game begins to change. The very fact of the firm's success creates its next set of problems and challenges to survival.

As a result of expanding sales, the firm's resources become stretched very thin. A seemingly perpetual and insatiable need arises for more inventory, space, equipment, people, funds, and so on. Day-to-day activities are greatly sped up and may even take on a frenzied quality.

The firm's operational systems (those needed to facilitate day-to-day activities), such as marketing, production or service delivery, accounting, credit, collections, and personnel, typically are overwhelmed by the sudden surge of activity. There is little time to think, and little or no planning takes place because most plans quickly become obsolete. People become high on their own adrenaline and merely react to the rush of activity.

11

At this point the firm usually begins to experience some, perhaps all, of the following "organizational growing pains":

- People feel that there are not enough hours in the day.
- People spend too much time "putting out fires."
- Many people are not aware of what others are doing.
- People lack an understanding of the firm's ultimate goals.
- There are not enough good managers.
- The feeling that "I have to do it myself if I want to get it done correctly" is prevalent.
- Most people feel that the firm's meetings are a waste of time.
- Plans are seldom made and even more seldom followed up, so things often do not get done.
- Some people feel insecure about their place in the firm.
- The firm has continued to grow in sales but not to the same extent in profits.

The CEO or founder must recognize these symptoms as a warning that corrective action must be taken immediately—before the firm gets into serious difficulty.

These symptoms are a warning that the firm has outgrown its "infrastructure." An organization's infrastructure consists of the operational support systems and management systems required to enable the organization to function profitably on a short- and long-term basis. As described further in Chapter One, a company's operational support systems consist of all the day-to-day systems required to produce a product or deliver a service and to function on a day-to-day basis. The management systems include the planning system, organization structure, management development system, control system, and corporate culture required to manage the overall enterprise on a short-term basis while preparing it for anticipated future growth and development. As we examined further in Chapter Three, when an organization is not fully successful in developing the internal systems it needs in a given stage of growth, it begins to experience growing pains. These growing pains are not merely problems in and of themselves; they are a symptom that there is an "organizational development gap" between the infrastructure required by the organization and the infrastructure it actually has. This, in turn, is a signal that a new stage of development has been reached—one that requires a change in the nature of the firm's management systems.

The Second Challenge for Entrepreneurs

When this new stage of development is reached, the firm must prepare to make a fundamental transformation or metamorphosis from the spontaneous, ad hoc, free-spirited enterprise that it has been to a more formally planned, organized, and disciplined entity. The firm must move from a situation in which there are only informal plans and people simply react to events to one in which formal planning is a way of life; from one in which jobs and responsibilities are undefined to one in which there is some degree of definition of responsibilities and mutually exclusive roles; from one in which there is no accountability or control systems to one in which there are objectives, goals, measures, and related rewards specified in advance as well as formal performance appraisal; from one in which there is only on-the-job training to one in which there are formal management development programs; from one in which there is no budget to one in which there are budgets, reports, and variances; and, finally, from a situation in which profit simply happens to one in which there is an explicit profit goal to be achieved. In brief, the firm must make the transition from an entrepreneurship to an entrepreneurially oriented, professionally managed organization.

As we will see in Chapter Fourteen, this is a time when the very personality traits that made the founder-entrepreneur so successful initially can lead to organizational demise. Most entrepreneurs have either a sales or technical background, or they know a particular industry well. Entrepreneurs typically want things done in their own way. They may be more intelligent or have better intuition than their subordinates, who come to rely on their bosses' omnipotence. Typical entrepreneurs tend to be "doers" rather than managers, and most have not had formal management training, although they may have read the current management best-sellers. They like to be free of "corporate restraints." They reject meetings, written plans, detailed organization of time, and budgets as the trappings of bureaucracy. Most insidiously, they think, "We got here without these things, so why do we need them?"

Unfortunately, at the stage of corporate development we are discussing, the nature of the organization has changed—and so must the firm's senior management. The owner-entrepreneur can deal with the situation in one of five different ways. He or she can

- Try to develop new skills and behavior patterns—difficult but quite possible;
- Resign, as Jack Tramiel did at Commodore International and as Loraine Mecca did at Micro D, and let others bring in a professional manager to run the organization;
- Move up to chairperson, as Steven Jobs did at Apple Computer, and bring in a professional manager while still staying involved;
- Continue to operate as before and ignore the problems, hoping they will evaporate;
- Sell out and start another entrepreneurial company, as did K. M. Siegel, the entrepreneur who founded Conductron, sold it to McDonnell Douglas, and then started KMS Industries.

Founder-entrepreneurs typically experience great difficulty in relinquishing control of their businesses. Some try to change their skills and behavior but fail. Others merely give the illusion of turning the organization over to professional managers. For example, one successful entrepreneur brought two very highly paid and experienced managers into his firm, made a great flourish about the transition, and then proceeded to turn them into "managerial eunuchs." After they had "failed," he was able to "reluctantly" resume control of the enterprise and plead that he had made every effort but the business obviously could not do without him.

There is no one pattern for a successful transition from an entrepreneurship to a professionally managed firm. Whatever path is followed, the key to a successful change is for the entrepreneur to recognize that a new stage in the organization's life cycle has been reached and that the former mode of operation will no longer be effective.

Making an Organizational Transition

Once the entrepreneur has recognized that the company's mode of operation must be changed, the inevitable question arises: "What should we do to take the organization successfully to the next stage of growth?" To answer this question satisfactorily, it is necessary to understand that there are predictable stages of organizational growth, certain key developmental tasks that must be performed by the organization at each growth stage, and certain critical problems that organizations typically face as they grow. This understanding, in turn, requires a framework within which the determinants of successful organizational development may be placed. We will present such a framework in Part One of this book.

Chapter One presents a holistic framework for successful organizational development. It deals with the issue of what makes an organization successful and profitable. Drawing on research and experience from consulting with many organizations, it presents a systematic approach to understanding the six critical variables in organizational effectiveness. It examines the six critical tasks of organizational development and tells what must be done to accomplish each. These six variables or tasks are conceptualized as a "pyramid of organizational development."

Chapter Two identifies seven different stages of organizational growth, from the inception of a new venture through the early maturity of an entrepreneurial organization, and to the ultimate decline and revitalization of a company. It then examines the first four stages of growth (the remaining three will be discussed in Chapter Thirteen). It also examines the relative emphasis that must be placed on each of the six critical developmental tasks at each stage of the organization's growth.

Chapter Three examines the growing pains that all developing organizations experience. It provides a method for assessing these growing pains and determining their severity. Senior manag-

ers need to be able to recognize such growing pains as symptoms
of the need to make changes in their organizations.

Taken together, the ideas in Chapters One, Two, and Three
provide a conceptual map of the tasks that must be done to manage
and develop an entrepreneurial organization. Part One also provides a guide for analyzing and planning the transitions that must
be made in moving a company from one developmental stage to the
next.

1 How to Build Successful Companies: The Pyramid of Organizational Development

●

The senior management of a rapidly growing entrepreneurial company must simultaneously cope with its endless day-to-day problems and keep an eye on its future direction. Furthermore, the managers of most such companies are going through the process of building a company for the first time. This is about as easy as navigating uncharted waters in a leaky rowboat with an inexperienced crew while surrounded by a school of sharks. The sea is unfamiliar, the boat is clumsy, the skills needed are not readily apparent or not fully developed, and there is a constant reminder of the high costs of an error in judgment.

Just as the crew of such a boat might wish urgently for a guide to help them with navigation, training, and ship repair, the senior managers of an entrepreneurial company may frequently wish for a guide to help them build their firm. The crew might also be glad to know that others before them have made the voyage successfully and to hear some of the lessons that the other voyagers learned in the process.

This chapter attempts to provide a guide for senior managers who are faced with the special challenge of building an entrepreneurial company. It gives a framework for understanding and managing the critical tasks that an organization must perform at each stage of its growth.

Six Key Organizational Development Tasks

Organizational development is the process of planning and implementing changes in the overall capabilities of an enterprise in order to increase its operating effectiveness and profitability. It involves thinking about a business organization (or any organization, for that matter) as a whole and planning necessary changes in certain key areas. Proper organizational development allows companies to progress successfully from one stage of growth to the next.

The framework for organizational development that is presented in this chapter is an outgrowth of several years of research and consulting experience with such organizations. It includes six organizational development areas or tasks that are critical in determining whether an organization will be successful at any particular stage of growth. Taken together, these six key tasks make up the "pyramid of organizational development" pictured in Figure 1.1. We will first identify and describe each key organizational development task individually and then examine the pyramid of organizational development as a whole.

Identify and Define a Market Niche.   The most fundamental prerequisite for developing a successful organization is the identification and definition of a firm's market and, if feasible, its "market niche." A market is made up of the present and potential buyers of the goods and/or services that a firm intends to produce and sell. A market niche is a place within a market where a firm can potentially develop a sustainable competitive advantage in providing goods and/or services to satisfy customer needs. This distinction will be discussed more fully in Chapter Seven, which deals with strategic planning.

The first challenge to organizational survival or success is identifying a market need for a product or service to which the firm will seek to respond. This can be either a need that has not yet been recognized by other firms or a need currently satisfied by existing firms. The chances for organizational success are enhanced if a firm identifies a need that is not being adequately fulfilled or that has little competition for its fulfillment. This challenge is faced by all new ventures; indeed, it is *the* challenge for a new venture to over-

Figure 1.1. Pyramid of Organizational Development.

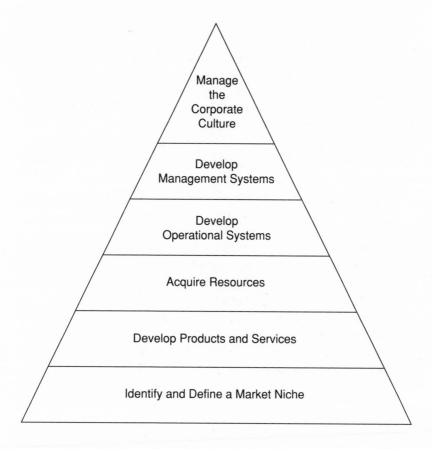

come. It has also been the critical test of growing concerns and has even brought many once proud and great firms to near ruin or total demise.

Many firms have achieved great success merely because they were one of the first in a new market. For example, Apple Computer grew from a small entrepreneurship in a garage to a $1 billion firm in a few years because its founders identified the market for a "personal" computer. Similarly, Dreyer's, a manufacturer of ice cream (which is a relatively undifferentiated product), went from sales of $14.4 million to sales of $55.8 million in just five years because the company saw and cultivated a market niche between the "superpremium ice creams" such as Haagen-Dazs and the generic (commodity) ice cream sold in most supermarkets. Pic 'N' Save became a company of more than $200 million in revenues by selling manufacturers' excess products. Ashton-Tate grew to more than $200 million and the third largest software vendor in the United States on the strength of dBASE, a program for storing, sorting, and managing information in a personal computer.

The reverse side of this happy picture is seen in firms that have foundered either because they failed to define a niche or because they mistakenly abandoned their historical niche. For example, a medium-sized national firm that manufactured and sold specialty clothing wished to upgrade its image and products and become a high-fashion boutique. However, it failed to recognize that its historical market was the "medium" market, and its efforts to rise out of this market were unsuccessful.

Similarly, Custom Printing Corporation, with more than $10 million in annual revenues found itself in difficulty after trying to upgrade its position in the medium-priced printing market. Attracted by the market segment where the highest-quality work was done (with accompanying high profit margins), the company purchased the best equipment available. It also hired a high-priced sales manager to recruit a sales force that could compete in the new market segment. However, the company had underestimated the strength of existing companies in that market niche, and it found itself unable to break into the higher-priced market segment as easily as its managers had hoped. Moreover, the additional investments it had made and the related increases in its overhead made the firm's cost structure higher than that of its former competitors, so it began losing business from its historical market niche. Thus the company found itself in a cost-price squeeze.

Many firms are able to survive merely because they have been able to identify a market need for certain goods or services; however, the firms that achieve the greatest success frequently have identified not only a market need but also a potential niche to capture. For example, Bud Knapp, chairman of Knapp Communications Corporation, perceived a niche for magazines geared to the relatively affluent consumer and proceeded to capture that niche with *Architectural Digest*.

The first task in developing a successful organization, then, is the definition of the firm's markets and potential niches. This process involves the use of strategic market planning to identify potential customers, their needs, and so on. It also involves laying out the strategy through which the firm plans to compete with others for its share of the intended market. The nature and methods of strategic planning will be described in Chapter Seven.

Develop Products and Services.   The second task of an entrepreneurial organization is "productization." This is the process of analyzing the needs of present and potential customers in order to design products and/or services that will satisfy their needs. For example, one group of entrepreneurs in the electronics industry identified the need for a solution to the so-called backup problem facing users of micro- and minicomputers. Such users needed a relatively inexpensive method of backing up the data on the disks used in their computers. This group of engineering-oriented entrepreneurs researched and developed a solution to the backup problem that used the technology called *tape streaming*. The result was a business that began to earn more than $30 million in annual revenues in just a few years.

Although many firms are able to correctly perceive a market need, they are not necessarily able to develop a product that is capable of satisfying that need adequately. For example, the firms of California's "Silicon Valley" were able to identify the need for a 64K computer chip, but the market for that product ultimately came to be dominated by Japanese companies and Motorola because of these companies' ability to mass produce the chip with a high degree of reliability. Thus, being the first to recognize a need is not necessarily sufficient.

The productization process involves not only the ability to design a "product" (defined here to include services as well) but also the ability to produce it. For a service firm, the ability to "produce" a product involves the firm's service delivery system, the mechanism through which services are provided to customers. For example, Domino's Pizza provides home delivered pizza. Both the pizza and "home delivery" are aspects of the company's "products."

Productization is not simply a task for relatively new or small companies; it faces large, well-established firms as well. Indeed, it can even face whole industries. For example, in the 1970s U.S. automobile manufacturers were unsuccessful in productizing their products to meet the changing needs of their market, including the growing need for reliable, fuel-efficient, economical automobiles. The same problem was faced by Xerox in the photocopying industry, U.S. Steel in specialty steels, and all U.S. television manufacturers. As a result, Japan emerged as a powerful competitor in markets that the Americans had once dominated.

The development of successful products depends to a great extent on effective strategic market planning. This involves understanding who your potential customers are, what their needs are, how they buy, and what they perceive to be value in a product.

The success of productization depends, to a very great extent, on success in defining the firm's market niche. The greater the degree to which a firm understands the market's needs, the more likely that its productization process will be effective in satisfying those needs. Productization is the second key development task in building a successful organization.

Acquire Resources.   The third major task of a developing organization is acquiring and developing the additional resources it needs for its present and anticipated future growth. A firm may have identified a market and created products but not have sufficient resources to compete effectively. For example, small competitors in the soft drink industry need to be low-cost producers. This requires high-speed bottling lines, which, at a cost of $1 million a line, the smaller firms simply cannot afford.

A firm's success in identifying a market niche and in productization creates increased demand for its products and/or services. This, in turn, stretches the firm's resources very thin. The organization may suddenly find that it requires additional physical resources (space, equipment, and so on), financial resources, and human resources. The need for human resources, especially in management, will become particularly acute. At this stage of development, the firm's very success ironically creates a new set of problems.

The company must now become more adept at resource management, including the management of cash, inventories (if a manufacturing company), personnel, and so forth. It is at this stage that an entrepreneur must begin to think in longer terms about the company's future needs. Failure to do this can be costly. For example, one entrepreneur told how he kept purchasing equipment that became obsolete for the company's needs within six months because of the firm's rapid growth. Instead of purchasing a photocopying machine that would be adequate for the company's needs as it grew but was more than currently required, for example, he purchased a machine that was able to meet only current needs. The result was that he spent much more on equipment than he would have done if he had purchased machinery that was adequate for potential future needs. Similarly, another entrepreneur found himself with insufficient space six months after moving into new offices that he had thought would be adequate for five years, because the company grew more rapidly than he had anticipated.

Develop Operational Systems. To function effectively, a firm must not only produce a product or service but also administer basic day-to-day operations reasonably well. These operations include accounting, billing, collections, advertising, personnel recruiting and training, sales, production, delivery, and related systems. The fourth task in building a successful organization is the development of the systems needed to facilitate these day-to-day operations—the operational systems. It is useful to think of a firm's operational systems as part of its "organizational plumbing." Just as plumbing is necessary for a house or building to function effectively, organizational plumbing is necessary for a business to function well.

Typically, firms that are busy developing their market niche and products tend to neglect the development of their operational systems. As a firm increases in size, however, an increasing amount of strain is put on such systems because the company tends to outgrow the organizational plumbing available to operate it.

For example, in one electrical components distribution firm with more than $200 million in annual revenues, salespeople were continually infuriated when they found deliveries of products they had sold could not be made because the firm's inventory records were hopelessly incorrect. Similarly, a medium-sized residential real estate firm with annual revenues of about $10 million found that it required almost one year of effort and embarrassment to correct its accounting records after the firm's bookkeeper retired. A $100 million consumer products manufacturer had to return certain materials to vendors because it had insufficient warehouse space to house the purchases (a fact no one noticed until the deliveries were at the door). A $15 million industrial abrasives distributor found itself facing constant problems in keeping track of customer orders and in knowing what was in its inventory. The firm's inventory control system, which was fine when annual sales were $3 to $5 million, had simply become overloaded at the higher sales volume. One manager remarked that "nothing is ever stored around here where any intelligent person could reasonably expect to find it."

Develop Management Systems. The fifth task required to build a successful organization is developing the management systems required for the long-run growth and development of the firm. These include systems for planning, organization, management development, and control. Management Systems are another component of an organization's infrastructure, or "organizational plumbing."

The planning system takes care of planning for the overall development of the organization as well as for scheduling and budgeting operations. It involves the processes of strategic planning, operational planning, and contingency planning. A firm may do planning, but still lack a planning system. The basic concepts and methods of strategic planning for entrepreneurially oriented professionally managed firms are presented in Chapter Seven.

The organization structure of the firm determines how people are organized, who reports to whom, and how activities are coordinated. All firms have some organizational structure (formal or informal), but they do not necessarily have the correct structure for their needs. The concepts and methods for design and evaluation of organization structure required at different stages of growth are presented in Chapter Eight.

The management development system sees to the planned development of the people needed to run the organization as it grows. Chapter Nine deals with management development and its role in making the transition from an entrepreneurship to a professionally managed firm.

The control system encompasses the set of processes (budgeting, leadership, goal setting) and mechanisms (performance appraisal) used to motivate employees to achieve organizational objectives. It includes both formal control mechanisms, such as responsibility accounting, and informal processes, such as organizational leadership. Chapter Ten deals with organizational control systems.

Until the firm reaches a certain size (which tends to differ for each firm), it can typically operate without formal management systems. Planning tends to be done in the head of the entrepreneur, frequently on an ad hoc basis. The organizational structure, if it exists, tends to be informal, with ill-defined responsibilities that may well overlap several people. Management development tends to consist of "on-the-job training," which basically means "You're on your own." When control systems are used in such organizations, they tend to involve only the accounting system rather than a broader concept of management control.

The basic organizational growing pain at this level of development is the decreasing ability of the original entrepreneur or senior executive to control all that is happening. The organization simply becomes too large for senior managers to be personally involved in every aspect of it.

Manage the Corporate Culture.   Just as all people have personalities, all organizations have a culture: a set of shared values, beliefs, and norms that govern the way people are expected to operate the business on a day-to-day basis. The culture may be implicit rather than explicit, but it can be identified by trained observers.

Values are what the organization believes is important with respect to product quality, customer service, treatment of people, and so on. Beliefs are the ideas that people in the corporation hold about themselves as individuals and about the firm as an entity. Norms are the unwritten rules that guide day-to-day interactions and behavior, including language, dress, and humor.

Organizational culture is a critical factor in an enterprise's successful development and performance. It can have a profound

impact on the behavior of people for better or for worse. Many
companies, such as IBM, Hewlett-Packard, and Domino's Pizza,
have achieved greatness at least in part because of a strong corporate
culture.

Organizational culture functions as an informal "control
system," because it prescribes how people are supposed to behave.
Japanese companies do not need as much as U.S. companies in the
way of formal controls because of their well-defined cultures.

Some managers believe that what is espoused as their corporate culture is actually the culture that affects people's behavior.
Unfortunately, this is often an illusion. For example, one rapidly
growing entrepreneurship in a high-technology industry stated that
its culture involved the production of high-quality products, concern for the quality of the working life of its employees, and encour-
agement of innovation. In reality, the firm's culture was less
positive. Its true concerns were to avoid conflict among its managers, set unrealistic performance expectations, avoid accountability,
and overestimate its performance capabilities. Moreover, the company saw itself as hard-driving and profit oriented, but its real culture was sales oriented regardless of profitability.

Sophisticated managers understand that their companies
compete as much with culture as with specific products and services. The CEO of a major New York Stock Exchange company once
said that he could predict a division's organizational problems as
soon as he had identified its culture. The sixth and final challenge
in building a successful organization, then, is to manage corporate
culture. The nature and management of corporate culture are examined in Chapter Twelve.

The Pyramid of Organizational Development

The six tasks of organizational development just described
are critical to a firm's successful functioning, not only individually
but as an integrated system. They must harmonize and reinforce
rather than conflict with one another. A firm's markets, products,
resources, operational systems, management systems, and corporate
culture must be an integrated whole. Stated differently, each variable in the pyramid of organizational development affects and in

turn is affected by each of the other variables. Thus, although the foundation of the pyramid of organizational development is the market, the market is affected by the company's culture. When the six variables function effectively together, the six key tasks of organizational development make up a "pyramid of organizational development." The management of an organization must learn to visualize this pyramid and evaluate his or her organization in terms of the extent to which its pyramid has been successfully designed and built.

We must also recognize that although an organization always contains the pyramid of systems that deal with the six key developmental tasks, the emphasis on the components or subsystems of the pyramid must be somewhat different at different stages of organizational growth. Before we can explore this idea further, we must examine the different stages of growth through which entrepreneurial organizations develop. This topic will be the focus of Chapter Two. First, however, let us examine an example of the building of the pyramid of organizational development at a successful company.

Successfully Building the Pyramid: The Example of IBM

International Business Machines Corporation (IBM) is a classic example of an organization that has been successful in building its pyramid of organizational development. It has achieved success in handling the six critical tasks of developing an effective organization not only individually but as a whole. Although IBM is much larger than the entrepreneurial organizations we are concerned with in this book, taking a closer look at what it has done can still be instructive. For one thing, even IBM was once a fledgling new venture. For another, IBM has demonstrated that even a company with sales exceeding $60 billion can act entrepreneurially, as it did when it introduced its PC computer.

Identify a Market Niche and Develop a Product. At its core, IBM is a market-driven company. It does not regard marketing merely in the narrow sense of sales and advertising; rather, it focuses on the market and market needs in the ways described in our discussion of the first two levels of the pyramid framework. Specifically, the company is concerned with identifying present and potential customer needs and then developing products to satisfy those needs. Although IBM has a reputation for product quality, the company's strategy is not to bring products to market that are of the highest possible intrinsic quality; rather IBM prides itself on its ability to develop profitable products that are of the quality level that its customers desire (that is, will purchase). While the Televideo computer was a more technologically sophisticated machine with a more powerful chip, the IBM PC became the dominant product in its market. Thus, one of the central tenets of the company's orientation is the satisfaction of customer needs. This is symbolized in the organization's culture as a concern for "customer service," but in reality it is broader than that phrase would suggest.

Acquire Resources and Develop Operational Systems. Unlike many entrepreneurial companies, even those with sales in excess of $1 billion, IBM has paid a great deal of attention to the next two levels of the pyramid of organizational development. The company has developed its resources and operational systems so that it has the operational infrastructure (organizational plumbing) to run efficiently and effectively on a day-to-day basis. The company takes as much pride in the excellence of its people, plant, equipment, and operational systems as it does in its products. This attitude, in turn, is based on the company's belief in its own excellence and in excellence as a criterion to evaluate its own performance. While many companies strive for excellence in their products or services, relatively few strive for excellence in all that they do. IBM is one of the exceptions.

Develop Management Systems. IBM has also developed an outstanding set of management systems, including systems for strategic and operational planning, management development, organization, and control. The company's comprehensive strategic planning system includes environmental scanning capability to identify and assess the implications of long-term trends. IBM also has a well-developed profit planning and budgeting system. All of IBM's planning is done on a regularly scheduled annual basis.

IBM's management development system and practices are one of the truly outstanding parts of its management system. IBM has invested heavily in management development, and it attributes much of its long-term success to this practice. The company requires that each manager go through what amounts to "basic management training" within thirty days of becoming a manager. Moreover, each manager must have forty hours of management development training each year. IBM uses the mechanism of management development not only to develop managerial skills, but also to institutionalize the organization's culture.

Organization of a company as large and complex as IBM is a considerable challenge, yet the company is well organized and functions effectively. The basic concept behind IBM's organization is decentralization with control. The company is organized into relatively autonomous divisions, all of which are coordinated and subject to centralized guidance and control. It is not merely a collection of loosely affiliated operating entities under a holding company management structure, like Beatrice Company; rather, it is an integrated organization with a balance between centralized planning and review and autonomous day-to-day decision making.

The company's control systems consist of an extensive reporting system plus periodic meetings for performance review. This company also monitors a number of variables over time to assess trends and deviations that may indicate problems. Finally, IBM has a well-developed performance appraisal system.

Manage the Corporate Culture. The highest level in the pyramid of organizational development is the corporate culture. Throughout its history, IBM has been aware of the role of corporate culture in the management of its organization. Under Thomas Watson, the firm formulated a set of three critical values that still persist today. These are customer service, excellence of performance, and respect for the individual.

Customer service, which has already been described in connection with the company's marketing orientation, is a broader concept than merely providing customer satisfaction. It comes closer to meaning a total commitment to understanding and trying to serve customer needs.

The concept of excellence has also been described briefly. It seems to be best captured by the phrase of one IBMer that "we try to do things the right way." When mistakes are made (and IBM, just like any other company, does make mistakes), people "swarm" over the problem to find its causes and correct it.

Finally, the company's notion of "respect for the individual" needs to be understood as something more than that phrase might imply. IBM's concern for its employees is not necessarily a selfless, humanistic concern, but it is a concern nonetheless. In spite of having hundreds of thousands of employees, IBM continues to operate within a culture that stresses the dignity and worth of each individual. The company has an open-door policy and practices that make it feasible for the individual to be heard. It assigns personnel officers to each operating division to serve as advisers on human resource issues to operating management. The company runs an annual morale survey to get feedback from people concerning their satisfaction with work-related issues. The IBM value of respect for the individual involves an implied reciprocity between the company and its employees: if employees will commit themselves to taking care of the company, the company will take care of them.

Companies such as IBM with "strong" (or well-defined) cultures tend to require less formal control systems than comparable organizations with "weak" or diffused cultures. This is a competitive advantage.

The Pyramid as a Whole.   IBM's management fully realizes that the six key development factors are not only important in themselves; they constitute a system. IBM seems to be managed as a holistic entity made up of interacting, mutually reinforcing systems. The company provides an outstanding illustration of an enterprise that has successfully achieved its pyramid of organizational development.

Summary

This chapter has presented a framework for understanding what makes an organization successful, effective, and profitable.

The framework includes six key areas in which organizations must succeed: (1) markets, (2) products or services, (3) resources, (4) operational systems, (5) management systems, and (6) corporate culture. For organizations to be successful, they must deal not only with each of these six areas individually and in sequence but also with the six as parts of a whole. We use the image of a "pyramid of organizational development" to describe this holistic approach.

IBM illustrates the power of developing a company in a way that is consistent with the pyramid of organizational development. However, companies need not be large like IBM in order to be able to do what IBM has done. In fact, the larger the company, the greater the difficulty in achieving a successful pyramid of development.

An organization does not have to be a billion-dollar company before a pyramid of organizational development is complete; a version of the pyramid exists at all different stages of organizational growth. The different stages of growth and the different emphasis on each part of the pyramid that is required at each stage will be the subject of the next chapter.

2 Identifying and Surviving the First Four Stages of Organizational Growth

All organizations pass through various stages of development. These stages are, at least in part, determined by the organization's size, as measured by its annual revenues. This chapter presents a framework for identifying and explaining the major stages through which all organizations grow and develop as they increase in size. It should be noted that this framework applies to a division of a large company as well as to an independent organization.

First, we will identify the various stages of organizational growth and examine the first four stages from the inception of a new venture to organizational maturity. Next, we will examine the emphasis on each level in the pyramid of organizational development that is required at each growth stage and explain the nature of the transitions to different stages. Then we will discuss the differences between an entrepreneurship and a professionally managed firm and what must be done to make the transition between these growth stages. Finally, we discuss some implications of this framework for the management of entrepreneurial organizations.

Stages of Organizational Growth

Seven stages of growth of a company's life cycle can be identified:

I.   New venture
II.   Expansion

III.   Professionalization
IV.   Consolidation
V.   Diversification
VI.   Integration
VII.   Decline and revitalization

The first four of the stages of growth characterize the period from inception of a new venture to the attainment of organizational maturity. This period includes the development of an entrepreneurship through the stage when the firm becomes a professionally managed firm. Stages V through VII all deal with the period of a company's life cycle after the attainment of organizational maturity.

Since the principal focus of this book is on the development of companies from entrepreneurship to the stage of becoming a professionally managed firm, this chapter will focus on the first four stages of organizational growth. We will return to the last three stages of organizational growth in Chapter Thirteen, which presents a preview of the challenges posed to continued organizational development success after an organization has reached maturity.

At each of these stages, one or more of the critical tasks of organizational development should receive special attention. The stages of organizational growth, the critical development areas for each stage, and the approximate size (measured in millions of dollars of sales revenues) at which an organization will typically pass through each stage are shown in Table 2.1.

Table 2.1. Stages of Organizational Growth.

Stage	Description	Critical Development Areas	Approximate Organizational Size (millions of dollars in sales)
I.	New venture	Markets and products	Less than $1
II.	Expansion	Resources and operational systems	$1 to $10
III.	Professionalization	Management systems	$10 to $100
IV.	Consolidation	Corporate culture	$100 to $500

A key word in this statement is *typically*. What this means is that for approximately 90 percent of the firms that have revenues in the range of $10 million to $100 million, they will typically have to encounter the critical issues of stage III.

There are, however, certain firms that will have to face these problems at a smaller size in their development, or much later in their development. For example, there may well be a $3 million firm that is facing the need to professionalize its management systems. Or a few firms may well reach $1 billion in annual revenue without really having to face the need to professionalize their management systems. Accordingly, we need to view the relevant range as designated for the transition to occur at each stage of development as a "normal curve." In statistics, a normal curve designates the percentage of "observations" that fall under the area of the curve. This means that statistically 68 percent of the "cases" of firms will fall under one standard deviation of the normal curve, while 95 percent of the cases will fall under two standard deviations of the normal curve. There are of course always certain exceptions to this. Similarly, there are exceptions to the revenue parameters used to mark the various stages of growth.

It should also be noted that the ranges of annual revenue used to designate the various stages of growth in Table 2.1 are based on manufacturing companies. My experience in working with a wide variety of organizations indicates that each stage of growth is reached somewhat earlier for service companies than for manufacturing firms. This occurs because of the greater complexity of a service company relative to a manufacturing company with the same annual revenues. This is, in turn, caused by the fact that manufacturing companies typically purchase materials that are semifinished to be used in their manufacturing process. Accordingly, the manufacturing company's revenues include a return for the components of cost of goods sold that are derived from other organizations' work. This means that the manufacturing company's "value added" is less than the comparable value added for a service company at a given stage of annual revenues. This does not mean that the manufacturing company makes less of a contribution than a service company, but merely that the service company that has a greater number of employees and no raw materials to be recouped as part of sales revenue has a relatively more complex operation than a comparably sized manufacturing company.

As a result of this phenomenon, I have found it useful to "convert" a service company's revenues into the comparable units of those of a manufacturing company. This process is similar to the conversion from the imperial system to the metric system, or from dollars into any foreign currency. Thus to convert a service company's revenues into comparable units of a manufacturing company, you should typically multiply the service company's revenues by a factor of 3.0. This means that the typical service company is three times more complex to manage than a comparable manufacturing company. Alternatively, it means that a $5 million service company is the *rough equivalent* of a $15 million manufacturing company. It should be remembered that this is an experienced-based adjustment that I have found useful, rather than a strict formula.

In the subsequent discussion, we will (for convenience) refer to a company at a given stage using the parameters for manufacturing companies as a base. The reader can "adjust" for service companies by using the service company adjustment factor of 3.0. Financial institutions, such as banks, savings and loans, and mutual funds can be viewed as service companies, under the framework. Distribution companies can be viewed as a hybrid manufacturing-service organization, and a multiple of 1.5 can be used as an adjustment factor.

Stage I: New Venture. Stage I of organizational growth involves the inception of a new venture. Stage I typically occurs from the time an organization has virtually no sales until it reaches approximately $1 million in annual sales. During stage I, the firm has to perform all the critical tasks necessary for organizational success, but the greatest emphasis is on the first two tasks: defining markets and developing products. This is represented schematically in the organizational development pyramid shown in Figure 2.1. Those two tasks are the tasks of survival.

Many firms have succeeded in establishing new ventures because the entrepreneur was able to identify a viable market and product. Earl Scheib, the "king of the no-frills auto paint job," is one entrepreneur who met this challenge. When he began painting

Figure 2.1. Developmental Emphasis in a Stage I Firm.

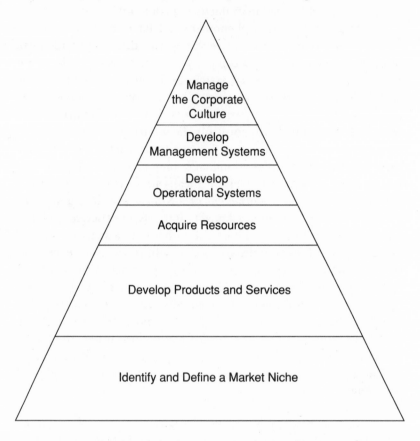

cars in his Los Angeles gas station in 1937, his original concept was to provide a no-frills face-lift for cars. Scheib built an entire business based on this concept. He had successfully identified a market niche that was not being served, and he proceeded to build a business to serve it. His company is now publicly held and in 1985 operated more than 275 shops for paint and bodywork on cars. Moreover, his concept has been copied by a number of competitors.

Another example of an entrepreneur who established a successful new venture because he was able to identify an unserved market niche is Thomas S. Monaghan, who founded the company known today as Domino's Pizza. Monaghan's concept was to provide pizza for home delivery, which at the time he founded his business was not commonly available. As he has stated, "When Domino's began delivering pizza, the only pizza places that delivered were those that had to deliver to survive."[2] Monaghan believed that there was an unserved market need for high-quality, reasonably priced pizza to be delivered to the home. Today his firm serves approximately one-half of the home delivery pizza market, a market Domino's Pizza helped create.

Other examples of new ventures that came about when an entrepreneur perceived a market niche to be served include Famous Amos Cookies, Federal Express, Kinder Care Day Care Centers, and Ashton-Tate, which markets popular database management software packages. Many other new ventures are reasonably successful and profitable but not as famous. They include businesses engaged in executive search, landscape design, printing, financial planning, restaurants, graphic design, repair services, catering, equipment leasing, and many more fields.

Stage II: Expansion. If an organization successfully completes the key developmental tasks of stage I, it will reach stage II. This stage involves the rapid expansion of the firm in terms of sales revenues, number of employees, and so on. For most firms, stage II begins at about the $1 million sales level and extends to the $10 million level.

Stage II presents a new set of developmental problems and challenges. Organizational resources are stretched to the limit when increasing sales require a seemingly endless increase in people, financing, equipment, and space. Similarly, the firm's day-to-day operational systems for recruiting, production or service delivery, purchasing, accounting, collections, and payables are nearly overwhelmed by the sheer amount of product or service being "pushed out the door."

The major problems that occur during stage II are problems of growth rather than survival. It is during this stage that "horror stories" begin to accumulate:

• Salespeople sell a product they know is in inventory, only to learn that someone else has grabbed it for other customers.

- One vendor's invoices are paid two and three times, while another vendor has not been paid in six months.
- A precipitous drop in product quality occurs for unknown reasons.
- Turnover increases sharply just when the company needs more personnel.
- Missing letters, files, and reports cause confusion, loss of time, and embarrassment.
- Senior executives find themselves scheduled to be in two widely separated cities on the same day at the same time, or they arrive in a distant city only to learn that they are a day early.

Organizational growing pains typical of a stage II company will be discussed in detail in Chapter Three. The relative emphasis on each key developmental task appropriate for stage II is shown schematically in Figure 2.2.

Many companies experience a great deal of difficulty during stage II and may even disappear. When this occurs, it is usually because the founding entrepreneur is unable to cope with the managerial problems that arise as the organization grows. A stage II company needs an infrastructure of operational systems that lets it operate efficiently and effectively on a day-to-day basis. Unfortunately, many entrepreneurs are not interested in such "organizational plumbing."

Some firms that are fortunate enough to have discovered an especially rich market niche find themselves growing very rapidly. Although most development of a firm's resources and operational systems ought to occur during the period when the firm is growing from $1 million to $10 million in annual revenues, it is not unusual to find firms with $30, $40, $50, and even more than $100 million in annual revenues with the operational systems of a stage II company. This kind of discrepancy between a firm's size and the degree of development of its operational systems leads to serious problems, but these may be masked in the short term by the firm's rapidly rising revenues. This often proves to be the case in the most spectacular examples of organizational failure, such as Osborne Computer. In an article on the rise and fall of Adam Osborne, Steve Coll states, "In retrospect, it seems clear that the company's accounting

Figure 2.2. Developmental Emphasis in a Stage II Firm.

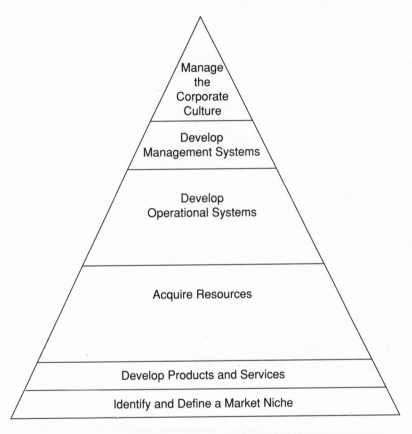

procedures were so slipshod that no one knew how things were."[3] Chapter Four will present several examples of companies that were successful at stages I and II but experienced developmental problems during their transitions.

Taken together, stages I and II, the new venture and expansion stages, constitute the entrepreneurial phase of organizational development. It is during these two stages of growth that the classic skills of entrepreneurship are most relevant. It is also during this phase that the need to make the transition from an entrepreneurship to an entrepreneurially oriented professionally managed firm begins to occur.

Stage III: Professionalization. Somewhere during the period of explosive growth that characterizes stage II, senior management realizes (or ought to realize) that a need for a qualitative change in the firm is arising. The company cannot merely add people, money, equipment, and space to cope with its growth; it must undergo a transition or metamorphosis and become a somewhat different type of organization, as illustrated in the Custom Printing example described in the introduction.

Until this point, the firm has been entrepreneurial. It has operated with a considerable degree of informality. It may have lacked well-defined goals, responsibilities, plans, or controls but still prospered. However, once a critical size has been achieved, many of these practices and procedures must be increasingly formalized. The need for this transition typically occurs by the time an organization has reached approximately $10 million in sales. The sheer size of the organization then requires more formal plans, regularly scheduled meetings, defined organizational roles and responsiblities, a performance appraisal system, and management control systems. These in turn require a planned program of organizational development.

The people who manage the firm must also change their skills and capabilities. Until this point, it was possible to be more of a doer or hands-on manager than a professional manager. At this stage, however, the organization increasingly requires people who are adept at formal administration, planning, organization, motivation, leadership, and control.

The relative emphasis on each key developmental task appropriate for stage III is shown schematically in Figure 2.3. As the figure indicates, the most important task during this stage is the development of management systems.

Although the professionalization of a firm ought to occur during the period when sales are growing from $10 million to approximately $100 million, the rate of corporate growth often outstrips the rate at which the enterprise's management systems are developed. This can lead to serious problems. An example of these problems can be seen in the history of Apple Computer. In 1984, Apple was essentially a stage II company in the process of making the transition to stage III, even though its corporate revenues were

Figure 2.3. Developmental Emphasis in a Stage III Firm.

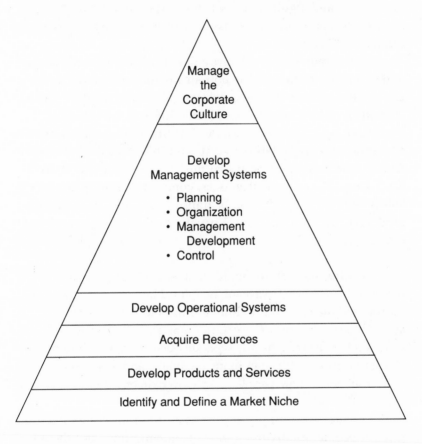

about $2 billion. Similar problems occurred at Maxicare, which had revenues of about $1.8 billion before downsizing and filing for bankruptcy.

Chapter Five will present the case history of one organization that made the transition from stage II to stage III successfully. It will examine the process through which this transition was accomplished and the problems that were encountered along the way.

Stage IV: Consolidation. Once an organization has made the transition to a professionally managed firm with workable systems for planning, organization, management development, and control, the firm must turn its attention to an intangible but never-theless real and significant asset: the corporate culture. Manage-ment of the corporate culture is the main task of stage IV of orga-nizational development.

Corporate culture can have a powerful effect not only on day-to-day operations but on the bottom line of profitability as well. During the growth that was necessary to reach stage IV (which typically seems to begin at about $100 million in sales), the firm has brought in new "waves" of people. The first wave probably arrived when the firm was relatively small and informal, during stage I. During this period, the firm's culture (values, beliefs, and norms) was transmitted by direct day-to-day contact between the founder(s) and personnel. The diffusion or transmission of culture was a by-product of what the firm did. Virtually everybody knew everybody else. Everybody also knew what the firm wanted to achieve and how.

During stage II, the rapid expansion of the firm most likely brought in a second wave of people. The first-wave personnel transmitted the corporate culture to this new generation. However, at an increased level of organizational size, especially once the firm develops geographically separate operations, this informal so-cialization process becomes more attenuated and less effective. The sheer number of new people simply overwhelms the socialization system.

By the time a firm reaches $100 million in revenues, a third wave of people usually has joined the organization, and the infor-mal socialization is no longer adequate to do what it once did so well. At this stage, the firm must develop a more conscious and formal method of transmitting the corporate culture throughout the organization. Many companies are currently trying to reshape their corporate culture in this way. The relative emphasis on each key developmental task appropriate for stage IV is pictured in Figure 2.4. Chapter Six will present the case history of one organization that is in the process of changing its corporate culture as it makes the transition to stage IV, and Chapter Twelve will examine the management of corporate culture.

Figure 2.4. Developmental Emphasis in a Stage IV Firm.

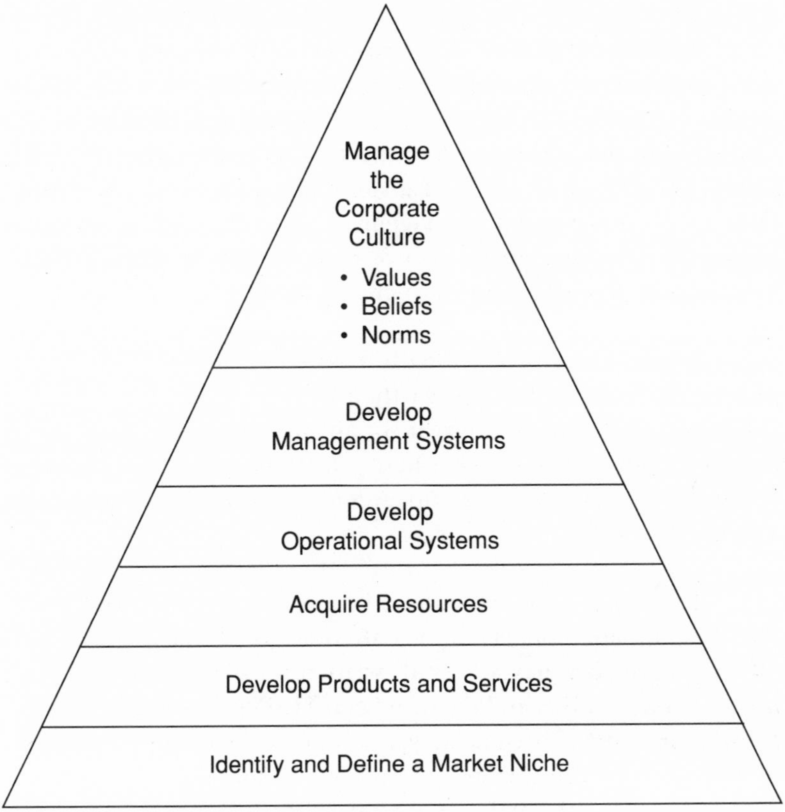

Manage
the
Corporate
Culture

• Values
• Beliefs
• Norms

Develop
Management Systems

Develop
Operational Systems

Acquire Resources

Develop Products and Services

Identify and Define a Market Niche

Differences Between Entrepreneurial and Professional Management

Stages I and II, taken together, make up the entrepreneurial phase of organizational development, while stages III and IV make up the "professional management" phase. As an organization passes from one of these phases of growth to the other, a variety of changes will occur in it.

There is a qualitative difference between an entrepreneurship and a professionally managed firm. The former tends to be characterized by informality, lack of systems, and a free-spirited nature. The latter tends to be more formal, to have well-developed systems, and to be proud of its disciplined, profit-oriented approach.

The most important differences between an entrepreneurship and a professionally managed organization involve nine key "result areas": (1) profit, (2) planning, (3) organization, (4) control, (5) management development, (6) budgeting, (7) innovation, (8) leadership, and (9) culture. Table 2.2 summarizes the principal characteristics of professional management as compared with entrepreneurial management in each of these key result areas. We will now describe these differences in greater detail.

Profit. In a professionally managed firm, profit is an explicit goal; it is planned, rather than being a residual or whatever is left over at the end of the year. In an entrepreneurial firm, profit is sought, but it is not an explicit goal to be attained. The entrepreneur(s) may be willing to invest and sacrifice current profits for a future "big hit."

Planning. Unfortunately, in many entrepreneurial firms, the plan, if there is one, is in the entrepreneur's head. A professionally managed firm has a formal, written business plan. Planning becomes a way of life, and the firm begins to develop a strategic plan for what it wants to become as well as operational plans at all levels of the company. Contingency or "what if" plans also are developed. The practice of informal, superficial, ad hoc planning is replaced by a regular planning cycle.

Organization. An entrepreneurial firm has an informal organizational structure with overlapping and undefined responsibilities. People are expected to do whatever is necessary, without regard to job titles or positions. This is fine when a firm is small. But as it grows, chaos can set in, with people simply not knowing what they are supposed to do. A professionally managed firm has a set of written role descriptions that clearly state responsibilities. These descriptions are designed to be mutually exclusive and exhaustive. They are intended to help people understand what their role is and to give focus to their efforts and use of time.

Table 2.2. Comparison of Professional Management and
Entrepreneurial Management.

Key Result Areas	Professional Management	Entrepreneurial Management
Profit	Profit orientation; profit is an explicit goal.	Profit seen as a by-product.
Planning	Formal, systematic planning: • Strategic planning • Operational planning • Contingency planning	Informal, ad hoc planning.
Organization	Formal, explicit role descriptions that are mutually exclusive and exhaustive.	Informal structure with overlapping and undefined responsibilities.
Control	Formal, planned system of organizational control, including explicit objectives, targets, measures, evaluations, and rewards.	Partial, ad hoc control; seldom uses formal measurement.
Management Development	Planned management development: • Identification of requirements • Design of programs	Ad hoc development, principally through on-the-job training.
Budgeting	Management by standards and variances.	Budget not explicit; no follow-up on variances.
Innovation	Orientation to incremental innovations; willingness to take calculated risks.	Orientation toward major innovations; willingness to take major risks.
Leadership	Consultative or participative styles.	Styles may vary from very directive to laissez-faire.
Culture	Well-defined culture.	Loosely defined, "family"-oriented culture.

Control. In an entrepreneurship, control of operations tends to be lacking or at least is often piecemeal. The firm usually lacks formal measurement or performance appraisal systems. A professionally managed firm, by contrast, has a formal, planned system of organizational control. This system makes full use of explicit objectives and goals, measurements of performance, feedback, evaluation, and rewards.

Development. Management development is planned in a professionally managed firm. The firm makes a conscious effort to develop the managerial skills of individuals and to prepare a pool of managers for the firm as a whole. In an entrepreneurship, however, management development is unplanned and tends to occur, if at all, through on-the-job experience. Although the entrepreneurial firm may avoid the cost of management development programs, people may become victims of the "Peter Principle" and cost the company through inefficiency, mistakes, and replacement costs.

Budgeting. In an entrepreneurship, budgeting tends to lack detail. There is little follow-up on variances or deviations from the budget. A professionally managed firm's budget system focuses on standards and variances. Managers are held accountable for performance compared against budget goals. Budgets are not "cast in concrete" but they are there to guide performance.

Innovation. By definition, entrepreneurial companies are oriented toward innovation. Many are willing to make major innovations in product, services, or operating methods. Some entrepreneurs even "bet the company" on an innovation because of the high payoff for success. They tend to need "quick hits" or fast payoffs. Professionally managed organizations tend to be oriented more toward incremental innovations. They are less likely to bet the company, and they often spread their risk among a portfolio of different products or projects. They are willing to take calculated risks, but they may seem relatively averse to risks, at least in comparison to entrepreneurial companies. There are exceptions to this, and established professionally managed companies such as Boeing and IBM are famous for having "bet the company" on new technologies a number of times during their history.

Leadership. In entrepreneurial companies, leadership typically ranges from very directive styles such as autocratic or benevolent autocratic to very nondirective styles such as a laissez-faire (see Chapter Eleven for a discussion of different leadership styles). In a professionally managed organization, the tendency today is toward more interactive styles, such as consultative and participative management, or, in a few instances, to consensus or team-oriented styles. Entrepreneurial organizations are more likely to have charismatic leaders than are professionally managed companies because of the nature of the process of selection for promotion in large organizations. Lee Iacocca is one exception, which indicates that the lack of charismatic leaders does not have to characterize professionally managed companies. Many of the best-managed companies are oriented to continuous, incremental improvements and long-term support of major innovations that do not require fast payoffs.

Culture. Culture tends to be loosely defined in entrepreneurial organizations. Usually it is not explicitly managed by the firm. Often the culture of an entrepreneurial organization is oriented toward a "family" feeling, which is feasible because of the firm's relatively small size. Professionally managed organizations are more likely to treat organizational culture explicitly as a variable to be managed and transmitted throughout the organization, and understand that culture is a source of sustainable competitive advantage.

Relevance of Differences. Our discussion of the differences between entrepreneurial and professionally managed firms is intended to be descriptive rather than evaluative. Both types have strengths and limitations. The significant point is that different styles are appropriate at different stages of organizational growth.

From an entrepreneurial organization's standpoint, it is clear that something inevitably will be lost as the organization makes the transition to professional management. However, something will also be gained. Just as a plant that has been successful in its pot must be transplanted if it is to continue to grow and develop properly, an organization that has outgrown its infrastructure and style of management must also make a transformation. Failure to do so will lead to a variety of problems.

Discrepancies Between Growth and Organizational Development

As we have seen, two independent dimensions are involved in each stage of organizational growth: size and the extent to which the enterprise has developed systems in each of the six critical development areas. An organization can be at stage III in terms of size, as measured in annual revenues, but only at stage II in its internal organizational capabilities, its infrastructure. For example, after only a very few years of existence, Osborne Computer was a stage IV company in size, but it was only a stage II company in organizational development.

An organization will face significant problems if its internal development is too far out of step with its size. As shown in Figure 2.5, the greater the degree of incongruity between an organization's size and the development of its infrastructure, the greater is the probability that the firm will experience organizational growing pains (the topic of the next chapter). Such a firm is like a thirteen-year-old boy who is well over six feet tall: He has the body of a man but, most likely, the mind of a child. As a senior manager in one organization stated: "We are essentially a $30 million company that happened to have $350 million sales." The manager meant that the firm had the operating systems and developmental structure of a $30 million company, but its growth had given it more than ten times as much revenues. Predictably, the company was in trouble, and was ultimately purchased by a competitor. In the next chapter, we will examine the nature of the growing pains that occur when an organization's size has outgrown its infrastructure.

Figure 2.5. Causes of Organizational Growing Pains.

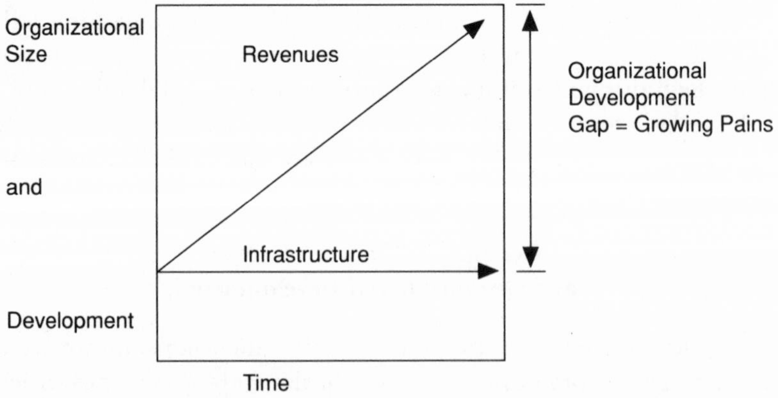

Managing the Transition Between Growth Stages

There are four steps by which the senior managers of a rapidly growing entrepreneurial company can assist their company to make a smooth transition from one stage of growth to the next. They are as follows:

1. Perform an organizational evaluation or audit of the company's effectiveness at its current stage of development
2. Formulate an organizational development plan
3. Implement the plan through action plans and programs
4. Monitor the programs for effectiveness

Each of these steps will now be examined in detail.

Perform an Organizational Evaluation or Audit. The first step in making a smooth growth transition is to apply the framework presented earlier to the organization, identifying its current stage of development and its strengths and weaknesses in the six key development areas. This can be done by performing an organizational evaluation or audit in each of the key areas—a systematic assessment, by means of data analysis and interviews with organization members, of the extent to which the company's organizational systems are adequate to meet the firm's current and anticipated future requirements. An organizational evaluation may be performed by the firm's management, but many firms prefer to have independent consultants make the audit in order to obtain greater objectivity. The findings of the evaluation represent a diagnosis of the organization at its current stage of development.

Formulate an Organizational Development Plan. Once the organizational evaluation has been completed, management must develop a master plan or blueprint for building the capabilities needed for the organization to function successfully at its current or next stage of development. This is the organizational development plan. It should include specific goals and action plans for the implementation of those goals. Typically, the first step in the planning process is strategic planning, which involves people at various organizational levels. Strategic planning will be described in Chapter Seven.

Implement the Organizational Development Plan and Monitor Its Progress. The third and fourth steps in preparing an organization for the transition to a new growth stage are implementing the changes set forth in the organizational development plan and monitoring their effects. This includes both developing new organizational systems (planning, organization, control) and developing management's capabilities through corporate education programs. Management development programs may focus on administrative skills (such as planning), leadership skills, or both. We will examine the role of management development programs in a case study in Chapter Nine and describe the types of leadership skills required in Chapter Eleven. Implementation of the organizational development program may also involve changes in the corporate culture, as will be discussed in Chapter Twelve.

Once the development program has been implemented, management needs to monitor its progress in meeting the developmental needs of the firm. Such monitoring allows senior managers to make changes in the program whenever they determine that it no longer meets its intended goals.

These four steps—diagnosing, planning, implementing, and monitoring changes in the organizational capabilities of a company—are the keys to making a smooth transition from an entrepreneurship to a professionally managed firm. The steps are the same regardless of the size, industry, or current stage of development of a firm.

It should be noted that these steps may appear simple, but they are often quite complex in practice. The transition process will typically require one to two years for a stage I firm, while three years or more may well be required in a stage IV firm. Some aspects of the change, such as changes in personnel (voluntary or otherwise), may be difficult to handle. However, where the process is suitably designed and well executed, the firm will almost always emerge from it stronger and more successful than ever.

Failure of senior management to take the necessary steps in negotiating transitions between each of the stages can have significant consequences. These range from stagnation and blocked growth to removal of the founders, as happened at Apple Computer and Maxicare. Or, the company may experience bankruptcy or take-over, as happened with Osborne Computer and People Express.

Managing the Transition: Humana Versus Maxicare

Maxicare and Humana provide examples of two companies within the health care industry that had different experiences with growth. These differences can be attributed to the degree to which each was able to execute the four transition steps adequately. These steps provide a measure of management control during rapid growth that increases the accuracy of decisions and the rapidity of response to problems.

Maxicare's problems in executing the transition steps may account for the difficulties that ultimately led to the resignation of its founders. In existence since the early 1970s, Maxicare began an aggressive acquisition program in 1982 before it had built up its own internal infrastructure. Two major acquisitions in 1987, however, nearly proved fatal. One of the acquisitions had more significant problems than had first been realized and Maxicare was unable to integrate the company without significant damage to itself. Although it was making more than $1.8 billion in revenues, Maxicare was still dealing with problems common to stage II firms. Moreover, the acquisitions also lacked an adequate infrastructure for their own operations. The net result was an organizational nightmare.

Industry analysts now attribute Maxicare's initial success to growth by acquisition rather than to savvy market analysis.[4] Maxicare's problems can be seen as the result of inadequate evaluation of its own and the acquisition's current strengths and weaknesses, as well as the lack of a plan that took these into account. This is a failure to adequately perform steps 1 and 2 in the process of managing the transition from one stage of growth to the next.

Similarly to Maxicare, Humana also followed an explosive growth through acquisition and construction period in the 1970s. However, Humana had built up a strong organizational infrastructure, which enabled it to better deal with the problems caused by rapid growth. It, too, experienced growing pains attributable to inadequate assessment and planning, and the firm had to divest itself of thirty low-profit hospitals, thus slowing its growth.[5] Characterizing Humana's approach to diversification into health insurance, CFO Bill Ballard noted, "We didn't study it to death."[6] However, the saving factor in Humana's difficulties with its insurance companies and ambulatory clinics was its management infrastructure, which permitted monitoring of its effectiveness in these areas. Seeing impending disaster, Humana made immediate and strong cutbacks in its operations,[7] actions that ensured the company's survival and made its return to a strong position possible. Humana's proficiency in performing steps 3 and 4 was, then, a key factor in its success.

Summary

This chapter has presented a framework to help senior managers understand and guide organizations at different stages of growth and development. It has described the first four major stages of organizational growth, from the inception of a new venture (stage I) to the consolidation of a professionally managed firm (stage IV). It has examined the degree of emphasis that must be placed on each level of the pyramid of organizational development at each stage of growth. It has also examined the differences between an entrepreneurial and a professionally managed organization. Finally, it has described the steps that must be taken to make a successful transition from one stage of growth to the next.

In the next chapter, we will examine the nature of organizational growing pains and present a method for measuring and interpreting them. Recognition and identification of these growing pains is a necessary part of the organizational evaluation process, which is the first step of the transition from an entrepreneurship to a professionally managed firm.

3 Recognizing Growing Pains and Assessing the Need for Change

When an organization has not been fully successful in developing the internal systems it needs at a given stage of growth, it begins to experience growing pains. This chapter examines in detail the most common organizational growing pains, showing through examples how these growing pains emerge in real-life companies. It also presents a method of measuring organizational growing pains and interpreting the extent to which they signal the need for further organizational development. Finally, it discusses the degree to which different sizes and types of business experience growing pains.

The Ten Most Common Organizational Growing Pains

As organizations enlarge, they often experience a variety of growing pains that signal that something has gone wrong in the process of organizational development. Such symptoms are especially likely to occur in a stage II company, where they warn of the need for a transition to stage III. The ten most common organizational growing pains are listed here:

1. People feel that "there are not enough hours in the day."
2. People spend too much time "putting out fires."
3. People are not aware of what other people are doing.
4. People lack understanding about where the firm is headed.
5. There are too few good managers.

6. People feel that "I have to do it myself if I want to get it done correctly."
7. Most people feel that meetings are a waste of time.
8. When plans are made, there is very little follow-up, so things just don't get done.
9. Some people feel insecure about their place in the firm.
10. The firm continues to grow in sales but not in profits.

Each of these growing pains is described in the pages that follow.

People Feel That "There Are Not Enough Hours in the Day." One of the most common organizational growing pains is the complaint that there is never enough time. Employees feel that they could work twenty-four hours per day, seven days a week, and still not have sufficient time to get everything done. They begin to complain about "overload" and excessive stress. Both individuals and departments feel that they are always trying to catch up but never succeeding. The more work they do, the more there seems to be, resulting in a never-ending cycle. People feel as if they are on a treadmill.

The effects of these feelings can be far reaching. First, employees' belief that they are being needlessly overworked may bring on morale problems. Complaints may increase. Second, employees may begin to experience physical illnesses brought on by excessive stress. These psychological and physical problems may lead to increased absenteeism, which can decrease the company's productivity. Finally, employees may simply decide that they can no longer operate under these conditions and may leave the organization. This will result in significant turnover costs and replacement costs related to recruiting, selecting, and training new people.

When many employees have the feeling that there is not enough time in the day, usually no one is suffering more from this feeling than the company's founding entrepreneur. The entrepreneur, feeling ultimately responsible for the firm's success, may work sixteen hours a day, seven days a week in an effort to keep the company operating effectively and help it grow. As the organization grows, the entrepreneur begins to notice that he or she can no longer exercise complete control over its functioning. This realization can result in a great deal of personal stress. We will see examples of this in the cases of Metro Realty and Tempo Products (Chapters Five and Six). This was also common at Apple Computer and Maxicare.

People Spend Too Much Time "Putting Out Fires."   A second common growing pain shows itself in excessive time spent dealing with short-term crises—"putting out fires." This problem usually results from a lack of long-range planning, and, typically, the absence of a strategic plan. Individual employees and the organization as a whole live from day to day, never knowing what to expect. The result may be a loss of organizational productivity, effectiveness, and efficiency.

Examples of the "putting out fires" problem are easy to find. In the case of Custom Printing, described in the introduction, a lack of planning caused orders to be needlessly rushed, resulting in excessive pressure on employees. Drivers had to be hired on weekends and evenings to deliver orders, some of which were already overdue. Similarly, at Maxicare the "surprises" that were encountered after acquisitions led to an almost endless number of fires.

In other companies, which we will discuss in more detail later, lack of planning produced other short-term crises. At Metro Realty, for example, it resulted in shortages of salespeople. Because of these shortages, Metro was forced to hire new people and put them to work almost immediately, sometimes without adequate training. This, in turn, contributed to short-term productivity problems because the new people did not possess the skills necessary to be good salespeople. You will see that at Tempo Products lack of personnel planning also created problems, but for different reasons. There, personnel were hired to "take up the slack" when business was good. Once the crisis was over, the company found it had a number of people that it simply did not know what to do with.

Fires were so prevalent at one $50 million manufacturing company that managers began to refer to themselves as "fire fighters," and senior management rewarded middle management for their skill in handling crises. When it became apparent that managers who had been effective in "fire prevention" were being ignored, some of them became "arsonists" to get senior management's attention.

People Are Not Aware of What Other People Are Doing. Another symptom of organizational growing pains is that many people are increasingly unaware of the exact nature of their jobs and how these jobs relate to those of others. This creates a situation in which people and departments do whatever they want to do and say that the remaining tasks are "not our responsibility." Constant bickering between people and departments over responsibility may ensue. The organization may become a group of isolated and sometimes warring factions.

These problems typically result from the lack of an organization chart and precise role and responsibility definitions as well as effective team building. Relationships between people and between departments as well as individual responsibilities may be unclear. As you will see in the cases of Metro Realty and Tempo Products, people can become frustrated by this ambiguity and begin creating their own definitions of their roles, which may not always be in the best interests of the firm. The president of Metro Realty vividly described this phenomenon when he said, "We were a collection of little offices working toward our goals without consideration for the good of the company."

The isolation of departments from one another may result in duplication of effort or in tasks that remain incomplete because they are "someone else's responsibility." Constant arguments between departments may also occur over territory and organizational resources. You have seen how this occurred at Custom Printing, and you will see in Chapter Six that Tempo Products suffered from the effects of the need to define and protect territory as well. It was also a critical problem at Digital Equipment (DEC), the minicomputer maker, prior to a 1983 reorganization, when there were eighteen different divisions, each focusing on its own product line to the exclusion of the overall corporate goals. Even as product lines evolved and began to overlap, the sales force continued to focus only on its own line to the exclusion of others. This resulted in some customers being called on by three or more DEC salespeople, each representing a different product group and sometimes even offering similar services for different prices. In essence, DEC was a company competing against itself.

People Lack Understanding About Where the Firm Is Headed. Another typical growing pain is a widespread lack of understanding of where the firm is headed. Employees may complain that "the company has no identity" and either blame upper management for not providing enough information about the company's future direction or, worse, believe that not even upper management knows what that direction will be. Basically, there has been a communication breakdown. This was one of the critical problems at Wang Laboratories that led to the resignation of Frederick Wang, son of company founder An Wang. It appears that the senior management at Wang failed to develop and/or communicate their strategy for maximizing market opportunities. As a result, salespeople became confused about which market Wang wanted to pursue. One former sales manager described this situation: "They pushed the sales force in so many directions that the reps in the field would say, 'What is it they want us to do?' "[8]

When insufficient communication is combined with rapid changes, as is often the case in growing firms, employees may begin to feel anxious. To relieve this anxiety, they may either create their own networks for obtaining the desired information or come to believe that they know the company's direction even though management has not actually communicated this information. Both these strategies were used by Tempo Products employees. Employees' speculations as well as "real" information obtained from people who were close to senior management circulated freely on the company's grapevine. Rumors were rampant, but in fact very few people really knew why certain changes were being made. Hence, employees experienced a significant amount of anxiety.

If anxiety increases to the point where it becomes unbearable, employees may begin leaving the firm. As we described in the introduction, this happened at Custom Printing. It should be noted that turnover of this kind can be very costly to a firm.[9]

There Are Too Few Good Managers. Although a firm may have a significant number of people who hold the title of "manager," it may not have many good managers. Managers may complain that they have responsibility, but no authority. Employees may complain about the lack of direction or feedback that their managers provide. The organization may notice that some of its components have significantly higher or lower productivity than others. It may also be plagued by managers who constantly complain that they do not have time to complete their administrative responsibilities because they are too busy increasing business. When any or all of these events occur, something is wrong with the management function of the organization.

As was the case at Custom Printing, the problem may be that the company has promoted successful "doers" (salespeople, office workers, and so on) to the role of manager, assuming that they will also be successful in this role. These two roles require significantly different skills, however. Thus, without proper training, many "doers" will fail in the manager's role. Their tendency to continue "doing" will show itself in poor delegation skills and poor coordination of the activities of others. Subordinates may complain that they do not know what they are supposed to do.

Problems like these suggest that the company is not devoting sufficient resources to developing a pool of managerial talent. It may be relying too much on on-the-job training rather than on formal management development programs. For example, during the days of rapid growth at Ashton-Tate, managers multiplied almost as rapidly as rabbits. One manager stated: "I was hired and then escorted to my department. The escort said: 'Here's your department. Run it.' " Similarly, rapid growth at Apple Computer led Steven Jobs to bring in "professional managers," including John Sculley, to help manage the firm, because the company had not developed a cadre of managers as it grew.

Management problems may also result from real or perceived organizational constraints that restrict a manager's authority. In the case of Tempo Products, you will see how the perception that only top management could make decisions greatly affected lower-level managers' effectiveness. One person at this firm described the managers as "people with no real responsibility." The feeling that only upper management has decision-making responsibility is common in firms making the transition to professional management. It is a relic from the days when the founding entrepreneur made all the firm's decisions.

People Feel That "I Have to Do It Myself If I Want to Get It Done Correctly." Increasingly, as people become frustrated by the difficulty of getting things done in an organization, they come to feel that "if I want to get something done correctly, I have to do it myself." This symptom, like lack of coordination, is caused by a lack of clearly defined roles, responsibilities, and linkages between roles.

As was discussed previously, when roles and responsibilities are not clearly defined, individuals or departments tend to act on their own because they do not know whose responsibility a given task is. They may also do the task themselves to avoid confrontation, since the person or department to whom they are trying to delegate a responsibility may refuse it.

Operating under this philosophy, departments become isolated from one another, and teamwork becomes minimal. Each part of the company "does its own thing" without considering the good of the whole. Communication between management and lower levels of the organization and between departments may be minimal because the organization has no formal system through which information can be channeled. You will see how the lack of coordination between areas can lead to productivity problems and inefficiencies when you read the Metro Realty and Tempo Products cases.

Most People Feel That Meetings Are a Waste of Time. Recognizing that there is a need for better coordination and communication, the growing organization may begin to hold meetings. Unfortunately, at many firms these meetings are nothing more than discussions between people. They have no planned agendas, and often they have no designated leader. As a consequence, the meetings become a free-for-all, tend to drag on interminably, and seldom result in decisions. People feel frustrated and conclude that "our meetings are a waste of time." For example, shortly after John Sculley joined Apple Computer he attended a management meeting at Pajaro Dunes, California, where Apple had many retreats. While

Sculley tried to focus on strategic issues, he had relatively little success in controlling the discussion. The traditional operating procedure for this group was for members to say whatever was on their minds, regardless of its factual base or relevance to the particular agenda item. As a result, it was difficult to accomplish the goals of such meetings in an effective manner.

Other complaints about meetings involve lack of follow-up on decisions that are made. Some companies schedule yearly or monthly planning meetings during which goals are set for individual employees, departments, and the company as a whole. These sessions are a waste of time if people ignore the goals that have been set or fail to monitor their progress toward these goals. As you will see, Metro Realty's budgeting process suffered from this condition. In a frustrating "yearly exercise," managers met and set goals, then met again the following year with no idea of whether they achieved the previous year's goals.

A further example of ineffective use of meeting time may appear in the performance appraisal process. In many organizations that are beginning to make the transition to professional management, performance appraisals are merely discussions between supervisor and subordinate. Objective performance goals may not be set or, if set, may not be monitored by employee or manager. Managers in these firms also tend to avoid providing negative feedback. Without such feedback, employees cannot learn what they need to do to improve performance. Because little real information is exchanged, performance appraisal meetings are a waste of both supervisor's and subordinate's time. In Chapters Five and Six you will see how Metro Realty and Tempo Products suffered from ineffective performance appraisals.

When Plans Are Made, There Is Very Little Follow-Up, So Things Just Don't Get Done. Another sign of an entrepreneurship with growing pains is a lack of follow-up after plans are made. Recognizing that the need for planning is greater than in the past, an entrepreneur may introduce a planning process. People go through the motions of preparing business plans, but the things that were planned just do not get done. In one amazing case, there was no follow-up simply because the plan, after being prepared, merely sat in a drawer for the entire year until the next year's planning process. When asked about the plan, one senior manager stated: "Oh that. It's in my desk, I never look at it."

In some cases there is no follow-up because the company has not yet developed systems adequate to monitor its goals. For example, many firms desire to monitor financial goals but have not developed an accounting system that can provide the information needed to do so. Metro Realty suffered from this deficiency.

In other cases, follow-up does not occur because personnel have not received proper training in setting, monitoring, and evaluating goals. They set goals that cannot be achieved or cannot be measured, or they do not know how to evaluate and provide useful feedback on goal achievement. These problems tend to appear most often in the performance appraisal process. You will read more about them in Chapters Five and Six.

Some People Feel Insecure About Their Place in the Firm. As a consequence of other organizational growing pains, employees begin to feel insecure about their places in the firm. Typically, the entrepreneur has become anxious abut problems facing the organization and has therefore hired a "heavyweight" manager from outside. This action may have been accompanied by the termination of one or more current managers. Employees feel anxious partly because they do not understand the reasons for these and other changes. When anxiety becomes too high, it may result in morale problems or excessive turnover.

Employees may also become insecure because they are unable to see the value of their position to the firm. This occurs when roles and responsibilities are not clearly defined and terminations are also occurring. Employees begin to wonder whether they will be the next to "get the axe." In an attempt to protect themselves, they keep their activities secret and do not "make waves." This results in isolation and a decrease in teamwork.

Entire departments may come to suffer from the need to remain isolated in order to protect themselves from being eliminated. This can lead to a certain amount of schizophrenia among employees. They begin to ask, "Am I loyal to my department or to the organization at large?" This happened at Tempo Products, as you will see in Chapter Six. Similarly, under Jack Tramiel (known as "Captain Jack") at Commodore International, people were insecure about their positions and a great deal of turnover resulted.

The Firm Continues to Grow in Sales But Not in Profits. If all the other growing pains are permitted to exist, one final symptom may emerge. In some instances, sales continue to increase while profits remain flat, so that the company is succeeding only in increasing its workload. In the worst cases, sales increase while overall profits actually decline. As you will see in the chapters that follow, companies may begin to lose money without having any idea why. The business loss can be quite significant, even though sales are up. There are many examples of entrepreneurial companies which have experienced this problem, including Apple Computer, Maxicare, Wang Laboratories, and Osborne Computer.

In a significant number of companies, the decline in profits may be the result of an underlying philosophy that stresses sales. People in such companies may say, "If sales are good, then profit will also be good," or "Profit will take care of itself." Profit in these companies is not an explicit goal but merely whatever remains after expenses.

In sales-oriented companies, people often become accustomed to spending whatever they need to in order to make a sale or promote the organization. For example, at Tempo Products, employees believed that it was important to the company's image to always "go first class." They made no effort to control costs, since they believed that no matter what they did, the organization would always be profitable. Organizations may also suffer because of systems that reward employees for achieving sales goals rather than profit goals. You will see examples of these problems in Chapters Five and Six.

Measuring Organizational Growing Pains

To assist the management of an entrepreneurial company in measuring the organization's growing pains, we have developed the questionnaire shown in Exhibit 3.1. This questionnaire presents ten organizational growing pains that have been identified in a

Exhibit 3.1. Organizational Growing Pains Questionnaire.

Growing Pain	A *To a very great extent*	B *To a great extent*	C *To some extent*	D *To a slight extent*	E *To a very slight extent*
1. People feel that there are not enough hours in the day.		x			
2. People spend too much time "putting out fires."		x			
3. Many people are not aware of what others are doing.	x				
4. People lack understanding of where the firm is heading.			x		
5. There are too few good managers.		x			
6. Everybody feels, "I have to do it myself if I want it to get done correctly."			x		
7. Most people feel our meetings are a waste of time.				x	
8. When plans are made, there is very little follow-up, and things just don't get done.		x			
9. Some people feel insecure about their place in the firm.				x	
10. The firm has continued to grow in sales but not in profits.	x				

Scoring

	A	B	C	D	E
11. Add the total number of responses in each column.	2	4	2	2	0
12. Multiply the number on line 11 by the number on line 12 and record the result on line 13.	5	4	3	2	1
13. Result of line 11 times line 12.	10	16	6	4	0
14. Add the numbers on line 13 in columns A–E and place the result on this line.	36				

wide variety of entrepreneurial companies with annual sales revenues ranging from less than $1 million to over $1 billion. Responses to the questionnaire are entered on a Likert-type five-point scale with descriptions ranging from "to a very great extent" to "to a very slight extent." By placing check marks in the appropriate columns, the respondent indicates the extent to which he or she feels each of the ten growing pains characterizes the company.

Scoring the Questionnaire.   Once the questionnaire has been completed, the number of check marks in each column is totaled and recorded on line 11. Each item on line 11 is then multiplied by the corresponding weight on line 12, and the total is recorded on line 13. For example, Exhibit 3.1 shows four check marks in column B. Accordingly, we multiply 4 by the weight of 4 and record the result, 16, on line 13 of column B.

The next step is to determine the sum of the numbers on line 13. This total represents the organization's growing pains score. It can range from 10, which is the lowest possible or most favorable score, to 50, which is the highest possible or most unfavorable score.

Interpreting the Scores.   Drawing on our research concerning the degree of seriousness of problems indicated by different growing pains scores, we have worked out the color-coding scheme shown in Table 3.1. More detailed interpretation of score ranges is as follows.

A green score represents a fairly healthy organization. It suggests that everything is probably functioning in a manner satisfactory for the organization at its current stage of development.

A yellow score indicates that the organization is basically healthy, but there are some areas of concern. It is like hearing from your doctor, "Your cholesterol is in the normal range but on the high side. It's something to watch and be careful about but not an immediate concern."

An orange score indicates that some organizational problems require attention. They may not be too serious yet, but corrective action should be taken before they become so.

A red score is a clear warning of present or impending problems. Immediate corrective action is required.

Table 3.1. Interpretation of Organizational Growing Pains
Questionnaire Scores.

Score Range	Color	Interpretation
1. 10–14	Green	Everything okay
2. 15–19	Yellow	Some things to watch
3. 20–29	Orange	Some areas that need attention
4. 30–29	Red	Some very significant problems
5. 40–50	Purple	A potentially dangerous situation

A purple score indicates a dangerous, perhaps deadly, situation. The organization is in distress and may be on the verge of collapse. There may not be enough time to save it.

If a firm's score exceeds 20, a more in-depth analysis to identify problems and develop recommendations for future action is probably required. Such a score may be a signal that the firm has reached a new stage in its development and must make major, qualitative changes. Failure to pay attention to a score of this magnitude can produce very painful results. For example, the questionnaire shown in Exhibit 3.1 was completed by Joe McBride, who was the CEO of Custom Printing, the firm we described in the introduction to this book. Custom Printing's score, based on Joe's perceptions, was 36. This "red" score tallies well with the fact that, as you saw, Custom Printing was in serious trouble.

Average Scores for Different Business Sizes and Industries. Table 3.2 presents average organizational growing pains scores of companies with different annual revenues based on our extensive research. As can be seen, companies of every size experience some growing pains. As organizations grow, growing pains tend to increase until companies reach a significantly large size. Our data suggest that the most significant problems begin to be experienced when a company's annual revenues reach $10 million (stage II to stage III organizations) and continue until revenues exceed $1 billion.

Table 3.3 shows scores broken down by type of industry. Clearly, timing of the occurrence of significant organizational growing pains differs across industries.

In the service industry, a time of concern seems to occur in the $100 to $499 million revenue range. The data suggest that it is

Table 3.2. Organizational Growing Pains by Company Size.

Size (Revenues)	Average Growing Pains Score
Less than $1 million (stage I)	27.00 (orange)
$1–$9 million (stage II)	28.00 (orange)
$10–$99 million (stage III)	29.00 (orange)
$100–$499 million (stage IV)	32.00 (red)
$500 million–$1 billion	32.00 (red)
More than $1 billion	29.00 (orange)

Table 3.3. Organizational Growing Pains in Different Industries.

Size (Revenues)	Overall	Service	High-Tech	Low-Tech	Finance
Less than $1 million (stage I)	26.56 Orange	26.38 Orange	25.78 Orange	28.10 Orange	25.60 Orange
$1–$4 million (stage II)	27.36 Orange	27.73 Orange	27.62 Orange	26.63 Orange	27.95 Orange
$5–$9 million (stage II)	28.56 Orange	27.25 Orange	28.55 Orange	31.17 Red	28.67 Orange
$10–$24 million (stage III)	28.97 Orange	29.60 Orange	30.00 Red	25.65 Orange	31.32 Red
$25–$99 million (stage III)	28.62 Orange	28.91 Orange	29.33 Orange	25.90 Orange	30.13 Red
$100–$499 million (stage IV)	32.33 Red	31.44 Red	34.59 Red	29.17 Orange	33.67 Red
$500 million –$1 billion	32.16 Red	31.75 Red	32.00 Red		35.00 Red
More than $1 billion	29.11 Orange	28.67 Orange	27.53 Orange	17.00 Yellow	26.50 Orange

very difficult to manage a large service company. Service companies in the less than $1 million range seem to have the fewest growing pains.

High-technology companies appear to experience significant problems when they reach the $10 to $24 million range of revenues. Problems then continue into the $500 million to $1 billion range. Low-technology companies, in contrast, experience significant problems in the $5 to $9 million revenue range, but they appear to resolve many of them by the time they reach $10 million in revenues. As can be seen in Table 3.3, in the financial industry growing pains increase until revenues exceed $1 billion and then they drop.

The information presented here suggests that entrepreneurs in different industries need to be concerned with growing pains at different periods of their organizations' lives. For those in the service, high-tech, and finance industries, a critical period occurs at the $10 to $24 million revenue range. For low-tech industries, this critical point occurs when revenues begin to exceed $5 million. These data also indicate that large ($500 million to $1 billion in revenues) financial firms experience the most severe organizational growing pains.

While the data presented in Table 3.3 indicate that there are certain stages of growth in which organizational growing pains are likely to be severe, these growing pains at any stage can be alleviated. This is best done through early detection of problems and careful plans for handling them.

Organizational Growing Pains, Growth Rates, and Infrastructure

As we have noted in this and the previous chapter, when an organization's growth outstrips its infrastructure, organizational growing pains will result. The more the firm is growing, the more difficult it will be for management to keep the organization's infrastructure at a level required to support the firm's rate of growth.

Based on our work with a wide variety of organizations we have identified five different rates of growth that characterize different categories of growth. Growth at the rate of less than 15 percent a year can be thought of as normal growth. This is relatively un-

spectacular growth, but the firm will double in size in approximately five years if it is growing at a rate of 15 percent per year. A
growth rate of between 15 and 25 percent per year can be thought
of as rapid growth. A rate of growth from 25 to 50 percent per year
can be considered "very rapid growth." Growth at a rate of 50 to
100 percent per year can be thought of as "hypergrowth." If the firm
is growing at a rate greater than 100 percent per year, it can perhaps
be regarded as experiencing "light-speed growth."

Based on our experience, it is extremely difficult for firms to
deal with growth rates greater than 50 percent per year. When the
rate of growth of a firm equals or exceeds what we have characterized as hypergrowth, a firm can become very dangerously close to
"choking on its own growth." This has happened to a number of
firms, including Osborne Computer, Maxicare, People Express, and
New World Pictures.[10]

Hypergrowth at New World Entertainment. New World
Pictures (NWP) was acquired in 1983 by two entrepreneurs. It was
the company founded by Roger Korman, king of "B movies."
Among his many successes, Korman had originally produced the
horror classic "Little Shop of Horrors."

Under Korman's leadership, the firm had found a market
niche producing low-budget movies, such as "Little Shop of Horrors." The new entrepreneurs, Larry Kuppin and Harry Sloan, were
highly ambitious and saw the possibility of turning NWP into a
diversified entertainment company, which they renamed "New
World Entertainment" (NWE). They had a brilliant entrepreneurial
strategy, which was designed to move NWP into other areas of
related entertainment where the firm could establish market niches.
They established New World Video and New World Television as
units of their company. They also acquired Lion's Gate Studios and
Marvel Publications. Three of these new units actually had relatively distinctive market niches. For example, New World Television produced such hit shows as "Crime Story" and "Santa
Barbara." The division as a whole was very well positioned to take
advantage of a need for relatively low-cost TV "product" for the
various networks.

NWE grew in revenue from $8.4 million in 1983 to more than

$450 million in 1987. In terms of the growth framework described above, NWE was growing at a "light-speed" rate. Although the firm was clearly successful in the extent to which it was growing in revenues, it was unable to develop its infrastructure to a sufficient extent that it could avoid the classic symptoms of organizational growing pains. By 1988, the firm was experiencing pressures on profitability as well as a wide variety of organizational difficulties. Thus NWE had come very close to "choking on its own growth."

When a firm grows as rapidly as NWE did, it is extremely difficult to avoid a gap between the organization size and its infrastructure. The ideal strategy for a firm that anticipates rapid growth is to build an infrastructure sufficient for the size of the organization it anticipates becoming prior to actually reaching that size. This means that management must make an investment in the future of the organization by investing in the operational management infrastructure. Most firms prefer to wait until they reach a certain size before investing in an infrastructure appropriate for that given stage of development. Unfortunately, by the time a firm reaches a certain size, there will be a significant lead time required to develop the infrastructure appropriate to that particular stage of growth. During the period that the firm is trying to "catch up" and develop its infrastructure, it will experience the classic symptoms of organizational growing pains. If these growing pains are allowed to reach the "red" or "purple" levels of degree of severity, the firm may well be in danger of failure.

What should a firm do to avoid the problems encountered at NWE? Most entrepreneurs are always concerned with the risk of failure if revenues are insufficient to cover expenses. However, many ignore the equally damaging risks of choking on their own rapid growth. To avoid the problems accompanying hypergrowth, a company must have an infrastructure that will absorb that growth. If a company anticipates rapid growth, then management must invest in building the required infrastructure *before* it is actually necessary. It is very difficult, and sometimes impossible, to "play catch-up" with organizational infrastructure. Some companies, such as Compaq Computer, have their infrastructure in place prior to their explosive growth and reap the benefits of this investment.

This strategy of building the infrastructure prior to growth is not merely appropriate for large companies, but for relatively small entrepreneurships as well. For example, in 1982 I met with the president of a service firm specializing in insurance-based benefit programs for executives when the firm had approximately $3 million in annual revenues. At that time, the author advised the CEO that it was probably premature to build the infrastructure to the extent that was being contemplated. However, the CEO indicated that he wanted his firm to grow to $50 million in revenue by 1987. He then proceeded to invest in professionalizing his company before it was actually necessary. This was a wise move, because the company actually grew to more than $65 million in revenue by the late 1980s.

Summary

Some people believe that the solution to problems of growth is to avoid growth. Unfortunately, very soon after an organization is founded, it must grow or it will die. Managers can, however, control the *rate* of growth, but it is unrealistic to try to remain at a given size or stage of development. This means we must learn how to manage growth and the inevitable transitions it requires.

This chapter has presented an in-depth discussion of the most common organizational growing pains. It has also presented a method for assessing the extent to which a company suffers from these growing pains. The company's score on the Organizational Growing Pains Questionnaire can suggest both the extent of its problems and specific needs for action. Finally, the chapter has provided information on the degree of organizational growing pains experienced by companies of different sizes and in different types of businesses. Variations exist here, but it is clear that organizations of all sizes and types experience some growing pains. As we may have suggested, severity of these problems can be affected by the rate of growth experienced by the organization. Managers of rapidly growing companies of any size or type must learn to recognize organizational growing pains and take steps to alleviate them so that their organizations can continue to operate successfully.

Part Two

Management Strategies
for Each Stage of
Organizational Growth

Part One of this book presented a framework for understanding the development of successful organizations. It explained the six key areas or tasks that make up the pyramid of organizational development. It also identified and examined the first four stages of growth of organizations. It presented the four major steps involved in making the transition from one stage of growth to the next. Finally, it described the organizational growing pains that result when a firm has not been fully successful in its development and presented a way to measure and interpret them.

Part Two will examine the issues involved in developing successful organizations at each stage of growth. It will also study the nature of the transitions that must be made in moving from stage I to stages II, III, and IV. It will draw on a variety of case studies of organizations at different stages of growth.

Chapter Four begins by discussing the steps involved in developing a successful stage I company. It gives several illustrations of firms that have been successful in accomplishing this stage of development and examines the problems faced by each company. Examples cited range from Domino's Pizza, Mrs. Fields' Cookies, and Federal Express to Liz Claiborne, Apple Computer, and Ashton-Tate.

Chapter Four also examines the process and problems involved in developing successful stage II organizations. It describes some growing pains that may result when the process of organizational development has not been fully successful, especially when a firm has not developed the operational systems it needs to function well at stage II.

Chapter Five describes the challenges of stage III and the case of a company that made the transition from stage II to stage III. It describes the company's situation, the nature of its growing pains, and the actions it took to make a successful transition between these stages. This case study also illustrates the most common problems involved in making the transition from entrepreneurship to professional management, especially in developing management systems. We also provide several other examples of companies that faced the challenges presented by this stage of development.

Chapter Six examines a firm that is making the transition from stage II to stage IV. It discusses the issues involved in managing corporate culture as a company grows.

4. The New Venture and Expansion Stages

This chapter deals with the issues involved in developing successful entrepreneurial organizations at stages I and II of organizational growth. It examines the tasks that must be performed to establish a successful new venture (stage I) and deals with the typical growing pains that arise during the expansion that takes place after a company has been successfully established (stage II).

Developing Successful Stage I Organizations

In the first stage of an organization's development or life cycle, the company is a new venture. This stage embraces the period from an organization's birth to the point at which it begins to experience rapid growth (usually at about $1 million in annual revenues). The first section of this chapter identifies the key problems or challenges involved in building a successful new venture and provides several illustrations of actual firms that have successfully met these challenges. It examines why these firms have been successful.

The Key Issues at Stage I. The key challenges or problems to be solved in developing a successful new venture are identifying a market need and finding a way to satisfy that need by providing a product or service. The skills required to solve these problems are essentially the classic entrepreneurial skills: the ability to see a market need, the willingness to make a risky investment to create a business that attempts to satisfy that need, and the ability to create an embryonic organization that is capable of providing the required products or services.

73

The primary basis of entrepreneurship is an idea. The idea may be the product of long, tedious planning and research or of a brilliant, almost accidental insight.

Hot Rock, Inc.: A Classic Entrepreneurial Success.   To understand the process of developing a successful stage I organization, let us review an actual example of a recent entrepreneurial success. In February 1983, two Harvard Business School students sipping coffee at Boston's Logan Airport casually began to discuss an idea for promoting record sales."[11] They wondered: What if ordering a record could be as easy as making a phone call? What if someone sitting in a living room could simply pick up the telephone and order a new album that he or she had just heard? One year later, the two student entrepreneurs had converted this concept into a successful business called Hot Rock, Inc. How did that happen?

The basis for the pair's ultimate success was a perceived market need. The two entrepreneurs, Michael Wigley and Jerry De La Vega, together with a third colleague, David Ishag, saw a potential solution to a problem that plagued the record industry: As the buyers of records grew older and became increasingly affluent, they had less time to shop. As a result, record companies became less likely to reach this segment of the market through the traditional channels of distribution. The entrepreneurs were also aware of the tremendous popularity of MTV and believed that it drew a broader audience than the eighteen to thirty-four age group that was the core market of record companies.

The basic concept of this new venture was elegant in its simplicity. By combining the convenience of telephone sales, the advertising penetration of MTV, and the market's demand for rock, the entrepreneurs identified a market niche that was not being satisfied. They put together a prospectus, raised $120,000 in venture capital, and began their firm. The target market was viewers of MTV, who were provided with Hot Rock's toll-free telephone number twenty-four hours a day.

After just a few months of operation, the firm projected sales of $6.7 million for its first year. It had successfully solved the critical problems of a stage I organization: identification of a market and development of a product or service relevant to that market's need.

Other Examples of New Venture Success.   There are many other examples of entrepreneurial success. Let us examine some of them to gain further insight into the process and skills required to develop a successful stage I company.

There have been a number of entrepreneurial successes in the computer industry, especially in microcomputers. One of the most spectacular success stories is that of Apple Computer. Apple was founded by Steven Jobs and Steven Wozniak. It was based on the perceived market for a "personal" computer: a small, relatively in-expensive computer that was "user friendly." Following this concept, the firm grew from being housed in a garage to having more than $1 billion in sales in 1983.

Adam Osborne, who founded Osborne Computer, had the concept of a relatively low-priced, easy to use computer that was also portable. His idea was a spin-off of the personal computer concept pioneered by Apple Computer, but Osborne identified a new market niche when he made his computers easy to carry. For a few years, Osborne Computer was one of the fastest-growing companies in business history. In 1981, the firm's first full year of operation, its sales were $5.8 million. By 1982, sales had grown to $68.8 million.

William Zimmerman founded Pic 'N' Save with the idea that the firm could buy manufacturers' excess inventory cheaply and sell it at large discounts to customers. The firm's merchandise constantly changes, as it shops the world for surplus goods. The company had grown to more than $235 million in annual revenues by 1984.

Another recent example of entrepreneurial success is Ashton-Tate. The firm's major product was dBASE II, a software package. Ashton-Tate was founded by Hal Lashley and George Tate. The firm took the name of George Tate and "Ashton," a large blue-and-yellow parrot. Ashton lives in his cage in the firm's offices in California.

Ashton-Tate's history is a vintage example of entrepreneurship. Initially, Lashley and Tate founded a part-time software distribution business. They then came across a software product developed by a third party and made an agreement to distribute it.

They named the product dBASE II. The product was an extraordinary success because it filled a market need and was marketed well.

Although many of the examples just cited are in the computer industry, high technology is not a prerequisite for entrepreneurial success. Federal Express is an example of a company based on a service rather than a product, and a relatively unsophisticated service at that.

Frederick W. Smith was the architect of Federal Express. At the time the company was founded, Emery Air Freight dominated the package delivery business. Emery had built a successful business on the assumption that the major cost in air freight involved weight and, therefore, air carrier charges. This notion made sense for heavy items but not for small packages or letters. Federal Express built a different system, geared to the goal of minimizing handling costs rather than air carrier costs. It focused on a different niche—small packages.

The success of both Debbi Fields of Mrs. Fields' Cookies and David Liederman of David's Cookies not only show that a new venture can be developed from a very old, familiar product; it also shows that more than one niche can be filled successfully within the same market. Both entrepreneurs created successful new ventures by developing stores to make and market over-the-counter chocolate chip cookies.

David's Cookies defined a market for consumers who prefer large chunks of chocolate in a thin, buttery cookie that is not sold until it cools. Mrs. Fields' Cookies, in contrast, defined a market for a more traditional chocolate chip cookie, with smaller chips in a larger-sized cookie that is served warm. Both firms have been quite successful.

Mitchell Kapor worked as a disc jockey, studied to be a Transcendental Meditation instructor, and became a mental health counselor. In 1979, he bought an Apple computer. He wrote two programs, called VisiPlot and VisiTrend, that simplified business graphs and charts. He then took the profits from these products, together with venture capital, and founded Lotus Development Corporation in April 1982. The firm produced the very successful program called Lotus 1-2-3. When the firm went public in October 1983, Kapor's stock was worth more than $80 million.

During its first year of business, 1983, Compaq Computer Corporation's sales zoomed to $111.2 million. The firm's product was a portable version of the IBM personal computer. It was compatible with the IBM PC and sold at a lower price.

In 1960, Thomas S. Monaghan and his brother borrowed $500 to open a small restaurant in Ypsilanti, Michigan, a small suburb near Detroit. Its name was Dominik's Pizza. Today, the firm is called Domino's Pizza; it has 5,100 stores and annual sales revenues in excess of $2 billion.

Monaghan originally went into the pizza parlor business because he liked to eat pizzas. He and his brother knew very little about the restaurant business. The firm was undercapitalized; as Monaghan explains, "I think I had $77 in my checkbook."[12] His original goal was to operate a pizzeria in order to generate enough funds to pay his way through architecture school. However, he soon found himself working more than 100 hours a week.

Monaghan's basic concept was to sell a pizza at a price lower than that charged by any of his competitors and to provide free delivery. The concept was an immediate success, and Monaghan found himself so busy that he did not have time to sit down and pay the bills.

The firm had five sizes of pizza, from six to sixteen inches. There was an enormous demand for six-inch pizzas, but they were unprofitable for the firm because of the labor and delivery costs. One day, Monaghan stopped the sale of the six-inch pizza. Suddenly, instead of losing four or five hundred dollars a week, he found himself making the same amount. As he put it, "I was rich!"

The keys to Domino's success were, first, the ability of its founder to identify a market niche and, second, his ability to build a business to satisfy it. Monaghan's concept was the simple notion of delivery of pizzas. This may not seem like a brilliant or unique strategy today, but it was a novel idea when Monaghan pioneered it. Monaghan states, "Basically, any place that delivered, you really wouldn't want to buy a pizza from, because if they had a good product they wouldn't have to deliver. Nobody delivered unless they were crazy or stupid, and I was both." Indeed, nobody wanted delivery except customers—so Monaghan focused on delivery as his competitive advantage. This led to his market niche, the place within the overall market where he had a strong foothold.

The basic idea behind the success of Liz Claiborne, Inc., was also simple. The concept was to develop lines of fashionable, well-made sportswear that could be worn to the office. To keep distribution costs low, the firm focused on department stores, thereby minimizing the need for a sales force. The Claiborne concept was successful, and the rest is history.

Keys to a Successful Stage I Firm

New ventures in computers, clothing, and cookies, not to mention package delivery, pizza, and rock records, would not seem to have much in common. Yet if we look closely, we will see that each of these diverse businesses demonstrated certain fundamental abilities. Possession of these abilities is the prerequisite for developing a successful new venture:

1. The ability to define a market need
2. The ability to develop, acquire, or provide a product or service that will satisfy the identified market need
3. The ability to build an organization that is capable of functioning on a day-to-day basis to provide the product or service

Let us discuss each of these critical factors further.

Ability to Define a Market Need. The most fundamental prerequisite for success as a new venture is the ability to identify and define a market need that is not currently being satisfied or that can be satisfied in a different way (higher quality, lower cost, and so on). Each of the firms we described was able to do this.

Apple Computer saw the need for a personal computer that the average person, not just the computer "hacker," could use. The company followed the same strategy with its Macintosh, which was initially advertised as the computer "for the rest of us." Adam Osborne perceived the need for a portable computer, and Compaq saw the need for a relatively inexpensive, IBM-compatible portable computer. Mitchell Kapor saw the need for certain computer software.

David Liederman and Debbi Fields saw an unsatisfied need for "gourmet" chocolate chip cookies. Tom Monaghan saw the need for home delivery of good pizza. The two Harvard Business School students saw an opportunity to satisfy the need for convenient purchasing of rock records. Frederick W. Smith saw the need for inexpensive, rapid delivery of small packages. Liz Claiborne saw the need for medium-priced fashionable clothing that could be worn to work.

It should be noted that the needs these entrepreneurs saw were not necessarily for a new product, although some of the products were new. Others, such as Mrs. Fields' and David's Cookies, were merely reconceptualizations of existing products or services.

Ability to Develop a Relevant Product or Service. The second major task in developing a successful stage I firm is providing a product or service that satisfies the market need the company has identified. Apple Computer was not the first firm to perceive the need for a personal computer, but it was the first to develop an acceptable product and market it successfully.

Some entrepreneurs do not succeed in developing successful new ventures because, while they are able to see the market for a product, they are not able to develop the required product or service.

Ability to Develop an Organization to Provide the Product or Service. The third requirement for a successful stage I company is the ability to develop an organization capable of providing the chosen product or service to customers. This involves developing the basic systems for day-to-day operation of the firm as well as finding the people needed to staff the organization.

If the three things just described are done well, a company will pass the first test of survival. It may then begin to grow rapidly, and this growth will create a new set of problems to be solved. These new problems are the subject of the next section of this chapter, which deals with the development of successful stage II companies.

Developing Successful Stage II Organizations

The second stage of organizational development is the rapid-growth stage. This stage begins after a firm has solved the three critical problems involved in establishing a new venture. It may start very quickly or only after many years.

Hot Rock, Inc.: Growing Pains.   Hot Rock, Inc., whose success in the new venture stage we described in the previous section, had hardly gotten started when it began to experience rapid growth. According to Michael Wigley, "We thought that our promos would generate between twenty-four and twenty-five calls a day, based upon our system's capacity and the demographics of our ads. As it turned out, we generated a lot more calls than expected."[13] By the firm's seventeenth day in business, it had already received 50,000 inquiries.

The firm grew at a rate of 19 percent a week for the first few months. At this rate of growth, it was not surprising that it overran its organizational resources, systems, and capabilities. Demand exceeded the firm's telephone capacity and computer capability twice over, and demand for cash forced the firm to sell an additional 39 percent of its holdings. The entrepreneurs found themselves working eighteen to twenty hours a day.

In brief, although Hot Rock was only a few months old, it had already begun to experience organizational growing pains that warned of a need to make the transition from a stage I to a stage II firm. It found that its resources (people, cash, inventory, telephone equipment, and computers) were insufficient to handle the volume of business it had generated, and its day-to-day operational systems were inadequate to support the volume of current and anticipated future business.

The name of the game had changed. The critical tasks facing the firm were no longer to identify a market and product or to provide more and more of the product; rather, they were to acquire the resources and develop the operational systems needed to facilitate anticipated future growth.

Unfortunately, many firms that successfully meet the challenges of growth stage I ultimately flounder in stage II. This happens because the problems of managing a rapidly growing organization are in many ways fundamentally different from those of setting up a new venture. A stage II firm requires capabilities different from those of a stage I firm, and the managers of such an organization require different skills. Not all organizations and all entrepreneurs, even those who were brilliant in stage I, can handle the required metamorphosis.

The "Osborne Syndrome."　One of the most spectacular and tragic examples of a firm that failed to make the transition from stage I to stage II is Osborne Computer. Because Osborne's experience is such a classic example, we call the phenomenon it exemplifies the "Osborne syndrome." This is the phenomenon in which an organization that has experienced rapid success as an entrepreneurial venture soon experiences equally rapid decline because it has failed to make the transition from an entrepreneurship to a professionally managed firm. As Adam Osborne himself has stated, "When you become an entrepreneur you can go up awfully fast, but you can go down just as fast. It's so ephemeral, like actors who end up committing suicide. One day they're famous, the next nobody knows who the hell they are."[14]

Osborne Computer began when Adam Osborne recognized the market for a portable microcomputer. Despite skepticism, Osborne produced and marketed his machines and, in doing so, created a new market. The firm experienced extraordinarily rapid growth, soon achieving more than $100 million in annual revenues and employing more than 1,000 people.

Osborne's success was the classic entrepreneur's dream come true; but it turned into the classic entrepreneurial nightmare when the firm experienced its now-well-publicized difficulties. When some suppliers sued to collect $4.5 million, Osborne filed for bankruptcy under Chapter XI of the Federal Bankruptcy code.

What caused the fall of Osborne Computer after its meteoric rise? Although the answer to this question is complex, a key to the basic problem was stated by Adam Osborne himself in reflecting on what had happened to his firm. As he said, the firm "had existed only eighteen months in terms of operation—hardly time to get my feet wet; all of a sudden the job was a whole different order of magnitude. I realized it was no longer an entrepreneurial operation in any conceivable way."[15] In spite of this recognition, Osborne was unable to make the required changes in himself or his company.

Unfortunately, there is a pattern in what happened to Adam

Osborne. Unless entrepreneurs learn from this story, they may someday find themselves experiencing the "Osborne syndrome."[16]

After the initial success of a new entrepreneurial venture, a rapidly growing firm will inevitably experience the kind of organizational growing pains we described in Chapter Three, just as Osborne Computer did. As we have stated, these pains are normal, but they are a warning, symptoms of a disease that can be fatal if left untreated. The "fatality" is the Osborne syndrome we have just described. The key to avoiding the Osborne syndrome is recognizing the warning inherent in an organization's growing pains and dealing with these symptoms before the condition becomes terminal.

Other Examples of Problems at Stage II. Let us now look at several other companies that experienced organizational growing pains strong enough to put them in danger of suffering the Osborne syndrome.

An industrial products distributor had grown from $3 million in annual sales to $15 million, but profits had not increased proportionately. Indeed, they had actually begun to decline. The firm's accounting information could not pinpoint the reasons for these profitability problems. Inventory had accumulated in the warehouse, but no one could say how much of each item there was or where it was located, since the firm's inventory control system was manual and not kept up to date. The firm hired an ever-increasing number of people to cope with day-to-day operational pressures, but many of these people worked without supervision because their managers were too busy "putting out fires." The sales staff included some outstanding people, but others were simply nonproductive. The firm was beginning to lose accounts because of a series of embarrassing foul-ups such as missed delivery dates, incorrect merchandise shipments, and erroneous billings.

A successful $35 million soft goods manufacturer that had grown rapidly suddenly found itself constantly struggling to "put out fires." Employees were unaware of what other employees were doing. The firm had the obvious goals of manufacturing and selling merchandise, but it had no concept of what it wanted to become. The firm did not have a profit plan or departmental budgets; it could determine profitability only at the end of the fiscal year, after the opportunity to correct problems had passed. It had no performance appraisal system, so people tended to do whatever they wanted to do. As long as the firm continued to grow in sales, these problems were "merely inefficiencies." When the economy suddenly turned sour, however, these growing pains almost became terminal, and the firm's venture capital group had the company's president replaced.

A $75 million women's clothing manufacturer began to experience high turnover and low morale, with people complaining, "If I want to get anything done around here, I have to do it myself." The firm had no plans, no goals, no formal organizational structure, no accountability, an almost incredible number of people running around doing things without direction, and a dizzying array of operational problems. No one seemed to know who should report to whom. The firm was still profitable because it had identified a market niche, but it had spawned competitors during the last few years, some of them people who had left the original firm. These competitors were now growing rapidly and seemed to pass the original firm in size and profits.

A $100 million consumer products manufacturer found that parts of the organization were making decisions affecting other parts without informing people, leading to costly inefficiencies and duplication of efforts. For example, materials delivered to a warehouse had to be returned to the vendor because of lack of space to store them. Fiefdoms had been built up at the senior executive level, and there was little communication except on a vertical basis. Since the firm was successful, people had got into the habit of "going first class" and operating with a "country club" mentality. Looming on the horizon, meanwhile, were some of the industry's bigger players, who had noticed the firm's success with its market niche and were planning their own entries.

Ashton-Tate had great success with a single product, growing from a garage-size operation to a significant firm. But after about three years of good times, it suddenly found itself in trouble. Management development was so minimal that one department head said, "I was walked to the door of my department and told: 'Here is your department; manage it.' " The firm also experienced difficulty in developing new products to repeat its earlier success.

Kierulff Electronics, a $350 million industrial components distributor that had grown explosively, found itself with extremely high personnel turnover. The firm was continuing to "push products out the door," but sales personnel were constantly infuriated to find that products they had sold and believed were in inventory could not be delivered because the firm's control system was hopelessly incorrect. The company was ultimately purchased by Arrow Electronics.

Maxicare grew rapidly through internal growth and acquisitions to $1.8 billion in annual revenues. The company's infrastructure was adequate for a much smaller sized firm, and Maxicare experienced all of the classic symptoms of growing pains.

All the firms just described were initially successful organizations. They experienced various problems or growing pains because of differences in size and/or market conditions. They all have the potential for experiencing the Osborne syndrome: meteoric success followed by equally rapid failure.

Keys to a Successful Stage II Firm

All the firms we described in the last section were diverse in their products and markets, yet experienced difficulties because of their failure to meet the challenges presented by rapid growth. Specifically, they were unable to acquire the required resources and to develop the increasingly complex operational systems that became necessary as they grew. Thus two factors are involved in developing a successful stage II firm:

1. The ability to acquire the resources
2. The ability to develop complex operational systems

These two factors make up a firm's operational infrastructure. We will discuss each of these critical factors further.

Ability to Acquire Resources. The ability to acquire and manage resources effectively is an indispensable element in the successful growth of a company. Without sufficient physical, technical, and human resources, a firm will be unable to meet the demands that growth places on organizations. For example, a $50 million furniture manufacturer with state-of-the-art production capability found itself at a competitive disadvantage because of a lack of adequate warehousing space and loading facilities. Customers complained about delivery delays and too much waiting time for their trucks.

People Express is an example of a firm that was able, despite failures in other areas, to acquire the physical and human resources necessary to support the growth of the company. It acquired remodeled planes from Lufthansa as its start-up fleet and made great effort to hire personnel who exemplified the "People type." Similarly, Federal Express developed a special recruitment plan that reflected a high-tech image in order to attract the type of employees it needed for a new electronic mail service. One of the keys to success at Humana has been the ability to acquire personnel (physicians) needed to attract the desired type of customers (patients).

The difficulties some entrepreneurs have in this area are related to acquiring resources for future needs as well as to meet current needs. The other difficulty is related to the second task in this stage: developing the systems that allow appropriate utilization of the resources.

Ability to Develop Complex Operational Systems. The second critical task in successfully meeting the growth challenges of stage II is integrating new operating systems into the organization. Federal Express was able to do this with a sophisticated tracking system using bar codes. Mrs. Fields' Cookies also developed an elaborate computer system that allowed the firm to maintain daily control over widely dispersed operations. Humana developed sophisticated information and control systems required for speeding the collection of receivables and for providing hospital managers with daily printouts of key variables to be monitored, such as patient satisfaction and drug inventory levels.

Osborne Computer required (but lacked) systems for control of inventories, cash management, and accounting information to facilitate the growth spurt that the company was experiencing. The industrial products distributor that had grown from $15 million to $43 million also had problems with its inventory management systems. A $35 million soft goods manufacturer lacked proper budgeting and performance appraisal systems and consequently found its staff "out of control." A $75 million manufacturer lacked both an adequate set of job descriptions and a set of overall plans or goals. Maxicare lacked the operational systems required by a $1.8 billion company. People Express, once hailed as a shining example of entrepreneurial success, suffered chronic understaffing, poor organization, and other operational systems required to facilitate the growth it was undergoing. The list could go on and on.

The basic problem all these companies faced was that the entrepreneurs who owned and managed them were more interested in the challenges presented at stage I than in those of stage II. Identification of a market and development of a product or service seem glamorous compared with the more mundane tasks involved in developing and refining the organizational plumbing or infrastructure. Unfortunately, while something like an accounting system may be unexciting, it is vital for a growing organization. The shipping dock may be a less elegant place than a well-appointed corporate headquarters, but if enough foul-ups occur at the shipping dock, they can render the headquarters an expensive albatross.

If entrepreneurs want to make the successful transition from stage I to stage II, they must force themselves to be concerned about the organizational plumbing or operational systems required for day-to-day performance. Their survival depends on it.

Managing the New Venture and Expansion Stages: A Comparison of Osborne and Compaq

Osborne and Compaq, two companies who entered the personal computer market around the same time with products geared to similar users, had very different outcomes. Part of the reason for Compaq's success and Osborne's decline can be seen in their respective approaches to the key developmental tasks at each stage of growth.

Compaq successfully met the challenges of growth. It was what might be called a professionally managed entrepreneurship from the beginning. From the outset, the company operated like a mature organization. Attention was directed toward securing adequate resources and developing a tight infrastructure. Compaq's founders were able to see the pressures beyond market and product development and plan for their response. As Rod Canion, one of Compaq's founders and president, remarked, "If you're growing slowly, problems can sidle up on you almost unnoticed. With high growth, if you don't get out of the way first, they knock you down flat."[17]

Identifying a Market and Developing the Product. Osborne and Compaq chose the same arena—the portable personal computer market—in which to attempt to carve out a niche. Both of these new ventures were highly successful. Osborne saw a need for a portable, inexpensive computer for the naive, first-time user that brought the cost of personal computing within reach of the consumer. Osborne reached $1 million in sales within the first two months and was generating $10 million per month the next year. Keeping a focus on the market, Osborne launched a subsidiary in the United Kingdom a month after the first computers were shipped.

Osborne's early days were fully focused on market and product development (stage I) tasks. The first computer was presented after just four months of development, and four months later the first units were shipped. This rush to market, however, resulted in over $140,000 of associated costs, since Osborne had to fix bugs that appeared in the field. Getting the product to the customer is an important part of productization, and Osborne acted to ensure availability to the customer. To guarantee adequate shelf space for its product, Osborne emphasized dealer relationships. Osborne Computer offered the dealerships attractive terms and did not compete with a direct sales force of its own.

For Compaq, the niche was a portable computer completely compatible with the IBM PC, the industry standard. The firm correctly identified a market for a small, compact, relatively lightweight computer that could be carried almost anywhere. Like Osborne, Compaq experienced phenomenal first-year growth, and recorded sales of over $111 million in its first year.

The need to get the product to the customer was met successfully by Compaq with a strategy similar to that of Osborne's. Compaq stressed the development and maintenance of good dealer relationships. Despite this similarity, Compaq dealt with the developmental task of productization in a fundamentally different way from Osborne. The product was not the sole concern at Compaq during its early days. Before production even began, attention was directed toward the infrastructure that would support the organization as it grew.

Acquiring Resources and Developing Operational Systems. Where the differences between Osborne and Compaq in handling key developmental tasks are most noticeable are in the two key issues to be faced in stage II. Osborne hired personnel and developed systems on an "as needed" basis. The first financial person was not brought in until February 1981—a month after incorporation and just six months prior to the first shipment of the product. Market planning problems were the impetus for development of good financial reporting and control systems. Quality control problems a year after the company was founded led to the addition of a vice president for engineering. This was followed a short time later with a major restructuring in response to manufacturing problems. Rather than anticipating needs, Osborne Computer was caught responding to problems. Its resources and systems were inadequate to handle the fast-paced environment of the industry and explosive growth of the company.

Compaq took a longer view of its needs and invested in the operational infrastructure (resources and systems) that facilitated its future growth. It hired computer programmers who averaged fifteen years of experience and drafted the best sales and marketing professionals possible from IBM. In establishing operational systems, Compaq again demonstrated the importance of professional management. According to John Gribi, Compaq's vice president and chief financial officer, financial controls and forecasting systems were in place well before production began.

Both of these companies successfully negotiated the first stage of growth. They were able to establish a new venture that provided a product to a market previously untapped. Where Compaq had the comparative advantage was its ability to successfully acquire the resources and develop the operational systems necessary to support its growth. While Osborne ended up in bankruptcy,

Compaq built a multibillion-dollar company that is now included in the Fortune 500 and has challenged IBM for technological leadership in the personal computer market.

Summary

This chapter has examined the development of successful stage I and stage II organizations. The keys to success at stage I are the ability to identify a market niche, provide a product or service appropriate to that niche, and develop the basic organization required to run the infant business.

If a firm is successful in stage I, it will begin to experience rapid growth. As a result, it is likely to develop a variety of organizational growing pains. These growing pains are normal, but they must not be ignored. They are the signal that it is time to begin the transition from an entrepreneurial to a professionally managed firm. Failure to successfully make this transition can lead to severe problems and, ultimately, to the Osborne syndrome (meteoric success followed by meteoric failure).

In the next chapter we will describe the problems and challenges involved in developing a professionally managed firm at stage III. We will present a case study of a firm called Metro Realty and show how it made the transition from stage II to stage III successfully.

5 The Professionalizing Stage: Developing Management Systems

The chapter examines the process of making the transition from an entrepreneurship (stage I or stage II) to a professionally managed firm (stage III). The first section of this chapter identifies the key problems or challenges facing the organization as it changes from an entrepreneurship to a professionally managed company. The next section describes, in depth, the case of Metro Realty, an organization that was successful in transforming itself from an entrepreneurship to a professionally managed firm. This case study provides an example of the problems experienced by a rapidly growing company and the kinds of programs that can help an organization formalize its management systems and overcome its growing pains. The final section provides several other illustrations of actual firms—including Federal Express, Apple Computer, Compaq Computer, and Mrs. Fields' Cookies—that have successfully met these challenges. It examines why these firms have been effective.

Developing a Successful Stage III Organization

During the entrepreneurial stages of growth (stages I and II), planning, control, and management development are done on an ad hoc basis in many firms, and a formal organization structure is practically nonexistent. Individuals and departments operate on a day-to-day basis, making adjustments in various systems to meet the demands of the environment in which the company operates. This may actually contribute to the success of entrepreneurial firms, but it can be quite detrimental once an organization reaches stage III. As organizational growing pains resulting from the rapid growth that characterizes stage II increase in severity, senior management begins to realize (or should realize) that a qualitative change in the nature of their firm is needed. The firm has reached the threshold of stage III.

The Key Issues at Stage III. The key challenge for a stage III firm is to develop and formalize the management systems that are needed in a professionally managed firm. In the third stage of a company's development or life cycle, the company is a nascent professional organization. This stage of professionalization usually occurs after a company has reached $10 million in annual revenues. Successful integration of management systems is absolutely required if the organization is to continue to prosper.

As described in Chapter One, these management systems include planning, organization structure, management development, and control. The systems help the company coordinate the functions of its personnel and departments, provide direction to its employees, and motivate employees to achieve organizational goals. Basically, management systems formalize many of the activities that earlier, when the organization was small and growing, were performed through face-to-face interaction with the entrepreneur.

The following sections will focus on a case study of Metro Realty, an organization that was successful in transforming itself from an entrepreneurship to a professionally managed firm. We will describe the company's history; the growing pains it experienced as it rapidly increased in size, personnel, and revenues; and the program its management designed to help the company overcome its problems and make the transition to a stage III firm. Although the case is about a real estate company, we have chosen it because the problems experienced at Metro are typical of those encountered at stage III. Specifically, it provides an example of the problems experienced by a rapidly growing company and the kinds of programs that can help an organization formalize its management systems and overcome its growing pains.

The company described actually exists, although its name has been changed and certain facts about its situation have been slightly modified in order to preserve confidentiality. The basic situation described here really occurred in this company.

Developing a Successful Stage III Organization:
The Case of Metro Realty

Harvey and Dolores Brown opened the first office of Metro Realty on July 5, 1938, in Center City, the heart of the metropolitan area. The company prospered and grew as a result of both the personal creativity and dedication of the founders and their ability to recruit people who could contribute to the success of the firm. In 1963 Harvey Brown died, and a group of seven investors acquired Metro Realty. The company was, at this time, still a small entrepreneurial enterprise emphasizing residential real estate. It had three offices and thirty employees.

By 1970, little had changed since the company's founding. Metro Realty remained small in terms of employees, office space, and revenue and operated under a "family-style" management system. Its staff still consisted of twenty-eight to thirty people occupying three offices. The president of the company, Bob Mitchell, was expected to supervise the entire company's functioning, much as Harvey Brown had done from the company's inception until his death.

Metro still operated very effectively as an entrepreneurial firm, as evidenced by its growth. Between 1970 and 1978, the total number of branch offices grew from three to eleven, and the total number of employees increased from 30 to 250. Revenues increased form $1 million to nearly $10 million in this same period. According to management, this prosperity resulted from the firm's ability to do certain things very well. These included knowing how to select locations, how to time moves, and how to recruit and train salespeople.

Growing Pains

Between 1970 and 1978, then, Metro Realty grew very rapidly in terms of sales, size, and personnel—and it was continuing to grow. By 1978, Metro included a management and leasing department, a loan and investment department, a referral department, an administrative department, and eleven branch sales offices, all seemingly operating successfully. Plans were even being made to acquire another realty firm, which would increase the company's size to twenty offices and about 500 employees.

Unfortunately, the organization's original infrastructure could no longer support the enterprise that Metro had become. Everyone from the president to the sales associates could feel the impact of the problems that the company's rapid growth was creating. As one branch manager put it, "The attitude that now exists is that the company wants to be larger than it is and is moving faster in this direction than can be accommodated by its organization structure, leadership, and personnel." Lack of coordination in functions and activities was leading to increasing frustration among employees. Certain aspects of the company needed to be changed if it was to continue to be successful.

Culture. According to the president of Metro, "Part of the real estate culture is to tolerate poor performers," and Metro was no exception. At Metro, poor performers were tolerated partly because the culture emphasized being "part of a family," and one could not very easily dismiss a family member. Managers also retained poor performers in order to avoid conflict. The culture promoted the notion that it was better to keep such people than to disrupt the system by dismissing them.

A third factor that contributed to the problem of poor performance was the concept of productivity promoted at Metro. "Productivity" was considered to include anything from sending out fliers and making phone calls to actually completing a sale. Only the last-named activity directly contributed to the firm's revenues, but all three activities were regarded as "productive" in and of themselves. One cultural belief of the firm seemed to be, "If a person looks busy, he or she is productive." With an increased number of personnel, this loose definition of productivity was becoming quite costly.

A final component of the firm's culture that may have contributed to retaining poor performers was an apparent lack of concern with the costs related to retaining these individuals. Traditionally, Metro had been concerned only with revenue production. Profit was not an explicit goal; it was simply the amount of money that remained after commissions and other costs had been paid. Cost control, therefore, was not an important consideration, since the company was not explicitly concerned with retaining income for future use. As the firm grew, however, a critical need arose to change the culture toward one that emphasized profit and considered both costs and revenues. This new culture would not be able to tolerate poor performers.

Roles and Responsibilities. The roles and responsibilities of different management positions had not been clearly defined at Metro. The organization functioned on an ad hoc basis, with responsibilities often overlapping. This lack of role definitions had not detracted from the functioning of the entrepreneurial firm, but it became a source of frustration as the company expanded. One manager, perhaps speaking for many, said that he was "fed up with the role confusion."

The ambiguity of role definitions also contributed to an unwillingness to accept responsibility. At Metro, it was relatively easy for managers to blame problems on other people or levels in the organization. There was no way to hold specific managers responsible for specific tasks, since responsibilities had not been clearly defined.

Planning. Like many activities, corporate planning at Metro was done on an ad hoc basis. Metro never had a written plan that outlined the financial and nonfinancial goals, objectives, and targets of the organization, and the size and success of the company had led its members to believe that such an effort was not warranted. As the organization grew, however, the need to plan for the company's future became apparent. The personnel at Metro began to desire some direction to guide their actions. It seemed that the company could no longer function effectively without goals.

Budgets and Accounting System. An important component of a company's planning process is a yearly budget that states financial goals. Unfortunately, the administrative systems necessary to help Metro know how it was performing financially and plan for its future were not formalized.

The budgeting process at Metro had traditionally been only

a yearly "exercise," since managers had no systems by which to monitor costs and revenue. They received little feedback from the organization concerning the amount they had spent or the profit they had earned. Most of the available financial statements provided information only on the performance of the organization as a whole, not on that of individual branch offices. The small amount of information on branch office performance that was available was often incomplete and/or inaccurate. Further, one branch manager suggested that he did not believe the accounting information that was being provided to him; he said he "couldn't understand where the numbers were coming from."

Metro clearly needed a more formalized budgeting process, but its underdeveloped accounting system did not support such an effort. Metro's system of accounting was described by an independent accounting firm as having "no thoroughly designed master plan." This system clearly needed to be revised.

Difficulties arising from the lack of an effective system to monitor costs and revenues began to surface in 1978. At this time the company began losing money although, according to the firm's president, profits for the industry were at an all-time high. In 1977, profits were $190,000, but in 1978 they fell to $130,000.

Control. Traditionally, Metro had operated with a "top-down" management style in which the president oversaw the entire company's operations. By 1978, however, it was clear that Metro had grown too large for this style to be effective. At this time the president described Metro as a "collection of little offices and divisions, each working toward its own goals without considering the good of the company." It was becoming evident that because of the expansion of the company in terms of profit as well as size, the president could no longer be the sole controller of its fate.

Performance Appraisal. Metro's performance appraisal system (or lack of such a system) contributed to its retention of poor performers. Performance appraisals, when they did occur, consisted of discussions in which only positive feedback was given. There was no system for evaluating progress in terms of meeting goals, since there was no goal-setting process. Negative feedback and suggestions for improving performance were rarely given, reflecting a culture that stressed conflict avoidance.

Decision Making and Leadership. Partly because of the lack of clearly defined roles and responsibilities and partly because of the traditional style of management, decisions were deferred to top management. Day-to-day decisions such as those relating to the purchase of office equipment, which should have been made by department heads or branch managers, were all presented to the president for approval. This resulted in a slow and ineffective decision-making process.

The tendency for upper management to make all decisions decreased the participation of other members in the decision-making process. This contributed to a lack of responsibility for actions taken and a lack of commitment to the decisions that were made. Management from the top down had been a successful way to make decisions when Metro was an entrepreneurial organization, but it had clearly become inappropriate for a firm that was ready to make a transition to professional management.

Communication. One branch manager remarked that while communication within each region was good, total company communication was poor. Communication between individual branch offices and the firm's upper management was especially ineffective. Branch managers seemed to feel that upper management was not giving them enough information for them to operate effectively. As one branch manager put it, "Upper management assumed we knew what was wanted or needed when we, in reality, didn't know."

Upper management was equally frustrated by its inability to communicate with the branch offices. As one manager put it, the lack of communication made it "too easy for a branch or region to run its shop its own way."

Recruiting. Metro Realty did not have a formal recruiting plan, since the company had traditionally been able to attract top job candidates without expending much effort and had never experienced staffing problems. As the firm continued to grow, however, it found it needed to formalize recruiting plans in order to ensure that all branch offices had an adequate number of personnel to meet the company's future goals.

In terms of recruiting, 1979 was a particularly critical year. Due to a downturn in the economy, fewer people were entering the real estate profession. It became quite evident that a recruiting plan was a necessary component of Metro's continued success.

Training and Development. Metro's major problem in the area of training and development was a lack of management development programs. Without proper training, most potential managers were not prepared to assume managerial roles. The lack of qualified managers indirectly affected the functioning of the firm.

Metro also lacked a standardized training program for sales associates. All sales associates were required to possess a state license as evidence that they had minimal competence in real estate sales, but additional training was usually needed. At Metro, each branch had traditionally offered its own on-the-job program. There was little standardization of the programs' contents, so the quality of the programs was potentially different at different branches.

Compensation. Metro's compensation system was designed to promote increased revenue at the branch level rather than profitability for the firm as a whole. The organization rewarded managers and sales associates for revenue production rather than the ability to meet financial and nonfinancial goals.

Branch managers were rewarded for the ability of their offices to generate revenue. This created certain inequities since their different locations meant that some branches automatically produced more revenue than others, regardless of the quality of the staff they employed. This compensation system led to a situation in 1978 in which two managers who possessed only marginal skills and had caused some difficulties for the organization were among the highest-paid managers in the firm.

Making the Transition

In 1978, Metro's Executive Committee, composed of the company's president, heads of the regional offices, and department heads, began to realize that the company was experiencing problems that required changes in its traditional operating systems. The committee felt that managers and brokers were too close to the situation to work adequately to resolve these problems, and so it hired an independent consultant to help the firm identify and alleviate its growing pains.

In 1978, Metro began a program designed to help it make the transition to a professionally managed firm. The consultant and the company president worked together to design the program, which would be implemented over a period of four years in order to reduce employees' resistance to change. This program was designed to be evolutionary rather than revolutionary. The purpose of the effort was not "Clean the house and throw out the garbage," but rather, "Repair what we can and throw out what we find to be irreparable after we have tried to fix it."

1978. After identifying the problems described in the last section, the consultant and president began planning an organizational development program for the company. The planning process included establishing goals for the firm's transition, designing programs intended to achieve these goals, and planning how and when these programs would be implemented.

The consultant began working with the organization's members to determine what sort of company Metro would become—that is, what the goals of the transition process would be. The group decided that the "new" organization would:

1. Have a decentralized system of responsibility with strong managers;
2. Be managed under a participative style of leadership;
3. Promote increased accountability;
4. Be profit oriented rather than strictly revenue oriented.

In order to achieve these goals, the organizational development program would focus on three major, interrelated areas: (1) organization and business planning, (2) management development, and (3) design and formalization of organization structure. Training programs in these areas would consist of lectures, group discussions, exercises, and individual counseling sessions. As the members of the organization began to put into practice what they had learned from their training, the consultant would be available to provide feedback.

The consultant and president established yearly priorities for the organizational development program. A long-term schedule was created, outlining yearly objectives and presenting suggested completion dates for various aspects of the program. This schedule is presented in Table 5.1.

Having outlined the goals and designed an organizational development program to meet these goals, the group devoted the latter part of 1978 to program implementation. In that year, members of the organization completed a business plan that outlined the mission, goals, objectives, and targets for the coming year (1979). This process was facilitated by giving the members training to how to design and use goals. Managers were encouraged to design goals for their individual areas of responsibility (branches, departments, or regions) as well as to contribute to the formal plan for the organization as a whole. People were also shown how to create and use a realistic budget.

Training in creating and using goals was but one part of a management development program that began to take shape in 1978. This program was intended to provide present and future managers with the skills necessary to become more effective in their positions. These skills included planning, budgeting, recruiting, performance evaluation, and decision making. The consultant provided seminars in each of these areas, with practical exercises in which the new skills could be applied. He also provided feedback on performance once the skills became a part of the managers' everyday work lives.

During 1978, management development efforts were concentrated on members of upper management, though the committee planned eventually to expand the program to include all present and potential managers at Metro. The president was a member of this first group of participants, and he also worked with the consultant on an individual basis. This close working relationship was intended to help the president make his personal transition from being the leader of an entrepreneurial firm to being the CEO of a

Table 5.1. Metro Realty Organizational Development Program:
Contents and Schedule.

1978	Plan organizational development program
	Identify problems
	Set goals
	Design programs
	Set schedule
	Begin program implementation
	Organizational planning
	  • Provide training in design and use of goals
	  • Provide training in creation and use of budgets
	  • Develop business plan for 1979
	Management development
	  • Work with president to develop skills necessary to make personal transition
	  • Work with upper management to help them develop skills necessary to make the transition to professional managers
	Organizational structure
	  • Present exercises aimed at facilitating discussion of roles and responsibilities
	  • Begin working toward consensus on definition of roles

1979	Review, revise, expand, and formalize programs
	Organizational planning
	  • Provide feedback on goals
	  • Increase ability to meet goals
	  • Develop more professional planning process
	Management development
	  • Continue work with president
	  • Expand group program to include branch managers and potential managers
	Organizational structure
	  • Formalize roles and responsibilities
	  • Provide written descriptions of roles to all employees

1980–81	Continue to review, revise, expand, and formalize programs
	Organizational planning
	  • Make planning an integral part of the organization
	Management development
	  • Continue work with president
	  • Formalize program for present and potential managers
	Organizational structure
	  • Put formalized structure into operation

professionally managed organization. This personal transition was a key element in the success of the overall organization transition process.

The management development program initiated in 1978 served as a forum in which role ambiguities could be discussed. Exercises were used to facilitate discussion of roles and responsibilities. The consultant provided information on the need to clearly define roles and helped group members resolve ambiguities.

1979. During this year, the programs begun in 1978 were reviewed, revised, expanded, and formalized. The planning process was refined and systematized. Regularly scheduled branch, departmental, and executive committee meetings were established to facilitate the setting of goals, objectives, and targets for the coming year. Through such meetings, goal setting became a participative process in which all organization members contributed to the formulation of the company plan. These meetings also served as a means of monitoring performance and providing feedback to the various segments of the organization.

During 1979, emphasis was placed on setting realistic financial and nonfinancial goals and working to attain these goals. The consultant provided feedback to managers on the strength of the goals they had set for their departments or branches and offered suggestions for improving their goal-setting skills.

During 1979, the firm also began to incorporate goal setting into its performance evaluation system. Evaluations were to be based on the extent to which employees met or exceeded the goals they had set for themselves. Compensation was to be contingent on the ability of people to meet their goals.

Management development programs were expanded during 1979 to include existing branch managers and potential managers. The program provided managers with the skills they needed to be more effective in their present positions and also prepared selected branch managers for promotion to upper-management positions. Selected sales associates were included in the program to ensure that the organization would have a pool of qualified potential branch managers to fill positions when needed.

By the end of the second year of the organizational development program, Metro had, for the most part, reached a consensus on role definitions. Written role descriptions were distributed to the organization's members so there would no longer be any confusion about responsibilities.

1980-81. Review and revision of the programs begun in 1978 and 1979 continued through 1981. By 1981, people were actively participating in the planning process, which was now an integral part of the company's operating systems. Management development programs had been formalized at all levels, and role ambiguity had been minimized.

Problems Encountered

As Metro began its transition from an entrepreneurial firm to a professionally managed organization, it encountered three critical problems. One of these problems, resistance to change on the part of the organization's members, was expected. The other two problems, a severe downturn in the economy and the departure of certain key personnel from the organization, could not have been planned for. We will now provide further discussion of these problems and their effects.

Loss of Personnel. In December 1978, one of the most successful managers at Metro left the company to form his own firm. This was a critical loss in a company that was just beginning to make the transition to a professionally managed firm, since at this point strong managers and a complete sales force are particularly necessary. There is also a need for everyone to pull together, and individuals who leave a firm at this time may discourage others from supporting the change effort.

The reason for the manager's departure was not clear. He may have simply "outgrown" the organization, so that Metro was no longer meeting his need for personal development and self-fulfillment. He may also have recognized that the organization was experiencing problems that he did not want to help it solve.

The manager made matters worse by taking quite a few salespeople with him when he left. As a result, at least two of the eleven branch offices became severely short staffed. Upper management at Metro had received little warning that this would occur. The net effect of the manager's actions was that while Metro was engaged in the already difficult task of working to overcome its growing pains, it also faced a short-term staffing crisis and a possible accompanying drop in morale.

The president of Metro responded quickly to the situation by rehiring Doug Perry, an experienced manager who had left the company only a year before. Perry was given the job of revitalizing the branch offices that had been devastated by staff departures. To accomplish this end, Perry took over as manager in one of the affected offices and, with the president's approval, promoted a company sales associate to the position of manager of the other affected branch. Both managers began an aggressive recruiting campaign, and within only six months the two branch offices were again fully staffed and functioning well. Because it was able to recruit quality people, Metro survived this crisis with relatively little adverse impact on its efforts to become a professionally managed firm.

Declining Economy. Having survived this staffing crisis, Metro suffered another blow in 1979 when the economy experienced a severe downturn. Real estate sales dropped suddenly and unexpectedly because of unprecedentedly high interest rates, vanishing mortgage funds, and uncertainty about the future.

The president of Metro suggested that this downturn was merely part of a cycle that occurs every few years. He pointed out, "This cycle begins with a period of prosperity like that which occurred in the late 1970s. Assuming that real estate is one of the best hedges against inflation, many people begin to buy houses left and right with the expectation that they can make profits without running any risks. This type of speculation cannot continue indefinitely. It eventually results in a declining market like that of 1979-80." At such times, he noted, weaker firms begin to fail as salespeople leave not only the firms but the industry itself and new people fail to enter the profession.

Nonetheless, the shift in the economy that occurred in 1979-80 was one of the most severe downturns the real estate market had experienced. The economic shift was especially threatening to

Metro because it occurred when the company was just beginning to make the transition to a professionally managed firm. In response to this threat, the president took the stance that Metro could be a "victim" or it could take advantage of the market. He chose the latter course of action and adopted a strategy that was intended to play on the strengths of Metro and to concentrate on the long term, making the most of opportunities. This strategy would allow Metro to respond when the market changed.

Metro Realty was fortunate in that it had a strong image in its community and also in that its management had prepared itself for possible economic downturns by designing contingency plans. The plan that the company adopted in 1979–80 promoted both cost containment and production. It also emphasized maintaining the sales force, since in such periods there are fewer people entering the industry and qualified people are at a premium.

All managers were asked to contribute ideas about specific expenses to cut, but the president had the final say in this effort. He decided that advertising budgets would be fixed, charitable contributions would be suspended, greater control of expense reimbursement to sales associates would be instituted, a freeze would be placed on the hiring of management and salaried personnel, and closing of nonproductive branch offices would be considered.

The company's strategy apparently paid off, since, despite market conditions, the company's performance in 1980 was one of the best in its forty-two-year history.

Resistance to Change.   Even after people realized that there were problems with the old operating systems at Metro, some individuals refused to take part in the changes necessary to solve these problems. They seemed to have a great desire to cling to old values and operating procedures. They showed their resistance to change in a variety of ways, including excuses for not adapting to procedures, justifications for using old practices, complaints that the changes were taking away the "family atmosphere" that people treasured, and, ultimately, outright refusal to adopt the new values and practices.

Some managers complained, "I just can't do it that way." The consultant replied, "Yes, you can, if you try"—and the president added, "You *will* do it that way." People who absolutely would not change were finally asked to leave since they were detracting from the transition process. By 1981, after a certain amount of struggle, most employee resistance had been reduced through adoption of the new strategy or through termination (both voluntary and involuntary) of the chief resisters. It now appeared that Metro Realty had, for the most part, successfully made the transition to a professionally managed firm.

Program Outcomes

Metro Realty's organizational development program was successful in helping the company make the transition from an entrepreneurship to a professionally managed firm, even in the face of the problems that were encountered. Fundamental changes in the organization, shown in Table 5.2, eliminated most of its "growing pains."

Culture. One of the most difficult changes Metro had to make was to replace its "family atmosphere" with an atmosphere that was more conducive to accomplishing the tasks of a professionally managed firm. This meant that managers had to learn how to confront conflict and eliminate poor performers. It did not necessarily mean that "a family feeling" could no longer exist. However, the dysfunctional aspects of this part of the firm's culture had to be eliminated.

Another component of the culture, the definition of productivity, also had to be changed. Individual productivity in the "new" organization was to be assessed in terms of profit contributed to the firm. This meant that people not only had to increase revenues; they also had to control costs. Something like mailing fliers could no longer be considered productive work in and of itself, but only as it contributed to the overall profitability of the branch and firm. If any activity was judged too costly in terms of the revenue it was expected to generate, it would be eliminated.

Profitability was also important in the evaluation of branch productivity. The executive committee decided that in the "new" organization, each branch would be regarded as a profit center in-

Table 5.2. The "Old" and the "New" Metro.

	Old	New
Culture	Poor performers are tolerated.	Poor performers are not tolerated.
	The company is a "family."	The notion of "family" remains but is modified.
	Managers avoid conflict.	Managers are able to deal with conflict.
	Productivity is loosely defined.	Productivity is closely related to profitability.
	Company concentrates on revenue production.	Company concentrates on profit production.
Roles and responsibilities	Roles and responsibilities are not clearly defined.	Roles and responsibilities are clearly defined.
	Responsibilities often overlap.	Responsibilities are agreed on and do not overlap.
	Role confusion causes frustration.	Written definitions distributed to all employees eliminate confusion.
Planning	No formal business plan exists.	Formal planning becomes an integral part of the organization.
	Company has no formalized goals, objectives, or mission.	Managers are taught how to design and use goals, and regularly scheduled meetings are used to evaluate progress toward goals.
	Little direction is given to personnel.	Personnel are asked to participate in planning a course of action for the company.
Budgets and accounting system	No formalized budget exists; budget process is only an "exercise."	Managers design and use realistic budgets.
	Finacial information is available only for the entire company. Information is often inaccurate or incomplete. Accounting system is underdeveloped.	A new accounting system provides information for all levels of the company in a timely manner.
Organization	Top-down management style is used.	Participative management style is used.

Table 5.2. The "Old" and the "New" Metro, Cont'd.

	Old	New
	Control is often ineffective.	Regularly scheduled meetings monitor performance and provide feedback.
Performance appraisal	Appraisal consists of discussion between managers and subordinates. Only positive feedback is given; little effort is made to improve performance.	Supervisors provide both positive and negative feedback and ways to improve performance.
Decision-making and leadership	Most decisions are made by top management; decision making is slow and often ineffective. Lack of participation in decisions leads to lack of commitment to decisions made.	Decision-making responsibility is distributed throughout the organization. Planning process encourages maximum participation by all employees.
Communication	Total company communication is poor; communication between upper management and branch managers is most ineffective. Poor communication contributes to branch managers' role confusion and control by upper management.	Clearly defined roles and responsibilities contribute to better communication. Regularly scheduled meetings increase communication between various levels of the organization.
Recruiting	No formal recruiting plan exists. With a growing number of branches, staffing is becoming a problem.	Recruiting is a planned activity. Managers are evaluated partly on their ability to set and meet recruiting goals.
Training and development	No management development program exists. No standardized training for sales associates exists.	Training department is responsible for training of sales associates.
Compensation	Compensation is based on ability of branch to generate revenue.	Compensation is based on ability of personnel to meet financial and nonfinancial goals.

stead of simply a revenue center. The goal of each branch manager thus was to have a profitable branch, which meant continuing to produce high revenues while controlling and being responsible for expenses. Profitability would become a measure of managerial success, and the management development program would help managers achieve this success by providing them with the skills they needed to be effective professional managers.

Roles and Responsibilities. Through the lectures, discussions, and exercises used in the management development program, the organizational structure of Metro was defined. Roles and responsibilities of position holders and formal links between various positions were identified, formalized, and distributed in written form to all employees so that there would no longer be any confusion about who was responsible for what.

Planning. Systems for planning were formalized. The organization developed an ongoing means of setting, monitoring, and evaluating goals. This included a series of branch, departmental, and executive committee meetings that facilitated the setting of goals, objectives, and targets for the coming year. The meetings also helped in evaluating progress toward goals. An important part of the planning process was the use of contingency plans whereby the firm attempted to determine what strategy to adopt in an optimistic or pessimistic market. Such planning helped the company weather the severe economic environment of 1979-80, when many less prepared companies failed.

Budgets and Accounting System. Organization members' ability to design and use budgets was developed through seminars presented by the consultant. In the first year or two that managers attempted to use the techniques described in these seminars, nearly all the branch managers failed to meet their budgets because of either unrealistic goals or inadequate monitoring of goals. By 1981, however, managers had become better able to meet their financial as well as nonfinancial goals.

To further promote this process, Metro implemented a new accounting system. In the new system, information was available on each level of the organization, from the organization as a whole to each region to the individual branch offices. There was initially a problem with the timeliness of the reports: Information was not being received at a rate conducive to effective monitoring of financial goals. In 1980, however, this problem was reduced when a computerized accounting system was installed. The new system increased the speed with which financial reports could be generated and distributed.

Control. A series of regularly scheduled meetings replaced the "top-down" management style as a means of control. These meetings helped to monitor performance and provide feedback to various segments of the organization, thus also serving to increase communication.

Executive committee meetings were held monthly. Members of this group, along with branch managers, formed the "planning committee," which met quarterly to prepare priorities and nonfinancial objectives, and to review plans and status reports. Department and branch meetings were also to be held monthly to review the status of goal achievement. Annual planning meetings, in which all the branch managers, department heads, regional managers, and administrative personnel were involved, were to be held in June and July of each year.

Performance Appraisal. A performance review system based on goal achievement was created. Evaluation sessions were designed to provide feedback (both positive and negative) to each employee on his or her performance and to provide specific direction for improvement in the coming year. Managers' performance was assessed according to how well they met their goals in profit, recruiting, training, planning, control, turnover, and reliability. Sales associates' performance was assessed in terms of performance toward goals in sales, number of contracts, open houses, and other areas deemed important by the individual manager and sales associate. Goals for all employees were established through mutual agreement between employee and supervisor and were to be congruent with the overall company goals.

Decision Making and Leadership. One purpose of defining roles and responsibilities was to distribute decision making responsibility to various levels throughout the organization—to decentralize responsibility, in other words. The president would no longer be responsible for all company decisions. Instead, managers would make the day-to-day decisions for their individual branches, regions, or departments.

The formal planning process developed at Metro allowed an even greater number of people to have a voice in the decisions that affected the company. The process was designed to encourage maximum participation by the organization's members. All those involved were to have input into decisions that would directly affect them.

Communication. Clarification of roles and responsibilities, along with the establishment of regular meetings, eliminated the communication problems that Metro had experienced. The company now had a clearly defined "chain of command" through which information could filter both down and up.

Recruiting. As part of the yearly plan, each branch manager was to set goals for the number of individuals he or she would recruit in the coming year. Each manager was also to devise an action plan for meeting these goals. Managers were encouraged to seek new employees at local junior colleges, through business contacts, or even at other firms. Part of each manager's performance appraisal was an evaluation of success in meeting recruiting goals.

Training and Development. In an effort to provide continuing education, Metro established a training department that was responsible for all programs given to Metro employees. The head of this department was to work with each branch to design programs that would meet the needs of the individual branch offices and the organization at large. The training department was therefore able to control the quality of the programs offered to employees and to ensure that all employees received sufficient training. As described previously, Metro also developed a formal management development program to help individuals become professional managers and to create a pool of potential managers.

Compensation. The objective of the new compensation system was to reduce the emphasis on increasing the revenues of individual branches and replace this with an emphasis on increasing the profit of the organization as a whole. To achieve this end, managers were to be rewarded for meeting or exceeding financial and nonfinancial goals. Common costs were to be allocated to branches and departments in proportion to their ability to generate revenues, thus reducing inequities in revenue generation between various branch locations.

Under the new system, each manager would receive a base salary plus a certain percentage of the company's profit, based on the extent to which that manager's branch had met or exceeded its financial goals. Such a system encouraged managers to exercise care in establishing budgets. It offered managers an incentive to meet or exceed budgets, thus increasing the profit of the firm as a whole.

The results of Metro Realty's original development program suggest that the company was successful at meeting the goals it had set for its transition.

1. The company now had a decentralized system of responsibility: Branch, department, and regional managers were responsible for setting and meeting their own goals.
2. Participative leadership was becoming a reality: All managers took part in a yearly planning process for their individual areas of responsibility and for the company as a whole. The president no longer had the ultimate decision-making responsibility.
3. Accountability had been increased: All employees were held accountable for meeting the goals they had set for themselves, and compensation was based on their ability to do so.
4. The organization had become more profit oriented: The culture had been changed to emphasize profit rather than revenue. Rewards were based on ability to generate profit for the company rather than simply revenue for the branch.

Postscript

In the late 1980s, after the firm called "Metro Realty" had made the successful transition to professional management, the owner was approached by a large national financial service company that was engaged in purchasing residential real estate companies throughout the United States. Metro Realty had been developed as a valuable property, and it was attractive to the company we will call "Diversified Financial Products, Inc." ("DFP").

DFP made several offers for Metro Realty and was turned down each time. Metro was attractive to DFP because the latter's strategic plan for diversification called for acquisition of one of the three leading residential real estate firms in each major population center. Finally, Metro accepted an offer from DFP. The owner of Metro joined DFP as a senior executive.

In a sense, the attractiveness of Metro to DFP was external recognition of the success of the professionalization strategy.

Other Examples of Success with Professionalization

Many other firms provide examples of successful transition to professional management. We will discuss some of these companies in order to emphasize the skills and processes that are necessary to the development of a successful stage III company.

Professionalization of Federal Express. In April 1973, Federal Express began transporting the first packages in its overnight delivery service. What Frederick W. Smith developed into the number one air freight service was initially an idea presented in a college paper in 1965. Convinced of the significance of a delivery service dedicated to small, time-sensitive packages, Smith weathered $27 million losses in the first two years. He set up a system and waited for the market to develop, struggling to obtain the necessary financing. From the 16 packages transported on its first night, Federal Express grew to 500,000 packages per night in 1985.[18]

The attention to planning and control necessary to develop a successful stage III company are seen in many of Smith's actions. Early on, while attempting to attract investors, he commissioned two feasibility studies, using 10 percent of the company's net worth.[19] In anticipation of a new two-hour delivery service, a recruitment strategy designed to identify a different type of employee was formulated. Control and planning were further facilitated by an advanced decision support system that allowed flexible budgeting and by computerized optical scanners that sort packages as they come into each of Federal Express's hubs. These, along with handheld devices carried by the truck drivers and mainframe-linked terminals in each truck, permit packages to be tracked as they move through the system.

An underlying ingredient in the development of professional management systems is a professional perspective. This was present at Federal Express and was exemplified by its chief executive. Smith, who the general public hails as the classic entrepreneur, sees himself "primarily as a professional manager. . . . The fact that I am also someone who saw an opportunity was coincident to that."[20] He recognized the qualitative differences between a $1.2 million and a $1.2 billion company that require different management styles.

Federal Express solved many of the challenges facing a stage III company. Despite this professionalization, however, industry observers have commented on its unique enthusiasm and entrepreneurial spirit, seen in bold and innovative product development and expansion into new territories.[21] Within a strong professional management structure, this spirit can provide the foundation for the next phase of organizational growth, that of consolidation.

Professionalization of Apple Computer.   One of the most famous examples of the importance of making the transition to professional management is Apple Computer. Its phenomenal early growth was followed by a period of alienation among the divisions, problems stemming from the lack of qualified middle managers, inadequate management control, and major product problems with the Apple III and Lisa computers that resulted from a tendency to ignore customer needs as well as inadequate control systems. John Sculley came into the firm in 1983 and over the next two years restructured the organization so as to focus its effort on one set of goals instead of differing goals based on the division in which one worked; hired more experienced managers; instituted management controls; and helped the company develop a better focus on the customer. He cut costs, decreased overhead, changed 25 percent of top management, and rationalized the product line.[22] Under Jobs, Apple was a company with revenues of more than $1 billion but with only a stage II infrastructure. Under Sculley, Apple professionalized its management capabilities and management systems.

Professionalization of Compaq. Compaq Computer, discussed as an example of successful passage through the new venture and early expansion stages, was also successful at making the transition to stage III. As discussed previously, from the very beginning Compaq's founder focused on creating and managing the management systems needed to maintain the firm's success as it grew. These included a formalized planning system, a financial control system, a structure that was designed for flexibility in order to meet current and future needs, and an emphasis on hiring and maintaining a cadre of skilled and experienced managers who can assist the company in meeting its goals. The company has, in essence, been a professionally managed entrepreneurship from its inception.

Professionalization of Mrs. Fields' Cookies. Prior to the firm's acquisition of La Petite Boulangerie, the success of Mrs. Fields' Cookies was also based on its ability to meet the challenges presented by stage III. With numerous and diverse outlets, Mrs. Fields' Cookies presents coordination and control problems not seen in more centralized companies. Its planning and control needs were well served by a sophisticated computer and telephone network system that permitted Debbi Fields to move responsibility and authority down the organization while allowing close control and implementation of product quality standards.[23]

Keys to a Successful Stage III Firm

Each of the companies discussed in this chapter met the challenges posed by professionalization that allows the development of organizations beyond the new venture and expansion stages. Several factors are involved in making the transition to stage III. These are

1.   The ability to plan and develop strategy
2.   The ability to develop an appropriate organizational structure and controls
3.   The ability to provide management development

In this section, we will discuss each of these factors. Chapters Seven through Ten deal with each of the factors on a more in-depth basis.

The Ability to Plan and Develop Strategy.   A primary factor in successful professionalization is the ability to plan for the future and develop appropriate strategies for maximizing market opportunities. Each of the companies cited in this chapter was able to do this. At Metro Realty, the organizational planning process taught employees how to formulate financial and nonfinancial goals and help the company develop systems for setting, monitoring, and evaluating these goals. As a result, Metro Realty was better able to meet the challenges presented by its environment.

Federal Express employed a complex decision support system and assumed developmental risks that required some time to show profit. It saw this as essential to company success. Apple Computer assessed its strengths and competitive needs and moved into the business computer market by developing a second strategy when the first proved unsuccessful.[24] In planning for its future growth, Compaq Computer designed and invested in sophisticated management systems long before they were actually needed. Domino's Pizza, a company described in Chapter Four, examined its traditional market and added drive-through service. It also provided a structure and mechanism for its franchisees to give input into planned organizational actions with the initiation of the position of national director of franchisee concerns.

The Ability to Develop an Appropriate Organization Structure and Controls.   A second major factor in developing a successful stage III company is developing an organizational structure and controls that will coordinate efforts and provide information and motivation to employees.

Metro Realty developed a formal organization structure that

allowed people to understand their roles, responsibilities, and reporting relationships. Through developing monitoring systems (such as performance appraisals and a budgeting system), Metro also created a control system.

Federal Express's Frederick W. Smith is a legend in employee motivation. He structured his firm to allow employees access to him and provided for an employee panel to hear grievances. Mrs. Fields' flat organizational structure combined with computerized analyses of sales and a telecommunications systems provides strong management control over standards while allowing store-level decision making.

The Ability to Provide Management Development. The third major factor for success at stage III is the ability to design and implement programs to provide present and potential managers with the skills needed to perform their roles effectively. At Metro Realty, a formalized management development program helped present and potential managers be more effective in their roles. Mrs. Fields' Cookies developed specific training programs to encourage employee advancement with the firm. Domino's similarly encouraged employees to become franchisees through a system that rewarded individual franchise managers for developing other employees. They also maintained rigorous training programs for manager trainees in which the trainers themselves must be certified in the company before being allowed to provide training.

Developing management systems can take a number of years, and there can be many obstacles to overcome, as happened at Metro Realty. However, if an organization is to continue to be successful as it grows, its management must recognize that problems exist and begin taking steps toward reducing them, no matter how painful the process may be.

Conclusion

Metro Realty's transition from stage II to stage III is typical of many companies in a variety of industries. As companies expand

and begin to experience growing pains, farsighted managers like those at Metro Realty, Federal Express, Apple Computer, Compaq Computer, and Mrs. Fields' Cookies recognize the need for a change and begin to develop and formalize management systems needed to overcome these problems.

This chapter—and the Metro Realty case in particular—teaches a number of lessons about making the transition from an entrepreneurship (stage I or II) to a professionally managed firm (stage III). The first lesson is that growing pains like those experienced by Metro are unavoidable. Entrepreneurial firms that are successful and therefore grow rapidly can expect to experience certain problems related to the fact that they have not had time to develop effective management systems. Other areas of the company have, justifiably, required more attention.

The second lesson is that management must recognize the symptoms of organizational growing pains and realize that it is time for a change. Management and others may prefer to ignore the problems or blame them on some fluke because no one wants to admit that the company's success is threatened. Some people may believe that the problems will disappear if the company keeps operating in the manner that has proved effective in the past. But this belief, as we saw in Chapter Four, can cause the organization to fall victim to the Osborne syndrome.

The third lesson is that the needed changes can be quite painful for those involved. People desire to cling to familiar, traditional ways of operating. Formalization of roles, responsibilities, planning, and control suggests to many people that the "warm" atmosphere of the entrepreneurial firm is being replaced by "cold" professionalism. Whether or not this actually occurs, management must remain steadfast in its efforts to transform the organization.

The final lesson to be learned from Metro Realty is that the transition process cannot be accomplished overnight; indeed, it may take years. This need for slowness is, in fact, an asset. Introducing change slowly can help to reduce employee resistance and anxiety. It is also important to help employees understand why changes are being made so they do not feel threatened and will know what to expect in the future.

This chapter has attempted to show how an organization can recognize the need for management systems and set about developing them. This critical challenge must be met if the organization is to make a successful transition from an entrepreneurship to a professionally managed firm.

6 The Consolidation Stage: Managing the Corporate Culture

This chapter deals with the issues facing companies at stage IV. It uses a case history to show the impact of corporate culture on the development of a successful stage IV firm. The history of this company will demonstrate how culture changes in unintended ways as a company grows, what problems arise as a result of those changes, and how an organization can manage cultural change in a way that lets it become a successful stage IV company. Chapter Twelve will present additional examples of firms that have faced the challenge presented in making the transition from a stage III to a stage IV company.

Developing Successful Stage IV Organizations

After a company has successfully professionalized its management systems, it must meet a further developmental challenge that involves making very different types of changes. At this point the organization has reached stage IV, and its main task becomes the consolidation and management of its corporate culture. Although every company, from its inception, possesses a culture, culture does not become a critical concern until the company is faced with making the transition to stage IV. At this stage of development, companies must become concerned with culture management if they are to continue to be successful. Otherwise, individual members of the company are likely to interpret cultural elements in ways that meet their needs but not those of the company. Sometimes, as in the case in this chapter, a company will reach stage IV and have to simultaneously focus on the development of its management systems and the management of its corporate culture.

The Key Issues of Stage IV. The key challenge faced by a stage IV firm is developing a system for explicitly managing the corporate culture so that it supports the development of a professionally managed firm. As we explained in Chapter One, corporate culture consists of the values, beliefs, and norms that govern the behavior of people in an organization. The culture reflects what the organization stands for in its products or services, the management of its people, and the way it conducts business. Culture can have a profound impact on an organization's success or failure. It can determine the degree of employee commitment to a firm and affect the way customers perceive the enterprise.

During a firm's early stages of growth, culture is transmitted informally through employee's day-to-day interactions with the entrepreneur. As the firm grows, however, the entrepreneur tends to have less time for contact with an ever-increasing number of people. Accordingly, unless a formal mechanism is substituted for the process of cultural transmission by osmosis, the firm will find that its people no longer have a shared vision of what the company is or where it is going. (The creation of a shared vision for a company is part of the managerial function of strategic leadership, which will be examined in Chapter Eleven.) Mrs. Fields' Cookies is one firm that has been effective in communicating and maintaining the values and vision of its founders. Despite the widespread locations of its stores, the standards, ideas, and values of founder Debbi Fields are part of the operations of each individual store. Randy Fields, husband of Debbi Fields, developed a technology for information flow and control that allows Debbi to directly reach the manager and personnel of each store.[25]

The next section of this chapter will examine a case study of an organization at stage IV. It illustrates how culture changes in unintended ways as a company grows and why the management of culture is critical, especially during stage IV.

As with Metro Realty, our example company actually exists, but we have changed its name and certain facts about its situation to preserve its confidentiality.

Tempo Products Unlimited: Background

From very modest beginnings, Tempo Products Unlimited (TPU) grew into a large, successful consumer products corporation with revenues exceeding $150 million.[26] Much of the firm's initial success could be attributed to its owner, Ronald Harrison, who was willing to take certain risks that allowed his company to grow and prosper.

In 1971, Ron Harrison founded Tempo Products Unlimited, a consumer products manufacturing company. This firm was small in employees, size, and revenues, and it manufactured only one product, which appealed to a limited audience.

The first few years of Ron's ownership involved constant struggle. Sales were not bad, but they could have been better. The company was not growing, though it seemed to be maintaining its market share. The turning point for TPU came when Ron and his small staff decided to implement some new product ideas and marketing strategies. These changes were very effective at increasing sales. By 1975, the company had revenues totaling $5 million and included about sixty people on its staff.

In 1978, Ron concluded that it was time for his company to expand further. Since he had great success with the new product line, he decided to invest in other products that might appeal to his target audience. He added two new products to the existing ones, and both met with great success. Ron and his company seemed to be doing everything right.

In the ensuing years, Ron invested in a few other selected products aimed at his target audience. By 1980, total company revenues were $100 million, and by 1983 they totaled more than $150 million. Personnel had increased to 650 in 1983. This rapid growth was very much the result of the entrepreneurial skills Ron Harrison possessed: the ability to identify a market niche, the ability to create and produce a product appropriate for that niche, the willingness to take risks, and the ability to attract talented people to assist him in building his enterprise. In short, Ron was a classic entrepreneur.

Elements of TPU's Culture and Their Attenuation

Tempo Products Unlimited had been successful at creating most of the operating systems it needed to remain profitable as it grew. Its accounting system and control system were reasonably well developed and were operating effectively. The company had implemented a planning system and was continuing to formalize it. In 1980, however, the firm's management realized that problems unrelated to operating systems were arising. These problems proved to be the result of unintended reinterpretations of the values, norms, and beliefs that had served the company well during its growth. TPU's original culture, management realized, was in the process of attenuating.

When TPU was small, Ron was the source of its corporate culture. He relied on close interaction with employees to disseminate his beliefs and his vision for the company's future. As the company grew, however, such interaction was no longer possible, and the company's culture became increasingly unclear to new generations of employees. Some of these employees therefore began to create their own values, beliefs, and norms. At times, this new culture was at odds with TPU's original culture.

As differing and sometimes opposing values, beliefs, and norms were translated into action, conflicts arose. People lacked a shared perception of what the company was and where it was going. As one manager said, "We don't know what business we're in. We have many employees who don't know what type of products we make." This form of "growing pains" typically occurs at about the time a company is ready to make the transition from a stage III to a stage IV firm.

Changes in certain elements of TPU's culture were particularly important. Let us take a look at these elements as they existed in the original company culture and then see how they were becoming attenuated.

TPU Is a Family. The culture at TPU had traditionally emphasized a "family atmosphere." In the company's early years, everyone knew everyone else, and everyone pulled together for a common cause: the success of the firm. This corporatewide family feeling was easy to maintain because most employees interacted with one another on a regular basis and also were able to interact directly with Ron, who provided the guidance needed to keep people working together effectively. However, as the firm began its rapid growth, the "family" became less cohesive because the size of the company made it impossible to have the number of interactions necessary to sustain it. This dissolution of a "family feeling" is a common occurrence in rapidly growing entrepreneurial firms.

At TPU, an employee's organizational "family" became redefined as either those who were of the same "generation" or those with whom the employee worked most closely. There were two generations of employees at TPU. The older one entered the firm in the years prior to its period of rapid growth (before 1975), while the new generation entered TPU after 1975.

The older generation of employees came to believe that they were the "true family members," the ones who had really built the company. They considered the new generation to be outsiders. Consequently, members of the older generation, many of whom occupied middle- and senior-management positions, believed that they were entitled to certain privileges that the new generation of employees should not receive. These privileges included access to people, information, and other resources.

This belief was supported, at least in part, by the emphasis that TPU's management placed on the use of confidential information. Only "family" members—that is, management—were entitled to such information, and members of the new generation who were denied access to it came to resent not being "in" on company activities and decisions. They responded by creating their own "family grapevine" through which they could circulate information. Management in turn came to resent the fact that, in reality, there was no confidential information; it was readily available to most employees through this informal system of corporate communication.

An individual's work group also became a "family." This made sense because interaction among individuals in a work group is usually high, so people have a good chance to create satisfying relationships. This definition of "family" was also influenced by the structure that evolved as TPU grew.

During the company's early development, its structure had

been loose. As more products and personnel were added, however, a more formal structure developed, with its basis in the various functions of the company. Each area, such as production or sales, came to see itself in isolation from all other areas. This "separate islands syndrome" led to duplication of services and inefficiencies within the organization. It also replaced the total "family" feeling with a feeling of identification mainly with the work group. As a result, employees began to experience conflicting loyalties. "Do I work for my group or for the corporation?" became a prevalent question. It was often answered with "I work only for my group."

Decision Makers Are Few and Invincible. Ron Harrison, as founder and owner, had obviously been responsible for providing the vision of what TPU was to become. In TPU's early years, this involved making most of the company's decisions and providing direction to employees. Employees accepted the fact that it was Ron's responsibility to make decisions involving his investment, and they supported him in whatever course of action he chose. The belief was that, as one manager put it: "Ron will decide. He knows what he wants the company to be. I don't worry about it because it's all in his head."

People wanted Ron to make the decisions because he had the uncanny ability to "always make the right one." This ability created the belief that Ron was somehow invincible, a superman that no one could surpass. The company's spectacular success reinforced this belief.

As TPU grew, the decision-making ability and "invincibility" that Ron alone had originally been thought to possess became attributed, through a halo effect, to anyone who occupied a senior-management position. Thus the belief became "Senior management will decide; they know what's right."

Because of this belief, it became an accepted practice to defer most decisions to senior management, even when the decisions could have been made at a lower level in the company. Inefficiencies resulted from this practice for three reasons. First, senior managers were no longer able to make rational decisions on some matters because they were too far removed from the daily activities that their decisions would affect. Their decisions were, therefore, sometimes inappropriate and sometimes made too slowly to be of value.

The second reason why inefficiencies arose was that deferring decisions to the upper levels of the company allowed lower-level managers to avoid responsibility for decisions that affected them or their areas. If lower-level managers failed to reach a goal set for them by senior management, they could claim that they were not accountable because "it was not my decision."

A final reason for inefficiencies was an excessive dependence on outside consultants. This was costly in terms of both time and money. Consultants seemed to be used in instances where decisions should have been made by the managers themselves. According to some people in the company, consultants were used so often because upper managers did not want to take responsibility for their own decisions.

In fact, senior managers came to deny that they had sole decision-making responsibility. They created policies suggesting that lower-level personnel should be involved in decision making. In practice, however, lower-level managers were still controlled and restrained by upper management's decisions. For example, one person said of TPU's budget process, "It lacks credibility because budget cuts are issued from the top after the budget is approved. This is seen as a mockery of the system, since people aren't given decision-making responsibility."

The lack of decision-making responsibilities made some managers feel powerless and therefore they did nothing at all. As one person pointed out, "There are too many managers who have no real authority because someone else can rule over them." This situation frustrated managers who were supposed to be invested with authority, but complaints seldom reached upper management because the notion of upper management's invincibility had come to mean that people should not challenge their superiors. Doing so was likely to result in adverse personal consequences.

This fear of reprisals for "making waves" contributed to the adoption of a "top-down" communication system that provided little opportunity for lower-level employees to communicate their ideas to upper management. In fact, it almost prohibited such communication. One employee said, "Subordinates tell managers what they want to hear, not necessarily what they believe."

Afraid to voice opposition, most lower-level managers simply accepted the need to seek direction for future activities from senior management and to do as they were told. One person described the situation this way: "Always being on the outside, doing just what you're told without explanations or understanding of long-range goals, gives employees the idea that they are a commodity and not a resource."

"Whatever It Takes, Get It Done with Excellence." One of the beliefs on which TPU was founded was that its products should be of the highest quality. People believed that Ron was willing to devote whatever resources were necessary to reach this goal. Cost was less important than the desire to produce excellent products. An implicit motto at TPU was, "Whatever it takes, get it done with excellence."

It appeared to both employees and outsiders that Ron also believed that to create excellent products, one must employ excellent people. This in turn fostered the belief that Ron was willing to spend more than his competitors to attract and keep such people. TPU employees believed that they were paid above the industry average. At least one person suggested, in fact, that TPU employees were spoiled by excessive rewards.

Ron's stressing of excellence in products and people had created a positive image of TPU in the eyes of both employees and outsiders and had made a major contribution to the company's success.

As TPU grew, however, these positive values came to be misinterpreted. The goal of product excellence came to mean "We are a first-class organization." This in turn was interpreted to mean "We always go first class." The implicit corollary of this was "Cost does not matter."

The goal of excellence in people was also misinterpreted. People came to believe that they could not help performing well, and they expected rewards regardless of what their actual performance was. The standard of employee excellence was redefined to mean "Whatever a TPU employee does is excellent."

Our Company Is Unique. TPU employees believed that their company was unique in both its good and its bad attributes. This belief was supported by policies and practices that Ron had created to help employees feel "special" and thus increase pride and motivation.

Unfortunately, as the company grew, this belief led to problems at the organizational level. TPU employees came to feel that the company's excellence rested on its "uniqueness" and that treating it like any other company would therefore jeopardize its survival. They believed that TPU was so unique, in fact, that it could not learn from the lessons of others. They complained about the proposed use of organization development methods that had proved successful elsewhere because "they won't work at a company like ours" and "we can figure out our own problems." The belief in "excellence through uniqueness" thus came to be used as a way to protect people against change and to excuse their resistance to modification attempts.

"Play It by Ear." TPU's early success was partly due to its ability to change to meet environmental requirements—to "play it by ear." Formal roles and responsibilities, a planning system, and well-defined operating systems did not exist in the early years, nor were they necessary for the company's success. TPU and its employees operated on a day-to-day basis, making whatever adjustments they needed to carve out a market niche. This was a very effective approach in an entrepreneurial firm, since it allowed for rapid change.

As the company grew, however, the practice of "playing it by ear" became dysfunctional. TPU's management realized that the company could no longer successfully operate on an informal basis and began taking steps toward formalizing its management and operating systems. Specifically, the firm became concerned with three levels of problems resulting from the "play it by ear" belief.

At the individual level, this approach meant that some employees did not have clearly defined roles and responsibilities. As the firm grew, role definitions were made for some positions but not others. Many of the positions that remained ill defined had been created when the company needed additional employees to cope with its rapid growth. Since TPU's management was relatively young and inexperienced, it had tended to add people without trying to reconceptualize the functions being performed or the organizational structure required to perform them. Ambiguous role definitions contributed to productivity problems when employees unknowingly worked at odds with corporate goals or did nothing at all. Furthermore, individuals in these positions sometimes believed that they could not be held accountable for their actions because their roles had not been defined.

At the management level, informality contributed to problems in communication. When TPU was a small company, informal communication met both employee and company needs. As the firm grew, however, the need for a formal communication system became apparent—but one was not created, because of the desire to cling to the old value of "playing it by ear." The lack of a formal system contributed to inefficiencies in production, duplication of effort, and misunderstanding between divisions.

At the organizational level, it became clear that the lack of a formal planning process and a clearly articulated culture were causing problems. Each division within the company was allowed to design its own strategic plans, but these plans were often formulated without considering the needs of other areas. Similarly, each area had its own financial and nonfinancial goals, and these sometimes conflicted with the goals of other areas. An integrated strategic plan was needed so that employees could understand and focus on company goals rather than just the goals of their particular work area.

Have Fun. While TPU's culture stressed working to achieve excellence, it also emphasized that people should enjoy their work. This element of the company's culture was based on Ron's desire to create a pleasant work environment to balance the uncertainty that is unavoidable in a growing, entrepreneurial firm. As Ron said, "I've tried to establish a spirit that we shouldn't take ourselves too seriously; we should have fun. You need to relieve the pressure of not knowing what the future holds."

Unfortunately, as the company grew, Ron's belief that people should have fun became transformed into a mandate that all employees "will have fun." In practice, this meant avoidance of conflict, since people believed that conflict was disruptive and not good for the company or its personnel. Avoiding conflict with senior managers became particularly important, since they could punish those who challenged them. It was also important, however, to avoid conflict with one's peers and subordinates—not to "make waves." According to one manager, it was generally accepted that "the best way to get fired is to talk too much" and that "80 percent of the terminations are of people who made waves across organizational lines."

Managers believed that it was better to avoid conflict with their subordinates than to disrupt the system by providing negative feedback or dismissing poor performers. One manager remarked that when subordinates were criticized, they either "cried or made excuses." Many managers therefore came to believe that it was better to say nothing at all. This contributed to retention of poor performers.

Do Your Own Thing and Do It Well. One belief that had existed at TPU from its inception was that people should be allowed to find their own levels of performance and that if excellence in products and work environment was stressed, every employee's standard would be high. In the company's early years, "Do your own thing and do it well" was carried out in practice as employees devoted a great deal of energy to making the company a success. Employees were motivated to achieve the standard of excellence implicit in "Do it well" because they were encouraged by others and, most important, by Ron to "Do your best." A high degree of interaction between Ron and his employees increased motivation, and inadequate performers could easily be identified and dealt with. The high degree of interaction also created a feeling of togetherness, so people's "own thing" usually fit in with the goals of the company. As the organization grew, however, people grew apart both physically and psychologically, and "Do your own thing" became distorted at three levels.

At the individual level, employees came to interpret "Do your own thing" as "Do what is best for yourself." This sometimes meant doing nothing at all, as suggested by one manager: "People

don't work around here anymore. They loaf, visit, chat, or wander
the halls." This distortion grew partly out of the lack of a clearly
articulated culture, partly out of the lack of formally defined roles
and responsibilities, and partly out of the belief that conflict should
be avoided at all costs. Without a well-defined and clearly communicated culture, it became acceptable to interpret "Do your own
thing" in many ways. Ambiguous roles led some employees to believe that they could create their own positions without considering
the goals of the company. Furthermore, some employees became so
frustrated by the lack of formal responsibilities or the overlap between their roles and those of others that they just gave up and did
nothing at all. Such behavior was allowed to continue because chal-
lenging it might result in conflict, and the culture stressed conflict
avoidance.

At the managerial level, "Do your own thing" came to mean
that managers could choose the leadership style that best met their
personal—but not necessarily the company's—needs. Managers differed in their ability to delegate and make decisions, and those with
well-developed leadership skills were sometimes dependent on those
who did not have such skills. Effective managers thus often became
frustrated because they were unable to attain their goals. One person
noted, "There are many different leadership and management styles
among TPU managers, and this has tended to create uneven delegation of responsibility and unclear decision making." The culture
was not strong enough to support the adoption of effective styles of
management, nor was there an institutionalized management development program in which managers could learn the skills they
needed to be effective in their jobs.

At the organizational level, one interpretation of "Do your
own thing" gave support to the "separate islands syndrome." Each
area came to believe that in order to fulfill its needs, it had to
compete with other areas for resources. This led individual areas to
become highly protective of their territories. As an example, area
managers often believed that if "outsiders" (such as consultants)
were able to audit their operations, they might lose resources and
even their jobs. The cultural belief became "Do your own thing, but
stay out of my territory."

In response to this fear, communication between areas became minimal. Some employees, in fact, said that horizontal communication at TPU was practically nonexistent. Lack of communication resulted in duplication of effort between divisions and a reduction in the ability of areas to work together effectively. For example, on one occasion production manufactured more of a product than the service center could store. The product had to be stored elsewhere, resulting in unanticipated costs. Production had failed to communicate its needs to the service center because the company's culture discouraged horizontal communication in the interest of "protecting one's territory."

Redefining a Culture

In 1980, TPU's senior management began to realize that certain aspects of the company's culture needed to be changed if it was to continue to be successful. Ron Harrison therefore worked with others to create an organizational development program to help TPU redefine its culture. The program was to emphasize four broad areas: (1) organizational design, (2) strategic planning, (3) management development, and (4) culture management.

Organizational Design. As TPU grew, its structure remained relatively unchanged. This lack of structural change, combined with certain cultural elements, resulted in a number of "growing pains." For example, when combined with the cultural element of "Do your own thing," the company's obsolete structure led to the "separate islands syndrome."

TPU's managers recognized the need for organization redesign. They realized that the design process not only should aim to alleviate current problems but should also plan for the company's next stage of development in order to avoid future problems.

It became evident to Ron Harrison that the company's redesign should include some changes in leadership. During TPU's first stages of development, Ron's unique skills as a risk taker, investor, and market niche identifier had contributed greatly to the company's success. This type of leadership is termed *strategic leadership* (see Chapter Eleven). Ron realized, however, that the $150 million company that TPU had become required different leadership skills for its continued success. At this stage of development, TPU needed a leader who was skilled at maintaining its day-to-day operations. This type of leadership is termed *operational leadership*. As will be explained in Chapter Eleven, Ron had two alternatives in meeting this need: develop the required skills himself or hire someone who had the skills that he had not adequately developed.

After much discussion with experts and consideration of the matter, Ron decided that his company's and his own needs would best be met if someone else were appointed to run TPU on a day-to-day basis. Ron could then assume the role of chief executive and remain responsible for strategic planning, new ventures, and organizational development. In 1982, therefore, Ron appointed Stewart Page, who had been an adviser to TPU for a number of years, to the office of president. Stewart was selected because he was familiar with the business and because Ron believed he could get the type of results that the company needed.

The change in leadership was communicated to employees through both word and action. The word consisted of a formal announcement of Page's appointment, and the action consisted of a number of changes in policy and practice that symbolized a change in the company's culture as well as a change in leadership.

Stewart Page made his presence felt almost immediately by reducing the company's "deadwood" in two ways. First, he asked people who had been "doing their own thing" without regard for the company's benefit to leave. Second, he analyzed positions for their contributions to the overall functioning of the firm, and positions that appeared to have no clear responsibilities and did not serve a critical function for the company were eliminated. Employees who occupied these positions were either terminated or relocated. During this period "heads rolled."

After the deadwood had been eliminated, a new and more formalized organization chart that clearly depicted how different positions related to one another was developed. Job descriptions were reviewed and revised, or created, to accommodate the changes made in the organization's structure. These new definitions of roles and responsibilities were communicated to employees both formally and informally so that all would clearly understand the way their jobs related to the total company's functioning.

Stewart Page also promoted cost control. He made it clear that the company would no longer tolerate excessive spending and that managers would be held accountable for their budgets.

Stewart set about reducing the "separate islands syndrome" by increasing communication across organization lines. He did this by creating a companywide operating committee that brought together individuals from various divisions within the company. This group also increased communication between middle and upper management by acting as the liaison between senior management and the rest of the organization.

Eventually, Stewart hoped to create operating committees for each product division. These committees would be responsible for setting, monitoring, and evaluating the division's goals. The creation of these committees was intended to move the organization's structure toward a focus on "profit centers" with functional general managers.

Through these actions and others, the change in leadership and the change in culture that it represented were communicated to TPU's employees. It became clear that several aspects of the old culture, including "playing it by ear," "doing your own thing," and operating in isolation from other areas of the company, were gone forever. The company was going to develop the culture of a professional firm, which included more formalized operating systems, making "your own thing" conform to the company's interests, and working together in an integrated, cooperative fashion.

Strategic Planning.   TPU had begun to implement a corporate planning process in the late 1970s, but this process had not been institutionalized and was not functioning effectively. In 1980, senior management became aware that a more formal corporate plan was needed and set about creating one. (For a complete discussion of strategic planning, see Chapter Seven.)

The initial challenge the company faced was to decide what business it was in. Creating a corporate identity is the first step in defining a corporate culture and designing a strategic plan. TPU had grown into a company with five divisions related to different products, and it lacked focus. Upper management therefore worked to clarify the company's identity through meetings and discussions outlining its present and future business growth opportunities. Corporate leaders eventually decided that TPU was in the business of producing small consumer items designed for the tastes of a special market segment.

Once this mission statement was agreed on, management began to create a strategic plan and to formalize the strategic planning process. Stewart Page established a planning department to concentrate on the long-term growth and goals of TPU and integrate the plans of various divisions.

Management Development. TPU had traditionally offered management development opportunities to its employees, but it had never had a formalized training program. Thus the quality of management training varied from year to year, depending on its frequency, content, and instructors.

Stewart Page and his senior managers recognized the need for formalized and continuing training programs. A belief in such programs was consistent with Ron Harrison's view that the key resource of TPU was people and that training could help to increase the value of this resource. Stewart, however, saw that these programs could also serve as a means of redefining and communicating the company's culture.

Both Ron and Stewart believed that it was important for members of upper management to understand and be able to perform their responsibilities effectively. Since the company's existing management training programs appeared to be insufficient, TPU's leaders asked an independent consultant to help them design new training programs for senior management. These programs consisted of counseling and skill-building sessions overseen by a professional trainer.

Stewart also recognized the need to improve the training programs offered to middle managers. Traditionally, these programs were not formal and attendance at them was not required. Thus, the quality of managers' training varied greatly. Stewart decided that the company needed a more formalized management development program that was precisely tailored to TPU's unique qualities and problems.

Working with an independent consultant, Stewart and other

members of upper management developed a program that both provided training to present and potential managers and helped the
company redefine and communicate its culture. The program consisted of lectures, readings, structured exercises, and group discussions, all focusing on the unique aspects and skill requirements of
being a manager at TPU. (An in-depth example of the use of a
management development program in a company facing issues similar to those at TPU is presented in Chapter Nine.)

Initially only selected middle managers participated in these
programs, although the programs were intended to eventually include all present and potential managers. This gradual implementation allowed the programs to be tested for their ability to meet the
company's needs. It also helped to reduce participants' potential
resistance to change.

Stewart hoped for three important outcomes from these management development programs. First, they should create a pool of
skilled managers, who would become the next generation of senior
managers to run the firm. Second, since participants were drawn
from different areas of the company, he hoped that the shared experience of taking part in the programs would create lasting relationships that could serve as linking pins between areas of the
company. Finally, he hoped that program participants would bring
back to their areas both new skills and the new definition of the
company's culture, which would then spread throughout the rest of
the organization.

Culture Management. In 1984, Stewart Page, Ron Harrison, and Catherine Forest Harrison (a senior vice president and
Ron's wife), began to focus on the management of TPU's culture.
Importantly, they realized that culture can be managed; it is not just
"there."

One of their first tasks was to define what TPU's culture was.
They began with an informal culture survey distributed to a sample
of employees at TPU. The survey asked respondents, who remained
anonymous, a series of questions about their satisfaction with various aspects of their jobs and with the company in general. It attempted to get them to answer the underlying question, "What do
you see as the company's personality?" The information obtained

was analyzed to determine what employees thought the current culture was. Interviews were then conducted with selected middle managers, asking them for their perceptions of the company's culture.

Stewart, Ron, Cathy, and other members of upper management now needed to decide what the definition of TPU's culture should be. They also needed to find ways to communicate the elements of this culture.

The firm also established a corporate communications department to articulate, design, and reinforce elements of the new culture. This department, headed by Mary Ryan, reported to Cathy Forest Harrison.

Another important ingredient in the process of cultural change and management at Tempo Products involved the formal and informal influence of Cathy Forest Harrison. As senior vice president in the firm, she was responsible for one of the major functional areas of the firm. She was also, however, a co-owner of the firm and a member of its board of directors.

Cathy's role in Tempo Product's development to a stage IV company and in the redesign and management of its corporate culture was both direct and subtle. As a member of the board of directors, she had a senior management perspective of what was happening in the company, but she also had the ability to think about the firm in a very different way than Ron and Stewart—both of whom were also board members—were able to. Ron was the classic entrepreneur. His skills have already been described, and he was the one who contributed the brilliant strategic vision to create the company. Stewart was the day-to-day administrator. One of his primary skills was problem solving. He was emotionally and intellectually prepared to make the difficult decisions involving people and resource allocation required at this stage of the firm's development. But successful development to stage IV also required a third type of thinking skill, the ability to think holistically about this organization and its developmental processes. Although both Stewart and Ron certainly possessed this third kind of skill to a considerable extent, in my judgment, of the three, Cathy Forest Harrison had the greatest talent for this type of thinking.

Based on her own analysis of the transformation taking place at Tempo Products, as well as on selected inputs from a consultant working with the firm, Cathy formulated her views and expressed them at board meetings, thus helping to shape the corporate culture. She also championed the corporate communications department (discussed further later), and served as senior management's representative to the organization by hosting a series of working lunches to meet employees, answer their questions about the firm's future direction, and, by her very presence, communicate the company's interest in people and their concerns. She was also a major player in the decision-making process involving all of the other aspects of the organizational development program just described, including the new corporate structure, the management development program, and strategic planning.

The New TPU Culture and Its Implementation

This section considers how the elements of the "professional" culture at TPU evolved from the entrepreneurial elements described in the first section of this case study. In some instances, the new culture promotes a belief, value, or norm that reflects a cultural element on which the company was based. In other cases, where going back to traditional elements would have been dysfunctional, new values, beliefs, or norms were created and communicated. Each element of the new culture that TPU's management created and the method used to reinforce it is described in the following pages.

TPU Is One Family, Not a Collection of Separate Families. TPU wanted to communicate to its employees the belief in a need to pull together as a company: "We can no longer operate as a group of separate entities, concerned only with ourselves."

The adoption of this belief was symbolized, in part, by the creation of the operating committee. This group increased communication between areas, although there was initially some resistance to the idea that the company could pull together. Individual areas feared that they would lose resources (power, people, materials) if they submitted to the new culture. People also still want to

138   Growing Pains

remain loyal to their work groups, since they found the most support there.

To reduce such resistance to whole-company loyalty, TPU
began promoting companywide activities such as picnics, parties,
and luncheons. These gatherings encourage individuals from different areas to talk with one another informally and thus establish
lines of communication. The result is that people feel more comfortable phoning an acquaintance in another area to find the
answer to a problem or question.

Another effort to reunite the company was the creation of a
newsletter and a formal corporate communications department
(mentioned earlier) which provides information on corporate activities and on the people who make up the company. In the biweekly
newsletter, individuals are honored for company service, recognized
for their participation in company-sponsored management development programs, congratulated on promotions, and even given
best wishes on birthdays and anniversaries. This publication is a
symbol that TPU cares about its personnel. More important, from
management's perspective, it also reduces employees' need to rely
on the "grapevine" for information. There are many key performers
in the company in addition to senior management. Previously, only
two people in the firm received recognition. However, with the
addition of the company newsletter and a new corporate awards
program, others besides senior managers now receive deserved
recognition.

*Decisions Will Be Made at All Levels of the Company, and
People Will Be Held Accountable for Their Decisions.* TPU's
management recognized the need to develop effective decision makers at all levels of the company and to eliminate the notion that
upper management must never be challenged. To accomplish these
goals, TPU began training individuals in effective decision-making
techniques and encouraging them to apply these skills.

Participants in TPU's management development program
are formally taught how to make effective decisions. They also learn
that certain decision-making responsibilities are theirs, not upper
management's. TPU's management hopes that as program participants return to their jobs, they will pass on these skills to others

through example and, wherever possible, through actual training of their subordinates.

Formalization of the strategic planning process has also helped distribute decision-making responsibility throughout the organization. Individuals are being encouraged to participate in decisions affecting them by setting goals for themselves, for their work groups, and for the organization at large. Management also stresses that employees will be evaluated on their success at meeting these goals. If employees do not understand or are unhappy with goals that have been set, it is their responsibility to clarify them.

A third way of promoting decision-making skills and reducing the practice of deferring decisions to upper management has involved the refinement of role and responsibility descriptions. These descriptions, in many cases, force individuals at lower levels of the organization to become decision makers because decision making is now defined as part of their jobs.

The new culture also stresses that no one is "invincible": everyone will be held accountable for decisions made, including senior management. The notion that senior management is invincible has been reduced not only by policy but also by example: Certain members of senior management who were not performing their jobs well have been terminated.

"Whatever It Takes, Get It Done with Excellence." The emphasis that TPU traditionally placed on excellence in products, people, and the company at large has been maintained in the new culture. However, excellence in people is no longer defined as "whatever TPU employees do." Rather, excellence has the more functional meaning of quality work and desire to "do something extra" for the good of the company. A new bonus system was created that supports this definition. This system rewards only those who perform above standard.

The management development program and the strategic planning process also reinforce this revised definition of excellence. Both of these efforts stress that individuals will be held accountable for achieving the goals they have set for themselves and that rewards will be contingent on meeting these goals. Participants in the management development program are taught how to recognize and reward excellence in order to increase employee motivation.

Another change in the definition of excellence is that the company no longer tolerates excessive expenditures. The "motto" now is "whatever it takes to get it done with excellence in a cost-effective manner." Managers are held accountable for meeting their budgets, and the notion of "always going first class" has been eliminated.

Our Company Can Learn from Others.   While TPU continues to promote the notion that it is a unique company, it now also wants employees to understand that it can learn from the experience of others. This belief has been promoted through the management development program, which is designed to meet TPU's specific needs and at the same time demonstrate techniques that have proved successful for other companies and other managers. These techniques include a performance review system that evaluates individuals based on observed performance; a strategic planning system in which goals are set, monitored, and evaluated; and an organization design that is functional for the kind of company TPU has become.

We Can No Longer "Play It by Ear."   TPU recognized that some of its growing pains resulted from a lack of formalized management and operating systems. It focused on replacing the "Play it by ear" cultural element with one that emphasized the planning, procedures, and policies of a professional firm.

At the individual level, the company carefully reviewed the roles and responsibilities of its employees. It got rid of most of its "deadwood" in the form of both nonfunctioning people and nonfunctional positions. This painful but necessary process not only improved the "bottom line" but also affected people in a positive sense. There is now little ambiguity about job roles, and employees are aware that each has a valuable contribution to make to the company.

The communication problems that the company experienced at the management level have been difficult to resolve, but TPU's managers have come to view the new management development program as an important step toward improving horizontal communications. Many groups of program participants developed a team spirit that continued after they returned to their individual areas, allowing them to feel comfortable in calling one another about problems. More than a few of these relationships have been maintained as the individuals have been promoted to higher levels within the company.

Just as participants in the management development program continued to help reintegrate areas on an informal basis, the strategic planning process—which emphasizes corporate rather than divisional planning—has helped to reintegrate the company on a formal basis. Each area is now responsible for its own financial and nonfinancial goals, but these are to be formulated with consideration for other divisions, not in isolation from them. The planning department is helping to coordinate this effort so that company interests will remain of paramount concern.

Even more significant than the steps just described was the firm's decision to improve horizontal communications through the creation of three separate product operating committees. Because of the nature of Tempo's products, the operating committee, consisting of representatives from different functional areas (production, sales, and so forth), is a highly effective tool for facilitating interdepartmental communication and decision making.

Have Fun, But Not All the Time. The new culture stresses that conflict cannot and should not be avoided. Rather, conflict should be confronted and resolved.

The first step in this process was to help individuals admit that conflict exists. TPU employees had operated for many years in what seemed, on the surface, to be a very smooth-running and peaceful atmosphere. However, like all organizations, TPU had underlying conflicts between people and areas. Traditionally, these conflicts had been ignored. In 1982, however, when Stewart Page was made president and major changes began, a great deal of conflict came to the surface and could no longer be denied.

The culture survey, conducted in 1984, also brought conflicts to the surface. The survey itself was evidence that management believed that not everyone was "having fun" and that some problems existed. It was intended to reinforce the belief that "It's all right to criticize, to be unhappy about certain things. Let's get them out in the open so we can resolve our problems."

The next step was to train employees to confront conflict. This has been accomplished, in part, through the management development program. Participants are shown how to deal with conflict, particularly how to give and receive criticism. Again, management hopes that participants will take both these skills and the new culture that they represent back to their jobs and start them filtering both up and down throughout the organization. As Cathy Forest Harrison pointed out, conflict is not necessarily bad. Senior management has fostered a new culture of accountability, and this has led to conflict. Moreover, the increasing sophistication of the finance department has led to its ability, mandated by senior management, to ask the "hard" questions, which leads to conflict.

Do Your Own Thing and Do It Well. This element of the organization's culture was positively redefined, in part, by the organization development program. The program helped redefine this value on three levels.

At the individual employee level, the new definition is "When you do your own thing, it should be congruent with the goals of the organization." To put this belief into practice, the company created procedures and policies that stress *real* excellence in performance and also emphasize that those who do not perform at the expected level will be dismissed. Management hopes that employees will come to recognize that those who strive for excellence will be rewarded, while those who do not will be forced to leave the company. Better definitions of roles and responsibilities act as guides to help employees determine what constitutes excellent performance. People will no longer be allowed to merely "wander the halls."

At the managerial level, managers are encouraged to use leadership styles that will help the company be more effective. (Chapter Eleven discusses the basic concepts and methods of increasing leadership effectiveness.) TPU's senior management hopes that, through the training that participants in the management development program receive, they will gain the skills necessary to be effective delegators and decision makers.

At the organizational level, the company focused on reducing the "Do your own thing but stay out of my territory" element of its culture. This was accomplished partly by the formation of the operating committee and partly by the management development program. The "team" feeling created among program participants helped decrease the need for territoriality.

Keys to A Successful Stage IV Firm

By the time a firm like Tempo Products reaches stage IV, the lack of a shared culture can produce a number of problems. Individuals are left to create their own cultures, which may not always be in the best interest of the company as a whole. Thus the key factor involved in making the transition to stage IV is the ability to develop a formal program of auditing the corporate culture and transmitting it to peer groups of employees.

To begin this process, management must first determine what the culture is. This can be a difficult process, since members are not always able to articulate values, beliefs, and norms. It is much like asking a U.S. citizen what it is like to be an American. However, interviews with organization members in which they are asked to relate stories about their lives in the company may provide some clues. Careful thought and analysis—including feedback to the organization for confirmation, refinement, or redefinition—is also important.

From the information provided by this cultural diagnosis, management can determine where it is in terms of culture. Then it can focus on redefining the company's culture and begin communicating the new culture to employees through changes in policies and practices like those described in the case provided in this chapter. A more in-depth examination of the culture management process will be presented in Chapter Twelve.

Given the complex nature of this process, attempting to articulate "what our culture should be to support our growth" and mapping out a plan to move the company from where it is (with respect to culture) to where it should be can take years.

Conclusion

The events we have described for TPU are typical of those that occur as companies attempt to make the transition from stage II or III to stage IV.

Several lessons can be learned from TPU's experience. The first is that the need to manage a firm's corporate culture is just as real and important as the need to manage cash or inventory. Culture can have significant positive or negative effects on operations and, ultimately, on the corporate "bottom line."

A second lesson is that cultural change is inevitable as an organization grows. Senior managers may think they know what the firm's culture is because they have a close association with the owner or founder, who directly communicates his or her vision to them. Unfortunately, as more and more new people enter the organization, the culture of the owner or founder is increasingly likely to become distorted because there is no longer much direct communication. The changes that occur are not necessarily malicious; they may simply arise from "noise" picked up through the process of cultural transmission.

A third lesson is that cultural change can reinforce and be reinforced by the broader process of organizational development that a firm must go through as it moves from stage II to stage III to stage IV. The culture that management wants to reinforce or introduce can be manifested in the firm's leadership style, its management development programs, its structure, and its strategic planning process. Indeed, the firm's culture *must* be consistent throughout all management systems if it is to become fully effective.

Another lesson concerns the process of cultural change. The change process must begin with an audit or assessment of what the firm's present culture is. This can be accomplished with a variety of tools, including questionnaires, interviews, and analysis of stories and internal corporate materials. Once the present culture has been identified, the organization must decide on the form of culture it desires and compare this ideal with the present situation. This comparison leads to identification of cultural gaps or desired cultural changes. The last step in bringing about cultural change is designing the strategy and action plan for introducing the desired changes.

A final lesson concerns the different kinds of management thinking required to develop an enterprise to a successful stage IV company. From our analysis of Tempo products it should be clear that organizational success at stage IV is more than merely a matter of products and markets, though they are an essential prerequisite. It is a matter of different modes of thinking as well. Classic entrepreneurial thinking is required for success at stages I and II. However, the successful transition from stage II to stages III and IV requires two additional modes of thought: the problem-solving mode and the holistic organizational development perspective.

At Tempo Products, all three of the senior managers (Ron, Cathy, and Stewart) possessed each of these different modes of thinking to some extent. However, each of them individually also possessed a comparative advantage in at least one mode. As a management team, they possessed all of the three key ways of thinking about their company.

Cultural change can be accomplished through a variety of methods. As seen at Tempo Products, several different ingredients were used, including a formal corporate communications program, informal family-style gatherings, changes in senior management attitudes, a culture survey, the use of a committee structure to increase interdepartmental communication, and management development. It should also be noted that the successful organizational development at Tempo Products was not without its problems. Moreover, although the roles of certain people are highlighted in this chapter, many other individuals played significant roles as well.

As this chapter has shown, cultural change in a corporation is complex and difficult, but necessary. It is the critical developmental task involved in building a successful stage IV organization and making the last part of the transition from an entrepreneurship to a professionally managed firm.

Part Three

Mastering the Tools
of Professional Management

Parts One and Two of this book presented a framework for understanding and managing the transitions of an entrepreneurial organization from one stage of growth and development to the next. Part Three will focus on the basic tools for managing organizations professionally. Specifically, we will discuss some of the major elements of a firm's management infrastructure, its management systems, and corporate culture. Management systems and corporate culture were described briefly in Chapter One, and their places on the pyramid of organizational development was shown in Figure 1.1.

An organization's management systems consist of (1) the planning system (including the strategic planning process), (2) the organization system (including the entity's organizational structure, its leadership practices, and its system for management development), and (3) the control systems. Management systems have a critical influence on an organization's performance and profitability.

A firm's planning system includes its processes for strategic planning, operational planning, budgeting, and contingency planning. In entrepreneurial companies these processes tend to be relatively informal, while in professionally managed firms they tend to be more developed.

The strategic planning process is a critical resource or tool for managing organizational growth and development. Chapter Seven presents the basic concepts and methods of strategic plan-

147

ning. It also explains the role of strategic planning in making the transition from an entrepreneurship to a professionally managed firm by using the example of one organization's strategic plan. Finally, it examines an organization's requirements for strategic planning at different stages of growth.

The way people are organized in a business enterprise can have a critical impact on overall operating effectiveness, efficiency, and, in turn, bottom-line profitability. Chapter Eight discusses the nature of an organization's structure and examines the alternative forms of structure. It also identifies criteria for the design and evaluation of organizational structure as well as presenting case studies of structural issues at different stages of growth.

Management development is another major tool for organizational development in entrepreneurial firms. As we saw in the case study presented in Chapter Six, the management development process can be used not only to train managers but also to shape or reshape the corporate culture. Chapter Nine examines the tools and functions of management development and presents a case study that shows how one company used the management development process in making its transition from an entrepreneurship to a professionally managed organization.

The organizational control system is another critical component of the firm's management systems. Chapter Ten discusses organizational control and its role in making the transition to a professionally managed firm. It explains the need for control and the nature and role of organizational control systems. It also presents a model of the key components of a control system and explains how they function to motivate and control behavior. Finally, it examines organizations' need for control at different stages of growth.

Another critical factor in managing and developing entrepreneurial organizations is leadership. Leadership is involved both in the day-to-day operations of firms and in their long-term organizational development. Chapter Eleven deals with leadership. It presents basic concepts and research findings concerning leadership effectiveness. It also distinguishes between strategic and operational leadership: The former is concerned with the overall process of organizational development, while the latter is concerned with the day-to-day management of the firm. Chapter Eleven examines the leadership styles available to managers in entrepreneurial organizations and presents the result of some research concerning the extent to which each style has been observed in such organizations. It also examines the key tasks that managers must perform if they are to be effective leaders and presents some research on the extent to which these tasks are actually performed by managers in organizations. In addition, it presents some case studies of leadership issues in actual organizations. Finally, it considers the nature of the leadership that is required at different stages of organizational growth.

The nature and management of a company's culture also have a significant impact on organizational success. Culture influences a firm's ability to develop the systems needed to support its growth. Like other variables in the pyramid of organizational development, culture must be effectively managed if a firm is to make the transition to professional management. Chapter Twelve describes the nature of corporate culture and how it is manifested in organizations. It also presents techniques for managing this variable effectively and describes the nature of corporate culture at different stages of organizational growth.

Part Three, then, gives a basic description of some of the most important of the managerial concepts and tools that can help entrepreneurs successfully manage their firms' transition from one stage of growth to the next. These tools provide an essential foundation for the successful management of entrepreneurial organizations at all stages of growth, but especially at stages III and beyond.

Figure III.1 summarizes schematically the relations among the key components of an organization's management system. As seen in the figure, the management process begins with the planning system, which articulates a firm's mission, objectives, and goals. Strategic leadership is involved throughout the planning process. The firm's plan and strategy determines how it ought to be organized (organizational structure). This, in turn, enhances the organization's operational systems and leads to the firm's results, which are measured by the performance measurement system.

The performance measurement system is a component of the company's control system, which also includes objectives and goals

Figure III.1. The Management System.

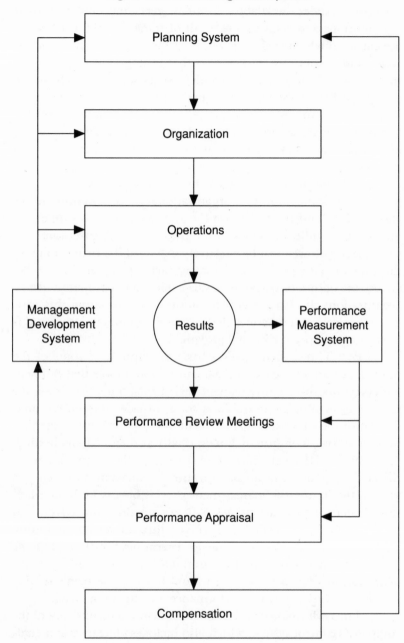

from the planning systems as well as performance appraisal and rewards (compensation). Performance review meetings as well as formal information are the mechanisms through which these components of the overall management system operate. The management development system helps the company and supports the other components of the management system by training managers in the skills required to do planning, to use the various forms of organizational structure, and to manage day-to-day operations (operational leadership). Input about the skills required by management development is received from the performance appraisal process.

Leadership—a key component of the management system—is not shown explicitly in Figure III.1, but it should be viewed as a part of the process of various components such as strategic planning (strategic leadership), operations, performance review meetings, and performance appraisal (operational leadership). Similarly, corporate culture is not explicitly shown in Figure III.1, but it must be recognized that corporate culture affects and is affected by all of the components of the management system.

7 Strategic Planning

Previous chapters have provided an overview of the things an organization must do to make a successful transition from an entrepreneurship to a professionally managed organization. This chapter focuses on one of the major tools available to help senior managers make this transition: strategic planning.

The strategic planning process is one of the managerial systems that an organization must develop if it desires to function effectively. Strategic planning plays a dual role. It is not only an important tool for managing organizations; it is also part of the process through which organizations make the transition from one stage of growth to the next.

Strategic planning is one of the major tools by which management can create a shared vision of what a company wants to become. The strategic planning process can also help to shape the corporate culture. The very act of instituting such a process, when one was not used in the past, signals to the organization's members that things are changing. It warns that planning must now become a way of life and that the firm has embarked on a program to professionalize itself. Strategic planning can also provide a sense of direction for a company and its employees as well as specific goals to motivate and guide behavior.

This chapter provides a framework to help managers understand the strategic planning process as well as a step-by-step approach to strategic planning in organizations. We will first introduce and define the basic concepts of the strategic planning process. We will then describe the steps involved in developing a strategic plan. To illustrate the nature of strategic planning, we will then examine the planning process at Metro Realty, the company introduced in Chapter Five. Finally, we describe the strategic planning process at each stage of growth.

The Nature of Strategic Planning

In its broadest sense, strategic planning involves deciding about the future direction of an organization and the organizational capabilities that will be needed to achieve the organization's goals. It involves analyzing the organization's environment to assess future opportunities and threats, formulating objectives and specific goals to be achieved, and developing action plans to attain them. An effective strategic plan must deal not only with a company's markets and external business opportunities but also with the internal organizational capabilities required for future growth.

There are two aspects of a firm's strategic planning process: (1) strategic issues to be addressed, and (2) components of the strategic plan. Each of these will be discussed in turn.

Strategic Issues

Although many people think of strategic planning as a number crunching exercise, its primary focus should be on strategic and related organizational development issues. The ultimate goal of the strategic planning process is to formulate a future direction for a firm. This is, in part, a statement of how the firm plans to compete in the marketplace. However, it should also define the direction for the internal development of the firm so that it will be enabled to compete effectively in the marketplace and achieve its long-term mission.

To articulate its future direction, it is necessary for the firm to address a wide variety of issues that are relevant to the market, competition, environmental trends, and organizational development.

Key Questions. Although for any organization there is a wide variety of questions that should be addressed by a given firm, there are seven generic questions that *must* be addressed by all organizations regardless of their size and their industry: (1) What business are we in? (2) What are our competitive strengths and limitations? (3)

Do we have a market niche? (4) What do we want to become in the long term? (5) Given what we want to become in the long term, what are the critical factors which will make us successful or unsuccessful in achieving this long-term mission? (6) What are our competitive strengths and limitations in each of the critical areas that will determine our competitive effectiveness? (7) What goals shall we set to improve our competitive effectiveness and organizational capabilities in each of these critical success areas? These questions are typically addressed during a series of strategic planning meetings.

Many companies are increasingly using annual retreats as a cornerstone of their strategic planning process. At such retreats executives are taken away from the normal environment of day-to-day activities and charged with the responsibility of thinking about the long-term direction of the enterprise. Regardless of the medium through which these questions are addressed, they must be answered as part of the strategic planning process. We will illustrate how these questions must be addressed in the context of a case study dealing with Metro Realty later in this chapter.

The Importance of Strategic Positioning. One of the primary strategic decisions that a firm has to make is to choose a market segment in which to compete. The choice of a market segment not only involves the nature of the product being offered, but the tier of the marketplace as well. The market for any product or service typically exists in terms of three different tiers or levels of the market. In order to position themselves effectively, companies must understand that customer wants differ at each tier.

The typical buyer in the tier 1 market is affluent enough to afford whatever he or she wishes. Accordingly, the primary concern is for the overall quality, service, and prestige of the product or service received rather than for the price per se. At the margin there may well be some buyers in the tier 1 category who have a significant concern with price. However, buyers in this price category typically are less concerned with price or even price differentials than they are with the other factors. For example, an individual who is purchasing an automobile in the tier 1 category may consider a Mercedes, a Jaguar, or some other luxury automobile and may very well not be concerned with a major differential in price between these particular products.

Viewed figuratively, the products and services in this tier can be thought of as ranging from a "Cadillac" to a "Rolls Royce." This is true not only for automobiles per se, but for all products and services that fit this particular quality categorization. The same kind of demarcation can be true for legal services or products provided by aerospace firms.

The second tier of the marketplace is usually significantly larger than tier 1 in terms of the number of customers in this segment. In terms of quality, the products in this category figuratively range from an Oldsmobile down to a Chevrolet. In tier 2, the buyer is concerned with a combination of quality, service, prestige, and price. Typically the buyer is making trade-offs between two or more of these variables. As before, this tier of the marketplace is not just applicable to automobiles, but to a full range of products and services.

In tier 3, the typical buyer is concerned primarily with price. Quality, service, and prestige are relatively unimportant. This particular segment is generally the largest of all three tiers of the marketplace. The buyer in this segment of the marketplace is looking for a "serviceable" product or service. It may well be a commodity or a generic brand. This tier can be symbolically represented by looking from Chevrolet down through Hyundai or Yugo automobiles.

To illustrate the fact that the three tiers of the marketplace do not merely apply to tangible products such as automobiles but to all other products and services as well, consider some examples, such as legal services, medical services, aerospace, and retailing. In Los Angeles there is a well-known law firm by the name of O'Melveny & Meyers. This firm operates in the tier 1 segment, and to paraphrase a well-known saying, "If you have to ask the price, you probably cannot afford it." In tier 3 we have a firm that specializes in being a legal service supermarket: Jacoby & Meyers. And in Los Angeles, there are certainly many tier 2 law firms. With respect to medical services, the urgent care centers that have emerged occupy tier 3 of the marketplace. Many of the HMOs occupy the lower portions of tier 2, while many private physicians are in various levels of tier 2. Tier 1 tends to be occupied by some of the elite private hospitals as well as by certain private physicians. In the aerospace sector, Hughes Aircraft had traditionally occupied tier 1 of the marketplace. It specialized in being able to do whatever was required by its "customers," which were subunits of the Department of Defense. Quality, rather than the cost, was the primary consideration. Today most aerospace firms occupy tier 2, because the customer is concerned with the trade-off between price, quality, and service. There are a few aerospace firms that occupy niches in tier 3. In the retailing sector, Saks Fifth Avenue and Neiman-Marcus occupy tier 1. Stores such as Bullock's and Macy's occupy tier 2, while tier 3 is served by Pic 'N Save.

It is typically very difficult for firms to compete in all three segments of the marketplace simultaneously. Only some of the largest firms have traditionally been able to accomplish this feat. For example, General Motors begins with its lower-priced Chevrolets and moves its customers all the way through its product ladder to the tier 1 version of its Cadillac. However, in the lower reaches of tier 3, General Motors does not compete with some of the less expensive foreign imports, and it does not compete in the highest levels of tier 1 with products offered by Mercedes and Rolls Royce.

IBM is essentially a tier 2 organization. IBM does not compete in the low-priced computer market (under $1,000). This market segment tends to be dominated by Atari and Commodore. IBM also has not traditionally competed in the upper reaches of the tier 1 marketplace, which are dominated by Cray Research, the entrepreneurial firm founded by Seymour Cray. Accordingly, one of the first strategic decisions that has to be made by a firm is to choose which segment or segments of the marketplace it will wish to compete in.

Market Segment Versus Niche. Determining a firm's strategic position is also important if the firm is to be able to build a market niche. The concept of a market niche must be distinguished from that of a market segment. Although many people use the terms *niche* and *segment* interchangeably, in our opinion they are not equivalent. A market segment is any subdivision of the marketplace. For example, we can define several different segments of the marketplace for computers, including mainframes, minicomputers, and microcomputers. Historically, IBM has dominated the mainframe market, while DEC has dominated the minicomputer market. With the emergence of the Apple Computer in the early 1980s in the so-called PC market, it began to have a dominant position, but it did not truly establish a sustainable niche. In 1981, when IBM introduced its PC computer, it captured between 30 and 35 percent of the PC market. This showed that Apple had not truly established a sustainable niche position, as we have defined it.

Sustainable Competitive Advantage. In this context, a market segment is any subdivision of the marketplace, while a niche is a relatively protected place in a market segment where an organization has a sustainable competitive advantage. Operationally, a competitive advantage is sustainable if it will last for at least two years. Accordingly, just by being the first company into a market does not mean the firm will establish a "sustainable competitive advantage."

The concept of a market niche, and in turn the notion of a sustainable competitive advantage, is important for two reasons. From an offensive standpoint, the primary advantage of a niche in a marketplace is typically that the price (and, in turn, the gross margin) of products is superior to that of competitors. This results in greater profitability and in the opportunity to reinvest those profits in a variety of ways. From a defensive standpoint, during periods of economic decline, holders of a market niche tend to suffer less than their competitors. Their products tend to sell to a greater extent than those of more generic or less established products and services.

A niche is also important defensively if a competitor wishes to "invade" the firm's market segment. For example, when IBM chose to invade the PC marketplace, Apple was unable to defend the entire market. However, Apple had established a niche in a smaller segment of the PC marketplace. Specifically, Apple had established a niche in the educational segment of the PC marketplace. By providing its computers at a lower cost to educational institutions and to teachers, Apple had familiarized instructors and students with their products and services. Accordingly, Apple had established a sustainable competitive advantage in that segment of the marketplace. This, in part, helped the company when IBM entered the PC market. In contrast to Apple's strategy, IBM's strategy was to establish a niche in the office computer segment of the PC market.

A niche can be established based on virtually anything, tangible or intangible. Since a niche is defined as a relatively nonperishable place in a market where an organization has a sustainable competitive advantage, the niche can be derived from having the largest possible sales force, control of a channel of distribution, superiority in product research and development, a proprietary product, or almost anything else that is nonperishable. IBM's niche in the PC market, for example, was based on its name and reputation for service. Ultimately, almost everything is a perishable competitive advantage. However, for relatively short periods or sometimes even longer, certain advantages may be able to sustain an organization.

The Strategic Planning Process

Even though all firms need to address certain key issues, there is no such thing as the ideal strategic planning process for any organization. The nature of the strategic planning process required for a company will differ depending on its stage of growth. There are, however, five phases that must be included in any strategic planning process. As shown in Figure 7.1, these five key phases are (1) the environmental scan, (2) the organizational assessment (or audit), (3) the business plan, (4) the budget, and (5) the management review. Let us now discuss each of these phases in more detail.

Phase I: The Environmental Scan

As seen in Figure 7.1, the first three steps constitute an "environmental scan." This is an attempt to assess the future external business environment in which the organization (business or not-for-profit) expects to operate. The environmental scan must include three things: (1) a market analysis, (2) a competition analysis, and (3) a trend analysis. Let us now discuss each of these steps in more detail.

Market Analysis. The first step in the environmental scan is to assess the organization's future opportunities. This, in turn,

Figure 7.1. Flow Diagram of the Five Key Phases in
the Strategic Planning Process.

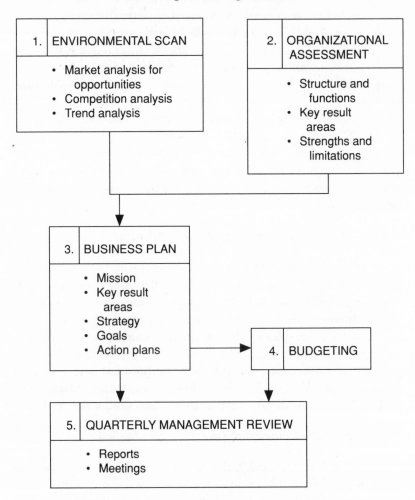

involves analyzing and defining the nature of the firm's business.
Management must answer the question: What business are we in?
Some organizations fail or at least do not prosper because they do
not really understand the nature of their business. For example,
during the nineteenth century and the early part of the present
century, the railroads were successful and powerful. However, they

viewed the answer to the question "What business are we in?" as obvious: "We are in the railroad business." Unfortunately for them, the "obvious answer" was not correct. They ought to have viewed themselves as being in the *transportation* business—the business of transporting people and goods. By defining their business as being railroads, they completely missed the significance of the development of air transportation, which ultimately eroded their strength.

Similarly, the Curtis Publishing Company was a great success during the early part of this century. Cyrus Curtis, a great entrepreneur, built a publishing empire with major properties such as the *Saturday Evening Post* and the *Ladies Home Journal*. Unfortunately, the company eventually failed because it had defined its business as the "publishing business." It failed to realize that in consumer media, advertising follows consumers, and one of its principal revenue streams was from advertisers. The managers of Curtis did not appreciate the implications of the new medium, television, and its impact on advertising revenues. Thus they chose to purchase a printing plant to vertically integrate the firm's operations, turning down opportunities to acquire NBC and CBS—a disastrous decision.

A more recent example of the strategic importance of business definition is Federal Express, which has attempted to define its business more broadly, only to pull back after suffering major losses. Federal Express is known for its role in the small-package delivery business. Its founder originally opened this market by attempting to sell his service to the Federal Reserve as a means of cutting down on the float period for checks. A more comprehensive business definition, however, and one that fits the original conception of the company as well, is that of being in the business of "moving information."

This conceptualization of the business coupled with the trend toward electronic transmission of information was the basis of Federal Express's two-year ZapMail venture. Heavy losses resulted in its abandonment, however, and the company has turned instead to warehousing and inventory management.[27] These new services point to a very different definition of Federal Express's business—away from that of information movement. As with the railroads and Curtis Publishing Company, time will prove whether or not Federal Express chose wisely.

Humana is another example of a company whose early days marked changes in its business definition, changes that proved successful. Initially founded as a chain of nursing homes, Humana briefly entered the mobile home market before finally defining itself as a hospital management company. To support this definition of its business, Humana embarked on a strategy of vertical integration. The primary goal was to increase its bed occupancy rates. The action plans Humana developed to achieve this goal included moving into health insurance and ambulatory care services. Despite some early problems in implementation, this strategy worked well for Humana.

An organization that is trying to decide what business it is in needs to understand what its markets are and what the customers in those markets need. It must answer the major questions: (1) Who are our customers? (2) What are their needs? (3) How do they acquire our products or services? and (4) What do they consider to be of value in a product or service? By focusing on these questions, the organization can define its business purpose in the marketplace. For example, a magazine publishing company such as Curtis must recognize that it serves two related but distinct groups of customers: subscribers, who read its publications, and advertisers, who wish to reach particular groups of people in order to market their own products or services. An organization must understand the needs of all its different segments of customers, especially when those needs differ significantly.

A good example of a concise business definition statement is that of Devon Industries, a rapidly growing health care products manufacturer: "Devon is in the business of solving nurses' problems." To implement this concept, Devon stays in close contact with nurses to learn about their problems and develop products that are actually "solutions" to these problems. For example, Devon developed the "light glove" to solve the problem of handling hot light bulbs in the operating room.

After analyzing the markets in which it desires to do business, the firm must define the products and services it will provide to satisfy the market's needs. We examined this process in Chapter Four.

Competition Analysis. The next step in an environmental scan is to assess the competition. What is the strength of our company relative to that of our competition? Does our company have a present or potential market niche? What distinguishes us from our competition? A well-thought-out and objective assessment of an organization's capabilities and those of its competition is an essential prerequisite to competitive success.

This is an essential step even for successful firms, because in order to continue its success an organization must understand what caused it. Xerox, for example, inappropriately believed its success was because "we are good managers," rather than the real reason: Ownership of the proprietary process that was the basis for photocopying (the "Haloid Process"). In contrast, a $75 million industrial products company was unafraid of Japanese competition because it understood that "customer service" was the competitive key to its market. Similarly, Devon Industries is able to compete among giants in its field because of its ability to create new products for well-defined market segments. The company is led by Dan Sandel, an entrepreneur who had a great deal of experience as a professional manager, and who has a genius for identifying new products.

Trend Analysis. The final step in the environmental scan is to survey the larger economic, social, political, legal, and cultural environment for emerging trends that may affect the firm in the future. The organization needs to try to answer such questions as: What will our industry be like in five years? What emerging trends in demographics, workforce values, the economic and political environment, technology, and so on might affect our organization? What potential opportunities and threats are implicit in those trends? What actions can or must we take to deal with them? The trend away from word processors and minicomputers toward personal computers and workstations brought about by the declining cost of microprocessors caught many office automation firms off guard. Failing to recognize this trend and take action on it led to declining profits at Wang, DEC, and Data General.

Phase II: The Organizational Assessment

The second phase of the strategic planning process is to conduct an organizational assessment that focuses on each of the six key organizational development areas in the pyramid of organizational development, described in Chapter One: markets, products and services, resources, operational systems, management systems, and corporate culture.

The organizational assessment may be done in several ways. It may involve a self-assessment of limitations in each area. It may also involve the use of questionnaires to be completed by a sample of people in the organization or by all of its personnel. Some firms use independent consultants to perform an organizational assessment; the consultants interview personnel and analyze operational data. This process, also called an *organizational audit*, is described further in Chapter Fourteen.

Phase III: The Business Plan

The third phase of the strategic planning process involves preparing a business plan. A business plan (also known as a *strategic plan* or *strategic development plan*) is a written statement of the future direction of an enterprise based on the environmental scan and the organizational assessment.

A business plan consists of five basic components: (1) the mission of the organization, (2) key result areas for planning, (3) objectives in each result area, (4) goals for each objective, and (5) action plans to attain them. Thus a strategic development plan is simply a written document that specifies a business's mission, key result areas, objectives and goals, and action plans. It focuses simultaneously on the firm's competitive strategy as well as the organizational capabilities required to implement its strategy and achieve its mission, objectives, and goals.

These five components of the business plan are shown schematically in Table 7.1, and each component is described below.

Mission.   A mission statement is a broad statement of what an organization or subunit wants to achieve during a planning period. It provides an overall sense of direction for decisions and actions. For example, a mission statement for Industrial Abrasives, Inc.—an industrial abrasives distributor—for a five-year planning period might be:

To develop into the leading full-service distributor of industrial abrasives in the western United States by 1996.

A mission statement for a medium-sized residential real estate firm might read:

To develop into a full-service residential real estate company, providing services throughout the northern

Table 7.1. Elements of the Business Plan.

	Mission *Key result areas* *Objectives* *Goals* *Action plans*
1. Mission	Broad statement of what the organization wants to achieve during the planning period
2. Key result areas	Performance areas that are critical to achieving the organization's mission
3. Objectives	What the organization wants to achieve in the long run in each key result area
4. Goals	Specific things that the organization seeks to attain by a specified time
5. Action plans	Activities that must be performed to achieve a specific goal

part of the state. In order to achieve this mission, we must add to our present service capabilities in guaranteed sales, condominium conversion, tract sales, investment counseling, and primary mortgages.

In addition to giving a broad description of what the firm wants to achieve, this statement specifies the principal service components that the firm must have in order to accomplish its mission.

A more abstract type of mission statement is this one, developed by a large national certified public accounting (CPA) firm:

Our mission is to develop a profitable, professional international accounting firm with a dynamic environment that will retain and motivate outstanding people who will provide high-quality services to business, government, and not-for-profit clients.

Mission statements can be developed not only for an organization as a whole but for specific subunits as well. For example, the mission statement for the personnel department of a bank with assets in excess of $1 billion is as follows:

The mission of the personnel department is to assist management with the attainment of its goals and objectives by:
1. Developing the capability to identify and meet the human resource needs of this bank
2. Developing the capability to help our human resources utilize their skills to the optimum

Mission statements are critical and powerful ingredients in business strategy. They guide the overall development of a company. For example, under Richard Ferris, the mission of UAL Corporation was to make the transition from an airline company to a diversified travel company. To achieve this mission, UAL acquired Hertz (the car rental company), Westin Hotels, and Hilton International. It also had the Mileage Plus organization (now known as MPI) and Apollo Travel. The concept was a brilliant notion of the use of synergy between organizational subunits. It was lost when Ferris was forced out of UAL for political reasons, as is examined in Chapter Eleven.

Key Result Areas. Key result areas are the areas of an organization's operation in which performance has a critical impact on the achievement of the overall mission. Unsatisfactory performance in a key result will inhibit the organization from achieving its mission.

Specific key result areas vary from organization to organization, and each firm must identify the ones that are relevant to its mission. In the industrial abrasives firm cited earlier, for example, the five key result areas were (1) profitability, (2) financial planning, (3) management and organizational development, (4) physical plant and equipment, and (5) marketing. The residential real estate firm defined two broad key result areas, financial and nonfinancial. The financial result area was further broken down into two major dimensions: (1) company profitability and (2) profit contribution by departments of the firm. The nonfinancial result area had five key result dimensions: (1) company integration, (2) services offered, (3) personnel development, (4) administration of the firm, and (5) research.

The key result areas for a particular department, division, or other subunit of a firm may differ from those of the overall organization. For example, the key result areas for the personnel department of the bank were the following:

1. Recruitment and selection of staff
2. Compensation and benefits administration
3. Availability of personnel data to meet management information needs
4. Turnover control
5. Advice on personnel matters to management and employees
6. Knowledge of EEO, ERISA, OSHA, and other regulations
7. Comunication
8. Training
9. Personnel research

Objectives and Goals. Objectives are relatively general statements that an organization or subunit wants to achieve in the long run in each key result area. Goals, by contrast, are specific, measurable things that the organization wants to attain by a specified time in order to achieve its objectives.

For example, an objective for a medium-sized manufacturer of electronic components might be "to increase our annual sales volume," while a specific goal might be: "Increase sales volume from current level of $150 million in 19XX to $180 million in 19XX." Similarly, an objective in the area of facilities and equipment might be "to increase our capability for inventory storage," while a specific goal might be "to relocate our Midwest branch by 19XX to a new site capable of handling 150 percent more inventory than existing facilities." In the area of profit, an objective might be "to earn a satisfactory return on investment." A specific goal might be "to earn a minimum of 18 percent ROI before taxes in each operating division."

Both objectives and goals are necessary. Objectives should not change very frequently during a planning period, while goals are subject to frequent change. For example, the objective of a marketing department for a large, Fortune 500 manufacturer of electronic equipment is to develop marketing programs for new products. A goal for 19XX is "to plan a campaign to introduce electronic toys into the market for the winter season."

Action Plans. Action plans specify the particular activities or steps that must be performed to achieve a goal. Although action plans are not necessary for all goals, they are useful for achieving relatively complex projects or tasks.

Phase IV: Budgeting

Once the overall strategy of a business has been developed, the next step is budgeting. Budgeting involves translating an overall business plan into financial terms. The budget then constitutes a performance standard against which actual performance can be assessed.

Phase V: Management Review

The final, but very important, phase of the strategic planning process is management review, the process by which management evaluates organizational performance. This phase is also part of the control process discussed in Chapter Ten.

I recommend quarterly management review meetings to focus on the strategic planning process. At these meetings, managers should present their results. Where actual results differ from plans, managers should explain the reasons for the differences. The use of quarterly meetings helps to reinforce the idea that strategic planning is a way of life in a company.

The specific steps in developing a plan are summarized in Figure 7.2, which shows that the development of a formal plan is a seven-step process, beginning with the analysis and definition of a firm's business. For example, the first two steps shown in Figure 7.2 are part of the environment scan phase, while step 4.0 is part of the organizational assessment phase as well as part of the development of a business plan as such (phase III). Thus the framework is presented as a conceptual overview of a very complex, iterative process.

Metro Realty: Development of a Strategic Plan

To illustrate the process and output of a strategic development plan, let us examine the planning process at Metro Realty, the medium-sized residential real estate company described in Chapter Five. The fact that Metro Realty is already familiar to you should make it easier to visualize the role of strategic planning in a firm's transition process. We will show how Metro followed the seven steps shown in Figure 7.2, which are the key steps in implementing a strategic planning process.

Analyze and Define Nature of Firm's Business

At the time the strategic plan was written, Metro Realty was in the process of evolving into a full-service residential real estate business. In the long run, the company was examining the option

Figure 7.2. Flow Diagram of Steps in the Planning Process.

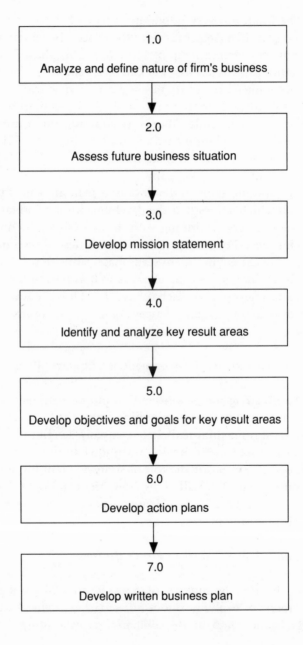

of becoming a full-service firm in the commercial as well as the residential market.

Assess Future Business Situation

As part of its annual planning process, Metro Realty identified alternative concepts of its business to guide its operations, provide direction for corporate efforts, and identify or help create a market niche or competitive difference for the company. Metro Realty's alternative concepts of its business are shown in Figure 7.3 and described below.

Specialist in Residential Real Estate Brokerage. This concept of its business (part A in Figure 7.3) sees Metro Realty as specializing in residential real estate brokerage with minimal support from other areas, which operate independently. This was, at the time, the firm's existing strategy. Following this concept, the company would add more brokerage offices and maintain other functional areas at their present levels.

Full-Service Residential Real Estate Firm. This concept (B) would mean becoming capable of serving *all* of a client's residential real estate needs. It would involve identifying the full set of services required in residential real estate and building the capability of supplying those services.

Concept B, in contrast to concept A, views loans, mortgages, relocation, leasing, and other areas as integral parts of Metro Realty, not merely as adjuncts. Under this concept the development of capabilities in these areas would be an important part of Metro's objectives. An analysis of Metro Realty's major competitors indicated that all but two were moving toward becoming full-service residential real estate firms.

Full-Service Real Estate Firm. This concept (C) would extend Metro Realty's service to commercial as well as residential real estate. At the time the plan was written, two of Metro's major competitors had developed in this direction. Although Metro's management felt that in the long run the company should consider devel-

Figure 7.3. Metro Realty: Alternative Concepts of Business.

A. Specialist in residential real estate brokerage
1. More offices
2. Mortgages
3. Leasing/property management
4. Special projects

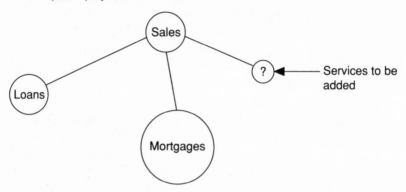

B. Full-service residential real estate firm

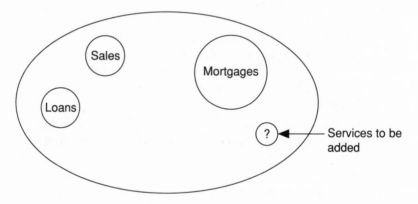

C. Full-service real estate firm

oping toward this type of business, revenues at the time were not sufficient to allow adoption of this concept.

In order to choose among these concepts, Metro's annual review and planning meeting analyzed the answers to a number of questions such as those shown in Table 7.2. On the basis of this

Table 7.2. Planning Steps and Related Questions.

Step No.	Planning Steps	Related Questions

1.	Analyze and define nature of firm's business	1.1 What is the nature of our business?
		  1.1.1 Services
		  1.1.2 Markets and customers
		  1.1.3 Competition
		1.2 What is the firm's market niche and competitive advantage?
		  1.2.1 Do we have a special niche in the market?
		  1.2.2 What distinguishes us from our competition?

2.	Assess future business situation	2.1 What will our industry be like in five years?
		  2.1.1 Trends
		  2.1.2 Opportunities
		  2.1.3 Threats

3.	Develop mission statement	3.1 What do we want to be like or to become in five years?
4.	Identify and analyze key result areas	4.1 What must the firm do during the next five years to achieve its mission? 4.2 What are the key result areas of the business? 4.3 What are our current strengths and limitations in each key result area?
5.	Develop objectives, goals, and targets for key result areas	5.1 What are our objectives in each key result area? 5.2 What are our goals and targets in each key result area?
6.	Develop action plans for implementing objectives, goals, and targets	6.1 What are our priorities for developing programs in various key result areas? 6.2 Who is responsible for developing programs in each key result area? 6.3 What steps must be taken to achieve objectives, goals, and targets in each key result area?
7.	Develop written business plan	

analysis, management decided that for the next five years Metro Realty should develop toward becoming a full-service residential real estate firm.

Develop Mission Statement

The planning meeting decided that the mission of Metro Realty was to develop into a full-service residential real estate company, providing services throughout the northern part of the state. A further aspect of Metro Realty's mission was to become the leading residential real estate firm in its geographical area.

Identify and Analyze Key Result Areas

In order to become a full-service residential real estate company, Metro Realty needed to add to its services capability in the following areas: marketing, guaranteed sales, condominium conversion, tract sales, investment counseling and sales, and primary mortgages. Other key result areas identified by Metro Realty were profit, profit contribution, corporate integration, personnel development, and administration. As we can see, the firm identified six key result areas. These include nonfinancial as well as financial aspects of the firm's performance.

Develop Objectives and Goals for Key Result Areas

In order to work toward the corporate mission of becoming the leading full-service residential real estate firm in the area, Metro Realty defined both financial and nonfinancial objectives and goals for the period 1981–1985, as follows:

Objectives.

Financial Objectives

• *Profit*—To develop profitability to a satisfactory level by 1983, through revenue increases and cost control.
• *Profit Contribution*—To develop the company so that there is a balanced profit contribution from each department.

Nonfinancial Objectives

- *Corporate Integration*—To achieve the integration of all parts of Metro Realty so that it functions as a single system rather than as a set of separate entities.
- *Services*—To review new and existing services in order to evaluate each and recommend addition, deletion, or expansion.
- *Personnel Development*—To provide education and training programs for management, sales associates, and salaried administrative personnel.
- *Administration*—To increase administrative efficiency by improving the management reporting system, adopting a planning system, and developing a control system, which includes incentive compensation and performance appraisal.
- *Research*—To develop the capability to do research on important aspects of the business.

Goals.

Financial Goals

- *Profit*—To reach profit in 1983-1985 of 10 percent (minimum), 15 percent (most likely), or 20 percent (ideal) of gross revenue, after all costs have been considered.
- *Revenue*—To base revenue on 8 percent inflation plus 1-2 percent "real" growth.
- *Costs*—To establish a standard figure for costs per employee, both direct and indirect, with the minimum figure being $750, the most likely being $850, and the maximum being $1,000.
- *Profit Contribution*—To spread the contribution of each department. Within the sales department, to redistribute the percentages of revenue contributed by different regions.

Nonfinancial Goals

- *Company Integration*—To expand and develop the relocation department in order to increase the number of referrals and integrate the department with the rest of the company.
- *Services*—To evaluate the possibility of new services in the areas

of guaranteed sales, condominium conversion, tract and subdivision sales, primary mortgages, and investment and counseling.

- *Personnel Development*—To develop the following programs:
  1. A management development and training program for present members of management and management candidates that will improve the quality of management as well as providing a necessary pool of future managers
  2. An indoctrination program of six full days for all new sales associates (presently provided by the realty class)
  3. On-the-job training for the salaried administrative group to instruct them in their duties and roles in the organization
- *Administration*—To increase efficiency by the following means:
  1. Development of the capability to provide accurate and timely accounting reports; analysis of all current reporting systems to decide whether they should be continued, discontinued, or expanded
  2. Completion of the implementation of the annual planning cycle, including development of a written annual corporate planning guide
  3. Development and implementation of a revised incentive compensation system for all managers
  4. Development and implementation of a performance appraisal and counseling system for all managers
- *Research*—To initiate research projects on the following topics:
  1. Competitive niche
  2. Growth
  3. Franchises
  4. Need for a marketing department or position

Develop Action Plans

The next step in the planning process is to develop action plans. It is not necessary to develop action plans for all goals. Only those goals that are sufficiently complex require these plans. For example, at Metro Realty an action plan would be required for a management development and training program. Exhibit 7.1 presents an action plan for Metro Realty's 1985 management develop-

Exhibit 7.1. Action Plan for Metro Realty's Management Development Program.

Action Plan No. 1

Key Result Area Personnel Development

Specific Objective To provide continuing training for branch managers

Specific Goal To increase branch managers' skill in time management, delegation; leadership

Date Program Development Begins March 1991   Estimated Completion Date June 1991

Program Coordination Responsibility K. Morgan   Plan Prepared by K. Morgan, Training Mgr.

Plan Reviewed by W. Rossin, Sales Mgr.   Authorized by T. Davis, President

Tasks	Responsibility	Hours		Date Start		Date Completed	
		Plan	Actual	Plan	Actual	Plan	Actual
1. Prepare program budget	W. Rossin	3		3/1		3/1	
2. Search for program design Consultant	K. Morgan	8		3/5		3/5	
3. Review consultant proposal	Rossin & Morgan	4		3/20		3/30	
4. Authorize contract	Morgan consultant	40		4/1			
5. Develop program materials	Morgan consultant	24		4/1		4/30	
6. Plan logistics	K. Morgan	2		6/10		4/15	
7. Distribute materials	K. Morgan	16		6/12		5/10	
8. Conduct program	Consultant					6/13	
9.							
10.							

ment program. It shows what tasks must be accomplished, who is responsible, and when these tasks are to be started and completed.

Develop a Written Business Plan

The next step is to prepare a written strategic development plan. A written business plan, such as the one illustrated for Metro Realty, also facilitates the control process, as discussed in Chapter Ten.

It ought to be noted that the strategic planning process is a dynamic, ongoing process. A strategic plan is simply a snapshot of the firm's future direction at a single point in time. The plan ought to be updated annually, and strategic planning ought to become a way of life rather than a one-time exercise. This is an issue for corporate culture management, as discussed in Chapter Twelve.

Ongoing Functions of Strategic Planning

Planning is a key component of a firm's management control system. It specifies what the organization seeks to accomplish. Stating the organization's mission or general direction provides a focus for its efforts. This in itself is a form of organizational control. The more specific statement of key result areas, objectives, and goals increases the degree and effectiveness of the control. A written plan, such as the one illustrated for Metro Realty, facilitates the planning aspect of the control process by providing criteria against which performance can be measured and evaluated.

Strategic Planning at Different Stages of Organizational Growth

Previous sections of this chapter have presented the basic concepts and methods of strategic planning for entrepreneurial organizations. They have also illustrated the strategic planning process in the context of an example company. This section discusses how strategic planning should differ at each of the first four stages of organizational growth.

Stage I. During stage I, strategic planning will probably be a very informal, even intuitive process done mostly or entirely by the entrepreneur. Our research has suggested that very few entrepreneurs do formal strategic planning in the sense described in this chapter.

As we saw in Chapter Four, new entrepreneurial ventures arise mostly from personal—sometimes almost accidental—insights. For example, the idea for Domino's Pizza grew out of a university student's personal need for income. Hot Rock, Inc., was born during an informal discussion at Logan Airport about business opportunities that might be developed to meet the requirements of a course in entrepreneurship.

Many times the entrepreneur is consciously or unconsciously following an informal strategic planning process at this stage. The entrepreneur often knows a particular business or industry, such as advertising, printing, publishing, ship repair, garment manufacturing, electronics, landscaping, insurance, or financial planning. Steeped in this knowledge, he or she perceives some market opportunity that is either not currently being served or not being served very well. For example, Thomas S. Monaghan, who founded Domino's Pizza, perceived that there might be a market for high-quality delivered pizza. Similarly, another entrepreneur, Fritzi Benesch—cofounder of Fritzi of California—perceived that there was a market for budget-priced blouses among teenagers and as a result created a business with more than $80 million in annual revenues. Her concept was that the blouse ought to be priced at what a teenager could earn during one evening of baby-sitting. Another entrepreneur who became interested in computers as a hobby found that there was a market for assistance to new buyers of personal computers who were not adept at setting up the machines and making them function. The large vendors, such as IBM and Apple, simply did not bother with this service. Still another entrepreneur, a university professor of accounting who had been successful with his own real estate investments, perceived the market for a financial planning and counseling firm aimed at relatively affluent investors.

Stage II. During stage II, the informal strategic planning process of an entrepreneurial company may begin to change in certain ways. The rapid growth of the organization places considerable demands on the entrepreneur's time and energy, and his or her focus is increasingly on day-to-day operations. This leaves less time and, most important, less emotional energy to do the strategic planning required for the future development of the company. Entrepreneurs in charge of stage II companies often work sixteen hours or more per day simply handling short-term problems and trying to keep up with the momentum of business. The entrepreneur may thus become a "one-minute decision maker," not by choice but by necessity. Unfortunately, the failure to do strategic planning is itself a kind of strategic plan, for the company that does not plan its future has implicitly chosen to allow the future to happen to the organization. As the great coach of UCLA's national champion basketball teams, John Wooden, used to say: "The failure to prepare is to prepare for failure." Similarly, to paraphrase Wooden, I believe that the failure to plan is to plan for failure.

At stage II a company does not need a very formal planning system, but it does need some strategic planning. Since the entrepreneur is likely to be more absorbed in other activities than was the case at stage I, it becomes necessary to substitute a system for what was initially a personal activity.

In essence, a formal strategic planning process is analogous to a "zone defense" in sports. If, for example, a college basketball team has a seven-foot center, the team is likely to have a comparative advantage in rebounding. If the team's center is only six feet six, the team is likely to be at a disadvantage in rebounding, but it may be able to compensate for this by using a zone defense. The zone defense is essentially a system in which people are positioned to perform certain tasks; in this example, they will be placed where they are most likely to give the defensive team a comparative advantage at rebounding. In effect, a seven-foot center is a one-person zone defense.

Similarly, if an organization has an entrepreneur who is brilliant at explicit or intuitive strategic planning, it may not need a formal strategic planning process. However, this presumes that the entrepreneur has the time and energy to perform strategic planning. When this ceases to be the case, the company must use a formal strategic planning process as a kind of zone defense to ensure that some strategic planning is accomplished.

During stage II, a company's strategic planning process can be reasonably simple. In a company with between $1 and $10 million in annual revenues, the process may consist merely of a one- or two-day meeting devoted to developing the corporate strategic plan, followed by departmental meetings to develop plans for each functional area in support of the overall corporate plan. Every company, even a relatively small one, ought to be able to devote one week a year to strategic planning at stage II. If this modest amount of time and effort is not spent, there is an increasing chance that external events that may profoundly affect the company will go either unnoticed or without response.

Stage III. By the time an organization reaches stage III, it needs to establish a formal process of strategic planning. This is the professionalizing stage of organizational development, and strategic planning is one of the key management systems of a professional firm.

From approximately $10 million to $25 million in annual revenues, the major focus can be on the overall corporate strategic planning process, with departmental or functional plans done more informally. By the time an organization has reached $25 million in annual revenues, however, it needs a more extensive strategic planning process. The corporate plan should be accompanied by formal departmental plans, and the overall amount of planning time and effort should increase.

By the time a company reaches the size of $50 to $100 million in annual revenues, the strategic planning process ought to be well in place. It should be beginning to be a "way of life" in the company. Generally speaking, a minimum of two to three years will be needed to institutionalize a strategic planning process in firms of this size. The first year will simply involve the process of learning the planning system's mechanics. During the second and third years, people should increase their planning skills.

How much time should management invest in strategic planning? A reasonable guideline is that management should invest the equivalent of at least one week per year on planning and perhaps up to 10 percent of its time. If less than one week per year is devoted to planning, management is planning to fail.

Stage IV. By the time a company has reached stage IV, the planning process ought to be well institutionalized. Strategic planning ought to be a topic in the company's management development programs.

During stage IV there can be a wide variety of refinements to the strategic planning process. At this point, for example, the company will have the resources to do more extensive market research analysis and environmental scanning studies.

A Final Note: Consultants and Strategic Planning Departments

A final issue involved in strategic planning concerns the role of external consultants and internal corporate planning departments in the planning process. The strategic plan ought to be based on line management's decisions rather than those of consultants or a planning department. Unless the plan is "owned" by line managers, it will tend to get ignored. Consultants or planning departments can, however, play a significant role as facilitators of the planning process. They can help to plan the overall process and serve as catalysts to its completion.

An internal planning department can serve as the source of market research and other competitive information. It can also aid in the logistical aspects of the planning process. External consultants can perform these facilitative roles, too. Moreover, because of their experience with other organizations, they can provide an independent, relatively objective perspective and raise questions that can be very useful for a company. For example, this simple inquiry can be a catalyst for a fresh look at some practice: "Other companies seem to be doing it this way. What is the rationale for your company doing it that way?"

Summary

This chapter has examined the nature of strategic planning for entrepreneurial organizations. It has presented a framework of the strategic planning process, described the components of a business plan, and presented a step-by-step approach for developing a written business plan. The chapter has also illustrated the steps in developing a strategic business plan, using an example of a company. Finally, the chapter has discussed how strategic planning should differ at each of the first four stages of organizational growth. This framework ought to be useful to entrepreneurial companies in designing or revising their own strategic planning process.

8   Organizational Structure

This chapter deals with one of the critical management systems of a firm: its organizational structure. An enterprise's "organizational structure" relates to the way people are organized to perform productive work and help achieve the firm's strategic business plan. The way people are organized, then, can have a critical impact on the overall success or failure of the firm. This suggests that organizational structure ought to be designed in such a way as to facilitate its business operations. However, in many firms the way people are actually organized comes not as a result of planning, but as the cumulative result of a series of ad hoc decisions. In addition, based on our research and consulting experience with many organizations, we have found that organizations require different structures to be effective at different stages of growth. Although a firm may have been adequately organized at a former stage of development, the company's success will facilitate its growth, which, in turn, will make it likely that a new structure will be required.

This chapter provides a framework to help managers understand how to design and use organizational structure as a managerial tool. It is also intended to assist managers in understanding what must be done to change an enterprise's structure as it grows and is faced with the need to make a transition from one stage of development to the next. First, we will define the nature and purpose of organizational structure. Second, we will examine the different types of organizational structures that exist in companies. Third, we will present some guidelines for the design and evaluation of organizational structure. Next we will examine a few case studies of structural problems faced by companies at different stages of growth. Finally, we will examine the nature of organizational structure changes required at different stages of growth.

Nature of Organizational Structure

An organization does not merely consist of people; it consists of the set of jobs or roles that have been patterned into certain specified relationships to achieve a purpose. An organization, then, can be viewed as a patterned arrangement of specified roles to be performed by people. It is something that management designs to help the organization achieve its mission, objectives, and goals.

A *role* is a set of expectations about how an individual will behave in a given job. The role consists of a group of *responsibilities* that an individual is expected to perform when he or she occupies the given role. These responsibilities, if the role definition is appropriate, should relate to the organization's key result areas. Stated differently, the overall organizational goals should be supported by a given department's key result areas, which, in turn, should be supported by the key results that are expected of an individual performing a specified role. For example, if one of the firm's goals is to increase revenue, a sales department key result area that supports this might be "Sales Revenue" and some of the key results for a salesperson that support the departmental key result area may include (1) sales revenue, (2) obtaining critical information from customers about their reactions to a product or service, and (3) other competitive information that is necessary to position the product in the marketplace. In brief, the set of organizational roles that make up the totality of the organization are "organized" into a structure that is designed to enable the organization to perform its tasks, achieve its mission, and achieve its goals.

The guiding principle underlying the organization of all the various roles that constitute an organization is that "form should follow function." This means that the form of the structure of the organization should be designed in such a way as to maximize the likelihood of achieving the overall "functions" that that structure is intended to perform. For example, if the function of an organization is to develop new products and services, then the structure (or "form") of the set of roles that comprise the organization should be organized in such a way as to maximize the likelihood that this function will be attained. Similarly, if the function of an organization is to produce a predesigned product and manufacture it as efficiently as possible, then the organization should be designed in such a way as to maximize the likelihood of that happening.

Alternative Forms of Organizational Structure

Given the strategic principle in designing organizations that "form should follow function," there are basically three pure "forms" that are available to management when designing an organizational structure. In addition to these three pure forms, there are an almost infinite number of hybrid forms or variations that are also available.

The three basic forms of organization structure may be described as follows: (1) the functional structure, (2) the divisional structure, and (3) the matrix structure. Each of these is described below. In addition, we will examine the strengths and limitations of each type and the situations in which they are most commonly used.

Functional Organizational Structure. As implied by its name, in the functional organizational structure, roles are organized according to the various functions that have to be performed to achieve the entity's overall mission. In a manufacturer, for example, the following functions are typically found: (1) engineering, (2) manufacturing, (3) sales, (4) personnel, (5) finance, and (6) administration. In addition to these basic functions, there may be a variety of other functions found in the structure, depending on the size of the organization. The functional structure is illustrated in Figure 8.1.

As can be seen in Figure 8.1, the functional type of organization is basically a system in which individuals report to a senior executive who is responsible for coordinating the overall operations of the company. Typical functions include sales, engineering, manufacturing, accounting, and administration. The heads of the various functional areas (such as manufacturing or sales) have their own organization, which consists of assistance in areas designed to support that particular functional area.

A variation of the functional structure that is typically found in organizations can be termed a "prefunctional organizational structure." This structure is most prevalent in the earliest entrepreneurial stages of development where there are relatively few people,

Figure 8.1. Functional Organizational Structure.

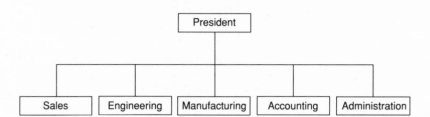

and the firm has not yet differentiated and specialized into various functions; rather, the same individual may perform a number of functions or parts of functions. Accordingly, if we were to try to diagram an entrepreneurial organization at stage I as a functional organization, you might find the same individual occupying several functions in the organization, as illustrated in Figure 8.2. For example, the president, Mark Booth, occupies three positions at Plastic Molding Corporation. He performs both the marketing and R&D functions while simultaneously functioning as president.

The primary strength of a functional structure is that it provides for greater specialization of function, allowing people to develop very specialized skills in each area. It also allows for the recruitment of people with predeveloped specialized skills in given functional areas. Accordingly, rather than having an individual who has only a general familiarity with manufacturing as its head, an organization can recruit an executive who is highly experienced and specialized in that area.

There are many very large organizations that continue to operate under a functional structure. However, as the size of an organization increases, the many advantages of a functional structure tend to be offset by certain critical disadvantages. One of the primary critical disadvantages of a functional structure is that as the operation increases in size and number of products, the focus of its executive is spread so thin that certain products receive considerable attention while others receive significantly less. A related problem is that as the size of the organization increases, the primary concern is with the overall efficiency of each functional area (such as man-

Figure 8.2. Prefunctional Organizational Structure: Plastic Molding Corporation.

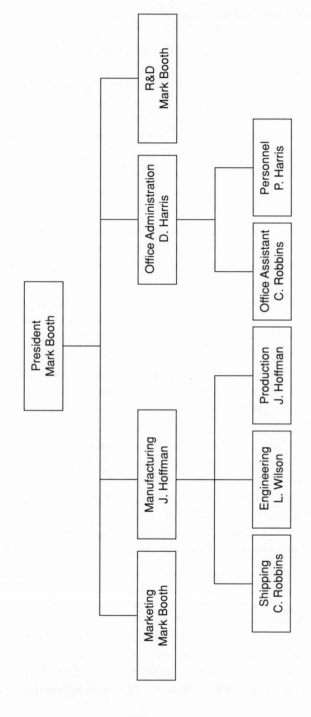

ufacturing or sales), rather than with a particular product's segment and its related customer groups. The functions may be efficiently producing products that are out of touch with the marketplace. Many large companies, such as Kodak and NCR, have experienced these problems to such a degree that they have changed from functional structures to different forms in recent years. Because of the problems, a different type of organizational structure has developed that strives to take advantage of key aspects of the functional system while also dealing with the problems of reduced focus and lack of in-depth concern for a particular product and customer grouping. This is known as the *divisional structure,* and is described in the next section.

Divisional Organizational Structure. As suggested above, the divisional organizational structure tends to group together related clusters of products and customers. A division may be set up to focus on a particular customer segment, and to produce and market products that are designed for that group. Divisions can also be structured around different technologies. A classic example of divisional structure was the one built by General Motors under the leadership of Alfred P. Sloan. Sloan, who was an MIT-trained engineer, guided General Motors to supremacy in the automobile industry, replacing Ford as the number one automobile producer in the mid-twentieth century.[28] The basic structural concept that Sloan used was to organize General Motors into several related divisions—Chevrolet, Pontiac, Oldsmobile, and so on—with each division focusing on a different customer market segment. The idea was to "grow" customers from one General Motors product to the next up to the ultimate, which was produced by the Cadillac division. Each division had some of its own functional aspects, but there were certain overall functions performed for the divisions by the organization as a whole.

As illustrated by this example, the basic concept of the divisionalized structure is to create divisions that focus on particular customer segments, and then to provide a certain "common" set of services to these divisions at the corporate level. Typically, these include capital allocation, finance, legal, and administrative services, among others. An example of a classic divisional structure is presented in Figure 8.3. As seen in Figure 8.3, InfoEnterprises is a producer of electronic instruments and computers with three operating divisions: electronic instruments, micro- and minicomputers, and mainframe computers. Each division is headed by a general manager, and each division uses its own functional structure. The corporate services group also reports to the president.

There is wide variation in the way organizations implement the divisional concept. Some organizations have corporate staffs that are considerably involved in the affairs of the divisions. These organizations tend to have large corporate staffs who play a role in the overall strategic planning process for the division, and may be actively involved in reviewing its operations. This may be termed the "M-type" divisional structure, because of the active management from the corporate staff. This was essentially the model that was used by ITT under Harold Geneen. At the other end of the spectrum, the corporation operates as a holding company, or in a certain sense as a "vertical bank." By this we mean that the corporation is essentially an investor, in that it buys businesses and allows them to operate in a very independent manner. In return, the businesses must meet certain performance standards, such as return on investment or cash generation. Some models of this style are Beatrice Company and Teledyne. Beatrice Company prides itself on having a relatively lean corporate staff.[29] It accomplishes this because Beatrice Company is essentially an "investor-type" corporate structure ("I-type" divisional structure), in which the various divisions are essentially part of a portfolio of investments. The basic concept is that each division must achieve, for example, an 18 percent pretax return on investment. If this does not happen, the division may be spun off. Similarly, Teledyne is an investor in many small entrepreneurially oriented companies, and the basic criterion for their maintenance is the ability to generate cash for the overall holding company.

Either of these divisional structure models (the I-type or the M-type) may be used, and both can be made workable and effective.

The primary strength of the divisional form is that it creates a focus on specific market segments. The primary disadvantage is that it results in duplication of functions in different divisions, and

Figure 8.3. Divisional Organizational Structure: InfoEnterprises.

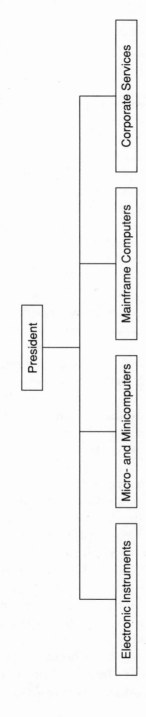

creates the need for coordination among divisions. This is what leads to additional corporate staff.

Matrix Organization Structure. The final "pure" type of organizational structure has been termed the *matrix*. This organizational structure was originally developed in the aerospace industry, although similar forms might have existed elsewhere for quite some time. In concept, the matrix approach is an attempt to achieve the best of both the functional and the divisional structures.

As shown in Figure 8.4, the matrix organization structure lists the various programs, projects, or products in the far left column of the matrix organizational chart. Each of these programs has a program manager. Where the organization is large enough, there is a manager who is responsible for coordinating all of the programs. On the other side of the matrix, over the vertical columns, we have the various functional areas. Each of these functional areas, such as engineering design, manufacturing, and so on, is headed by an executive who is responsible for the functional specialization. The matrix operates by having the program managers "borrow" people from the various functional areas to work on their programs. When the program is finished the people are returned to the functional pool. For example, a large aerospace company that is involved with the design of a new aircraft for the Department of Defense will borrow engineers and assign them to that particular project. When the responsibilities of those given engineers are completed, they will return to the overall engineering pool to be reassigned. In this structure, an engineer might also be simultaneously involved in more than one project.

The basic strength of the matrix structure is that it permits a focus on the customer and the product, and also allows functional specialization. The major disadvantage or limitation of the matrix structure is that it requires a high degree of coordination to be effective. The keys to successfully operating a matrix structure are conducting regularly scheduled meetings to review the status of work and having the ability to deal with the inevitable conflict that arises when employees are responsible to more than one supervisor (a program supervisor and a functional supervisor) and possibly involved in more than one program (where they are now responsible to mul-

Figure 8.4. Matrix Organizational Structure: Ultraspace Corporation.

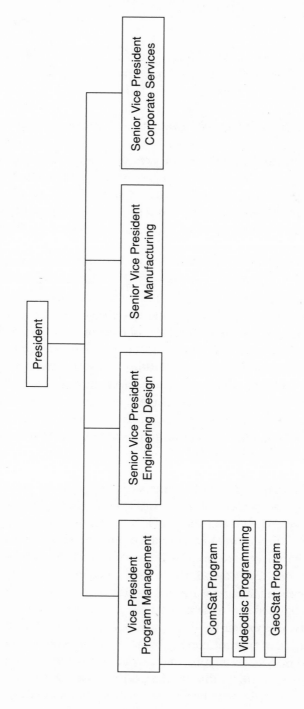

tiple supervisors). Accordingly, the matrix structure requires a considerable amount of training in work-related interpersonal skills to ensure its smooth operation.

Criteria for Design and Evaluation of Organizational Structure

As can be seen from the preceding discussion, organizational structure is a major tool available to management since it is something that management creates or designs. There are a few guiding principles of organizational structure that are relevant to the choice of a particular form of structure, and to the overall design of the structure.

As discussed previously, a basic principle underlying the design of an organization is that: "Organizational form should follow organizational function." There are three other specific criteria that should be used to evaluate the effectiveness and efficiency of an organizational structure (1) span of control, (2) number of levels in the organization, and (3) the extent to which the structure maintains consistency in the interrelationships between individuals' roles and the key result areas necessary to achieve the organization's mission. All of these factors, discussed below, need to be evaluated within the following context: the nature of the business the organization is operating in and the organization's stage of development within the organizational life cycle.

Span of Control. This variable relates to the number of people who occupy roles or positions that report directly to a given manager. The greater the manager's span of control, the lower the cost of supervision of individual employees. The cost of supervision (per employee) decreases as the span of control increases, because supervisory costs are allocated over a greater "base" of employees. However, a manager is limited in the number of employees that can be supervised before he or she begins to do an inefficient job. Conversely, it is expensive to employ more managers than is necessary. An effective span of control balances the decreasing per-employee supervisory costs against the increasing costs of managerial inefficiency. As a rule of thumb, if a position has fewer than three direct reports, it is likely to be unnecessary; if it has more than nine direct reports, effective supervision is not likely to occur unless the manager is very experienced and uses sophisticated leadership methods (see Chapter Eleven).

Layers of the Organization. Any organization structure can also be viewed in terms of the number of levels of roles that have been aggregated to make up the structure. A level of a set of roles consists of a group of positions that are comparable in terms of the nature of the work done. There are basically five pure (or distinct) types of levels of work in organizations, shown in Figure 8.5, and these create an organizational hierarchy. Each of these organizational levels is described briefly below.

The first or *entry level* in the organizational hierarchy is the level at which technical or individual contributor work is performed. People who occupy this level of the organizational hierarchy are typically involved in doing a wide variety of "technical" work like computer programming, sales, and all clerical work.

The next level may be termed the *first-line supervisory level.*

Figure 8.5. Organizational Hierarchy.

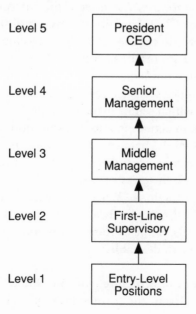

People at this level may still be doing a certain amount of technical work, but are beginning to have more responsibility for the supervision of the technicians or other individual contributors at the organization. Individuals who are first-line supervisors have no other managerial employees reporting to them, but only other technical or individual contributors.

The third level in the organizational hierarchy can be termed the *middle-management level.* The function of middle management is to supervise one or more levels of other managers, which may include first-line supervisors or other middle levels of managers. Organizations can ultimately have a number of middle levels of management. However, regardless of the number, the primary function for the middle managers is a supervisory and coordinating function, and a liaison between first-line supervision and senior management.

The fourth, relatively distinct level of an organizational hierarchy is the *senior-management level.* This level of management is concerned with the overall planning and direction of the enterprise.

The fifth level that can be distinguished is the *chief executive* and/or *chief operating officer level* of the enterprise. The chief executive officer, or CEO, has ultimate responsibility for the overall planning and direction of the enterprise. The chief operating officer, or COO, has primary responsibility for the execution of the overall strategic planning implementation in terms of day-to-day operations. These two positions can be treated as a single "level" of the organization to which senior managers report.

Although in actual practice organizations may have a significant number of levels that deviate from these five relatively "pure" levels, for the purposes of understanding organizational structure it is helpful to think in terms of these five levels as performing relatively distinct functions. When an organization has a greater number of levels, this is merely a variation on the overall theme of the five basic levels. Some of these "variations" may be functional, and others may be undesirable.

Consistency of Structure with Key Result Areas and Corporate Mission. Given the principle that "organizational form should follow organizational function," the basic organizational structure should be designed to facilitate the organization's performance in achieving its overall corporate mission. This may mean that units are designed to address specific key result areas. For example, if one of the key result areas of the organization is new product development, then an organizational unit may well be established for product research and development. Similarly, if another key result area relates to sales, the organization should have a unit that deals with issues involving sales and marketing.

The basic analysis used when evaluating the consistency of organizational structure with corporate key result areas is to determine the extent to which all key result areas are reflected within existing organizational units. For example, one key result area may be customer service. This does not necessarily mean that the organization must have a customer service unit; however, the organization must in some way have an individual or group of people who are directly responsible for the performance of customer service.

Unless key result areas are somehow linked to organizational units, there is a tendency for organizations not to perform responsibilities in these areas. These key result areas tend to be neglected in favor of other tasks that may seem more pressing. Examples of this phenomenon have occurred in the key result area of product development, which has led to the divisionalization of many organizations. For example, Medco Enterprises, a $20 million medical manufacturing firm discussed in Chapter Fourteen, experienced difficulty using the functional form of organizational structure because coordination problems emerged with respect to new product development. Rather than a unit that was focused on a particular market segment, Medco had separate functional units for engineering, sales, and manufacturing, which created a variety of problems with respect to the timeliness and appropriateness of new products. The company ultimately shifted to an organizational structure in which one key organizational unit was responsible for the combined functions of design, manufacturing, and sales. This change shifted the focus of product development and sales to a single organization unit, rather than requiring the coordination of three separate units with differing responsibilities for a much wider range of products.

Organizational Structure Analysis

In many firms where organizational structure has not been well designed, problems arise because of a proliferation in the number of roles that are grouped together, the span of control that managers have, and the number of levels in the organization. As organizations grow, they tend to add jobs and levels in a piecemeal manner to meet current expediencies. If this process continues, the entire organization develops a very ad hoc character. Indeed, the result can be an "organizational Frankenstein." At this point, it is necessary to review the entire organizational structure in light of these overall changes in the level and scope of business activities.

During the past few years, a variety of new approaches have been developed to facilitate such analysis of organization structures. The basic objective of these analyses is to determine whether "value" is being added by particular positions in different levels of management. In general, these approaches can make a useful contribution to organizations at any stage of growth; however, they should not be viewed as precise formulas, and should not be implemented without seasoned judgment. This is typically an area that requires the assistance of independent consultants.

This section briefly describes an approach termed *organizational value analysis,* which has been developed for the purpose of analyzing an organization's structure to determine whether the various positions and levels included in the structure are making an optimal contribution to the overall value of the enterprise.[30]

Organizational value analysis consists of a set of different types of procedures and activities designed to assess the organization's structure in terms of six critical factors or dimensions. Each of these factors can be identified in terms of a basic managerial question that needs to be addressed:

1. Do the current roles within the firm contribute to company objectives? Are there roles that can be eliminated?
2. Are reporting relationships clear and structured in a way that facilitates managers' accountability?
3. What is the appropriate number of subordinates reporting to each manager?

4. To what extent do managers feel that their subordinates have the skills and knowledge needed to be more autonomous?
5. How effectively do interdependent departments coordinate with each other?
6. Are control systems maximizing and monitoring an accountability that reduces the need for direct supervision?

Each of these questions involves a critical factor of organizational structure. For example, the first question deals with whether a position makes a contribution to a company, and the second question relates to the clarity of organizational relationships. To the extent that reporting relationships are clear and structured in a way that facilitates manager accountability, motivation is enhanced and coordination problems are minimized. The third question focuses on the number of subordinates reporting to a manager and relates to the variable called "span of control." As previously noted, the more people a manager can supervise, the fewer managers are required by that organization. Increasing the span of control allows an organization to reduce both the number of managers and the number of management levels. However, the variable of span of control is dependent on the capabilities of managers' subordinates. An organization's requirement for managers decreases to the extent that subordinates acquire the skills and knowledge needed to be more autonomous, which in turn reduces the overall cost to the organization and enhances its competitive position. The effects of the extent to which subordinates are autonomous is addressed in the fourth question. The fifth question relates to the "macro" or broader aspects of organizational structure and the interrelationship among departments, while the sixth relates to the impact of control systems on organizational structure.

Answering these six questions involves performing several related analyses, as part of an organizational structure assessment or audit. One analysis is what may be termed an "organizational role analysis." This involves looking at the specific activities and responsibilities being performed in the organization to determine the most logical grouping of these activities into specific organizational roles. This is addressed to the first two questions cited above, and is described below.

Organizational Role Analysis. At the most fundamental level, organizations need to be concerned with how people spend their time. To the extent possible, organizations want to focus people's efforts on key responsibilities. This means they want people to spend their time on the things that are most important to the organization, which are typically reflected in the key responsibility areas or key result areas defined for each individual.

In this context, one way of looking at the concept of a person's "role" is to think of it as an acronym, as shown here:

R = Responsibilities
O = Objectives
L = Linkages with other roles
E = Evaluation measures

This means that the letter *R* represents a person's responsibilities, the letter *O* relates to a person's objectives, the letter *L* relates to the linkages of a person with other people in the organization, and the letter *E* relates to the measures that will be used to evaluate the person's performance. Stated differently, a person's role prescribes the key responsibilities that that individual is accountable for achieving. These key responsibilities relate to specific organizational objectives that must be achieved. The person's role relates to others' roles in the organization, and these linkages need to be predefined because it is the collective set of these roles that in turn makes up the overall organizational structure. Finally, the person's performance in a role needs to be evaluated, and there is a set of evaluation measures available for assessing this performance. These evaluation measures should be based on the person's performance of his or her key responsibilities. Thus, the term *role* encompasses some very specific dimensions of performance that form the basis of an individual's efforts in an organization. The organization will lose an opportunity to motivate and focus an individual's performance on its goals if the individual does not understand his or her role.

Organizational role analysis looks at the components of an individual's role, both separately and in relation to other roles in the organization. In essence, then, it focuses on the contribution made by individual roles as well as the relationship between these roles. As an organization grows, the roles that people occupy will undoubtedly change. Most of this change occurs in an ad hoc fashion. Accordingly, it is periodically necessary to do a systematic analysis of each role, both individually and in relation to the other roles that make up the organizational structure. When we have conducted such analysis, we have frequently found superfluous positions and levels of an organization, which leads to reduced efficiency and profitability.

Organizational Cost-Effectiveness Analysis. Another perspective for evaluating organizational structure relates to the notion of cost effectiveness. In principle, it may be possible to structure an organization in such a way that no errors occur, product quality is always achieved, and customers are always satisfied, but the costs of operating this organization would be prohibitive. In practice, a variety of trade-offs will have to be made. Different forms of organizational structure require different costs, and each organization needs to find the optimal level and type of structure that balances costs incurred with effectiveness achieved.

Organizational cost-effectiveness analysis can be used to focus on questions 3 through 6, dealing with different aspects of structural analysis. It is especially useful for focusing on the cost consequences of span of control (the third question) and some of its underlying causes (questions 4 and 6).

To assist managers in examining cost-effectiveness issues, it is essential that various components of organizational expenses be analyzed over time to identify any patterns that may exist. This is because specific costs tend to fluctuate in accordance with some measurable activity, such as sales revenue or number of employees, and the organization must track these costs over time. For example, an organization should try to determine the cost of supervision per employee supervised. This is, in essence, an issue that relates to the span of control. If a manager earning $30,000 a year is supervising three people, the cost per employee supervised is $10,000; but if that same manager is supervising ten people, then the per-employee cost of supervision drops to $3,000. While this does not mean that a manager should be supervising an infinitely large number of em-

ployees, there is obviously some reasonable range within which the
cost of supervision per employee should fall, and this range should
be a balance between the costs incurred in supervising employees
and the corresponding benefits gained from this supervision. A
company that has been tracking costs over time can determine
whether unfavorable trends are beginning to emerge. For example,
perhaps the span of control of managers is decreasing to too great
an extent. If management has been tracking the correct costs, they
will detect this trend and can take action to change practices with
respect to the number of people being supervised by each manager.

A Holistic Perspective. As can be seen by the preceding discussion, each of the two facets of analyzing organizational structure
interrelate to some extent. Although we have identified six key dimensions of organizational structure, these are not the only issues
that need to be examined. Management must learn to take a "holistic" look at an organizational structure to determine whether all
the functions that must be performed have been defined, are being
adequately performed, and are being performed in the most cost-
effective manner. Organizational value analysis is an approach that
helps managers accomplish this.

Case Studies of Organizational Structure

The next section of this chapter looks at organizational structure issues from a different perspective. Specifically, we will examine cases of organizational design in order to identify some of the
strengths and limitations affecting organizations at different stages
of growth. We will focus on stage II and stage III companies since
it is at these stages that organizational structure becomes a critical
variable. However, since organizations of all sizes must focus on
designing and managing structure so as to allow the firm to continue growing from one stage to the next, we also provide examples
of larger firms that faced organizational structure issues.

Design Corporation. Figure 8.6 shows the organizational
structure of Design Corporation, a stage II company. This firm
specializes in interior design for industrial and commercial enter-

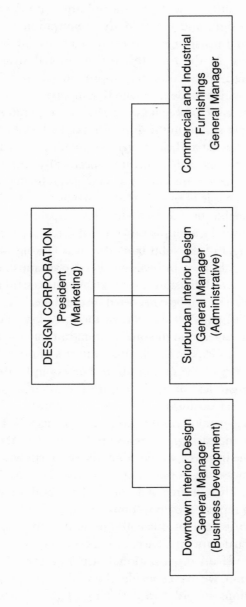

Figure 8.6. Organizational Structure of Design Corporation: (Managerial Strengths in Parentheses).

DESIGN CORPORATION
President
(Marketing)

Downtown Interior Design
General Manager
(Business Development)

Surburban Interior Design
General Manager
(Administrative)

Commercial and Industrial
Furnishings
General Manager

prises. As can be seen in Figure 8.6, the organization has three divisional units: downtown and suburban units that specialize in interior design, and a subsidiary organization that specializes in purchasing furnishings required for commercial and industrial organizations. At the time this organizational structure was being used, Design Corporation had approximately $3 million in annual revenues, which made it a stage II company.

The basic problem facing Design Corporation was not in its structure per se, but in the difficulties caused by the lack of managerial and other capabilities of various people occupying key positions in the organizational structure. Specifically, the basic marketing strength of the organization was in the entrepreneurial founder who occupied the role of president. The manager of the downtown office had reasonable business development capabilities, but was somewhat lacking in administrative capabilities, as was the president. The manager of the suburban office was lacking in business development capabilities, but was an effective administrator. The operation of the third division was reasonably successful as a stand-alone entity, and will not be considered further here. The net result of the various skill gaps on the part of the three key managers (the two general managers and the president) meant that each individual was trying to compensate for the inadequacies of other individuals in a different part of the organization. For example, the president was doing a great deal of marketing for the suburban division because of the lack of business development capability on the part of that division's general manager, while the manager of the suburban division was increasingly responsible for some of the administrative work of the firm as a whole. Since the president was deeply involved in the business development of one of the divisions, he obviously did not have sufficient time to devote to the organizational development needs of a rapidly growing company.

While none of this could be seen from looking at the organization structure on a sheet of paper, when evaluating the appropriateness of an organizational structure for an entrepreneurial organization, we must consider the skills of the players who occupy key positions in order to determine if the structure truly makes sense. In other words, looking at the structure on paper alone would seem to indicate that it made sense, but when we examine the skills of the various managers in the firm, this structure is one that is clearly inappropriate for this organization.

There are structural as well as nonstructural solutions to the problems described in this situation. A structural solution would be to add the role of executive vice president to the firm. The executive vice president would be responsible for the day-to-day administration of the organization, which would free up the president to devote time to long-range planning, organizational development, and business development, as well as to train the general managers to do business development. This solution would obviously add to the cost of operating the organization. Another approach, which might not be politically acceptable to the president, would be to promote a general manager to president, and have the president "withdraw" to a chairman of the board–type advisory position, or retire from the company. For example, this type of solution occurred both at Apple Computer, when John Sculley replaced Steven Jobs, and at Cray Research, when Seymour Cray was replaced by John Rollwaggen.

Sometimes the president of a company does not wish to perform the roles and responsibilities required of a CEO. This is a very typical occurrence in firms that have been founded by an owner-entrepreneur who was particularly interested in either marketing or product development. In such cases, the president should seriously consider the possibility of hiring a professional manager who will be responsible for running the organization on a day-to-day basis. In some cases, it may even be feasible to have the president report to the professional manager who has been brought in to run the organization. For example, the president of a medium-sized firm in a service business brought in a professional manager to run the organization. This individual was given the title of vice president and chief operating officer. After a period of time it became apparent that the president's real interest was in serving as the manager who coordinated all service operations, and not in running the company as a whole. Since the operations managers reported to the COO, the president was actually reporting to the individual he had hired. This solution worked very well in this particular company. Another solution is for the president to bump himself or herself upstairs to the role of chairman of the firm, and to bring in a president who is responsible for running the organization on a day-to-day basis.

Hitek Manufacturing. Hitek Manufacturing Company was a rapidly growing, stage III manufacturer of high-technology products. The firm has recently achieved revenues of approximately $75 million. Up until the time the firm's revenues were approximately $50 million it was organized in a functional fashion. The firm had developed a number of products, but was experiencing certain difficulties in the coordination of new-product development and with the successful introduction of these new products into the marketplace. This was due, in part, to the fact that the existing functional structure emphasized the more successful existing products. The firm realized that it needed to have a steady stream of new products, and that one way to enhance the development of new products was to have them developed in a division that was focused on a particular product market segment. Accordingly, when Hitek reached approximately $50 million in annual revenue, the firm made the decision to take steps to transition itself from a functional structure to a divisionalized structure.

Except for the president of Hitek, all of the senior managers were functional specialists in areas such as sales, marketing, manufacturing, and product development. Hitek realized that to ensure the successful transition to a divisional structure, it had to develop senior managers who were capable of operating as general managers. Accordingly, part of the company's organizational development plan was focused on the development of some of its functional managers as potential general managers. By the time the firm had reached $75 million in revenue, it had two people who were thought to be very likely candidates as general managers, and a third individual who was thought to possess the capabilities of being the general manager of a smaller division. Hitek was able to successfully introduce the divisional management structure.

Digital Equipment Corporation (DEC). In the early 1980s when DEC sales were approximately $4 billion, its organizational structure seemed to be contributing to product development problems, a lack of coordination between different areas within the company, and an inability to effectively meet customer needs. DEC consisted of eighteen separate product divisions that concentrated on specific industries and had responsibility for developing their own strategic plan, while at the same time having to contract with central departments for engineering, manufacturing, and sales.[31] Over time, the divisions began to suffer from what we have called the "separate islands syndrome," with each division focusing on its own needs often to the exclusion of overall company needs. The groups began to fight for control of the centralized functions that contributed to delays in product development. In early 1983, DEC undertook a reorganization intended to overcome these problems and reduce the infighting. DEC's president Kenneth H. Olsen consolidated the twelve U.S. product groups into three regional management centers, each having profit and loss responsibilities as well as their own sales force and administrative staff. The sales force was to focus on accounts rather than markets. Engineering and manufacturing were placed within one area.

Unfortunately, the "organizational structure fix" did not solve, but seemed to increase, DEC's problems for at least a short time. New-product development all but stopped and a number of senior managers left the company. "We spent three years planning the reorganization," sighs Olsen. "It was good planning but not quite good enough."[32] By 1986, however, DEC seemed to have overcome its problems and the structure was functioning effectively. All divisions understood and were working toward the same goals. An effective development process led to a range of new products being released on a timely basis, and the sales force was being professionalized through the hiring of experienced salespeople. (Previously DEC had used entry-level engineers to sell its products.)

Organizational Structure at Different Stages of Growth

This section examines the organizational structure requirements of various kinds of firms at different stages of growth. It is intended to provide some guidelines for the design and selection of organizational structure, rather than offering a precise formula for selecting a particular organizational structure.

Stage I.   A stage I organization usually has what we have termed a "prefunctional organizational structure." This means that the typical organization at stage I has a number of individuals who simultaneously perform a wide variety of responsibilities. The same individual may be performing marketing and administrative tasks because the organization is not yet at the size where it can precisely define its structure in terms of specialized functions.

Although the above situation is probably typical of most stage I organizations, it is possible that a stage I organization has made the transition to a functional structure. this can only be determined on a case-by-case basis, without any precise rules being given.

Stage II.   A stage II organization will typically have annual revenues from $1 million to $10 million if it is a manufacturing company, or from approximately $350,000 to about $3.3 million if it is a service company. Stage II organizations are usually organized according to functional specialties. They will have made the transition from a prefunctional stage but are probably not yet ready for a divisionalized form of structure.

Stage III.   Organizations at stage III, ranging from $10 million to $100 million in annual revenues for manufacturing companies, and one-third of these values for service organizations, can be viewed in terms of three substage groupings: stage III(A) from $10 million to $25 million, III(B) from $25 million to $50 million, and III(C) from $50 million to $100 million.

During stage III(A) the organization typically has a functional organizational structure. As the firm grows in size, there is an increasing need for coordination in the development of new products and services, as well as in their manufacture and distribution. At some point, the firm will begin to neglect some of its products and services. The "more important" products and services receive primary attention, while newer products, or those that are less significant in terms of current sales revenue, will be somewhat neglected. This could become a serious problem, because some of the newer products have not yet achieved significant sales revenue but may be vital to the firm's long-term development. Accordingly, sometime during this period of development the organization may wish to consider moving toward a divisionalized structure. The primary advantage of a divisionalized structure is that it allows a group of people to focus on the development, marketing, and distribution of a common set of products and services.

For many companies, the transition from a functional structure to a divisionalized structure begins to occur during stage III(B). This transition involves the development of managers who will become general managers of the various divisions. Since most managers prior to this time have been technical or functional specialists in an area such as engineering, sales, or production, they now need development that will enable them to coordinate all of the various functional areas. This is a task of management development, which will be examined further in Chapter Nine.

Another organizational problem that increasingly becomes apparent during stage III(B) is the need for greater coordination of overall operations than is probably feasible when a single individual serves as president. Sometime during this period, the president of the organization becomes stretched very thin. This means that the individual is simultaneously involved in so many aspects of both day-to-day and long-term operations that he or she begins to feel increasingly torn apart.

What has happened is that the size of the organization, and the corresponding complexity of its operations, have combined to make it extremely difficult for a single individual to hold everything together. At this point the president of the organization needs to think seriously about bringing in an executive vice president or chief operating officer.

There are two major transitions that need to be made at this time. The first transition requires a role change for the president, who will give up this position to become the chief executive officer. This involves the transition from a role focusing on both the day-to-day operational issues and the long-term development of the organization, to a role in which the CEO is concerned about the organization's long-term development, strategic planning, and organizational development. The introduction of a COO who is now responsible for coordinating the day-to-day operations is the second transition being made by the organization. The changes in the CEO's role will be examined further in Chapter Fourteen.

By the time the organization reaches stage III(C) these two transitions should be completed. This means that a COO will be in place, and that the organization probably will have a number of divisions. It should be noted, however, that there are exceptions to this pattern. Many organizations will reach $100 million without a COO or any divisions. There are examples of billion-dollar organizations that still have a functional organizational structure. This is not to say that these organizations operate without problems; rather, it is merely to say that they have still maintained their functional organizational structure and that some of their operational problems are being caused by this structure.

Stage IV.   By the time a firm reaches stage IV, it has either made the transition to a divisionalized structure or is in the process of doing so. The challenge at stage IV is for a divisionalized organization to consolidate the cultures in the various operating divisions, making them reasonably consistent with the overall corporate culture. These issues will be further discussed in Chapter Twelve, which deals with the management of corporate culture.

Summary

Organizational Structure is the patterned arrangement of specified roles to be performed by people to achieve a purpose. When properly used, it is a tool that helps management increase productivity and makes it more likely that people will perform the tasks required of them to help the organization achieve its mission.

There are three primary forms of organizational structure: functional, divisional, and matrix. Each form has its particular strengths and weaknesses, and the limitations of each can be controlled through the proper attention of management. Each of these forms of structure becomes more appropriate to use as a firm progresses through the organizational life cycle. It is therefore important that management match the organization's stage in its life cycle with the appropriate organizational structure. Three case examples were presented to illustrate this concept.

Several different criteria were presented to assist managers with determining the effectiveness of their structure. For example, one criterion is the need for an effective span of control; another is the importance of linking the organization together at these levels: (1) the organization's mission, (2) the roles of the departments, and (3) the job roles of the individuals within those departments. The criteria presented in this chapter will help managers customize their organization's structure to meet its particular requirements.

9   Management Development

Management development is another major tool available to the senior management of an entrepreneurial organization that is trying to make the transition to a professionally managed company. It can help to meet one of the greatest ongoing needs of rapidly growing entrepreneurships, the need for managerial talent and for the next generation of managers. Many CEOs of such firms are familiar with the cry, "We just don't have enough good managers!"

Management development can provide people with the skills they need to effectively manage a firm. But sophisticated companies such as IBM, Hewlett-Packard, and Motorola recognize that management development is more than a tool for training people in new skills. It is also a tool for educating managers in the company's corporate culture: its values, beliefs, and norms.

This chapter begins by discussing the general role of management development in organizational development and transitions. It then examines this topic further by describing how one company, Knapp Communications Corporation (KCC), used its management development program to assist it in making the transition to a professionally managed organization.

The Nature of Management Development

Management development is the process of building the present and potential performance capabilities of an organization's managers. It can focus on managerial skills, attitudes, and experiences as well as the manager's perception of his or her role.

As has been noted, one of the critical problems in growing entrepreneurial organizations is the lack of sufficient good managers. To repair this lack, a firm can hire experienced managers from outside the organization, develop them from within, or do both. Most successful firms use both external recruitment and internal development.

Management development is just as real an investment as the investment in plant and equipment. It is an investment in the human capital of an organization—the skills, knowledge, and experience of people.[33] It is an investment in the infrastructure of an organization.

Some of the country's most successful and progressive organizations invest heavily in management development. At IBM, for example, management development is a way of life. It is woven into the fabric of the organization.

Within thirty days of being appointed a manager at IBM, an individual must begin a program of basic management training. This program teaches the fundamental skills needed to perform effectively as a first-line supervisor. IBM also requires that each manager have a minimum of forty hours of additional management development training each year. At IBM, management development is viewed as an ongoing process, and the firm has made a significant commitment of resources to it.

Management development is also a key element in the success of Domino's Pizza. At Domino's, management development is a part of a sophisticated training effort that extends throughout the company and includes about 400 company-certified trainers. Further, training and development are integrated throughout the Domino's Pizza organization. According to Jim Corbin, national director of operations, "Everyone within operations is responsible for training. In fact, we say around here that in order to move up in the company, you've got to train your replacement."[34] Well-trained managers are essential to Domino's growth since eligibility for a franchise depends on having successfully managed a store for one year. Domino's manager-in-training (MIT) program consists of six classes taken over six to ten months plus on-the-job training overseen by a supervisor. The program is tied to an overall performance evaluation system. New responsibilities and evaluation criteria are included as the trainee managers progress.

Employee development at Domino's is not limited to the MIT program. Franchisees have a training program that addresses their needs. Courses in contracts, marketing, site selection, and store construction are given. Supervisors, who oversee the operation of six to eight stores, are also included in Domino's efforts to increase the capabilities of their managers.

Many successful smaller entrepreneurial organizations also provide training to ensure adequate managerial talent when needed. Companies in a wide variety of industries and of varying sizes such as Westec Security, Medical Engineering Corporation (Surgitek), Copyspot, Windham Hill Productions, and Twentieth Century Investors have all created management development programs. The entrepreneurs of these organizations recognize that one of the critical factors in their company's ability to continue to grow successfully will be the presence of sufficient managerial talent. As the owner of one firm that had grown in about seven years to more than $100 million in revenues stated: "We have plenty of product and expansion ideas, and I can borrow money for expansion from a bank; but my critical need is for people who will be capable of managing what we plan to become." In response to this kind of need, Melvin Simon & Associates—one of the largest shopping center developers in the United States—established The Simon Institute, an in-house management development program for senior executives designed to provide advanced leadership and organizational development skills.

Although management development can play a positive role in building managers, it is not a panacea. It cannot be expected to turn people into "managerial wonders" overnight. The development of managers takes time. Consequently, it is useful to regard management development as a process of "building managers."

Functions of Management Development

Management development has several functions, all of which are especially relevant in organizations making transitions from one stage of growth to the next. The most obvious is to enhance the skills of the firm's managers. Management development can also be used to (1) help define or redefine the corporate culture, (2) help promote the style of leadership that the organization desires, and (3) serve as a reward to or recognition of good managers. Let us discuss each of these uses further.

Shaping the Corporate Culture. One of the most powerful uses of management development programs is to help articulate and communicate the corporate culture. Programs may communicate culture by various means, such as by using example cases to describe "how we do things here at General Products Corporation" and identifying "heroes" who personify corporate values and serve as models to be emulated.

At Domino's "hustle" is the predominant attitude and its management development programs inspire it. One MIT requirement, skills in pizza making, is one of the most celebrated events in a national competition held annually. This reinforces the training program, which, in turn, instills the Domino style and culture.

Promoting Leadership Style. Another major function of management development is to communicate the leadership style that is acceptable in the organization. Some firms, such as IBM, promote a version of "contingency theory," which postulates that the appropriate style of leadership depends on the nature of the situation. (This approach is described in Chapter Eleven.) Other organizations promote a single style of leadership. For example, Motorola promotes participative leadership.

Rewarding and Recognizing Managers. Some organizations use participation in management development programs as a reward. A reward program may be held at an off-site location, such as a resort, and the entire event will be designed to be a pleasurable experience. Closely related to the reward concept is the use by some organizations of selection for management development as a form of corporate recognition. It is intended as a signal to both the individual and the rest of the firm that the person is valued.

Management Development Required
at Different Organizational Levels

Each of the different levels of the organizational hierarchy (described in Chapter Eight) requires a different mix of skills, attitudes, and responsibilities to be performed. Moreover, each of these levels of the organizational hierarchy can be viewed by the manager as a different "stage of career growth." Therefore, the content of management development programs should differ depending on the level of managers involved.

In the entry-level or "doer" role, the emphasis is on the performance of specific tasks. People occupying these roles can be viewed as "individual contributors." These individuals will typically not be involved in management development programs; rather the emphasis in their training should be on technical skills.

The first-line supervisory role will, of course, still involve the performance of technical work, but the individual occupying the role of supervisor must make the transition to a role in which the primary responsibilities involve the management of people rather than the direct performance of technical work per se. This is the first level at which an individual must begin to make a personal and professional transition to a different kind of role, one in which he or she is required to think and act like a manager rather than a technician or doer of specific tasks. It is the key management development task at this level.

The next level in the hierarchy, middle management, requires a further change in an individual's concept of his or her role, skills, and attitudes. The key challenge at this level is to learn how to "manage managers."

Positions at the fourth level of the hierarchy include vice president, senior vice president, and executive vice president. Since the primary function of this senior-management level is to provide leadership and direction for the overall enterprise, the key management development task is to learn the skills of organizational development and strategic planning as well as how to manage other senior managers.

At the final or ultimate level of the organizational hierarchy, the level of CEO and/or COO, the key task is to learn how to guide the organization through the inevitable transitions required during its life cycle.

Critical Dimensions of Management Development

Given the above, the basic problem faced by a manager (and, in turn, the primary function of the management development process) is to make a transition from one level of the organizational hierarchy to the next. Based on our experience in working with managers in a wide variety of organizations, as well as research on the nature and determinants of management success and failure, we believe that there are three critical dimensions that a person must manage effectively in order to be successful at a given level of the organizational hierarchy. These three dimensions are

1. The person's concept of his or her role;
2. The skills demanded by the new role;
3. Certain attitudes or psychological factors.

We believe that if a manager is to be successful in a given organizational role, he or she must manage each of these critical dimensions in a way that is appropriate for the role and level of the organization at which the individual is operating. In addition, when an individual is promoted from one level of the organizational hierarchy to the next, the individual must make a transition on all three of these dimensions if the person is to continue to be successful in the new role. This section examines the specific nature of these three dimensions and the changes that are required for successful career transitions to occur.

Change in Role Concept. The most fundamental dimension of a successful transition to a management role involves changing the concept of one's organizational role from a performing role (doing) to a managerial role (supervising the work of others). This is an essential prerequisite to a management development transition, but it is not simple.

People do not typically exist independently of their jobs or organizational roles. For most of us, the work we do helps define ourselves to others as well as to ourselves. People ask, "What do you do"? We tend to answer, "I am an accountant (salesperson, engineer, manager, and so on)." They ask what we do, and we describe what we *are,* because our professional roles are fused with our overall identity. It is not surprising, then, that when we change occupational roles we have some difficulty in making the transition from being the kind of person we were in our old role to being a new kind of person as required by our new role.

Part of the difficulty involved in making a successful transition from an old role to a new one involves the very way we think about our job or role. A *role* is a set of expected behaviors. This means that we expect people who have the role of manager, president, or engineer to behave in certain specified ways. Similarly, we expect people who occupy the role of accountant, secretary, or clerk to behave in certain ways. These "role expectations" are grounded in our culturally derived concept of the specific roles with which we are concerned.

To be successful in a given role, a person must master the requirements of the particular role: its responsibilities, skills, and even its psychological requirements. Slowly and subtly, the role fuses with the person. Then, abruptly, the person may be promoted and suddenly faces the need to master a new role.

When a person first becomes a manager, he or she will be aware to some extent that the new role requires different activities, responsibilities, and even new ways of thinking. Unfortunately, however, few people have a very clear or specific concept of just what those new demands are until some time after they have been in the role, and by the time they realize what was required they may already have failed on the job.

The first challenge facing any person who is making the transition to a managerial role is, then, a change of self-concept to reflect the new role. This, in turn requires

1.   An understanding of the concept held of the old role;
2.   An understanding of the concept required by the new role;
3.   An action plan for change.

Whether people are explicitly aware of it or not, a most fundamental and profound change occurs when we make the transition from performing some technical job to doing the job of a manager. It is analogous to going from a player's role to a coach's role in some sport. The player's role is analogous to the doer role, while the coach's role is analogous to the first-line supervisor's role.

A second major aspect of a person's role concept that must

be changed in a successful transition to a managerial role involves changing the way he or she spends time; performance activities must receive less and supervisory activities greater emphasis. The newly promoted manager may feel more comfortable doing the work that he or she used to do rather than the newly required activities. Typically a manager must spend a considerable amount of time in planning (deciding what to do, when to do it, who should do it, and so on), reading materials and reports, meeting people, and talking on the telephone. These are very different types of activities from the performance activities of jobs such as engineer, accountant, and salesperson.

The manager must first recognize that more than just his or her title has changed. The new role demands that there be a shift in the percentage of time spent on various activities. An increasing amount of time will have to be spent in meetings, reading, and planning and much less time will be involved in doing technical work itself. Although this may seem simple for a person to recognize, in practice it is often difficult to accomplish. For example, a person promoted from a position as engineer to the position of "engineering project manager" may like to do engineering work rather than performing the new job requirements, since many people simply "re-create" their old jobs by becoming "hands-on managers."

Change in Skills Possessed. The second dimension of the successful transition to a managerial role involves making a change from a role in which the primary emphasis was on technical skills to one in which there is relatively greater emphasis on interpersonal and administrative skills.

In a performing or doer role, a person must typically possess technical skills to be effective. This is true of a wide variety of entry-level roles such as accountant, computer programmer, engineer, or salesperson. However, once the person reaches even the first managerial level in an organizational career hierarchy, the nature of the role requires a change in the skills required to perform its responsibilities.

Managerial roles typically require work-related interpersonal skills such as motivation, communication, and leadership. These skills are required in order to supervise people and handle day-to-day people-management issues. Management roles also require administrative skills such as planning, supervision of people, conducting of meetings, budgeting, performance evaluation and counseling, and control. Individuals must develop these skills in order to be effective in their new roles.

Based on extensive work with managers and organizations over the last twenty years, we have formulated a framework that helps explain the kinds of skills managers must develop at different stages of the organizational career hierarchy. This framework, which is entitled the *pyramid of management development* and is shown in Figure 9.1, comprises five different levels of skills that managers must develop over their careers to be effective in managerial roles. These five levels are (1) core management skills, (2) operational management skills, (3) organizational management skills, (4) organizational development skills, and (5) transition management skills.

The *core management skills* are a set of generic skills required of all managers regardless of the organization they are operating in or the level at which they are operating. These include time management effectiveness, delegation effectiveness, interpersonal effectiveness, and operational leadership effectiveness (see Chapter Eleven for discussion of the nature of operational leadership.) They can be thought of as the foundation skills required of all managers, whether at Apple Computer, Pepsico, or a fifty-person quick print shop.

The next level of skills in the pyramid of management development are the *operational management skills*. These are skills required to manage day-to-day operations and supervise people. They include recruitment, selection, training, day-to-day supervision of people, performance appraisal, management of meetings, and project management. Together with the core management skills, these are the skills required by first-line supervisors.

The next level of skills are the *organizational management skills*. These skills include planning, organizing people, designing control systems, and management development. They are skills needed by a wide variety of middle managers.

At the senior-management level, the next level of skills that

Figure 9.1. Pyramid of Management Development Skills.

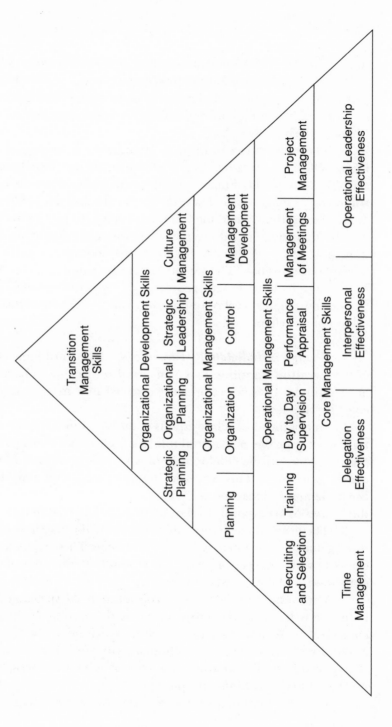

needs to be developed are *organizational development skills.* These skills include strategic planning (see Chapter Seven), organizational planning, organizational design (see Chapter Eight), strategic leadership (see Chapter Eleven), and corporate culture management (see Chapter Twelve).

The transition to the ultimate organizational career level, the CEO/COO level, requires the development of the final level of skills in the pyramid of management development. These are *transition management skills.* These skills relate to managing different kinds of transitions. First, the CEO and COO need skill in managing the transitions of taking the organization from one stage of growth to the next, which has been the subject of discussion throughout this book. The second kind of transition management skills concerns how to help people in the organization make the transition from one level of responsibility to the next, which is the subject of this chapter.

Change in Individual's Psychology. The third dimension of the successful transition to a managerial role involves changing one's attitudes from a performance-oriented to a managerial-oriented psychology.

One of the most subtle aspects of the transition to a managerial role or from one managerial role to a higher-level management position concerns the development of what may be termed a *managerial psychology.* This dimension has previously been termed the *Inner Game of Management* by Flamholtz and Randle.[35] Each of these facets of managerial psychology will be examined in turn.

There are three critical dimensions of the psychology or inner game on which managers need to change. These relate to the degree to which they feel in control over results, their source of self-evaluation, and their need to be liked.

With respect to the need for control, to make the successful transition to a management role, an individual must make the psychological transition from a situation in which he or she has relatively direct control over the results of activities for which he or she is responsible to one in which the control is indirect because it involves the efforts of other people.

In a technical or player's role, control over results is at a maximum. For an accountant, computer programmer, engineer, or salesperson, performance frequently determines the results. However, as soon as the position of first-line supervisor is reached, the relationship between personal effort and control over results becomes more indirect and tenuous. This fact is difficult for many (if not most) people to accept, and yet it must be accepted if they are to make the successful transition to a management role.

When this "decreasing degree of control" phenomenon is not accepted by a manager, he or she typically tries to reestablish the feeling, if not the reality, of control. For example, he or she may want to "be involved in everything," or have all "significant" decisions checked before they are made. The results are typically negative in two respects. First, the manager is bogged down in detail and, in reality, is doing not just his or her own job but the work of other people as well. Second, the procedure can lead to lower productivity of subordinates who are continually checking with the boss, as well as their reduced motivation and professional development. The manager copes with these problems by working harder and harder.

The "desire for control syndrome" is a fundamental problem for many managers. It gets worse as a person moves higher and higher up in the organizational hierarchy, and there are even examples of CEOs of major corporations who never fully make the psychological transition.

A second psychological aspect of the transition concerns the individual's source of self-evaluation. An individual promoted to a managerial position must develop the capacity to evaluate himself or herself based on the performance of the people being managed rather than on his or her own performance.

Since a manager's job is to utilize others to achieve organizational goals, he or she must increasingly derive his or her personal satisfaction from the performance of the people reporting to him or her. This is analogous to a basketball coach who derives self-esteem from the team's ability to win a championship rather than from the personal ability to play offense or defense.

To effectively make the transition to derive one's self-esteem from the work of others, managers also need to learn how to feel comfortable in managing people who may possess greater technical knowledge or skill than they do.

A manager is not necessarily the most capable person from a technical standpoint. Even if he or she did possess greater technical knowledge or skills at one time, as people develop and new people are brought into an organization, it is common to find himself or herself supervising people with superior technical skills or even technical skills the manager does not possess at all. For example, a marketing manager may be supervising someone who understands the advertising media better than he or she does, or a controller may be supervising an accountant who has a greater knowledge of computers. It is a personal challenge to accept and feel comfortable in such a situation. People who do not achieve this tend to hire only weaker people, and this, in turn, can lead to ultimate failure. One situation that illustrates this problem was faced by David Robbin, when he was president of the residential real estate division of a diversified national real estate company. Robbin, who was a lawyer by training, found himself managing the presidents of five residential real estate companies. Each of these individuals had substantially more experience in the real estate industry than did Robbin. Yet he had to manage them and maintain their respect even though they had more technical knowledge than he did.

The third aspect of managerial psychology that must be developed is learning how to manage one's need to be liked so that it does not interfere with an individual's capacity to be a manager. Specifically, a person may have to overcome the desire to avoid conflict, increase the ability to provide support to people, and also learn to feel comfortable in telling or asking people to do the things required to accomplish goals.

An individual must develop the ability to deal with conflict and not merely avoid it. Many people in our society not only prefer to avoid conflict, but actually cannot or will not confront it, because they fear others will no longer "like" them if they "make waves." Yet by its very nature a managerial role frequently places a person in a situation in which conflict can only be avoided at considerable cost to the organization. A successful manager must develop the capacity to face and deal with conflict. For example, a manager must frequently face the necessity of providing criticism to subordinates, and may find this task distasteful. Unfortunately, it may be essential to provide negative feedback to help employees develop.

In spite of this need, people who possess this ability are relatively rare, and are sometimes assigned this as a "role" in an organization. For example, Todd Lundy, who is currently a partner with the CPA firm of Altschuler, Melvoin, and Glasser, performed the role of "designated critic" at another CPA firm. It was recognized that Lundy had the ability to face and deal with conflict, while many of his partners did not.

Similarly, many individuals feel uncomfortable in either asking or telling other people what to do because this may lead to conflict if people do not want to do what they are asked. However, it is a manager's job to direct the efforts of others. Managers must learn to manage their need to be liked so that it does not interfere with this task.

An individual must also develop the ability to provide positive feedback to personnel. Our culture does not reward flattery. Indeed, so strong is the cultural taboo against flattery that there is a bias against praise as well. Yet the human need for self-esteem is fundamental, and praise for work done well is a valued reward. The manager must develop the ability to provide legitimate praise to his or her subordinates, since the absence of praise is functionally equivalent to criticism.

In brief, the third critical dimension an individual needs to manage in order to make the successful transition from one level of management responsibility to the next is his or her own "managerial psychology." An individual must learn to manage his or her source of self-esteem, need for control, and need to be liked in such a way as not to interfere with being an effective manager.

The Three Dimensions as a Whole. The three critical dimensions of management development required for a successful transition to a management role are, then, the individual's concept of his or her role, the skills required, and the person's managerial psychology. Table 9.1 schematically summarizes the previous discussion linking the five different levels of management with the three critical dimensions of management success. This table shows

Table 9.1. Critical Aspects of Management Development Transitions.

Five Levels of Organizational Career Hierarchy	Role Concept	Skills	Managerial Psychology
5. CEO/COO	"Head Coach"	Transition Management Skills: the ability to provide a common vision for the direction of the organization.	"Leader"
4. Senior Manager	Increased emphasis placed on supervisory activities of: • planning • reading • meeting • coaching These supersede time previously spent performing technical "hands-on" tasks.	Organizational Development Skills: strategic planning; organizational planning and leadership to position the organization in response to long-range needs identified through strategic planning; management of corporate culture.	• Becoming comfortable with increasingly indirect control over results, a phenomenon produced by delegation. • Learning to evaluate one's own performance based on the excellent performance of others. • Learning to handle conflict and provide feedback to subordinates.
3. Middle Manager		Organizational Management Skills: development of managers; departmental planning, organization, and control to produce a coordinated effort to achieve collective goals.	
2. First-Level Supervisor	"Assistant Coach" or "Player Coach"	Core and Operational Management Skills: delegation, time management, recruiting, training, performance appraisal, supervision. The focus is on day-to-day activities.	

Table 9.1. Critical Aspects of Management Development Transitions, Cont'd.

Five Levels of Organizational Career Hierarchy	Role Concept	Skills	Managerial Psychology
1. Technician	"Player" (Doer)	Technical Skills directly related to "hands-on" performance of tasks.	"Follower" • Has direct control over results. • Self-esteem is based on what *the follower* does. • Believes that being liked will get him or her ahead (avoids conflicts).

that as the individual moves from one level of the organizational hierarchy to the next, the role concept must change from a player's role at the entry-level position of a technician to the role of a kind of "head coach" as he or she reaches the level of CEO/COO. It also shows that the skills must move from technical skills directly related to hands-on performance of the task at the entry level to increasingly higher levels of skills shown in the pyramid of management development as the individual moves up the organizational hierarchy. Finally it shows that the individual must also make a psychological transition from playing the role of a follower or doer to that of a leader as he or she moves to the highest levels of the organizational hierarchy. The primary function of management development is to help people make the transitions required at each level of the organizational hierarchy.

Knapp Communications Corporation: Management Development in the Transition to Professional Management[36]

To illustrate the role of management development in making the transition from an entrepreneurship to a professionally managed organization, we will examine the way it was used by Knapp Communications Corporation (KCC). Under the leadership of C. T.

Knapp, founder and chairman, and H. S. Cranston, president, KCC used management development as part of an overall strategy to professionalize the firm. Management development helped the firm achieve certain aspects of development at both stages III and IV of corporate growth.

Corporate Background.   In the mid-1960s, Cleon ("Bud") Knapp acquired *Architectural Digest* from the estate of his maternal grandfather. *Architectural Digest,* the cornerstone of what was to become Knapp Communications Corporation, was at that time a small-circulation Southern California magazine of interior design. For several years, Knapp worked to create a new product from the magazine he had purchased, and it ultimately became the leading magazine of interior design throughout the world.

Beginning in 1975, KCC experienced extraordinarily rapid growth. It acquired a second magazine, *Bon Appetit.* Revenues increased from $2 million in 1975 to $100 million in 1982. Personnel increased from about 30 in 1975 to more than 450 by 1983.

The firm's founder had the classic skills required for entrepreneurial success: the ability to identify a market need and niche, the ability to produce a product appropriate for that niche, the willingness to risk, and the ability to attract talented people to assist him in building the enterprise. KCC's period of growth also occurred because it had learned to do some fundamental things very well. Specifically, the firm had learned how to identify a magazine market need, redesign an existing magazine to gear it to the market's requirements, and produce and sell the "new" publication.

During KCC's process of growth Knapp was well aware of the need to make the transition to professional management. By 1983 the company had already taken steps to develop its management systems and capabilities. The firm had initiated a strategic planning process, engaged in a corporate reorganization, and begun a series of management development activities for middle-level executives.

Growing Pains.   A key step in the process of professionalizing KCC focused on management development as a way of solving certain problems that had come to plague the company. One problem was a lack of managerial talent. As KCC grew, it was forced to promote to managerial jobs many people who were talented doers and technicians who had not been trained as managers. Such people quickly found themselves stretched beyond the limits of their experience and formal training. The firm grew so fast that it was always on the treadmill of hiring new people and promoting others before they were prepared to assume managerial responsibilities. These people were managers in title only.

A related problem was that since KCC merely continued to add people as it grew rather than reconceptualizing its organizational structure, it was in essence an overgrown version of a small company. As one person stated, "We were a $5 million dollar company that happened to have $75 million in sales."

Adding to these difficulties, employees at KCC had fallen into the "Superman syndrome." (As noted throughout this book, many companies suffer from this same problem.) The company's founder was viewed as a genius; even articles in the popular press credited him with the "Midas touch." People were used to kicking problems upstairs to Knapp. He was an authority without being authoritarian, and many people correctly assumed that his decisions would be better than theirs. Unfortunately, the firm had exceeded the size where one person could deal with everything—but neither the management systems nor the managerial personnel were yet in place to substitute for "Superman," who found even his considerable abilities stretched to the limit. The firm had simply been so busy keeping up with its rapid growth that it had no opportunity to "grow" the systems and managers it now required.

Another set of problems created by the firm's success involved its culture. One manifestation of this was in employees' financial expectations. Since the firm was successful, Knapp had been generous with compensation and bonuses. Some people therefore began to expect compensation and bonuses as entitlement rather than as rewards for effort. Others expected to be rewarded lavishly for merely average performance. People began to regard bonuses as a "base" part of their compensation.

The firm's success also led to a kind of organizational hubris. Many people began to believe that because KCC produced excellent products, it must also be excellent in everything else it did, including personnel management, administration, and so on. This was an admirable performance standard. Unfortunately, however, it was viewed not as a goal to be attained but as a reality. The firm had also begun to become ethnocentric; that is, many people had begun to think in terms of "the Knapp way" of doing things. The firm had done things its own way from the beginning, and that had worked out very well. This led to the belief that "We are different from and better than everyone else in publishing." Although this type of self-confidence can often lead to a self-fulfilling prophecy of success, it can also have the negative side effect of causing people not to seek or to ignore new ideas from outside the organization.

Another dimension of the cultural problem was attenuation of KCC's original culture. As we have seen, this often occurs in organizations that have reached growth stage IV. Basically, as more and more people entered the firm, they found increasing trouble in understanding the corporate culture because it could no longer be effectively transmitted through face-to-face interaction, the means of communication on which KCC had traditionally relied.

Objectives of KCC's Management Development Program

Although KCC recognized the need for a formal program of management development to facilitate the growth of its future executives, there was some dissatisfaction with prior efforts in this area. The firm had offered a variety of management development sessions for its present and potential managers, but there was no overall concept of these programs' goals. The management development activities had been presented by a wide range of instructors from both inside and outside the company, and the quality of their programs varied widely. The programs offered had been open to all who wished to attend, which led to significant differences in the knowledge and abilities of those enrolled in any particular program at the same time. Finally, the programs offered were geared to the development of managerial skills, but they failed to deal with other equally important but more subtle aspects of management development.

Because of these problems, KCC decided to experiment with a different approach to management development. It arranged for an overall program of management development that was geared to meet a broad range of management development needs, including (1) developing a cadre of future managers, (2) developing a managerial viewpoint, (3) developing managerial tools and skills, (4) reestablishing the firm's value system, and (5) initiating a "cascade effect." We will now look more carefully at some specific objectives of KCC's management development program.

Develop a Cadre of Future Managers. One of the major objectives of KCC's program was to develop a cadre of future managers who would be able to move into middle-management positions as the firm continued to grow. The idea was not only to develop individual managers but to try to create a company team analogous to the one that existed during the firm's initial stage of development. This peer group, senior management hoped, would grow together as the firm continued to develop. The plan was to bring this group together in the program, enable them to interact, and hope that this would lead to future informal interactions that could help to overcome the "separate islands syndrome," the condition in which each functional area of a company operates so totally independently that effective coordination does not occur.

Develop a Managerial Viewpoint. Another major objective of the program was to help people begin to think and act like managers rather than technicians or doers. Although many individuals occupied managerial positions, they had not yet begun to think or behave like leaders. The goals in this area were to teach people what a manager was, that a manager was a leader, what the differences between a manager and a doer were, and what each individual would have to do to make the transition from a "doer" psychology to a managerial and leadership psychology.

Develop Managerial Tools and Skills. Another objective was, of course, to help participants develop their skills as managers and to learn about the tools available to managers. KCC conducted a needs assessment to identify the skills that should be taught. This assessment involved both interviews with potential course candidates and discussions with selected senior managers in the firm. The firm's president, H. S. Cranston, also suggested skill areas he felt were important, including understanding of the management role, people management skills (including motivation and communication), and accounting skills for nonfinancial managers.

Reestablish the Firm's Value System. Bud Knapp recognized that the firm's basic values had not been accurately transmitted to newer employees. He also understood that the informal mechanism through which this cultural transmission occurred in the past would no longer function, because of the firm's size. For this reason, one of the explicit objectives of the management development program became reestablishment of the firm's value system. In meeting this objective, the most important part of the program was to be the establishment of the idea that the values of a business enterprise are the enterprise's most important aspects. Some specific values to be emphasized concerned standards of excellence.

A basic cultural assumption that management hoped to reestablish through the program was that the only form of control that is effective or worthwhile is that resulting from self-motivation. As stated by Cranston, "The belief that one must do one's best can only be a personal obligation and cannot be imposed. If demonstrated, however, it can be emulated by others, provided it is based upon a value system that goes beyond the desire for material fulfillment."

Another implicit goal of the management development program was to cause people to realize the futility of searching for panaceas or easy answers. Management wanted to avoid the "current management guru syndrome," in which everyone blindly studies "the work" in the latest best-selling book on management techniques.

Initiate a Cascade Effect. KCC's management hoped that the new program would initiate a "cascade effect" in which the participants in the program would go back to their posts and motivate changes that would cascade down through the organization as the trained people were promoted and managed more and more employees. The group was intended to motivate changes upward in the organization as well, in that the very existence of a cadre of trained junior managers could motivate others to develop their skills and "buy into" the value system being demonstrated by the class graduates.

Nature of the Program

KCC's management development program was intended to be of high quality, rigorous, and demanding. Designed by a management development firm consisting of experienced university educators, it was of a quality and difficulty comparable to MBA-level courses at a leading university. No explicit rewards were offered either as inducements to enter the program or as recognition of its successful completion. Participants in the course would receive a "Certificate of Completion" and a token memento but no bonuses or salary increases. The primary rewards were intrinsic: the satisfaction of meeting demanding standards—of being able to say, "I did it!"—and of the experience itself.

Unlike most management development efforts, the program developed at KCC was designed as an integrated course. The course was to be conducted over a nine-week period. It would include case histories, films, role-play simulations, and exercises as well as selected readings and lectures. A binder of materials was prepared for each participant. Each participant had to complete three written assignments during the course. Participants needed a grade of "B" or better to pass the course.

Some of the example cases used in the program drew on existing materials. However, five case histories were specially written for the KCC context. These new case histories were intended to increase the meaningfulness of the concepts and tools presented by showing their relevance to day-to-day problems faced by managers in that firm and to increase the familiarity of each participant with other areas of the corporation. Role plays, also specially designed for KCC, were intended to increase the meaningfulness of program materials by means of both experiential learning and contextual relevance.

Impact of the Program

In order to assess the extent to which KCC's management development program was able to achieve its objectives, we administered a questionnaire at both the beginning and the end of the course. This questionnaire was designed to assess the overall extent to which an individual had made the transition from a performing to a managerial orientation, based on four specific dimensions that have been hypothesized to be key elements of the required transition: (1) the person's concept of his or her role, (2) the types of skills possessed, (3) the psychology of managing one's self, and (4) the psychology of managing others.[37] The third and fourth components of this questionnaire are both aspects of an individual's managerial psychology, cited above. Responses to this questionnaire showed that the program had made a significant difference in the students' thinking.[38]

During the period in which the course was conducted, the class evolved, as hoped, from an ad hoc group to a cohesive group. A considerable degree of "we-feeling" developed, and the class even set up its own unofficial graduation. In part, this was an effect of the well-recognized "common fate syndrome," the affection that develops among individuals who have shared a demanding experience.

Management Development at Different Stages of Organizational Growth

This section examines the different needs for management development that companies have at the first four stages of organizational growth.

Stage I.   At the earliest stage of growth, most organizations do not have formal management development programs for their people. Management development takes place, if at all, through on-the-job training. Although some management development would be desirable for companies in stage I, the cost of establishing an in-house training program is usually prohibitive at this point.

In spite of this, stage I is a good time to begin establishing the organization's cultural attitude toward management development. The firm can hold an annual one-day in-house seminar on a management development topic, or it can support attendance at public seminars. It can purchase and distribute management books to its employees or purchase management magazines for circulation. Employees can also be encouraged to participate in continuing education programs or even acquire MBAs. Most significantly, the founding entrepreneur can serve as a role model and stress, through word and behavior, that management development is important in his or her firm.

Stage II. During the early part of stage II, a firm can continue the same approach to management development that was recommended for stage I. After the firm has reached approximately $5 million in annual revenues, however, it is probably ready for and can afford some form of in-house management development as well.

The principal management development goal for a stage II company is to ensure that all its managers understand at least the basic skills of management. At this point most people will be first-line supervisors; that is, they will be managing one level of personnel rather than managing other managers. Such people require training in the fundamentals of supervision, including people management skills (motivation, communication, performance appraisal, conflict management), as well as in basic skills in work planning and organization and personal time management. They should understand the fundamentals of delegation and the need to begin to think and act like a manager rather than a doer. Stated differently, they require development of the skills at the first two levels of the pyramid of management development as shown in Figure 9.1.

The principal advantage of using an in-house program to provide this training is that the program can be tailored precisely to the firm's people and their needs. A firm may find it useful to have an outside professional management educator help in designing and implementing the program. The firm can typically find such assistance at a local university.

Stage III. By the time a firm has reached stage III, it ought to be in the process of developing an in-house program of management development. At this stage, the key organizational development issue is professionalizing the firm and its management systems.

To accomplish the transition to professional management, the organization must change the way it thinks about itself and the way it operates. The founder/entrepreneur will no longer be able to fully manage all aspects of operations personally. He or she will have to use other managers as surrogates. This does not—or should not—mean that the entrepreneur simply uses these managers as extra "arms and legs" to perform specific tasks; rather, there should be real delegation of authority. The entrepreneur must learn to trust managerial subordinates to perform their responsibilities well. This, in turn, means that these people will have to think like entrepreneurs or business people rather than simply as functional specialists. To accomplish this change, some form of management development is typically required. The management development program at Metro Realty, described in Chapter Five, is one good example.

Assuming that an organization has already laid the foundation for management development in stage II by providing a basic supervisory skills program for its people, a major management development goal for a stage III company will be to reinforce these basic skills. Such skills are not simply learned once and then fully retained. People get into and out of habits, and skills must be reinforced. For example, one function of the five-year driver's license renewal test is simply to motivate people to read the test booklet again and remind themselves of what they ought to be doing. Although most people probably consider it a nuisance to go through the test, it is likely to make them remember long-forgotten parts of the "rules of the road." Doing so reinforces the way they ought to be driving.

The primary goal of stage III management development, however, is to provide the advanced skills of managerial leadership, strategic planning, departmental organization, and control systems required by people who are or will be managing other managers. The skill of strategic planning was described in Chapter Seven, and effective leadership is discussed in Chapter Eleven. These are the skills at level 3 of the pyramid of management development.

Stage IV. After a firm has reached stage IV, it will have a greater degree of discretionary resources. Wise officers planning for the successful long-term development of their enterprises will then want to invest considerably in building human assets through management development programs. They will realize that their firms are competing not merely in products and technology but in people as well.

A stage IV company definitely ought to have an in-house management development program. Our KCC example presented a model of the type of thinking that should underlie a stage IV company's program.

A typical stage IV company will have its own human resources department and training staff. In addition, most firms supplement their in-house staff by using either outside university educators or consultants to help design and deliver management development services.

The primary goal of a stage IV management development program is to train and develop people with either a general-management or a senior-management perspective. The need for managers at stage IV relates to the consolidation of the enterprise as well as to preparation for future growth and development. There is a qualitative difference in the type of managerial skills and capabilities required by managers at this stage. The skills shown at levels 4 and 5 of the pyramid of management development must be developed by these senior executives.

A stage IV organization is a very significant entity. A great deal of effort is required to manage the internal organization and the business of such a firm. To accomplish this task, managers require a holistic perspective. They need to think in terms of the pyramid of organizational development both for the care and feeding of the existing enterprise and for the development of new entrepreneurial ventures that will replicate the growth cycle that the parent company has already gone through.

Training people to think strategically and conceptually about the development of an organization requires a more sophisticated type of management development. It requires the use of case histories and exercises designed to broaden the perspectives of people who are used to thinking in narrower terms as functional specialists. Yet it is essential if a firm is to maximize its chances to grow and develop successfully.

Investment in Management Development

Management development is an investment, and all firms need to make such an investment. If you owned an expensive automobile, such as a Mercedes, you would or should be prepared to spend 5 percent of the car's value on maintenance to protect the asset. Managers are frequently far more expensive than cars and other machines. Yet companies fail to invest in management development either as "preventive maintenance" to avoid managerial obsolescence, or to enhance the manager's skills and, in turn, increase the human asset's value.

Although no precise guidelines can be given, I recommend that a company invest between 5 percent and 10 percent of its annual payroll on management development. If a firm is investing less than 5 percent, it may experience costly personnel replacement costs as a result of "the Peter Principle" and related turnover.

Some managers may feel that these are costly investments, and they are, but the alternative is to incur the opportunity cost of lost profit that is frequently caused by ineffective management. For example, one medium-sized consumer products manufacturing company that failed to invest $60,000 in a management development program for all of its top managers found it cost the firm $1,500,000 in losses from ineffective management by one member of the group.

Summary

This chapter has examined the role of management development in making the transition from an entrepreneurship to a professionally managed firm. Management development is the process of building the present and potential performance capabilities of managers. However, it also serves the functions of helping to shape corporate culture by promoting a desired leadership style as well as recognizing and rewarding managers.

There are three key dimensions of management development, including an individual's (1) role concept, (2) skills, and (3) managerial psychology. Each of these three dimensions must change as a person moves through the organizational hierarchy.

This chapter has also presented a case study of how an entrepreneurial company can use management development to help make the transition to a professionally managed firm. The case illustrates the various functions and uses of management development in making this transition. Knapp Communications Corporation used the management development program not only to increase people's skills but also to help reestablish the firm's culture, to create a cadre of managers who would serve as role models in the organization, and to promote a new style of management in the company. Although this is not the only model of using management development, it provides a powerful tool for companies in the process of moving from stage II to stage III or IV. The chapter has also examined the different levels of management required at different stages of organizational growth.

10 Organizational Control Systems

All organizations, no matter what their stage of development, require some form of control system. When the organization is very small, the entrepreneur can control what is happening through day-to-day involvement and observation alone. The required coordination and information needed for decisions will appear almost by osmosis. The owner will have a "feel" for what is happening, what the problems are, and what needs to be done; and this will be enough.

As the enterprise increases in size and gains additional people, however, the entrepreneur's ability to maintain control over all aspects of its operations will begin to decrease. The organization will begin to experience growing pains related to ineffective control systems. For example, people either deny responsibility for tasks or do everything themselves because there are no clearly defined roles and responsibilities. A company can find that its profits are low even when sales are increasing because it has no way of knowing where it is financially; this comes about when the company has not developed formal performance monitoring systems. A firm may experience a high degree of duplication of effort and decreasing productivity because of poor coordination between people and departments. All these problems suggest that one of the critical challenges facing entrepreneurs in rapidly growing companies is the need to be able to control what is happening.

Companies hire people, give them specific jobs and responsibilities, and expect them to perform well and achieve the enterprise's goals. However, the managers of successful organizations know that this is not enough. They realize that in order to be reasonably certain that the company's objectives will be achieved, they must have some way of trying to influence or channel people's behavior. In short, an organizational control system is required.

Organizations use a variety of methods to gain control over people's behavior, including personal supervision, job descriptions, rules, budgets, and performance appraisal systems. These methods are all a part of the organizational control system.

As we explained in Chapter Four, a formalized control system is necessary to make the successful transition to a professionally managed firm. This chapter describes the use of organizational control as a managerial tool to help in making this transition. First, we present a framework for understanding how to design a control system. Next, a case study is provided that highlights some of the issues facing a firm in designing a control system to meet its needs as it grows. We also provide a description of how control systems should differ, based on a company's stage of growth.

The Nature of Organizational Control

The term *control* has a variety of meanings. For our purposes, it is defined as the process of influencing the behavior of members of an organization. An organizational control system may be defined as a set of mechanisms designed to increase the probability that people will behave in ways that lead to the attainment of organizational goals. This definition brings out two important aspects of organizational control: (1) It is intended to motivate people to achieve goals, and (2) it can only influence the probability that people will behave in the desired ways.

Control Motivates People to Focus on Goals. The ultimate objective of organizational control is to try to motivate or influence people to achieve organizational goals. Its intent is not to control people's behavior in predefined ways but to influence them to make decisions and take actions that are likely to be consistent with the organization's goals.

Ideally, the objective of the control system is to increase the congruence between the goals of the organizational members (individuals and groups) and the organization as a whole. This is important, because individuals will be most motivated to work toward the goals of the organization if, by so doing, they are also able to satisfy their own goals. It should be pointed out, however, that while there is usually some degree of correspondence between the goals of organization members and those of the organization as a whole, total congruence is rarely attained.

Control Influences the Probability of Goal Achievement. There can be no guarantee that all people will always behave in ways consistent with organizational objectives all the time. Rather, there is a specified probability or likelihood that such behavior will occur. Control systems are intended to increase the *likelihood* that people behave in the ways desired by an organization.

Tasks of Control Systems

In order to motivate people to behave in ways consistent with organizational goals, control systems must perform three tasks. First, they must be able to influence people's decisions and actions in an appropriate direction. As we have seen, without an effective control system, people are likely to make decisions and act in ways that fulfill their own personal needs and goals but not necessarily those of the organization. At Tempo Products, for example, employees and departments "did their own thing" without considering the needs of the company as a whole. This resulted in a number of people and departments that did nothing at all or that, consciously or unconsciously, worked at odds with the goals of the company. It also resulted in duplication of effort between departments, which contributed to increased costs.

Control systems must also coordinate the efforts of diverse parts of an organization. Even when people are trying to act in the best interests of a company, they may find themselves working at cross-purposes. As we saw in the case of Custom Printing, lack of coordination can result in duplication of effort, production delays, and other inefficiencies. At Custom Printing, there were a large number of rush orders because coordination between sales and production was poor. When orders were rushed, many had to be redone because of mistakes in production, which resulted in unanticipated delays for customers and increased costs for the company. Lack of coordination between shipping and production contributed to shipping delays and resulting customer dissatisfaction.

The third task of control systems is to provide information about the result of operations and people's performance. This information allows the organization to evaluate results and make corrective changes as required. Even if individuals, groups, and the organization have common interests, problems may occur that require correction. At Custom Printing, for example, few people knew whether they had met their goals because there was no way to monitor their performance. This resulted in a number of unmet goals for which there were no repercussions. People could not be held accountable, since they had no way of knowing what their performance was. Similarly, managers at Metro Realty could not be held accountable for failing to meet their budgets because the information necessary to monitor financial goals was not available. When profits began to decline, the company was unable to take corrective action because it did not have adequate information on income and expenses. At Tempo Products, a lack of adequate information contributed to poor performance and ineffective operations. Employees did not know how to improve their performance because managers were reluctant or unable to provide both positive and negative feedback. The result was that, even when individuals were performing poorly, they continued to operate in the same fashion as they had before the evaluation.

Control Systems at Mrs. Fields' Cookies.   At Mrs. Fields' Cookies, the three functions of control systems—to influence the direction of action, to coordinate activities, and to provide information on performance—are operating with a high degree of success. The system, developed by Randy Fields and based on standards set by Debbi Fields in her first store, gives top management control over widely dispersed operations.[39] A variety of computer programs designed to minimize administrative paperwork and maximize managerial decisions are the heart of the system.

Using the telephone and personal computer, each store manager has access to the information needed for that day's production, can receive feedback on how sales are going compared to similar operations, and can communicate with the corporate office. The actions and decisions of individual store managers are guided through the standard embedded in the programs. One program provides hourly sales figures by product that managers need to meet their sales projections. It also tells when and how much of each type of cookie dough to prepare based on similar previous days' sales figures. An hourly update is provided based on the data the manager inputs. Another program projects crew schedules. Despite the detailed programmed information, the system is seen as providing adequate information for corporate control requirements and as an aid to managerial decision making, not a substitute for it.

Programs for personnel administration and maintenance increase effective coordination efforts with the main office. Repair orders are sent by computer to corporate offices where a work order is generated. When the work is complete, it is signed off by the manager—again on computer—and payment is made through headquarters.

Communication is a key element in any control system, and Mrs. Fields' system provides a link between the individual store managers and founder Debbi Fields. Through computerized phone mail link, Debbi can relay information and concerns by voice to individual managers. Conversely, each manager, using another program, can send Debbi messages that are answered by her or one of her staff within forty-eight hours.

Design of Organizational Control Systems

An organizational control system is a system designed to control some sort of organizational activity, such as sales, production, or engineering. More formally, it may be viewed as a set of mechanisms designed to increase the likelihood or probability that people will behave in ways that help to achieve organizational goals in a specified key result area.

We refer to the activities or functions that a control system is intended to influence as the "operational or behavioral system." This is simply the "target" or intended focus of the control systems. For example, if we want to control sales, then the operational or behavioral system might be (1) a single salesperson, (2) a sales department, or (3) the entire sales of an enterprise.

Key Parts of a Control System. The four basic components of a formal system of organizational control are (1) objectives for the performance of the activity or function, (2) goals for performance on each specified objective of the activity or function, (3) a method of measurement for monitoring the performance of members of the organization, and (4) a method of administering rewards to motivate and reinforce performance (the evaluation/reward process). These four components actually constitute what may be termed a company's "core control system," a formal mechanism for planning and communicating objectives and goals, measuring, reporting and evaluating performance, and rewarding performance.[40] The relationships among these four components are depicted in Figure 10.1. We will now describe each of these components further.

Objectives. As described in Chapter Seven, objectives are the things an organization wants to achieve in a given result area. For purposes of this discussion, it is useful to think of two types of objectives, ultimate and instrumental. Ultimate objectives are broader and tend to be related to the primary mission of the organization. They might be such things as earning a satisfactory return on the assets used in the business, developing a new market for a product line, or expanding the scope of the business to meet a competitive threat. For example, Kawasaki Motors has as one of its corporate objectives an increase in market share of 1 percent each year for the next five years.

Instrumental objectives (subobjectives) are the means by which the ultimate objectives are achieved. For example, the firm that has as its ultimate objective the development of a new market for a product line would have instrumental objectives dealing with desired sales of that product for a given period, production objectives for the product, and marketing campaigns and costs. Some instrumental objectives are stated in monetary terms through budgets, while others are part of the broader planning process.

Both ultimate and instrumental objectives help to direct or

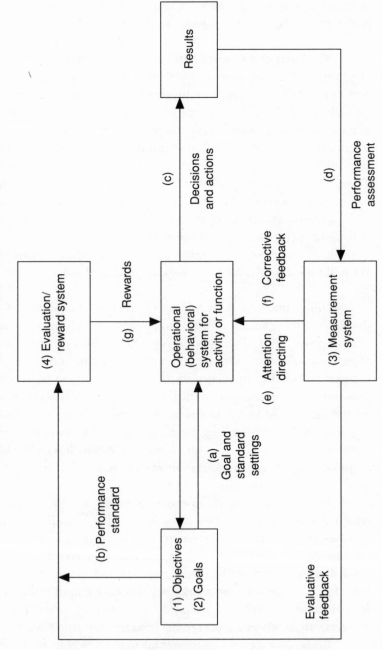

Figure 10.1. Model of Organizational Control Systems.

channel the efforts of people in an organization. They are both means to achieve desired ends and a form of ends in themselves.

Goals. As described in Chapter Seven, goals are specific, measurable, and time-dated. A goal states what performance ought to be in order to achieve a given objective. The objective of a salesperson may be to generate revenue for the firm, while the goal for the revenue may be last month's (or last year's) sales plus 5 percent. Goals may be based on management judgment, expectations, or historical data.

Goals may be used to establish desired performance levels, to motivate performance, and to serve as a benchmark against which performance can be assessed. For example, "standard costs" can be used in a manufacturing plant as a goal to motivate employees to control production costs and also as a way to evaluate their performance.

Goals are intended to facilitate control both before and after performance. *Preperformance control* is motivation of performance before the operation or behavioral system is executed. Goals in this area are intended to bring about desired performance levels in people. *Postperformance control* uses goals as standards in evaluating actual performance and as a basis for rewards, the fourth component of organizational control systems.

Measurement and Reporting System. Measurement is the process of representing the properties or qualities of objects in numerical terms. In organizational control systems, measurement has a dual function. One purpose is to provide information that can be used for evaluating performance and making corrections in goal-directed behavior. This is the informational function of measurement. The accounting system, with its measures of financial and managerial performance, is a part of the overall measurement system that contributes to the informational function. The informational function also draws on nonfinancial measures of performance such as market share, production indices, and measures of product quality.

Measurement also plays another role in control systems. The very act of measuring something has an effect on people's behavior because people tend to pay more attention to the aspects of jobs or goals that are measured. For example, at Custom Printing, employees tended not to pay attention to scrap losses until a measurement system to monitor them was put in place. This aspect of measurement may be termed the *process function*. It is related to Marshall McLuhan's notion that the medium is the message.[41] The medium of measurement is itself a stimulus. As the managing partner of a national CPA firm stated: "What gets measured gets counted."

An effective control system ought to measure all major goals because of the process function of measurement; otherwise, some goals may be ignored. For example, if a store uses an incentive pay plan that compensates employees on the basis of sales volume as a performance measure, those employees will tend to compete for sales and ignore unmeasured functions such as stock work.

Reporting or feedback is also an important part of an organizational control system. A variety of reports, ranging from financial statements to cost reports and performance reports, provide information about the results of operations to management and others.

Performance Evaluation and Reward System. The final component of an organizational control system is the evaluation and reward system, which facilitates both preperformance and postperformance control. Evaluation determines how well individuals and groups have done in meeting organizational goals. Evaluative reports generated by the measurement system—containing such items as net income, budgets compared to actual, and return on investment—generally are used in performance evaluation. Through evaluation, the organization decides how individuals and groups will be rewarded.

Rewards are desirable outcomes of behavior required by organizations. Organizations offer a wide variety of rewards, ranging from monetary items such as compensation or bonuses to recognition and promotion. Rewards can be extrinsic or intrinsic. When people perform tasks because work is interesting, their rewards are intrinsic. When people perform tasks because of the rewards they expect to receive from others, such as praise or pay, the rewards are extrinsic.

Whatever the nature of rewards, they should reinforce positive performance and modify negative performance. Further, the rewards must be *seen* as being linked to desired behavior in order to be effective as motivators.

Sometimes organizations fail to offer rewards that motivate people to perform desired behavior, or they offer rewards for one type of behavior while actually trying to motivate another: "the folly of rewarding A, while hoping for B."[42] For example, a business manager may be rewarded only for not exceeding his budget, even though the firm hopes that he will also pay attention to personnel development. Similarly, an organization that wants to motivate people to be good planners but rewards only "fire fighters" may soon find that some managers become "arsonists."

Rewards can be useful in motivating employees before behavior occurs because of the expectation of rewards in the future. Once good performance occurs, rewards reinforce the behavior and lead to the greater probability of its happening again. Behavior that is not followed by a reward is less likely to happen in the future.

All the components of the control system affect the operational or behavioral system for an activity. As shown in Figure 10.1, the control system's process of objective and goal setting initially channels effort. Once set, the objectives and goals become performance standards that function in both preperformance and postperformance control. In their preperformance function they serve as inputs to motivate desired behavior in the operational system, while in their postperformance function they are inputs to the evaluation and reward subsystem. Measurement directs attention toward measured dimensions of goals and provides corrective and evaluative feedback. Organizational rewards serve both preperformance and postperformance control functions. Preperformance, they are a source of arousing motivation toward organizational goals. Postperformance, they reinforce or extinguish behavior.

Illustration of Control System. To illustrate the feasibility of applying the model of organization control just described, we will examine the application of the model in a manufacturing plant. As seen in Exhibit 10.1, the plant has five key result areas: production volume, quality, safety, energy utilization, and scrap.

Exhibit 10.1. Control Model's Application in Manufacturing Plant.

Key Result Areas	This Year's Goals	Last Year's Actual	This Year's Performance											
			Jan.	Feb.	Mar.	Apr.	May	June	July	Aug.	Sept.	Oct.	Nov.	Dec.
1. Production Volume														
2. Quality														
3. Safety														
4. Energy Utilization														
5. Scrap														

All of these key result areas are different in nature. Production volume is something that can be easily quantified. Energy utilization and scrap can also be measured but in a different way. Quality and safety require still a different type of measurement.

The company has established goals for each of these five key result areas, as listed in the column titled "This Year's Goals." The firm also shows last year's actual performance in the next column. In addition, this year's performance is tracked on a monthly basis in the adjacent columns.

Virtually any company or any unit of a company can use a format similar to that shown in Exhibit 10.1 to apply the control model to its operations. This approach can be used for the company as a whole, a division, a department, or even an individual such as a salesperson. Indeed, I observed an example of the application of this framework on a visit to China in 1983 in a chemical plant located in the city of Shanghai. The plant manager was using a blackboard to list the key result areas, current performance goals, prior year's actual performance, and historical best performance, as well as to track the actual performance of the plant to date. Whenever an employee walked past the blackboard, he or she got a quick glimpse at how the plant was performing to date.

Design and Evaluation of Control Systems Effectiveness. The effectiveness of a control system is measured by the extent to which it increases the probability that people will behave in ways that lead to the attainment of organizational objectives. If a control system sometimes leads to goal congruence and sometimes to goal conflict, it is ineffective, or at least less effective than might be desired.

To be effective, a control system must identify all behaviors or goals that are required by the organization. If the system does not identify all relevant goals and seek to control them, people may simply channel their efforts toward some desired but uncontrolled behavior. In addition, in order to be effective, the control system must actually lead to the behavior it is intended to (or purports to) produce. For example, a control system may be intended to motivate people toward achieving both a budgeted profit and personnel development. If it produces this effect, it is said to be "behaviorally valid." If it leads to behavior that is in conflict with these goals, it is "behaviorally invalid." In general, a control system cannot be expected to lead to behavior that is totally consistent with what is desired, but it must have some degree of behavioral validity if it is to be effective.

A control system's effectiveness also depends on the extent to which it repeatedly produces the same behavior, whether this behavior is intended or not. This quality is called the control system's *behavioral reliability.* A control system may have a high degree of behavioral reliability but lead consistently to unintended behavior, or a system may lead to intended behavior but do so irregularly.

Lack of Production of Dysfunctional Behavior. When a control system is ineffective, dysfunctional behavior can result. There are two types of dysfunctional behavior: goal displacement and measurementship.

Goal displacement is a lack of goal congruence created by motivation to achieve some goals sought by the organization at the expense of other intended goals. Goal displacement may be caused by several things, including suboptimization, selective attention to goals, and inversion of means and ends.

Suboptimization occurs when the performance of an organizational subunit is optimized at the expense of the organization as a whole. It is caused by factoring overall organizational goals into subgoals and holding individuals and units responsible for those subgoals. It is a common problem and is difficult to avoid in large, complex organizations.

Selective attention to organizational goals is closely related to suboptimization. It occurs when certain goals of the organization are pursued selectively, while other goals receive less attention or are ignored. In this case, a rule or guideline that is part of the control system is followed absolutely, even if it contradicts or prevents achievement of the goal. The original goal is replaced by the goals of following the rules. A third type of goal displacement is caused by the inversion of means and ends. This occurs when a control system tries to motivate attention to certain instrumental goals, which become ends in themselves because of rewards and thereby prevent achievement of other goals.

Measurementship involves a lack of goal congruence created by motivation to "look good" in terms of the measures used in control systems, even though no real benefit is produced for the organization. It involves manipulating the measures used by a control system—playing the "numbers game." There are two primary types of measurementship: "smoothing" and falsification.

Smoothing is an attempt to time activities in a way that produces the appearance of similar measures in different time periods. For example, a manager may wish to smooth the calculated net income in two adjacent periods. If profit is expected to be unusually high during the first period, this figure can be smoothed by incurring expenditures then that otherwise would have been made in the second period in the prior year.

Falsification is the reporting of invalid data about what is occurring in an organization in order to make a person or activity look good in the management system. A large toy company, for example, was charged with manipulating sales by intentionally accounting for certain transactions incorrectly in order to show good earnings for the stock market.

Problems related to dysfunctional behavior point to the importance of designing and implementing effective control systems at each stage of organizational development.

Superior Alarm Systems: Case Study

This section builds on the framework for control systems presented previously in this chapter and applies it to a case study of an actual control system in an organization. We will examine the control system at Superior Alarm Systems, a medium-sized distributor of electronic automotive alarm systems.

Superior Alarm Systems is a rapidly growing distributor and installer of electronic alarm systems for automobiles. The firm was originally founded in the early 1980s as an "electronics boutique," where individuals could purchase stereo systems, alarm systems, and other electronic devices for installation in automobiles. With demographic changes, the firm noted a rapid growth in the market for original equipment and replacement alarm systems, and by 1985 had totally redirected its focus to just the installation of these electronic systems.

The original location of the firm was a single store in a major metropolitan area in a large Western state. The firm emphasized a variety of competitive aspects, including the use of original equipment, materials, competitive prices, rapid service, quality of installation, and field service by means of radio-dispatched trucks. As the firm began to grow, it targeted new geographical markets. By 1986 the firm had organized a franchise operation, and had established ten locations throughout the state.

Each of the franchises is organized with a branch manager, a number of installation technicians, and an administrative assistant. The administrative assistant's function is critical to the effectiveness of the operation of the branch since he or she has the primary contact with the customer and is required to relay most of the critical information concerning sales and/or repairs. The installation and repair technicians are also critical to the effective operation of the firm. Incorrect installation or faulty repair creates significant customer ill will and substantial cost to the company. The "branch manager" is actually an owner/operator, who has an investment in the franchise. Depending on the size of the branch, the branch manager may also function simultaneously as an installer/technician or even as a salesperson. In some of the larger branches, there may be one or more full-time sales personnel.

By 1989, the firm had grown to approximately $25 million in annual revenue. It was growing at an average rate of 22 percent a year, and because of rapid growth both in terms of the number of branch operations and in terms of the total volume of sales there had been relatively little time to develop the infrastructure of the organization.

Development of Control Systems.   Certain aspects of the Superior Alarm control systems were more developed than others. The company had developed a relatively sophisticated strategic planning process. The firm had been involved in numerous formal planning exercises over several years since its inception, including planning meetings that involved a considerable amount of discussion concerning problems facing the company, identifying alternatives, assessing their strengths and limitations, searching for information that was relevant, and formulating a broad concept of where the firm wanted to go. These sessions were the basis for the firm's decision to franchise, for example.

One problem with the planning process was, according to the firm's administrative staff as well as the branch managers, that it did not tend to result in a set of specific goals and objectives for the firm, or a set of priorities to guide them in carrying out their overall efforts. The frequent complaint was that many of the plans that were made at the beginning of the planning year tended to be "bumped" by more immediate problems handed down by top management. The introduction of unplanned projects, or crises that tended to emerge, resulted in shifts in the focus of energy, and resulted in neglect of many of the projects that had originally been agreed to at the beginning of the year. There was a sense that the firm was making progress, but that a great deal of the progress was in an ad hoc or piecemeal manner. The bottom line was that many of the participants in the planning process sessions expressed uncertainty about how the content of the meetings would be translated into action.

Although the overall planning process was extensive, there had never been formal consideration of what the company's key result areas ought to be. Accordingly, although the branch managers and, in turn, the installation technicians understood in general what their role was, there was not a specific set of key result areas for which they were held accountable. Similarly, there was not a specific set of goals or objectives for which they were held accountable.

Another problem with the firm's control system related to the nature of its objectives and goals: Only a few were quantifiable. When objectives and goals were measurable, the level of performance expected was frequently unrealistic. For example, the times that were available as "standard times" for installation were thought by all but a few of the most talented and experienced installation technicians to be unrealistic. As a result, many of the employees found the standards to be demoralizing. Moreover, the enforcement of the standards was relatively uneven. Some branch managers tended to stick to standards and to evaluate installation technicians negatively whenever their performance was below standard, which was quite frequently. Other branch managers, who recognized that the standards were not wholly realistic, tended to ignore them.

One strength of the measurement system of the firm was that it was organized on a "responsibility accounting basis." This meant that the firm had good information concerning the profitability of each individual branch. At each branch, the company had institutionalized a monthly financial review of the data. A representative from the home office met with the branch manager and examined the monthly financial report. They also discussed issues involving branch performance on such key factors as market share.

Within each branch, however, the process of performance review was relatively uneven. With the exception of an examination of overall bottom-line profitability, there did not tend to be a review of performance in key result areas that supported that profitability. Discussions of "problems" would occur as they emerged. There was no systematic attempt to identify the critical success factors of the branch, to measure the branch's performance in each one of those factors, and to examine it in depth.

With respect to performance appraisals of each employee, there was an uneven emphasis by the different branch managers in evaluating their subordinates. While it was company policy that employees were to be reviewed based on their performance on a yearly basis, some individuals indicated that over two years had passed since their last review. They also reported that feedback on their performance ranged from some very specific, constructive criticisms to more global assessments of their performance. Many individuals indicated that they were not really sure how they were being evaluated by their managers, or whether they were valued or not valued by their managers. One stated, "Well, I'm still here, so I must be doing okay."

At this stage of the firm's development there was not a well-designed compensation program. The administration of compensation increases was on ad hoc basis. Some individuals had not received a salary increase in more than two years. Further, there were no specific guidelines for salary increases that would be allocated in relation to different levels of performance, such as excellent performance, good performance, or satisfactory performance. Individuals reported that they did not have a clear idea as to how their performance would result in increases in their compensation.

Improvements in the Control System An analysis of our description of the control system at Superior Alarm indicates that there are a number of problems in the design of that system. There are problems both in the individual components of the control system and in the overall integration of the system. In this section, we will examine some of those problems and make suggestions about how they can be improved.

Goals and Objectives. As described in Chapter Seven, objectives and goals are the output of the firm's planning system. A company's strategic planning system should result in a statement of its mission, its key result areas, its objectives, and its goals. In the case of Superior Alarm, the planning system does not provide a foundation for an effective control system in these areas. The basic problem with the planning process at Superior Alarm is that it is not producing a well-defined statement of key result areas. The key result areas are necessary to provide an overall focus for the branch manager and in turn for the installation technicians and the administrative assistants. Once the key result areas for each branch are identified and defined, it is necessary to further improve the planning process at Superior Alarm by generating a set of objectives related to each key result area. The next step is to generate goals related to each objective which, by definition, are specific, measurable and time-dated. These steps will help overcome the problems faced by branch managers, installation technicians, and administrative personnel. To help avoid the problem of setting unrealistic goals, the branch manager, installation technicians, and administrative personnel should participate in the process of setting these goals. It is particularly important that great care be devoted to ensuring that the goals are measurable, specific, and time-dated. Otherwise, they will not provide an effective basis for comparison with actual performance.

Measurement Systems. A measurement system permits a company to represent the performance of a branch or individual in quantitative terms. At a company such as Superior Alarm, the measurement system includes the accounting information system, sales management system, and other sources of information. Although there seems to be ample financial information to assist managers, there does not appear to be an adequate source of financial information concerning performance in the branches.

The company will need to do an analysis of each of its key result areas in order to ensure that measurements are available to assess performance on each of these key factors. The measurements do not all have to be in dollar terms. Some can be in monetary terms; others can be in nonmonetary terms. Some measurements can even be what may be characterized as "go/no go" measurements. This means that a manager can do an informal rating of whether something has happened or not happened. For example, we might be able to assess the level of customer service by the number of written complaints or letters of praise received. Ultimately, the home office might conduct a telephone sample of customers and have the interviewer generate a judgment as to whether the service provided was "satisfactory" or "unsatisfactory." By then tabulating the number of satisfactory versus unsatisfactory responses, we can generate a "measurement" of branch performance in this key result area.

Rewards. A significant problem with the firm's control system is the lack of linkage between objectives, goals, measurements, and rewards. The firm's compensation system does not appear to be linked to its objectives and goals. Individuals do not perceive that they are rewarded based on their ability to achieve goals and objectives. Since people do not perceive a clear linkage between goals and objectives and compensation, there is unlikely to be a great deal of "ownership" of the goals and objectives. People may very well be motivated, but the firm's reward system is neither enhancing nor channeling their motivation directly toward the goals and objectives that the branch seeks to attain.

To improve its control system, the firm will have to do an analysis of its overall compensation system. To be effective the compensation system should ideally provide incentives for an individual to achieve the goals and objectives that the organization wants to attain. An increasing number of entrepreneurial firms are relying on compensation systems that have a significant component based on incentive compensation. In such circumstances, people are generally provided a base salary that is relatively competitive, as well as opportunities for substantial increases in compensation linked to the achievement of individual and company objectives and goals. Wherever feasible, a company should attempt to tie incentive compensation to measurable factors. However, even where this is not feasible, if management can identify the key factors it wishes people to focus on, and indicate how incentive compensation will be based on those factors, it will result in enhanced motivation of performance.

Control Systems at Different Stages of Organizational Growth

No single control system is ideal for every organization. Each organization is different and requires a different type of system. The major factor that determines the amount of control a given organization requires is the company's stage of growth.

Stage I. Even the smallest organizations need some type of control system, but at stage I, control typically is relatively informal. Usually, the entrepreneur can exercise control during stage I simply through his or her day-to-day interaction with people in the organization. By the very fact of constantly being there, the entrepreneur is able to observe what is happening and be on top of almost everything. At this stage, the entrepreneur still knows all the company's employees. He or she is able to observe what most of them are doing and suggest modifications when necessary.

Even in this informal stage, however, the basic functions of control need to be exercised. The organization should have a basic budgetary system and an accounting system. The latter can be a manual system at stage I, although a computer-based system is preferable. (Several existing software packages are appropriate for stage I companies.) At stage I, a company can get by with a relatively informal performance appraisal system, but there ought to be some regular appraisal process.

Stage II.   As soon as a firm reaches stage II, its control needs increase dramatically. The entrepreneur no longer has the time to handle control single-handedly, nor can he or she personally interact with all of the growing number of employees. There is increased need for the kind of coordination that only a formal system can bring. If the entrepreneur fails to recognize the need for a more formal system, the company is likely to experience difficulties.

During stage II, a company ought to be beginning to develop a formal planning system that includes the basic elements described in Chapter Seven. It also needs a more formal control system to help carry out its plan. It will most likely need to change its basic accounting system to some kind of "responsibility accounting system," which provides information not only on overall financial performance but on product-line profitability and business segment profitability as well.

In stage II, the evaluation and reward component of the control system must also be developed further. Job descriptions specifying responsibilities are required. Some sort of "management by objectives" approach ought to be introduced, accompanied by a formal performance appraisal system. The firm's compensation program also ought to become more systematic and include an incentive component that is linked to performance. Failure to make these changes during stage II may lead to the feeling that the organization is "out of control."

Stage III.   By the time a company has grown to stage III, it requires more sophisticated and powerful methods of control. This is the stage at which the company must develop a formal control system along with other components of its management systems.

As we have noted, planning at stage III needs to be brought down to the level of individual products or profit centers. Similarly, the company's budgeting system needs to be brought down to the level of individual products or profit centers.

The company's accounting information system will typically need to be reconceptualized to provide a greater amount of information for management control. By the time a firm reaches stage III, it ought to have a well-developed set of management reports dealing with the nonaccounting information that is required to monitor the business.

By this stage, performance appraisal linked to management by objectives also ought to be a way of life. A formal performance appraisal system should be in place, and management development programs should have taught the firm's managers how to use it effectively.

If management did not lay the foundation for these systems during stage II, they will be more difficult and costly to develop during stage III. If the firm still has not put the systems into place by the time it reaches the later phase of stage III, it is likely to experience serious growing pains. These may be masked temporarily by continually rising sales if the firm is in a favorable market. Unfortunately, when the market ultimately turns, the company may find itself facing a "scissors effect" of simultaneously reduced revenue and increased costs. This can prove fatal.

Stage IV.   By the time a firm reaches stage IV, its basic organizational control system should be in place. Most of the changes to be made at this stage are (or at least ought to be) merely refinements.

The planning system will become more sophisticated. Moreover, the budget process may be refined to include features such as flexible budgeting (budgeting based on different assumptions about the economy and related level of business). The accounting information system ought to be able to generate accurate, timely, comparative data.

Performance appraisals oriented toward performance against plan should be regularly scheduled, and employees should expect that deviations from standard will require factual explanations.

In short, by the time a company reaches stage IV, its organizational control system ought to be well developed, functioning smoothly, and in place as an integral part of its overall corporate culture.

Conclusion

When an organization passes the size at which the entrepreneur can personally function as its control system, the owner will increasingly be stretched thin, and with the addition of other employees and managers, the need for coordination will grow. There will also be a need for information about problems being encountered in various aspects of operations, including receivables, inventories (if any), and sales. Thus there will be a growing need for formal controls to supplement the personal involvement of the entrepreneur.

Unfortunately, organizations do not have to be very large before it becomes extremely difficult, if not impossible, for the entrepreneur to perform all functions of the control system. In fact, by the time a company reaches $1 million in annual revenue, it becomes highly unlikely that the entrepreneur alone will be able to exercise effective control. This chapter has described the basic concepts that the entrepreneurial firm can use to develop the type of control system required at its particular stage of organizational development.

1 1   Effective Leadership

One of the most critical managerial functions in entrepreneurial organizations is leadership. Effective leadership is a prerequisite not only to successfully making the transition from one stage of a firm's development to another, but for that matter to operating effectively at any stage.

Leadership can have many styles. U.S. managers have come to recognize that Japanese managers use a leadership style different from those used most often in this country. They have also begun to appreciate that there are significant differences in management style among U.S. organizations.[43]

The purpose of this chapter is to provide basic concepts, ideas, and research findings concerning leadership effectiveness. The framework we present is a synthesis of various schools of leadership research. A basic premise underlying our discussion is that the two key factors in effective leadership are (1) the choice of the correct leadership style for a particular situation and (2) the performance of certain key tasks of leadership.

The entrepreneurial manager needs to select a style of leadership appropriate for an organization's current stage of growth. To aid in this selection, we will examine the nature of organizational leadership and point out two different types of leadership relevant to entrepreneurial organizations: strategic leadership and operational leadership. We will then examine a variety of different leadership styles and the factors that must be considered in selecting a leadership style. We will also present some research findings relating to the nature of leadership styles found in entrepreneurial companies. After a brief discussion of leadership theories, we will describe the key tasks an effective leader must perform. Next, we will present some case studies of leadership in actual organizations. Finally, we will consider the nature of effective leadership at different stages of organizational growth.

The Nature of Leadership

Leadership is the process whereby an individual influences the behavior of people in a way that makes them more likely to achieve organizational goals. Under this definition, leadership is an ongoing process, not a set of traits that a person possesses. The process involves understanding, predicting, and controlling others' goal-directed behavior. The leader's ultimate objective is to create a goal-congruent situation—a situation in which employees can satisfy their own needs by seeking to achieve the goals of the organization. Leadership, then, like organizational control, is behaviorally oriented and goal directed.

As noted earlier, two general types of leadership are relevant to the management of entrepreneurial organizations, strategic leadership and operational leadership. *Strategic leadership* is the process of influencing members of an organization to plan for the long-range development of the firm in the six key areas making up the pyramid of organizational development: markets, products and services, resources, operational systems, management systems, and corporate culture. It is oriented toward the development of the organization as a whole and of the organization's ability to function in its environment. Lee Iacocca's performance at Chrysler was a fine example of strategic leadership. *Operational leadership,* in contrast, is the process of influencing the behavior of people to achieve operational goals. This dimension of leadership is concerned with the day-to-day functioning of the enterprise.

Both types of leadership are essential for the long-range survival and growth of an entrepreneurship, yet a single individual may not possess the ability to perform both leadership functions. For this reason, some organizations appoint both a chief executive officer (CEO), who is responsible for strategic leadership, and a chief operational officer (COO), who is responsible for operational leadership. This occurred at Tempo Products, as we explained in Chapter Six.

Styles of Leadership

A quarter century of research has failed to confirm that there is one style of management that is best for all situations. Rather, there are a variety of styles, each of which may be effective or ineffective depending on the circumstances. This notion has been called *contingency theory* or *situational leadership*.[44]

The following pages describe six basic styles of leadership.[45] These styles constitute a continuum that proceeds from a very directive to a very nondirective leadership style, as summarized in Figure 11.1.

It should be pointed out that this is only one of a variety of leadership classification schemes. The major point to draw from it is that in their purest form, these styles are indeed different and may therefore be appropriate for different situations with different personnel.

Figure 11.1. Continuum of Leadership Styles.

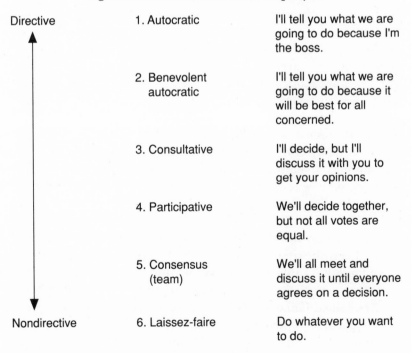

Directive	1. Autocratic	I'll tell you what we are going to do because I'm the boss.
	2. Benevolent autocratic	I'll tell you what we are going to do because it will be best for all concerned.
	3. Consultative	I'll decide, but I'll discuss it with you to get your opinions.
	4. Participative	We'll decide together, but not all votes are equal.
	5. Consensus (team)	We'll all meet and discuss it until everyone agrees on a decision.
Nondirective	6. Laissez-faire	Do whatever you want to do.

The Autocratic Style.   The autocratic style is a very directive style of leadership. A manager who uses this style promotes the notion that he or she has the authority to make all decisions and does not feel the need to explain the decisions' rationale to subordinates. This style can best be characterized by the statement "I will tell you what we're going to do because I'm the boss," or "Look, I'm head of the department; I'm being held responsible. I will tell you what we're going to do, and that's that." This was the style of leadership used by Harold Geneen at ITT. It was also the style of Steven Jobs, when he was at Apple Computer. It is a style commonly observed in Fortune 500 as well as entrepreneurial organizations.

The Benevolent Autocratic Style.   The benevolent autocratic style is a "parental" style of leadership: The leader acts on the assumption that he or she knows what is best for the organization and the individuals involved. The degree of direction used in this style is essentially the same as with the autocratic style, but the style is more benign. A manager who uses this style will usually explain the rationale behind decisions, while an autocratic leader will not. Instead of simply issuing directives, a person adopting this style might say, "I'll tell you what we're going to do, because that will be best for all concerned." Where an autocratic leader might say, "As a condition of coming to work here, you are obliged to accept what I say," a benevolent autocrat might say, "This is what I want you to do, but I've taken your needs into account." This style of leadership was used by the Watsons at IBM. It is also the classic style found in many entrepreneurships during the initial stages of organizational development. For example, it was the style of Jack Tramiel, who was called "Captain Jack" when he was head of Commodore International.

The Consultative Style.   The third style of leadership is qualitatively different, at least to some degree, from the first two. A person adopting this style reserves the right to make the final decision but actively seeks the opinions of others concerned first. To illustrate the difference between this style and the other two, suppose a manager is presenting the organization's goals for the coming year. An individual operating with the autocratic style might say, "This is what we're going to do. These are our goals for next year." A benevolent autocrat might approach the situation with, "This is what the organization needs, and here is how it will affect you." In contrast, a manager utilizing the consultative style might say, "Here is what I think our goals ought to be for the next year. What's your reaction?" This manager will still make the ultimate decision, however. This is a version of the style used by Robert McNamara when he was president of the Ford Motor Company. John Sculley was a consultative leader when he first came to Apple Computer from Pepsico. He stated, "This is what we want to do, but I want your input."

The Participative Style. Inherent in this fourth style of leadership is the idea that a decision should be made on the basis of group input. This does not mean, however, that all votes on an issue are equal. The leader still reserves the right to make the final decision, as in the consultative style.

The basic difference between the participative and consultative styles is the manner in which others' opinions are solicited and used. In the participative style, the group actually helps to develop ideas rather than just giving input on the manager's ideas. In the consultative style, the manager might come into a group and say, "Here is what I think we should do. Give me your reaction." The manager using a participative style, on the other hand, may have an idea about what the group should do but basically will say, "Here are the problems. Let's discuss them together and come up with recommendations. Then I'll make the final decision." In the latter instance, the manager might begin a meeting by expressing his or her own stance, but the group will be allowed to participate in solving the problem by making recommendations. It should be noted that some companies have "mandated" the participative management style. For example, Motorola has "autocratically decided" that it will be a participatively managed company. Managers with fifteen to twenty years of experience were "encouraged" to develop skills as participative leaders. The late Don Estridge, who led the team that created the PC for IBM, used more than one style. However, when IBM made the decision to switch from the 80286 to the 80386 chip, he acted as a participative leader.

Bob Daniel, CEO of United Technologies Corporation (UTC), is a practitioner of the participative style of leadership. He used a participative style in getting UTC to deal with a classic "turnaround" situation. Specifically, he took his executives to a retreat for several days where, with the assistance of an outside consultant as a facilitator, the group analyzed and discussed the situation at UTC. During the process Daniel was more of a listener than a participant. Finally, on the last day, he summarized the group's decisions and said, in effect, "Fine, let's do it." This approach is in sharp contrast to the style used by former UTC CEO Harry Gray, who was a more autocratic manager.

The Consensus (Team) Style. The consensus style represents another qualitative shift along the continuum of styles. A leader adopting this style uses the same format as one utilizing the participative style, but in this case, the leader's vote is virtually equal to all others. This leader does not reserve the right to make the final decision but rather emphasizes the importance of developing group consensus on the matter at hand. A person using the consensus leadership style might say, "Let's meet, discuss the problem, and reach an agreement on its resolution. I will run the group only as a facilitator because I believe that if you all agree to something, you will be highly motivated to achieve it. I will not, therefore, exercise a high degree of authority." A group with a leader who uses this style is thus given more responsibility than in the other styles.

The consensus style can also be thought of as a "team leadership style." This means that the leadership that is frequently exercised by a single individual under the more directive styles of leadership has been delegated as responsibility to a team of individuals. Although this is a complex style, an increasing number of firms have been experimenting with it for a number of years. These include large established firms such as Delta Airlines and entrepreneurial firms such as Compaq Computer. This style has been used very successfully under Rod Canion at Compaq to expand the firm from a new venture into a multibillion-dollar Fortune 500 organization. At Compaq, this leadership style is known as "the process."

The team style of leadership is also used by Jim Stowers, Jr., at Twentieth Century Investors, a mutual fund investment management company with more than $7 billion in assets. Stowers has long believed in the value of a team approach to portfolio management, and has extended this philosophy to the management of the company, where an increasing number of decisions are made by the firm's executive committee operating as a team.

The Laissez-Faire Style. The most nondirective style of leadership, laissez-faire, places the responsibility for task accomplishment completely on the subordinate(s). A leader utilizing this style essentially says, "Do whatever you want to do."

There are two versions of this style, one positive and one negative. A leader operating under the positive version promotes the notion that highly trained individuals do not need a great deal of direction. This type of leader thus gives his or her subordinates considerable independence. Such a leader might say, "You are a professional. You know what your job is. Do whatever you have to do to get it done." The more negative version of the laissez-faire style might be characterized by the statement "Do whatever you want to do. Just leave me alone." This is an "abdocratic" style, an abdication of authority and responsibility. The positive laissez-faire style was used by former President Ronald Reagan, when he was governor of California. Former President Reagan was also criticized for using a negative laissez-faire style while he occupied the White House. The style was also used by Don Estridge in IBM's PC division at Boca Raton. Similarly, it has been used by Fernando Niebla, CEO of Infotec, a rapidly growing entrepreneurial firm in the aerospace industry.

Leadership Styles in Entrepreneurial Organizations. Our research and consulting work has shown a wide variety of leadership styles among CEOs and other managers of entrepreneurial organizations. The most common styles, however, were the consultative and participative styles. The participative style was somewhat more common in high-technology manufacturing and service organizations, while the consultative style was more common in low-technology manufacturing. Perhaps as a reaction to the behavioral literature of the 1960s and 1970s, there seemed to be relatively few managers who used autocratic or benevolent autocratic styles.

Factors Influencing Choice of Leadership Style

It is important to understand that a manager does not have to always use the same leadership style. An individual may adopt a variety of styles, each suited for a particular situation. We have found that consideration of six key factors can help managers in entrepreneurial firms decide which style is best at a given time. The first two factors we will discuss are the most important; they probably account for 80 to 90 percent of the influence on leadership effectiveness in a given situation.

Nature of the Task.   The aspect of a work task that is most important to consider is probably the degree of programmability of the task. If a task is highly programmable (that is, the optimal steps for its completion can or may be specified in advance), then a directive style of leadership is appropriate. If the task is nonprogrammable (that is, the nature of the work necessitates a great deal of variation in individual procedures), a directive style may be difficult or impossible, and a more participative or nondirective style will be required. In other words, the greater the degree of programmability of the task, the more appropriate it is for a manager to say, "This is the right way to do this task; we know it's right because we've studied it and worked out the best way to do it." Where the task is less programmable, the manager must use a more interactive or laissez-faire approach.

Nature of the People Supervised.   This factor is really made up of a variety of subfactors, including people's skill and education levels, their degree of motivation, and their desire for independence on the job. This latter subfactor refers to the degree to which workers prefer to do their jobs on their own and then return with results as opposed to wanting more interaction, feedback, and supervision.

Taken together, all these subfactors can be thought of as a single variable called *potential for job autonomy.* The more highly educated, highly motivated, highly skilled, and in need of independence a person is, the higher his or her potential for job autonomy. Conversely, a person with low motivation, low task-relevant skills, and low need for independence has a low potential for job autonomy.

People with different potentials for job autonomy require managers with different leadership styles. A nondirective style (consensus or laissez-faire) will be most appropriate with workers who have a high potential for job autonomy, while a very directive style is appropriate with workers who have low job autonomy. A more intermediate style of leadership is needed when workers do not fit one or the other extreme. For example, a person who is highly motivated and working at a job that requires a high degree of nonprogrammability but is not very skilled may require a leader who adopts a style somewhere in the middle of the continuum, either consultative or participative, at least until the person becomes more experienced.

Figure 11.2 shows the relationship between the two factors we have just described and the six leadership styles described in the previous section. As can be seen in the figure, a high degree of programmability combined with a low potential for job autonomy would ideally require a directive style. At the other extreme—low programmability and high job autonomy—a nondirective approach would be most effective. The other two cells show intermediate conditions where an interactive approach would best fit the situation.

Supervisor's Style. If a difference exists between a supervisor's preferred leadership style and one or more subordinates' style(s), it will be difficult for the subordinate(s) to justify their own style unless the supervisor allows the use of it. A subordinate may feel a need to change his or her style to make it closer to that of the supervisor. In other words, supervisors have a tendency to consciously or unconsciously evaluate their subordinates on the basis of their own leadership styles. The manager in the superior position in such a situation may need to recognize that people can use different styles and still be effective.

Peers' and Associates' Styles. The dominant style of his or her peer group can also influence a manager's choice of leadership style. For example, if most managers in a particular group use a

Figure 11.2. Factors Affecting Choice of Leadership Style.

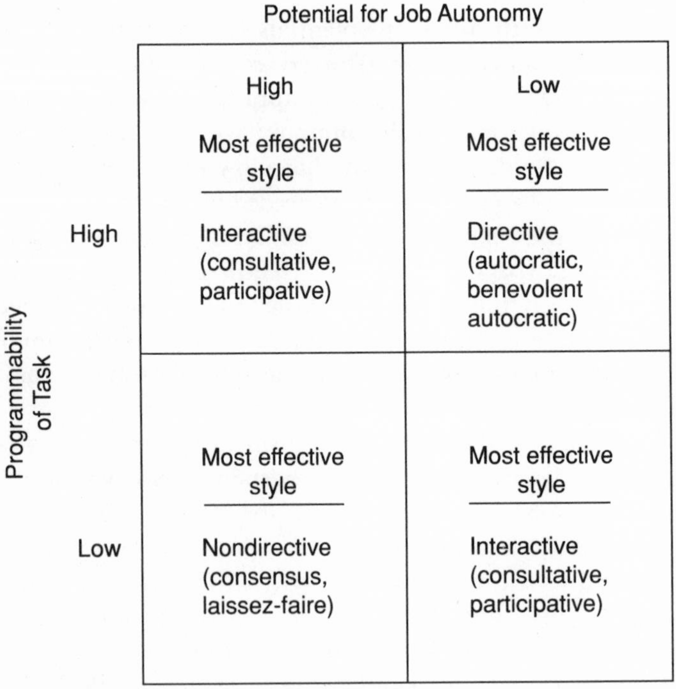

Potential for Job Autonomy

	High	Low
	Most effective style	Most effective style
High	Interactive (consultative, participative)	Directive (autocratic, benevolent autocratic)
	Most effective style	Most effective style
Low	Nondirective (consensus, laissez-faire)	Interactive (consultative, participative)

Programmability of Task (vertical axis label)

consultative style and a few use a benevolent autocratic style, the latter individuals will feel some pressure to change their style to make it more like that of the majority.

Amount of Available Decision Time. People are much more willing to accept a directive leadership style in crisis situations than in situations where nothing needs to be decided in a hurry. If someone in a roomful of people says, "I see smoke," people will not expect to be asked to form groups and discuss alternatives for action. Most individuals will probably be quite comfortable with someone's saying, "Stand up and calmly walk out the door, down the hall, and out into the street."

Nature (Culture) of the Organization. Each organization has norms concerning the type or types of leadership style(s) felt to be appropriate for its members. These norms affect all members of the organization. For example, as noted earlier, Motorola recently autocratically decided that it would become a participatively managed organization. People were asked to change their leadership styles to become participative managers. If they could not or would not, they were explicitly or implicitly encouraged to leave. This organization essentially said, "Look: To compete effectively with the Japanese, we are going to have to be a participative organization, because the kind of people we're attracting want a say in what they're doing. Therefore, we will be participatively managed."

These, then, are the factors that affect the choice of leadership style. They can be analyzed to determine what kind of style would be most appropriate in a particular situation with particular types of personnel.

Leadership Theories

In the study of leadership, the initial emphasis was on attempting to identify the personal characteristics of effective leaders. After more than two decades of research, this approach was abandoned in the mid-1950s because a set of consistently valid and reliable predictive factors could not be identified. This does not mean that such factors absolutely do not exist; it could mean that the statistical tools used were not powerful enough to detect them. In any event, the leadership "trait" theory was abandoned, and a leadership process approach was adopted. This new approach proved to have much greater predictive value.

The leadership process approach is based on the premise that leaders can be developed. Instead of being born with certain personalities, as the trait theory suggested, this approach suggests that leaders can learn what to do to be effective. Further research was then conducted to determine what differentiates effective from ineffective leaders. Two key factors, task orientation and people orientation, were identified as being important characteristics of effective leaders.

For a time, these two factors defined two divergent schools of thought about leadership. The school of neoscientific management argued that concern for task made a leader most effective,

while the "human relations school" argued that concern for people
and their needs was the critical variable. However, empirical research showed that neither factor alone was sufficient to explain
leadership effectiveness. Both factors appear to be important and
independent dimensions of leadership. An effective leader needs to
be concerned about both task performance and the nature of the
people being supervised. These two dimensions of effective "operational" leadership can be subdivided further, as will be discussed
later.

Two Sets of Effective Leadership Tasks

There are two different sets of leadership tasks that must be
performed in organizations. One of these can be termed the "macro"
tasks of leadership. These are tasks of what we can call "strategic
leadership." These include establishing a strategic vision for a firm,
monitoring and managing the process of organizational development, and managing the corporate culture. The other set are the
"micro" tasks. These are the tasks of operational leadership, which
include all of the day-to-day things that must be performed to influence people to produce the products and services that the organization offers to the marketplace.

Key Tasks of Strategic Leadership

There are three key tasks of strategic leadership: (1) strategic
vision, (2) organizational development, and (3) management of corporate culture. Each of these tasks is described in turn.

Strategic Vision. The first task of strategic leadership involves formulating a strategic vision. This is a vision of what the
firm is likely to become. Drawing on the concepts of strategic planning, we can think of it as essentially akin to a mission statement.
For example, under the leadership of Richard Ferris of UAL Corporation, the vision was to have UAL make the transition from an
airline to a full-service travel company. This vision or mission was
the basis for the expansion of UAL in a variety of directions. The
mission led to a concept that was designed to energize the organi-

zation. Unfortunately, Ferris was not able to "sell" his vision either to some key employees within UAL or to the investment community. One key aspect of the strategic vision component of strategic leadership is the vision concept per se, while another dimension is the ability to motivate people to "buy in" to the vision.

Organizational Development. A second key dimension of strategic leadership involves organizational development. In this context, the term *organizational development* refers to the whole process of influencing the members of the organization to build the various key aspects of the pyramid of organizational development that have been described throughout this book. The task of strategic leadership is to motivate the ongoing development of the organization as a way of life. Once the strategic vision has been articulated, the next challenge is to translate that vision into the organization's choices with respect to its markets, products and services, resources, operational systems, management systems, and corporate culture. For example, Rodney Putz, president of Simon Management Company—a division of Melvin Simon & Associates, one of the largest shopping center developers in the United States—initiated an organizational development program designed to help the division continue the transition from an entrepreneurship to a professionally managed firm. In initiating this program, he was performing the organizational development function of strategic leadership.

Management of Corporate Culture. The third key aspect of strategic leadership concerns the management of the firm's culture. As we have previously suggested, one of the key tasks of management is to "manage" the firm's culture. This task ultimately falls to the chief executive officer of an entity, whether it is a corporation as a whole or a subdivision. The execution of this function can, however, be delegated. The next chapter will examine the nature of organizational culture and how it can be managed.

Key Tasks of Operational Leadership

Research has identified five specific tasks that further define the people and task orientations of operational leadership that were described earlier.[46] In other words, to be effective as operational leaders, managers must perform five key tasks, which we will describe in the following pages. Each of these tasks can be effectively performed using any of the leadership styles previously defined. As we have noted, the best style to use depends on the situation.

Goal Emphasis. An effective leader emphasizes the attainment of goals through goal-setting processes, focusing on goals, and monitoring of goals. The late Rensis Likert, an internationally noted behavioral scientist, pointed out that to be effective, a leader has to demonstrate a "contagious enthusiasm for the achievement of organization goals."

Note that in this emphasis on goals, the effective leader's style can range from autocratic to laissez-faire. An autocratic leader might simply say, "Here are our goals." At the other extreme, a laissez-faire leader might say, "Let's agree on what our goals are, then you figure out how to achieve them." At the intermediate level, a person with a participative or consultative style might say, "Here's what I think our goals should be. What do you think?"

One of my favorite examples of the succinct application of goal emphasis was observed in an executive committee meeting at Surgitek, a rapidly growing medical engineering subsidiary of Bristol Meyers. Surgitek's CEO, Bob Helbling, was asked how he might implement the concept of goal emphasis. He turned to the vice president of sales and stated simply, "Sell something."

Interaction Facilitation. An effective leader must be able to coordinate people and facilitate effective interaction among them. An effective leader can either manage meetings or create them in a way that allows people to work together effectively and cooperatively. Someone with a directive leadership style might accomplish this by saying, "We're having a meeting. This is our agenda, and this is what we're going to accomplish." A more nondirective way to do the same thing might be to act as a facilitator at a meeting, helping to summarize what people are doing and asking nondirective questions.

Work Facilitation. The third thing an effective leader does is to help personnel achieve their goals by facilitating their work.

This can be accomplished in a variety of ways, including helping to schedule a task, making suggestions about how it should be done, providing reference materials, and suggesting knowledgeable sources of information regarding task procedure. A very directive way of facilitating work might be to say, "This is the way you should be doing your job." At the other extreme, a person using a laissez-faire style might simply ask nondirective questions or suggest that people look in certain areas for help.

Supportive Behavior. A fourth task of an effective leader is to provide supportive behavior in the form of both positive and negative feedback to subordinates. Positive feedback is important, since it serves to reinforce appropriate goal-oriented behavior and thereby increase the chances that the behavior will continue to be performed. Negative feedback, in the form of expressed dissatisfaction with work and constructive criticism, tends to eliminate dysfunctional behavior.

A directive leader might express supportive behavior with "No, John. Don't do it that way. Do it this way." A person using a more nondirective style might handle a similar situation with "I'm going to have to evaluate what you do on this project. You do a self-assessment at the same time. Then, let's meet and compare notes, and we'll see where we need to go from there." An extremely nondirective approach might be to say, "You've just completed the project. I want you to review your documentation and critique it. What have you done well? What have you done poorly, and how will you better this in the future?"

Personnel Development. The effective leader helps to develop people. He or she motivates people to be concerned about their future development and to analyze their specific needs for development. As was the case with the other factors, the leadership style used to perform this task can range from directive to nondirective, depending on the personnel and the nature of the work being done. A directive approach might be to say, "I think you should go to a management training program." A nondirective approach might be to say, "What do you see as your developmental needs? I want you to think about them and to decide what you want to do to meet them."

Performance of Key Leadership Tasks in Entrepreneurial Organizations. Our research with entrepreneurial organizations has led to certain general findings. We have noted, first, that there is a consistent underemphasis on the leadership task of goal emphasis in such organizations. Perhaps because entrepreneurs are so goal oriented themselves, they may expect their subordinates to be equally goal oriented and therefore they may not perceive the need for further direction. Second, we have found a consistent tendency for the supportive behavior task to be performed in entrepreneurial firms to a somewhat greater extent than is usual. The larger the firm, the more emphasis it is likely to place on this task.

Case Studies of Leadership

The previous sections have presented a framework for understanding leadership effectiveness. This section examines some case studies of actual managers facing particular leadership problems in organizations of different sizes.

The Erik Brandin Case. Erik Brandin is a relatively young man who became the general manager of his family's business, Copyspot. Copyspot is a rapidly growing firm specializing in the quick copy and quick print business. The firm was founded by Erik's parents, Bob and Evie Brandin.

Erik got into the firm in a classic entry-level position. He learned the firm from the ground up, doing everything from sweeping the floors to working on the machines and serving customers.

In the mid-1980s, Bob and Evie Brandin were getting ready to turn the business over to their son. However, Erik had not received any formal management training or development. Since he did not have any background as a manager outside of his experiences at Copyspot or any formal training, Erik developed his own concepts of what was appropriate to do to be effective as a leader. As he states, "My idea of being a leader was to be the best at everything that had to be done. I had to be able to do everything that was required in the firm. I hoped that I could lead by example." This concept of leadership led Erik to be a classic "doer." Instead of being a "hands-on manager" in the sense that he was still involved in the operational aspects of the business, Erik did all the operational aspects of the business. Unfortunately, he did not become a role model for people in the organization. Instead, people simply let him do everything that had to be done. As he says, "It was a classic case of the tail wagging the dog."[47]

While Erik was so busy with all of the operational aspects of the business, the longer-range aspects required to build an effective business were being neglected—that is, there was little focus on the organizational development task of strategic leadership. Although some of the operational systems were in place, the firm lacked most of the management systems required. There was no planning. The organizational structure was ill defined. There were no control systems. There was no management development. There was a corporate culture but it was unmanaged.

The firm had experienced rapid growth. At one point, it doubled in size, going from $1 million to $2 million in a very short time. However, in spite of the increase in revenues it was earning less at that point than it had previously. The family began scratching its collective head, wondering what had gone wrong.

Erik and his family decided that he needed to become more effective as a manager, and they sought outside assistance to help him develop. During his management development process, Erik was exposed to the leadership framework that has been presented in this chapter. He learned that there were a variety of different styles of management, and he came to realize that he was using the laissez-faire style. He also learned about the various key tasks of leadership effectiveness that had to be performed and was able to identify those he was underemphasizing.

At first, Erik made a 180° switch from a laissez-faire to an autocratic style of leadership. As he describes it, "I went from being a nondirective manager to being a version of Mussolini." Over time he began to moderate his style of leadership and began to use the whole range of leadership styles available as a manager. He began to focus more on the functions of strategic leadership. He initiated a planning process that led to the development of the strategic plan for Copyspot. He focused on organizational development in terms of the operational and management systems of the firm. He organized the firm in terms of a series of profit centers, with each of four departments being their own profit center. He established control systems to motivate the managers to focus on their contribution to profitability. The managers were motivated to contribute to the firm's performance because their bonuses depended on their contribution to profits. He instituted other control systems dealing with operational aspects of efficiency.

One significant difficulty Erik faced was in coming to terms with the need to deal with conflict. Prior to Erik's development as a manager, people might well come late but little was done as a consequence. People might mess up a job or irritate a customer and there were few consequences. Once he understood that his role included goal emphasis, supportive behavior, and personnel development as key tasks of operational leadership and that he needed to overcome the problems involving the need to be liked (discussed in Chapter Nine), Erik became more willing to deal with the issues that inevitably occur on a day-to-day basis. As he stated, "I was too nice a guy to deal with conflict. I was a lousy manager but I was a very nice guy."

At Copyspot the transition of Erik Brandin from a doer to a manager—which included learning how to be an effective leader— was the catalyst for a transition of the firm as a whole from an entrepreneurship to a entrepreneurially oriented professionally managed firm.

The George Frazer Case.   George Frazer was president of Helix Inc., a rapidly growing company that produced high-technology components for a specialized market. George's partner in the enterprise was its founder, Charlie Bowman. Charlie was the idea man whose designs had led to the development of new products. He had brought George in to manage the business on a day-to-day basis.

Before his exposure to the framework on leadership effectiveness presented in this chapter, George was managing the R&D department and Charlie was managing the manufacturing function. This arrangement seemed logical to both individuals since Charlie had the detailed background and knowledge of the product, while George had been an engineer himself and was responsible for supervising the other engineers as well as the administrative aspects of the firm.

Unfortunately the firm was experiencing a wide variety of difficulties. The problems ranged from unsatisfactory profitability (the firm was actually incurring a loss) to morale problems among the staff.

When George and Charlie reviewed their own styles in light of the continuum of leadership styles presented above, George concluded that he could be classified as a classic autocrat, while Charlie could be thought of as a laissez-faire manager. Charlie might even be thought of as an "abdocrat." If we examine the nature of the situation in which George and Charlie were managers, we see that George was supervising highly motivated, highly experienced engineers and scientists who did not want or need a great deal of direction. This conflicted with his style as an autocrat. Charlie was supervising a wide range of people in manufacturing. Some of these were highly experienced operators, but most were relatively new and inexperienced. They required a great deal of direction and training.

One option available to the entrepreneurs was to develop new leadership styles. George would have to develop a more non-directive leadership approach, while Charlie would have to become more directive. Another option available was for them to simply reverse roles, with George assuming responsibility for manufacturing—which required greater direction—and Charlie assuming responsibility for R&D. Given the needs of the firm, they chose the latter alternative.

In less than sixty days after the organizational change took place, there was a fundamental change in the situation at Helix. As George stated, "I'm now running manufacturing and telling everybody what to do and they think I'm training them. Charlie, on the other hand, is sitting in his cubicle reading technical magazines and drinking coffee and ignoring the R&D staff, and they think that's just great." In addition to the change in morale, the company turned its profit situation around in very short order. This case study illustrates the very significant impact of leadership effectiveness on a firm's bottom line.

The Ken Walker Case. With an engineering degree in hand, Ken Walker obtained an MBA degree at a very prestigious institution. He was bright and articulate. After a period of considerable success in a number of organizations, he found himself as the president of a rapidly growing high-technology company. The company, which had been purchased by a Fortune 500 organization, was semiautonomously managed by its parent. The firm was expected to prepare a strategic plan and to submit it for approval, but day-to-day operations were left to the direction of the senior management of the entrepreneurial subsidiary. The firm's revenue had grown rapidly, and it was a classic stage III firm with revenues in the range of $50 to $100 million.

In his M.B.A. program, Ken had learned about the benefits of "participative management." He understood that there was a great deal of research that indicated that when people participated in making decisions they were likely to experience a sense of "ownership" of those decisions, and would be more motivated to help implement them. Accordingly, throughout his career he had attempted to use participative leadership to the maximum extent feasible.

The situation he faced at Technology Systems Corporation, where he was president, was a bit more complex. He reported to an individual by the name of John Mortenson, who was the group vice president and was responsible for overseeing a number of subsidiary companies including Technology Systems. As is typical of any large Fortune 500 company, there were certain things that Mortenson found he had to tell Ken to do simply to be consistent with overall corporate policy, procedure, and direction. Still, however, Ken felt it was best if he tried to get people to "buy in" to these decisions. As a result, at the weekly executive committee meeting that the firm conducted, Ken would present problems and ask all of his senior executives to participate in making the decisions. For many of these decisions, the participative approach worked quite well. However, there were times when decisions that were reached by the executive committee could simply not be implemented because of constraints of meeting the requirements imposed by John Mortenson and the parent company. Instead of addressing this issue directly, Ken would simply bring the issue back up the group and try to guide the discussion in such a way that the group ultimately reached a decision that would be acceptable to John and the parent company.

Over time people came to perceive that Ken's style was not really one of true participative leadership. They realized that whenever a decision was reached that Ken felt uncomfortable with, for whatever reason, he would keep bringing the decision back to the executive committee. Finally, as a result of an organizational development and team building effort, Ken was provided feedback that people were aware of this situation and found it frustrating. They felt that too many hours were wasted in meetings reaching "decisions" that were not really true decisions.

After considering this problem, Ken decided on a different approach. He announced to the group that henceforth there would be several different categories of decisions. One type of "decision" would be those in which he had to adopt a benevolent autocratic style. This meant that he would present to the group what he felt had to be done given the various constraints that the firm was operating under. He would explain why it had to be done and what the rationale and what the benefits were for everyone concerned. These were to be known as *benevolent autocratic decisions*. In turn, he expected the members of the senior executive group to support those decisions to the maximum extent feasible. The second category of decisions were those he termed *consultative decisions*. Consultative decisions were to be those where he had a strong view of what needed to be done, but could be convinced to change his view if the discussion presented strong enough arguments. The third category of decisions were *participative decisions*. These were to be decisions in which the group could meet and decide as a group but he had to retain the right to make the final decision. The fourth category of decisions were to be *consensus or team decisions*. These would be decisions in which the executive committee would meet as a group and reach whatever decision the group felt was appropriate, and his vote would simply be one of the group. While this system of leadership was not a panacea, it resulted in the elimination of what had become a time-consuming process, as well as a process that had become damaging to morale.

The Richard Ferris Case.   As noted in Chapter Seven, when Richard Ferris was CEO of UAL Corporation, he was known as a forceful leader who held strong opinions. He was not known for his ability to build consensus for his views, but, rather, he expected people to support the direction he provided.

Ferris was brilliant in one function of strategic leadership but unsuccessful in another at UAL. His basic strategic vision was to have UAL make the transition from an airline company to a diversified travel company.

On the strength of this vision, UAL put together a company that included United Airlines, Hertz, Westin Hotels, and the Hilton International hotel chain. This provided the traveler with transportation as well as lodging. In addition, the company had acquired the company that ran its "frequent flier" program (Mileage Plus— known as MPI) and also had its own travel company, Apollo Travel.

Travelers had an incentive to utilize all of UAL's components because the Mileage Plus program gave credit for mileage when cars were rented from Hertz or the traveler stayed at Westin or Hilton International hotels.

Unfortunately, the brilliance of the strategic vision articulated by Ferris was not matched by equal skill in managing people at UAL. He did not get the support of the pilots and other key people at the airline company. In fact, he alienated many people. Moreover, he did not "sell" his concept to the Wall Street community, and UAL's stock did not reflect the potential value of his strategic concept.

In the late 1980s Ferris changed the name of UAL to "Allegis" to reflect the company's reorientation to a diversified travel company rather than merely an airline. Soon afterward, he was forced out and the company's name was changed back to UAL. Hertz, Westin, and Hilton International were sold. Ferris's strategic vision was completely dismantled, not because it did not work, but because of a lack of diplomat-level leadership skills to key internal and external constituencies.

Effective Leadership at Different Stages
of Organizational Growth

Previous sections of this chapter have presented the basic concepts and research findings concerning leadership effectiveness that are relevant to managers in entrepreneurial organizations. This section deals with the question of how leadership should differ at various stages of organizational growth.

The task of leadership in rapidly growing organizations needs to be viewed from two different perspectives. First, one of the central problems of an organization is to choose the style of leadership that is appropriate to the "situation" in which the organization finds itself. During the first two stages of organizational growth, we typically find that an organization requires a great deal of nurturing and an open-ended commitment on the part of senior managers to enable it to survive. This tends to be accompanied by a more directive style of leadership. Typically we will find entrepreneurial organizations in which the autocratic or benevolent autocratic styles of leadership are used during these stages.

As the organization grows to stage III and becomes professionalized, it tends to bring in functional specialists and people with greater experience. These people usually have significant ideas of their own about how organizations can be managed, and if the organization is to benefit from their abilities, the style of leadership must be transformed from a more directive style to a more interactive or even a nondirective style. In the latter stages of organizational growth—stages III through VI—we typically see a range of styles from consultative through laissez-faire.

In stage VII, which is concerned with the revitalization of organizations, we may again see the initiation of an autocratic or benevolent autocratic style of leadership.[48] At this stage, the organization is in crisis, and the situation requires some decisive action. At this point, people are more willing to accept direction, and even expect it. Hence, when Lee Iaccoca came into Chrysler he was expected to provide decisive—that is, directive—leadership. He was brought in because he had knowledge of the automobile industry and presumably the leadership capabilities to help Chrysler overcome its crisis.

We will now take a closer look at the leadership requirements during stages I through IV.

Stage I. During the first stage of organizational development, it is likely that the entrepreneur, either individually or together with a small team, will be responsible for all major decisions in the organization. This will include both operational and strategic decisions. It is also likely that the entrepreneur will be in the best position to make most of those decisions. He or she will have an open-ended commitment to the business, and the firm will still be small enough for the entrepreneur to be on top of almost everything. Accordingly, it is likely that the benevolent autocratic or autocratic style of leadership will be used and will be acceptable to most members of the organization.

At this stage, the entrepreneur will probably be concerned more with work facilitation and supportive behavior than with the other key leadership tasks. While the organization is relatively small, goal emphasis will occur almost by osmosis—that is, by day-to-day interaction of employees with the founder(s). Since there will be relatively few people, formal interaction facilitation also will not be necessary. People will interact in the natural course of their transactions. Similarly, personnel development will occur simply as a by-product of on-the-job training and probably will not require formal training programs.

Stage II. During stage II, it is likely that the style of leadership used in stage I will still be reasonably effective. However, emphasis will increasingly have to be placed on the performance of the five key tasks of leadership.

It is surprising how soon the clarity of goals begins to break down as organizations increase in size. An organization does not even have to exceed $1 million in annual revenues before this lack of clarity can arise. Thus there will be an increasing need for goal emphasis. Similarly, even with a relatively small number of people, a growing need for interaction facilitation will occur. Meetings for the purpose of communication rather than for making decisions will have to start being regularly scheduled. During this stage the entrepreneur's time will be increasingly filled, but the need for work facilitation will not diminish. Since the organization will be high on its own adrenalin, the need for positive support may not be intense, but the rapid growth of the enterprise will lead to hiring mistakes and, therefore, to an increased need for corrective feedback (a part of support). The need for personnel development will also be increasing during this growth stage.

Stage III. The critical factor in leadership effectiveness during stage III will be the need to begin to make a transition from a directive style to a more interactive style, such as the consultative or participative style. This means that the entrepreneur must begin to give up some degree of control and learn how to delegate authority rather than merely delegating tasks. Delegation of tasks involves telling people what you want them to do, while delegation of authority means letting people be responsible for an area—letting them have a say in setting the goals to be achieved as well as in deciding how those goals are to be accomplished.

The transition in the style of leadership that must be made at this stage is complex, and many entrepreneurs never accomplish it. Their failure in this regard places their companies in jeopardy, because organizations outgrow the entrepreneurs' ability to make all decisions. (Changes in leadership style that a CEO must make during this transition are discussed further in Chapter Fourteen.)

Entrepreneurs during stage III need to begin developing a trained cadre of managers to whom they can feel comfortable in delegating authority. They need to make sure that these managers know how to perform the five key leadership tasks.

Stage IV. The key leadership need in stage IV is to articulate and spread the company's culture through the organization. This means that managers must be trained to use a more participative or consultative style with their subordinates. The leader also needs to help create and transmit a shared vision of what the company is to become. When the company was smaller, the concept of its future direction could be communicated more informally. By the time a firm reaches stage III or stage IV, however, senior management must exercise the process of strategic leadership to develop and communicate this common vision. This can be done through the strategic planning process described in Chapter Seven.

Summary

This chapter has defined leadership as a process and has presented information that should help managers make that process more effective. It identified six different leadership styles, ranging from very directive to very nondirective. It noted that there is no one most effective style; the most effective leadership style in a particular situation is determined by a variety of factors, including the nature of the task being performed and the nature of the people being supervised.

This chapter also discussed the key tasks that effective leaders perform. Effective leaders are both task oriented and people oriented. In performing the function of strategic leadership, effective leaders articulate a vision, focus on organizational development, and manage the corporate culture. In performing the function of operational leadership, they emphasize goals, facilitate interaction and work, are supportive of personnel, and encourage personnel development.

Each manager has the potential ability to choose a leadership style to fit any situation and group of people. This ability can be improved by increased awareness of the factors that influence the choice of effective leadership style and by increased development of the skills needed to accomplish the tasks that effective leaders perform.

12 Corporate Culture Management

Chapter Six provided a brief introduction to corporate culture and its management through the use of a case study. In this chapter, we focus on defining corporate culture and providing you with some tools for managing your own corporate culture.

Although the concept of corporate culture is abstract and may seem somewhat elusive, it is nonetheless real and can have a decisive impact on corporate success and profitability. Every organization, from a small entrepreneurship to a multibillion-dollar firm, has a corporate culture whether it knows it or not. The corporate culture is much like a personality in that it changes over time as a result of a firm's own development or changes in the environment that, at times, may send conflicting messages. As we stated in Chapter Seven, for example, strategic planning can shape the culture through providing a vision. However, if the organization's performance appraisal process (a control system) does not reward individuals for pursuing that vision, individuals will receive conflicting messages about their organization's culture and will be left to select their own meaning.

The basic issue is that unless the cultural change process is adequately managed, a firm may find itself with a culture that does not support the goals it wants to or needs to achieve.

In this chapter, we first describe the elements of corporate culture and how culture is manifested in organizations. Next, we provide a description of how culture changes and how this change process can be managed to maintain an organization's effectiveness as it grows. In the final section of this chapter, we describe the nature of corporate culture at different stages of growth.

The Nature of Corporate Culture

As previously defined, corporate culture consists of values, beliefs, and norms. Values are the things an organization considers most important with respect to its operations, its employees, and its customers. These are the things an organization holds most dear— the things for which it strives and the things it wants to protect at all costs. Beliefs are assumptions individuals hold about themselves, their customers, and their organization. Norms are unwritten rules of behavior that address such issues as how employees dress and interact. The corporate culture is, in essence, a guide to behavior as well as a mechanism for creating expectations for the future with respect to rewards and action.

While values, beliefs, and norms are constructed around a range of organizational variables, we believe that how the corporate culture is defined with respect to three areas has the most impact on an organization's success. These areas are (1) customer orientation, (2) orientation toward employees, and (3) standards of performance.

Customer-Client Orientation. The importance attached to how the company views its customers or clients as well as the assumptions employees hold about the nature of their customers and clients can have a profound impact on how the company operates and thus on its success.

In the early days of the personal computer industry, for example, it was assumed that the customer was someone very much like the founder of most personal computer companies (a belief). He or she was a hobbyist who enjoyed tinkering with electronic gadgets, and the company's only responsibility was to give the customer the minimum essentials for him or her to develop a do-it-yourself system. There was little emphasis on quality or service and, in fact, many of the early products offered few features and often were "dead on arrival." The focus of the early entrepreneurs in this industry was more on creating a product than on satisfying customers and growing a business (a value). To support this view of the customer, norms developed around product advertising and selling. Most products were sold through advertisements in technical journals, and frequently the product was, at best, only in the initial stages of development at the time the advertisements were placed. Products were sold through the mail or by word of mouth, and in conversations with customers as well as in advertisements, the technical specifications of the product were emphasized rather than "what the product could do." The latter was the responsibility of the customer.

As the industry matured and the customer base began to include people other than computer enthusiasts, the most successful companies developed (or in the case of IBM, maintained) an emphasis on customer service and a desire to meet customer needs through the products they offered. If the company was to grow, customers now had to be viewed as technically unsophisticated with a desire to buy and utilize a "friendly" system to solve complex problems. The customer became a valued member of the product-design team in at least an indirect way as companies began to rally around the value of "listening to our customers" rather than the earlier "selling our customers what we think they need." Norms developed to support this shift, including the tendency to now emphasize service and capabilities instead of the technical aspects of the product, training to assist employees in better meeting customer needs, and methods for collecting information about customer needs. Unfortunately, even companies like IBM, which has traditionally placed a tremendous emphasis on customer service, failed to listen to its customers and produced at least three personal computer products (including the PCjr and Portable Computer) that customers did not want. The company suffered as a result.

Some companies have been very effective at developing and communicating to their employees their values with respect to customers. Employees at Disneyland, for example, refer to their customers as "guests." The word was chosen carefully to send a message to Disneyland employees about the company's customer orientation. It is intended to have an impact on the way employees interact with customers and, in fact, employees are trained to make customers feel "at home." The goal is customer satisfaction, which hopefully will encourage them to return to the park in the future.

Employee Orientation. The second critical cultural area is the view people hold about themselves and others within the organization itself. Again, as was true with customer orientation, there are two components to the value: how people are viewed with respect to their roles within the firm and how important people feel. Some companies devote a great deal of effort to satisfying employee needs and making them feel valued. At the extreme, these organizations develop a strong competitive team spirit that is directed at other companies and even at departments within the same company. At the other end of the spectrum are those companies in which employees are viewed as replaceable. Somewhere in between are companies where some employees are considered valuable assets (by themselves and everyone else) but where other employees are considered "second-class citizens."

As discussed in Chapter One, IBM has traditionally emphasized commitment to employees. Employees are made to feel like a member of the IBM family, and the belief is fostered that the company will "take care" of employees. This is supported, in part, by IBM's practice of lifetime employment that has survived even in the face of declining profitability. The result of this belief and the value IBM places on its people is a strong commitment and loyalty to the organization.

After the IBM PC became an overnight success, the leader of the task force that developed this product, Philip D. "Don" Estridge, was approached by several other personal computer firms (including Apple Computer and Sun Microsystems) and offered salaries as much as four times what he was making at IBM. He turned down all of the offers, in essence because of his commitment and loyalty to the IBM family. Unfortunately, other members of the original PC team had not been so affected by IBM's culture. While the employees of IBM-component and software manufacturers were growing rich from their efforts, IBM provided PC team members with one-shot "merit award" cash bonuses, which had no effect on salaries or benefit packages. Further, the corporate office began to move "outsiders" into key positions in the PC group, thus reducing the autonomy and authority that had been a significant incentive for many individuals. The actions sent the message to many members of the PC team that they were no longer as valued by the company for the contribution they had made. The end result was that many members left the company.[49]

As was the case with IBM's PC division, it is fairly easy to identify organizations that have problems with their orientation toward employees, because these firms usually experience very high turnover. Conversely, organizations that are successful at making employees feel valued (by whatever means) tend to experience relatively low turnover. (We do not wish to imply that employee orientation is the *only* cause of turnover, but it is often a significant one.) Compaq Computer devotes a great deal of attention to hiring employees that will "fit in" with their culture and then helping these employees feel valued through the input they have into decisions. Their strategy seems to work because they have one of the lowest turnover rates in the industry.

A variety of norms are associated with this cultural variable. How employees dress defines who they are in an organization. In the early days of the personal computer business, the standard "uniform" for employees at Apple Computer (and other PC firms) was a T-shirt and jeans. The message communicated was that the atmosphere at the company was relatively unstructured and it allowed people the freedom to be creative. Employees who violated this dress code were viewed as outsiders and, hence, John Sculley took great care when he arrived at the company from Pepsico to change from suits to the more casual attire that was consistent with Apple's culture.

Performance Standards. Performance standards include things like what and how much employees are held accountable for, the level of quality expected in products, and the expected level of customer satisfaction.

Accountability. In some companies, employees believe that they are held accountable only for coming to work on time. In others, employees are held accountable for achieving goals that will assist the organization in meeting its mission. Sometimes the defintion of accountability can become distorted, as was the case in one $35 million high-technology manufacturing company that had traditionally placed a high value on "commitment." Over time, employees came to believe that commitment meant spending eight to nine hours a day at work, regardless of what they were doing during that time period.

The norm was to come to work early and to never leave the office prior to 5:00 (if possible staying until 5:30) as a way of showing commitment. While the company had many employees "working," they were having difficulty meeting their goals because employees were focused on an inappropriate standard of performance.

Quality. With respect to quality, at one extreme, quality takes a backseat to increasing the bottom line while at the other, companies find themselves in financial difficulty because they want to offer their customers only "perfect products" (for example, "No product will be released before its time"). IBM's commitment to customer service and product quality is exemplified in what came to be known as the "Power Supply Brigade."[50] Just before the official introduction of the PC in August 1981, a problem was discovered with its power supply that could result in an electric shock being administered to the user. The PC team decided that they would fly a team of engineers from product center to product center to install a piece of insulation that would prevent the problem from occurring in any of the products once released. While they feared that customers would view this in a less than favorable light (the release of a product with quality problems), the opposite occurred: Customers viewed it as showing that the company really valued service. In contrast, at a much smaller high-technology company, each employee wore a button stating that "Alpha Corporation loves contented customers." Yet when faced with a product problem just prior to its introduction, senior management said: "Ship it. We'll fix it after it's been delivered." The company knowingly released defective products, which sent the message to employees that quality really was not valued. Subsequently, employees smirked whenever there were discussions about quality.

Customer Service. With respect to customer satisfaction, some companies—as was true of firms in the early years of the personal computer industry—believe that customers will be satisfied with whatever product is offered, while others believe that there is a need to achieve a high degree of customer satisfaction and have designed systems to promote this.

As previously mentioned, the performance standards in the

early days of the personal computer industry were low in terms of quality and reliability of products. Customers were satisfied with whatever they could get in terms of products and technology. As the industry matured, however, those companies that continued to adhere to "hobbyist" standards of performance for both products and employees found themselves on the brink of Chapter Eleven. Even though it survived as a company, Texas Instruments lost hundreds of millions of dollars in the home computer business because it failed to listen to what its customers wanted with respect to products and service.

At the other extreme, the dramatic success of People Express—before it experienced difficulties in coping with growing pains—was due, at least in part, to a major emphasis on customer service. Similarly, Nordstrom, which operates in a highly competitive market, has an emphasis on customer service that has played a major role in its success.

How an organization defines and manages each aspect of its corporate culture can have a profound impact on its success, as will be discussed in the remainder of this chapter.

The Impact of Corporate Culture on Organizational Success

Culture influences every aspect of the pyramid of organizational development, and every level of the pyramid has an impact on culture. This is illustrated by the value one $500 million manufacturing firm placed on relationships. One of the reasons this firm had grown so large and been so successful was because of the relationships that it had developed and maintained with its customers. As the firm grew, this became not only an important part of the firm's culture with respect to customers, but also with respect to its employees. Rewards and, in fact, the organizational structure reflected the value placed on forming effective relationships. On the company's organization charts, there seemed to be no consistent use of the titles given to positions at each level of the organization. Reporting to the president were vice presidents, executive vice presidents, and senior vice presidents. While the responsibilities of these positions did not vary a great deal, the titles were different. So, what explained the variation in titles? In talking with people at the company, it appeared that those individuals at any level that had developed the best relationships with those at the next level were rewarded with the most desirable titles. The cultural belief was, "Success depends on developing good relationships," and the structure reflected this.

In this example, the structure developed out of the culture, but in other cases the culture is influenced by the structure. This implies that since culture supports and is supported by all levels of the pyramid of organizational development, an organization cannot just simply decide to change its corporate culture without making changes in its operations and structure. Organizations that focus on culture and ignore these other areas are wasting their resources. If, for example, a firm decides it is going to make the transition to a culture that rewards planning, but fails to design and implement a strategic planning system in which individuals are rewarded for their performance, the culture will remain unchanged.

Real Versus Nominal Corporate Culture

Many organizations develop "culture" or "philosophy" statements that articulate their values, beliefs, and norms. These may be displayed on walls or in employee handbooks, and if an employee is asked about his or her company's culture, these sheets of paper appear. Unfortunately for many companies, the information printed on the pieces of paper is, at best, a slight exaggeration of the company's real culture and, at worst, a wish list of what the company would like to be but is not. In the case of Apple Computer, for example, in the early 1980s there was a well-articulated statement of "Apple Values," but the real culture included some beliefs that detracted from the company's performance. In the case of U.S. automobile companies in the 1960s, the nominal culture was that "We produce the best automobiles in the world," while the real culture was, "If you can get it to drive out the door we can sell it." The real culture ultimately led to the irreversible entry of Japanese automobile manufacturers into the U.S. market.[51]

We refer to the statements presented on paper as the "nominal" culture and the culture that people actually operated under as the "real" culture. The difference between the "nominal" and the "real" cultures of a rapidly growing $25 million manufacturing firm is illustrated in Table 12.1 The nominal culture suggest that this firm has some very positive values and beliefs that support its continued success. The problem is, however, that people's behavior is influenced by the real culture. The real culture led people to "hide" product-related problems rather than solve them (that is, to avoid conflict and responsibility); to blame other people when things went wrong; and to focus their attention on the bottom line because "as long as the product is selling, we must be making money."

At this company, the system and structure were not in place to support what the company wanted its culture to be—in other words, the culture was not being effectively managed—and the result was that this company could not effectively influence people's behavior to achieve its goals. Among other things, it did not have a well-defined system to reward people for doing what it needed them to do, and there was no quality control system in place. Further, quality control personnel were viewed as unneeded interruptions rather than as important members of the production team.

As this case illustrates, the real culture is not the antithesis of the nominal culture; rather, it merely bears no relationship to it. The real culture of any organization can be identified by examining a variety of factors. These "manifestations" of culture are discussed in the next section.

Table 12.1. Nominal Versus Real Culture: An Example.

Nominal Organizational Culture
1. Quality products.
2. Ethical dealings with vendors.
3. High quality of working life for the employee.

Real Organizational Culture
1. The firm is sales oriented rather than profit oriented.
2. Current standards of performance seem to be unrealistic.
3. The company appears overly optimistic abouts its capabilities.
4. There is a lack of accountability.
5. Personnel tend to avoid conflict.

Manifestations of Corporate Culture

An organization's culture is manifested in a variety of ways. Aside from people's behavior, an organization's culture is reflected in (1) the language people use; (2) the things that act as symbols and the meaning attached to them; (3) the rituals performed within the company; and (4) the rewards provided by the company as well as the recipients of these rewards (known as "heroes"). Each of these will be discussed below.

Language. The words and phrases people use to refer to themselves, events, or the organization are manifestations of the organization's culture. At Domino's Pizza, the company's success is reflected in their jargon, which is called "Dominese" and which permeates the corporation and fosters the culture of teamwork and recognitic n for performance. As previously mentioned, Disneyland employees refer to customers as "guests." In addition, they refer to themselves as "cast members." This communicates to all employees, even the maintenance people, that they are like actors playing their defined role within the organization.

Organizations also use language to give special meaning to events. For example, when the number of employees doubled at Apple Computer in a period of three months in 1980, this came to be known as the "Bozo explosion," because of the influx of experienced managers and engineers. The hobbyists who were the original "family members" at Apple believed that these "professional managers and engineers"—dubbed "bozos"—would destroy the entrepreneurial spirit. To reinforce their point, the Apple loyalists created pins with pictures of Bozo the clown with a line through his face.

Culture is also manifested in the language used to talk about the organization itself. With respect to organizational development, perhaps the most feared word is *bureaucracy.* The meaning attached to this word for many employees of entrepreneurships is that of a slow-moving dinosaur that seldom gets anything accomplished. The problem is that "bureaucracy" often becomes equated with "professionalized," even though the latter is a state to be desired and an organizational form that is necessary for continued success. Managing language during the transition process, then, can be critical.

Symbols. Things within an organization to which special meaning is attached are known as *symbols*. Depending on the organization, symbols may include furniture, awards, and dress (uniform). In many companies, the type of furniture or office an individual has symbolizes his or her value to an organization. In one $100 million manufacturing firm, the type of telephone people had was a significant symbol of status. One individual, who occupied an open cubicle, lobbied very strongly for a speakerphone because this symbolized a higher status than the traditional phone that had been provided. While a speakerphone was somewhat impractical in an open environment, the meaning attached to the phone was so strong that its practicality was secondary in this individual's mind.

If managed properly, symbols can be used to motivate people to achieve the organization's goals. At Knapp Communications (whose management development program was the subject of Chapter Nine), H. Steven Cranston, the former president, gave people a small "K" pin for exceptional service to the company. When these pins started appearing around the company, employees would come to Cranston asking what it took to earn a "K." To earn a "K," in fact, an individual had to work toward achieving the organization's goals. This activity, in turn, reinforced the company's culture.

Symbols can also serve to communicate the organization's values to the outside world. For example, Don Estridge, head of IBM's PC division, began giving his managers a red rosette lapel pin as a morale booster and to symbolize that they were part of something special. The red rosette came to symbolize the PC division to the outside world: At product introductions, members of the team could be identified by the single rosebud they wore on their lapel.

Rituals. Special events and traditional ways of doing things are what we refer to as rituals in companies. Examples of corporate rituals include retirement parties, company picnics, Silicon Valley's afternoon beer busts, and annual meetings. Generally, rituals are intended to communicate the values and beliefs related to a company's people orientation.

A few years ago, we were able to witness the retirement "ritual" at General Ribbon, a manufacturing firm. We were in a meeting with Bob Daggs, the president, and he informed us that we would have to break in about ten minutes because he needed to be at an employee meeting in the company's cafeteria. He explained that one of the company's employees was retiring. When we arrived in the cafeteria, it was already filled with employees sitting and standing along the walls. The retiree was seated at one of the tables nearest the front; the table was otherwise empty. The president asked us to be seated at the table, and he approached a microphone that had been set up in the front of the room. Bob explained why they were there (basically to honor a loyal and long-term employee), mentioned the employee's years of service, and called her up to the microphone. He thanked her for her contribution and presented her with a pen-and-pencil set embellished with the company logo, and an envelope containing a monetary gift. He then told the employees that there were donuts and coffee for everyone and that they should say good-bye to the retiring employee. It is difficult to capture the spirit of the event, but the goodwill of all was evident.

While the entire presentation lasted no more than fifteen minutes, the values and beliefs it communicated and reinforced were much longer lasting. First, it showed that the company values all of its employees and their service. Second, it reinforced the belief that loyalty and service will be rewarded. Third, it indicated that the company believes its employees are part of a family. The sharing of food (in this case simply coffee and donuts) added to the family atmosphere. Finally, it suggested that the leadership of the company is interested in and concerned about its employees.

Like other aspects of culture, however, rituals must be managed, or the values and beliefs they are intended to reinforce can become distorted. At Apple Computer, for example, the annual meetings served as "pep" rallies for employees as much as to present the company's latest products and report on profitability. At the 1985 meeting, the Macintosh product team sat in the front row of the auditorium, while members of the Apple II product team were forced to watch the proceedings on closed-circuit television a few blocks away. Further, the presentation focused almost exclusively on the Macintosh, without mentioning the tremendous income provided to the company by the Apple II. The "second-class" citizenship that this communicated to the Apple II team greatly reduced their morale, while at the same time instilling in the Macintosh team that they were the corporate heroes. The mismanagement of this important ritual contributed to a significant split between the two divisions and led, at least indirectly, to cofounder Steven Wozniak's resignation from the company.

Rituals can also be mismanaged when employees no longer understand their intent. Examples of this mismanagement include the afternoon beer bust—which becomes a time for employees to "drown their sorrows" at the company's expense rather than a way for employees to informally share ideas and get acquainted—and the meeting that is held each week because "we've always had it," even though attendees agree it's a "waste of time."

When, however, a ritual has been effective at communicating its message and employees embrace it, they may choose to maintain it even at significant cost to themselves. At Hewlett-Packard, for example, during a period when the company's performance was less than expected and significant cuts were being made across various operations, employees voluntarily raised money to sponsor the corporate picnics. The implication of this is that employees clearly understood that the company valued them and that the picnic was only in jeopardy because of the company's performance. Further, the company had effectively communicated the belief that employee loyalty was valued, and employees chose to express their loyalty by sponsoring the picnic themselves.

Rewards. These are monetary and nonmonetary things that the company gives employees for behavior consistent with the company's culture and its goals. Examples include bonuses, company-sponsored vacations, employee-of-the-month awards, certificates of appreciation, and items embellished with the company logo presented in recognition of service of a particular kind. The gold "K" used at Knapp Communications is an example of the latter type of reward. Knapp Communications also uses certificates to recognize employees who complete their management development programs. These certificates are prominently displayed in employee offices, and the message communicated by this reward is that the company values education.

Domino's Pizza is another company that effectively utilizes rewards to foster its values of teamwork, customer service, and high performance standards. National awards go to winners of annual competitive events and to individuals and stores with the fastest/greatest sales record. Recognition of a different kind is given to poor performers. The slowest delivery times are recognized by inscription of the store's name on a plaque placed near the slowest elevators at corporate headquarters. Finally, founder Thomas Monaghan's impulsive gift of his tie to an especially successful manager has become a tradition, and hundreds of these awards are presented annually.

As is true of the other manifestations of culture, rewards must be managed or they can communicate values and beliefs and promote norms that are at odds with the company's goals. One small $2 million service firm had instituted a "manager-of-the-month" program intended to reward the "best manager." Unfortunately, the program had become a popularity contest rather than a way to recognize behavior consistent with the company's goals. The criteria for determining who should receive this reward were vague, and employees were asked to vote on who they believed to be the best manager. This process was adversely affecting morale because, while the most popular managers "won," those that were working hard to meet their goals were sometimes overlooked. Eventually, it might be expected that the good performers who were not rewarded for their behavior would simply give up.

How Corporate Culture Changes

Corporate culture does and should change over time. Culture does change over time as the organization grows and as new people are added. We will refer to these types of change as "uncontrolled." Culture should change over time to support organizational growth. We will refer to this type of change as "controlled" or "managed." These two change processes will be discussed briefly below.

Uncontrolled Change. The corporate culture of an entrepreneurship is dictated principally by the founder and the few people he or she initially hires. Everyone understands the culture and "buys into" it. It is very easy for the entrepreneur to influence and maintain the culture when he or she can have direct contact with all employees on a daily basis. However, by the time there are four or five generations of employees, it is almost impossible for people at the lower levels of the organization to have any direct contact with those at the top who articulate the culture. Therefore, the culture that those at the bottom of the organization adopt may be very different from that which the founder and the original family want to promote.

Such different perceptions result from the tendency of individuals to interpret the corporate culture in ways that meet their own needs. In the absence of a well-managed culture, this can lead to the original culture's becoming very distorted. This can be a subtle, and almost imperceptible process. We provided examples of such reinterpretations of the culture in the Tempo Products case presented in Chapter Six. In addition, if the culture is not managed, then there can be a "clash" between the old and new cultures that can affect the company's success. During the rapid growth phase at Apple Computer, for example, differences in style between the original hobbyists and the professional engineers and managers hired during the "Bozo explosion" precipitated a clash of cultures typified by the label attached to this period in the company's life. The cultural differences, along with the organizational structure, contributed to a lack of cooperation and communication that led to, among other things, quality problems with the Apple III.

Given our previous discussion of the relationship between culture and the organization's infrastructure, any time a change is made in a particular area of the company, there will be an impact on culture whether or not the organization has planned this change. When Apple adopted a nine-unit divisionalized structure in 1980 and then consolidated this structure into two major divisions in 1983 under Mike Scott and John Sculley, respectively, adequate emphasis was not placed on the cultural implications of these changes. As a result, in both cases the managers of the various divisions were left to create their own cultures and "fiefdoms." This was manifested by symbols like the T-shirts of the Macintosh division and the pirate flag they flew over their building, showing that they were somehow different from others at the company. The reorganization of 1985-1986 was, in part, a reaction to a culture that had gotten out of control, and in this effort John Sculley made it a point to explicitly deal with the cultural ramifications of the new structure he was implementing.

This was accomplished by, among other things, meetings with managers at all levels to explain the "new" culture and structure as well as a more formal culture management process designed by Apple's Human Resource department. Scully was careful to communicate to employees through words and action that he wanted to preserve the entrepreneurial spirit while at the same time professionalizing the firm.

Planned Change.   As suggested above, each time an organization changes any aspect of its operations, there is an impact on culture. If an organization is to be successful as it grows, culture must be managed at each stage so that the values, beliefs, and norms support the other changes taking place. As we discussed in Chapters Two and Six, culture does not become a critical factor until a company reaches $100 million in revenues, but that does not mean that it should or can be ignored. For example, in a $50 million manufacturing company, strategic planning was done but because the culture and other systems did not support it, it was nothing more than a yearly paper exercise. The company had not found ways to explicitly manage its culture so that it supported planning.

At Apple Computer, in 1983—after a period of spectacular corporate success—the implicit corporate culture included the belief that "We work here, so we must be brilliant."[52] As a result, the company became somewhat isolated from its environment, offering what they called "insanely great" products (Steven Jobs's phrase) to customers, but not often listening to what the customers wanted. This cultural belief also contributed to wasted resources and missed product deadlines because control systems were not created to monitor behavior. For example, the disk drive for the Lisa computer was unreliable and expensive, even though Apple had invested more than four years in its development. This fact was not discovered until months before this computer was scheduled for introduction.

In making the transition to professional management, a company must shift from unplanned to planned systems of cultural change and management. This is the subject of the next section.

How to Manage Your Corporate Culture

As a result of organizational growth and a lack of time to focus on culture management because other systems have taken precedence, a firm may find itself with a culture that is no longer appropriate for its size. When this occurs, usually by the time a firm reaches $100 million, culture management must become a priority.

For some firms, the problem is simply identifying and finding ways to better manage the existing culture, while in others the dominant culture needs to be changed to support the other changes that are taking place in the organization. In both cases, however, the challenge becomes one of finding a way of managing the culture so that it supports the operations of the larger firm. Using the area of strategic planning, Table 12.2 presents an example of the "competing" cultures one firm faced as it began to focus on managing its culture. The top-value, belief, norm, or hero definition is consistent with the culture needed to support an entrepreneurship, while the bottom is consistent with the culture needed to support a more professionalized firm. In the entrepreneurship, the culture emphasizes the ability to simply respond to market opportunities. It is "reactionary." This can be a strength for a small firm as it attempts to establish itself in a market. The professionalized firm's culture, however, needs to focus on promoting planning as a way to anticipate and design, in advance, responses to environmental opportunities and threats. This "proactive" approach is important, because if the changes made are inappropriate, they can be quite costly. Further, firms in a competitive environment that are "reactive" are usually at a competitive disadvantage because they respond to, rather than are prepared for, threats and opportunities.

The goal of the management process is to create a culture that is consistent with the firm's current stage of growth. As mentioned previously, this top tier of the pyramid of organizational

Table 12.2. Example of Entrepreneurial and
Professional Cultures.

Values:	We value "fire fighters." versus We value planners.
Beliefs:	Our success is based on our ability to respond rapidly to changes in our environment. versus Our success depends on our ability to anticipate and plan for changes in our environment.
Norms:	We do not plan; we react. versus We know what direction we are going in at all times.
Heroes:	The Arsonists and Fire Fighters. versus The Planners.

development does not become critical until a firm reaches $100 million in revenues, but it needs to be managed throughout the development of the organization.

There are three basic steps in the process of culture management: (1) analysis of current culture; (2) determination of what the culture should be, given the firm's current stage of growth; and (3) developing and implementing a plan for transforming and/or maintaining the corporate culture. Each step will be described in turn.

Analysis of Current Culture. The first step in the culture management process is to perform a "cultural audit" to determine what the culture currently is. Since the emphasis is on the "real" culture, not the nominal culture, we recommend ignoring written culture statements (at least initially) and focusing instead on what people have to say about the culture they "live and breathe." As explained earlier, culture is a very fuzzy concept, and if one asks an employee to describe his or her firm's culture, in most cases the employee will either pull out the company's philosophy/culture statement and begin to read it or will look at the interviewer as if he or she is speaking a foreign language. In other words, the direct approach is not effective in gathering information on this subject.

A somewhat more indirect approach that has been very effective for researchers and managers alike is to ask employees to write or tell short stories about their experiences in the firm. Employees should be asked to tell a story or two related to critical incidents they have personally experienced or heard about that occurred at the company. Another effective method is to have them construct a story that describes their first day on the job. The construction of these stories can take place on paper, and they can then be read aloud in a group setting or told to interviewers.

The next step is to extract from the stories critical elements of the company's culture. Examples of elements of Tempo Products' culture that were derived from the stories employees told are presented in Chapter Six. The identification of these elements may be done by the employees themselves or by an independent observer. Whatever the case, once the elements have been identified and summarized, they should be circulated to employees for further elaboration or feedback.

An example of two stories that were told by employees at a stage IV service firm and the elements of the culture that they identify are provided in Table 12.3. As shown in this table, the stories suggest a number of elements of this organization's culture, including concern for quality, the importance of extra effort, concern for people, the importance of first impressions, the concern that people feel valued, and the importance of treating people with respect.

As a result of such analyses, a number of competing "subcultures" may be identified. For example, each department may adhere to slightly different values. This is important information in the culture management process because the goal of this process will be to blend all of the competing cultures so that they support the overall corporate goals.

In analyzing stories, it is useful to identify how culture is manifested in the organization. What symbols are important to people? How do they talk about themselves, their customers, and company events (language)? What rituals are important? Who receives rewards (the heroes), for what, and what types of rewards are important to people in this firm? This is important information not

Table 12.3. Stories and Their Elements.

Story 1:	Not long after I began working here, I was reviewing some artwork that had been submitted. As usual, I was hoping to be able to approve the work and get the project rolling. The artwork was all right. In fact, it was probably more than just all right. But still it wasn't perfect. It fell into that gray area of being almost what you had in mind.
	I showed it to my boss. Like me, she agreed that it was okay, would do the job, and be just . . . fine. We stood a minute looking at the work, each of us wishing it were a bit something more, but recognizing that maybe sometimes okay is good enough. Then my boss turned to me and said, "I want to love this!" And in that moment we both agreed that it was worth it to get that extra something we wanted from the artwork.
Story 2:	When I arrived at the company, Allan was working the reception desk and while I was filling out my application he offered me coffee, decaf, tea, hot chocolate, milk, and water. Every time he offered, I said, "No thank you. I'm fine." When I met with the president, the first thing she asked me was if Mark had offered me coffee or tea and I said that he had, but that I didn't want anything. I was fine. After I interviewed with the president, she took me into the sales department to meet Jerry, the manager. When I met him, he asked me to tell him about myself in two minutes. I started telling him what my experience was and what I had done. He stopped me and said, "No, tell me about yourself." I was very impressed. So far, everyone at this company had been interested in who I was as well as in what I had done.
	After I met with Carol, I met another member of the sales team and the first thing he asked me was if anyone had offered me coffee or tea or something to drink. I said that they had and I was fine, really! Well, I came back for a second interview the next week, and then started work two days later.

Element of Culture Extracted from These Stories

1. We value quality in our products.
2. We take the extra effort to "do it right."
3. We care about our employees.
4. First impressions are important.
5. We want to make everyone who comes in contact with us feel like they are valued.
6. We treat people with respect.

only in terms of identifying the current culture, but also in terms of identifying how to manage these manifestations of culture in order to promote a more professionalized culture.

The outcome of the cultural audit will be a list of the elements of the current culture and their meanings. Some managers also find it useful to develop a list of the systems or structures (elements of the company's infrastructure) that promote each of the various cultural elements as a way of identifying possible targets for change.

Identification of the Appropriate Culture. In beginning to explicitly manage an organization's culture, the key question is, "What should our culture be, given our current stage of development?" In the final section of this chapter we provide some general guidelines for the elements of corporate culture at different stages of development.

Whatever the stage, however, it is senior management's responsibility to answer this question, and in doing so it should focus not only on what the current culture should be, but on what the culture should be in five years. From brainstorming sessions, senior management should construct a set of values and beliefs that it deems will meet the firm's needs. These can be a set of three to five key phrases, each with a paragraph to explain their meaning or simply a list of the key elements of the culture. If a company chooses to utilize a list, then senior management should develop its own written definition of each element so that there can be no misinterpretation of its meaning.

We recommend that the culture statement contain no more than five to seven key items so as to help employees remember them. For example, there are only three basic values in the culture of IBM, one of the most effective organizations with respect to culture management. The three core values are: respect for the individual, service to the customer, and excellence in what we do. These values have been the foundation of IBM's culture since its inception. In spite of having more than 400,000 employees, the company is sufficiently well managed that if an "IBMer" is awakened in the middle of the night he or she can recite the values. This is the intent of a culture statement: not only that employees remember it, but that they live and breathe it.

Transformation and/or Maintenance of the Corporate Culture. Once the new culture has been identified and articulated, the next step for many companies is to transform the current culture into one that will better support the firm's stage of development. For others, it is simply to develop a way of ensuring that the existing culture is effectively communicated to all employees.

Changing the corporate culture usually involves focusing on changing other systems, since culture affects and is affected by everything else in the pyramid of organizational development. This is why it is important to identify those aspects of the infrastructure that are supporting the old culture and those needed to support the new. Similarly, each time a change is made in the infrastructure, senior management needs to consider the cultural implications.

John Sculley, at Apple Computer, said that he wanted to maintain the "entrepreneurial spirit" while at the same time professionalizing the firm. Sculley made a number of changes in the organizational structure (including eliminating divisions and re-centralizing control) and putting in new systems to promote accountability in order to instill in employees the value that would be placed on operating as a professionalized corporation. The company, however, continued to focus on and reward new-product development.

Data General, recognizing a change in its market toward consumer-oriented products, refocused its values toward customer services by training salespeople how to interact more effectively with the "new" customer and by managing sales meetings in such a way that any disdain for customer service was eliminated. Further, the company was restructured so as to better meet customer needs through timely new-product development. Responsibility for product development, which had traditionally been in the hands of engineers who operated on their own time schedules and fairly autonomously, was given to R&D teams that are held accountable for meeting deadlines.

Sometimes it is the case that the need for culture change arises because of an acquisition or merger. In this case, senior management must perform an audit of each of the cultures, identify areas of overlap and conflict, and determine the best way to "blend" the cultures. This may mean that some values of one or both firms will need to be significantly changed or, perhaps, eliminated in order to support the firm's growth. The culture's management is, however, essential in assisting the company in making a smooth transition since it has such a tremendous impact on employee morale.

During the late 1980s, the Southern California–based Vons Grocery Store chain acquired a large number of Safeway's stores in Southern California. For the acquired Safeway stores, the transition to becoming a Vons store took place gradually, with Vons senior management exercising care in how they transformed the Safeway symbols and rituals into those of Vons. To symbolize the transition, truck drivers were given caps that bore the logo, "VonWay," indicating Vons desire to have Safeway blend it with Vons. The house brand labels also went through a gradual transformation from Safeway to Vons, and so did the store signs. Commercials emphasized that while the name had changed, the personnel remained the same ("Our name has changed, but they haven't changed me"). Finally, Vons decided to continue the company picnic for Safeway employees even though Vons does not hold such events. This served to communicate the message that the new acquisitions (of people) were valued not only for what they were but for what they brought to the company.

While corporate culture change is a necessary part of the transition process, culture must be managed on a continual basis in order to ensure that it supports the company's goals and operations. The values, beliefs, and norms must be communicated and constantly reinforced because as a company continues to grow, new employees will need to understand what the culture is and what it means.

Senior management is ultimately responsible for the culture management process. Moreover, senior management actually serves as the role models for the rest of the company. It is important, then, for senior management to not only communicate the culture through its words but also through its actions. At Wang Laboratories, for example, An Wang decided in the early 1980s to decentralize management decision making. Unfortunately, employees continued to complain that Wang still made most of the major decisions. The nominal culture said, "We believe in providing all of our managers with the authority they need to make decisions." But the behavior, for whatever reason, stated, "Only senior management will decide." A positive example is that of a $35 million manufacturing firm where employees equated commitment with hours worked regardless of actual productivity. A memo was sent out stating that there was a commitment to reduce people's hours, but that the company wanted people to work smarter—not longer—hours. Senior management decided that they would no longer arrive at the office before 7:30 A.M. and would leave the office by 5:30 P.M. Through their behavior, they attempted to show their employees what the new value would be: We value productivity, not just hours worked.

A second way to manage corporate culture is through training programs. Orientation programs can serve as a way to provide new employees with an understanding of the corporate culture, as well as of how the infrastructure works to support this culture. Again, however, while the words are important, the other elements of this program—for example, whether the president welcomes them in person or in a video, the first impression left by their immediate supervisor, and the tone of the meeting—can leave a lasting and sometimes distorted perception of the company's values. In the absence of such formalized programs, employees are sometimes left to their own devices to read the handbook and identify "what's important here."

Management development programs can also serve as a means of conveying the corporate culture, as discussed in Chapter Nine. They help to build a sense of teamwork and, at a minimum, usually communicate to employees that the company values training and professionalized management. Further, management development programs provide managers with the skills they need to support and use the organization's systems in ways that reinforce the corporate culture.

Another way that corporate culture can be managed is through personnel selection. This can be proactive or retroactive. Proactively, the goal is to select personnel who will promote the values, beliefs, and norms of the firm and who are not at odds with the culture. While this is a very time-consuming process and takes a great deal of planning and execution, it can be very effective. Compaq Computer utilizes this mechanism as one way of managing its culture. Even if an individual possesses superior technical skills, he or she will not be hired if the company believes that he or she cannot readily adopt the firm's culture. Similarly, IBM spends time explaining to applicants what the negatives about working at IBM are, hoping that self-selection will lead to a group of people who understand and accept the company's culture.

Retroactive personnel selection usually occurs during culture change. The goal is to eliminate those individuals who will not support the new culture or, at a minimum, move them into positions where they can do little to harm the cultural change process. Some companies bring in outsiders—called "hired guns"—to perform the "terminations." Usually, in these cases, the entrepreneur realizes that he or she cannot do what needs to be done and either moves up or out of the company, as happened with Steven Jobs at Apple Computer.

In other cases, the culture eventually becomes so strong that other employees force the cultural "violator" out. The person who refuses to adopt the new culture becomes an outsider and leaves of his or her own volition. Individuals who leave under these circumstances sometimes say that "the company just wasn't any fun anymore."

Finally, corporate culture can be managed through the administration of rewards. As discussed in Chapter Ten, it is important to ensure that rewards are linked to the behavior needed to achieve organizational goals and objectives as outlined in the strategic plan. The company should be trying to create corporate heroes out of those individuals who best exemplify this behavior. These individuals can, in turn, act as role models for others. This is why it is not only important for employees to understand what they are being rewarded for, but to publicize achievement as a way of motivating others to exhibit the same behavior. Employees at Knapp Communications became very interested in working for a gold "K" and in so doing were working toward the company's goals. In other companies, the best performers are rewarded with bonuses. The reward structure and system must constantly be reevaluated to determine that it is motivating employees to be concerned with the appropriate goals and that these goals have not become distorted.

Corporate Culture at Different Stages
of Organizational Development

While the particular elements of a corporate culture will differ, culture should change to meet the demands at each stage of development. This section discusses some of the key dimensions of culture at the various stages of organizational development.

Stage I. The culture of most small organizations emphasizes flexibility, ability to respond quickly to the environment, and the notion that the company is a "family" with the entrepreneur serving as the parental figure. The organization seems to be constantly moving and, while there is a certain amount of anxiety about the firm's future, there is also a great deal of excitement. Technical wizardry and innovativeness are valued and, often, the technicians are the corporate heroes.

Culture is communicated through direct interactions with the entrepreneur. Employees, in fact, look to the entrepreneur for direction, and so he or she is able to almost daily define and reinforce the corporate culture as well as to monitor and correct it. Very few entrepreneurs choose to commit their values to paper at this stage of development. While this is not an absolute necessity, it can serve as a basis for communicating values as the firm grows. Whatever is placed on paper, however, should be supported by the daily operations of the firm.

Stage II. The corporate culture of the stage II firm is very similar to that in stage I. The firm still values responsiveness, but now there is a tendency for this to mean "crisis management." The firm still values flexibility, but now this means something like being flexible and creative enough to operate with less than adequate resources until personnel interviews are completed or until the new facilities are ready. The firm also still values the family, but now there is an extended family living within the same "house," and one's loyalty seems to depend more on which leader (regardless of level) one is most exposed to. Corporate heroes tend to become those people who are the best fire fighters and problem solvers.

It is at this stage of development that the corporate culture of most firms begins to become distorted. Since all employees can no longer have direct contact with the entrepreneur, they are left to develop their own interpretations of the corporate culture, based on what they have heard. Since the entrepreneur cannot be there to monitor behavior, he or she must depend on other managers to do so, but they also each have their own interpretations of the culture. If the company has not yet developed the strategic planning, control, management development, and organizational structure consistent with this stage of development it may be placed at a further disadvantage because, even if it can develop the appropriate culture, there will be no support for it.

At this stage of development, a company should devote at least part of its planning time (as discussed in Chapter Seven) to articulating the culture that will support its efforts and to devising ways to communicate it to employees. Again, if there is an existing culture statement, it may need to be revised to reflect the needs of the current stage of development. In this regard, it should mention a shift toward planning and control in at least an implicit way as well as an emphasis on meeting responsibilities and goals. Further, as suggested in Chapter Ten, the reward systems should be reviewed and changed, if necessary, in order to support the behavior required to meet the organization's goals.

Stage III. It is at this stage of development that the culture of a firm will make a fundamental shift toward promoting professional management. The culture of a stage III firm should promote planning as a way of life, accountability for meeting departmental and individual goals, a commitment to training employees to become professional managers, and other behavior consistent with the professionalized firm. However, if the planning, control, management development, and organizational structure systems are inconsistent with the requirements of this stage of development, then the culture will be as well.

At this stage, the culture is, of necessity, still being implicitly

managed in most cases. However, senior management can increase
the probability that its culture will support its professionalization
efforts by at least considering the impact proposed organizational
changes will have on what it believes to be the corporate culture and
how that might be managed. In other words, it can build into its
change efforts a cultural component that redefines existing elements
and clearly articulates new elements. However, the effort needed to
explicitly manage these elements may need to be postponed until
the systems and structure are at least nominally in place.

Stage IV.   By the time a firm reaches stage IV, it needs to
develop a formal method for managing its corporate culture. Corporate culture management should become an important part of the
planning process and resources should be devoted to: (1) performing
a cultural audit to identify potential problem areas; (2) clearly articulating the existing culture and the new culture, if different; and
(3) developing a plan for transforming and/or maintaining the corporate culture. The latter step should include a process for monitoring the culture on a regular basis to ensure that it is promoting
the organization's goals.

Conclusion

A clear understanding of the meaning and importance of
corporate culture remains elusive for many managers. Some managers choose to deny the existence of a culture in their organizations; others are intimidated by the thought of trying to identify
anything so "fuzzy," let alone of finding ways to manage it.

This chapter has attempted to address these issues. We examined the nature of corporate culture and how culture is manifested
in organizations. We also described methods that can be used to
identify an organization's culture, and to manage it so as to increase
organizational effectiveness. In brief, managers must first determine
what their current culture is through performing a culture audit.
Next, they must determine what their culture should be, given their
stage of growth, and finally they must design and implement a plan
for managing the corporate culture.

Every organization has a culture and culture can have a profound impact on organizational success because it supports the other changes needed to make the transition from entrepreneurship to professional management. It is, then, important for managers to understand and learn how to manage the culture as their organizations grow.

Part Four

Role of the Entrepreneur in a Growing and Changing Company

The previous sections of this book have examined the organizational issues that face companies making the transition from an entrepreneurship to a professionally managed firm. But some organizations will have the opportunity to grow beyond stage IV. This growth will present a new set of problems that are different in nature from those encountered during the first four stages of growth.

Chapter Thirteen presents a preview of the future organizational challenges encountered beyond stage IV. It examines the advanced stages of growth after a firm has become professionally managed. Stage V requires a firm to diversify because it can no longer rely on its initial product line for future growth. As a result of stage V, a company typically develops new businesses, which leads to the problems faced at stage VI. Once a firm has diversified, either through internal growth or acquisition, the new businesses must be integrated. This is the developmental focus of stage VI. Finally, stage VII requires that an organization deal with the inevitable forces leading to decline, whether they are caused by market saturation, erosion of management's entrepreneurial skills, or the organization's own success. All organizations will ultimately encounter decline and must revitalize. In the revitalization process, management must again give its full attention to the entire pyramid of organizational development.

Chapter Thirteen examines each of these issues and provides guidance to assist the CEOs as well as other senior managers in planning for the future development of their enterprises at the advanced stages of organizational growth.

Although all members of an organization are profoundly affected by its transition, no one is more influenced by the changes involved than the organization's senior management, especially the CEO or founder(s). The transitions required may lead to a great deal of organizational and personal trauma, as in the case of Apple Computer, which lost both its founders, Steven Wozniak and Steven Jobs. These men, who were responsible for the founding and development of a $2 billion organization and for the technical innovation and entrepreneurial vision that created Apple, were replaced by John Sculley, a professional manager brought in from Pepsico by Jobs himself.

Other entrepreneurs face a similar fate unless they are able to change along with their companies. Chapter Fourteen deals with some of the personal, professional, and organizational transitions that the founder or CEO of an entrepreneurial organization must make if the organization is to continue to grow successfully and profitably. The issue here is not whether entrepreneurship or professional management is better. Both are valuable, but each is suitable for a different stage of organizational growth and development.

Chapter Fourteen begins with an examination of the personal issues facing the CEO during organizational transitions and the alternatives available to him or her. Next, it considers the organizational issues facing the CEO and the steps the CEO can take when faced with the need for an organizational transition. Finally, Chapter Fourteen offers some additional advice to CEOs concerning their role, their organization, and its management during the transition process.

13 Managing the Advanced Stages of Growth: A Preview of Future Challenges

The previous chapters of this book have dealt with the issues encountered by rapidly growing entrepreneurial organizations as they move through the first four stages of growth: from a new venture (stage I) to consolidation of an established firm (stage IV). If management has accomplished the developmental tasks described throughout this book, then on completing stage IV, the firm has become a "professionally managed organization."

Some firms will have the opportunity to grow in size beyond stage IV. This growth will present a new set of organizational development problems that are quite different from those during stages I through IV, the transition from entrepreneurship to professional management.

This chapter is intended to assist the senior managers of such firms in planning for the future development of their enterprises by examining the stages of growth that will occur beyond stage IV.

It is also intended for senior managers of organizations that have already reached those stages of growth and are either encountering certain developmental problems or wish to avoid the classic problems at each stage.

We will first describe the nature of each of the later stages of growth, then examine the key problems and challenges that organizations must confront as they advance to each of them.

Nature of Problems Beyond Stage IV

The problems encountered beyond stage IV are quite different from those of the prior stages of growth. In stage I, the essential problem is to find a market and develop a product that is appropriate for that market. In stage II, the central problem for the organization is to develop the operational infrastructure. This includes development of both the resources needed to facilitate future growth and the day-to-day operational systems required to run the firm. In stage III, the central problem is to begin the professionalization of the organization. At this point, the firm needs to focus on developing its management systems, including its systems for planning, organization, management development, and control. In stage IV, the key issue is to consolidate the organization by beginning to manage its corporate culture, and reinforce the transition to professional management. In brief, prior to stage V, the firm's management problems all center around the issues of locating an initial market, developing a product, and building the operational infrastructure, management systems, and corporate culture needed to run a firm that has reached approximately $100 to $500 million in annual revenue (for manufacturing firms), or approximately one-third of this for service firms.

On reaching stage V, the firm's problems change in nature. Unless it has somehow managed to retain its entrepreneurial spirit, it must now reestablish itself as an entrepreneurial company, returning to the set of skills that gave it its original success. Ideally, the firm will have retained its entrepreneurial orientation throughout stages I through IV. In reality, the firm is likely to have lost its entrepreneurial spirit to some degree, and must now seek to reestablish it.

The Stages of Growth Beyond Stage IV

The advanced stages of organizational growth, the critical development areas for each stage, and the approximate size (measured in dollars of sales revenue) at which an organization will pass through each stage are shown in Table 13.1. These are the stages of growth beyond entrepreneurship. They represent the transitions

Table 13.1. Advanced Stages of Organizational Growth.

Stage	Description	Critical Development Area	Approximate Organizational Size (in sales)
V	Diversification	New products: replication of the stage I–IV cycle	$500–$1 billion
VI	Integration	Integration of different business units	$1 billion plus
VII	Decline and Revitalization	Revitalization of organization at all levels of the pyramid of organizational development	Varies

which must be made by all entrepreneurially oriented professionally managed firms if they are to continue to be successful in their future growth. In this section, we describe, in depth, the stages of growth beyond stage IV.

Stage V: Diversification.   After an organization has completed the consolidation stage, the next developmental challenge it faces is typically to diversify. This problem usually arises because the firm's original product or product line has become relatively mature and will not facilitate sufficient future growth to sustain the organization at its current rate of growth, its historical rate of growth, or its immediate future growth expectations. This problem is simply a result of the phenomenon of market saturation.

When a firm initially introduces a product as a new venture, the market is typically unsaturated, and there is relatively little competition. As the firm becomes successful it typically attracts competitors. For example, Apple Computer found the market for the personal computer, but attracted a host of competitors, including IBM. The presence of competition decreases the firm's profit margins and erodes its market share over time. A related phenomenon is that as the market for the new product becomes increasingly saturated, the new venture's rate of growth cannot be sustained for its given product vehicle. An example of this phenomenon is Ashton-Tate's highly successful dBASE II, the first version of its product for database management. As the potential users of dBASE were reached, and as new competitors have entered the marketplace, the need has been for Ashton-Tate to identify new product "vehicles" to continue its growth. Yet, by early 1989, the company had not been fully successful in accomplishing this task and was, as a result, posting significant losses.

One way of thinking about the difference between the issues faced by the firm during stages I through IV, and the issues faced in stage V, is to consider the analogy of a "product" as an oil field. The central problem in petroleum exploration is to find a new oil field. Once a field has been found, the organization builds up an infrastructure to tap the oil well and convert it into marketable products. As the size of the business increases, the firm has to build its business around that oil well. The central issues here are developing the capability to tap the oil well and marketing its products. From this standpoint, the oil well is essentially a resource that the firm is drawing on. However, this resource has a finite life, which means it will not last forever but only until all of the oil has been pumped out.

By analogy, most consumer and industrial markets are very much like "oil wells" in that they will not last forever. They may produce a "gusher" that leads to very rapid growth for an organization, but over time the oil wells will inevitably play themselves out. When a firm builds up its organizational and management infrastructure to tap an oil well, it usually does so with the intention of remaining a "going concern." This means that if the organization is to continue to exist, it must find other oil fields that it can begin to extract resources from. Accordingly, if the firm is to become more than a one-time venture, it must use some of the resources earned from tapping the oil well to invest in exploration of other oil fields. It should be hiring geologists to search for additional oil fields, spending additional resources in drilling test wells, and so forth.

Companies in totally different businesses from petroleum exploration and refining will find it useful to think of their business in terms of the oil well analogy just described. A company's entrepreneur identifies a new market, which is analogous to a petroleum corporation finding an oil field. The company then develops a product that is accepted by consumers, which is again analogous to a firm beginning to tap the oil in the field. The firm then builds up the operational management infrastructure necessary to operate the day-to-day business, while simultaneously preparing an infrastructure that is necessary to continue the operation after its first product has been "used up." Thus, the challenge of stage V is essentially analogous to the firm's finding another oil well. If the firm is prudent, it will not wait until its markets are sufficiently "dried up" to begin locating new markets and building new products. Accordingly, it will be engaged in a process of research and development designed to identify new oil fields and begin their production while its current oil fields are still producing.

Typically, an organization can only expect that a given "product vehicle" will carry it to the range of $100 to $500 million in annual revenue. As discussed previously, this is simply the "normal curve" for this phenomenon, and certain companies may not experience the need for a new product vehicle until significantly after $500 million in revenue. There are examples of a number of firms which have reached a billion dollars in annual revenue before they experienced the need for a new product vehicle; however, these firms are the exception rather than the general rule. The upper limit for growth through a single product or line of business may be reached well before a firm generates $500 million in annual revenues. For example, Ashton-Tate, which develops, manufactures, and markets computer software, began facing the problem at about $80 million in revenue.

When a firm fails to diversify the result can be stagnation or even bankruptcy. For example, Cuisinarts, Inc., well known for its upscale food processors that were highly popular in the 1970s, filed for bankruptcy under Chapter Eleven of the Federal Bankruptcy Code in 1989. The food processing business had become saturated, and though the company still controlled about 45 percent of the food process market, it experienced difficulties.

Cuisinarts had not done effective strategic planning and failed to capitalize on its famous name. By the time it filed for Chapter Eleven, the company had only recently begun branching out to items such as cooking utensils, hand blenders, and other cooking products. Cuisinarts had defined its business as the "food processing business" rather than more broadly. Unfortunately, its traditional market dried up before Cuisinarts found a new one.

Thus, the central problem of stage V is to diversify the firm so that it is no longer dependent on its initial product vehicle. The challenge is to establish one or more new-product vehicles that will enable the firm to continue to grow successfully. These may or may not be in the same business as the firm's initial product vehicle. Stated differently, the firm may have to diversify outside of its initial business segment. The firm may be developing multiple businesses. Thus, stage V is a time when the business should be making two transitions: from one product vehicle to the next, and from a single business to a set of businesses. This can be accomplished both through internal development of new products and markets and through acquisitions of other organizations. However, if corporate acquisitions are made without an adequate infrastructure, the results can be disastrous as in the case of Maxicare and Campeau Corporation. Robert Campeau, a successful Canadian real estate developer, purchased Allied Stores and Federated Department Stores, both U.S. retailing giants, but found the acquisitions to be undigestible. Campeau Corporation ended up filing Chapter Eleven protection under the U.S. Bankruptcy Code. The company simply did not have the adequate organizational resources and infrastructure to manage its acquisitions.

Stage VI: Integration.   In the process of making the transition to stage V, an organization sets in motion the forces that require it to move to stage VI—integration. During stage V, the firm will have made the transition from a single-product-line company to a multiproduct company, as well as from a single-business to a multibusiness company. This means that by the time the organization completes the diversification process begun in stage V it will consist of a set of (at least partially) related businesses.

By the time an organization completes stage V, it will most likely be divisionalized. As explained in Chapter Eight, the firm will have overcome the problems associated with using a functional structure to manage a multiproduct business. The divisions that result from this process are themselves each businesses and are potentially capable of being stand-alone entities.

For example, Hughes Aircraft Company had approximately $8 billion in annual revenue when it was acquired by General Motors in the late 1980s. It became a subsidiary of General Motors, which had more than $90 billion in annual revenue at that time. Hughes Aircraft itself comprised several divisions, some of which had more than $1 billion in annual revenue. For example, the Space and Communications Group, a division of Hughes Aircraft, was itself a multibillion dollar business.

The phenomenon of having a number of businesses within a larger entity is not only found in large, established companies such as Whittaker Corporation, Teledyne, and IBM; it also exists in many smaller organizations. For example, Aerotek, a rapidly growing stage III company with $40 million in revenues, has three independent divisions.

Another version of the need for integration of different businesses arises from the acquisition of different companies in the same industry. When a company grows by acquiring other firms, there is a potential problem of integration. For example, Maxicare made two major acquisitions that increased its size from $500 million to $1.8 billion in annual revenue. Maxicare then had to deal with the problems of integrating these companies, which had different operational systems (such as payroll and benefits) and different corporate cultures. Unfortunately, Maxicare had overextended itself, and the company had to declare bankruptcy. The company then had to proceed to liquidate many of its operating units. Similarly, when the Southern California Safeway stores were acquired by Vons, the latter had to deal with merging the two different systems and cultures. However, Vons handled the task much better than Maxicare. For example, Safeway had a long history of participation in company employees' associations. Vons chose not only to continue this practice, but to adopt it in its other operations. This and other company efforts have resulted in successful integration of the two formerly competitive units.

The key challenge at this stage involves integrating the operations and businesses of the enterprise while maintaining the firm's entrepreneurial spirit. The company has a simultaneous need to have some degree of centralized control over the diverse operating units and to allow divisional managers sufficient freedom to be entrepreneurial in managing their operations. Many companies do not do a good job of striking this delicate balance and lean too much toward organizational control. The price is a loss of entrepreneurial instinct and culture and the creation of institutional bureaucracy that is more concerned with form than with substance.

At this stage it may also be the case that certain corporate-wide systems will need to be "adjusted" in ways to meet the needs of a new division while at the same time maintaining control. In one $100 million subdivision of a Fortune 500 firm, for example, problems were created because the parent firm mandated that certain operating systems would be used that did not adequately meet the needs of the smaller firm. Further, the parent firm's culture promoted cautiousness, while the subsidiary needed to respond quickly to take advantage of market opportunities. Finally, the compensation system of the parent firm could not reward behavior that contributed to business development since it was structured, instead, to maintain the status quo. Without careful management and negotiation with the parent firm, such practices can adversely affect a division or subsidiary's ability to succeed.

The problem of integration is, to a great extent, a function of organizational size, complexity, and geographical dispersion. The greater the size of revenues (and, in turn, personnel and transactions), the greater the degree of geographical dispersion, and/or the greater the degree of business variety, then the greater the problems of organizational integration are likely to be.

Stage VII: Decline and Revitalization.   All organizations, regardless of their greatness or past success, will ultimately experience a period of decline. In the late nineteenth century, the railroads were the dominant enterprises, but they failed to use their resources to move into other aspects of transportation. In the early part of this century, U.S. Steel was the hallmark of our economy, but it did not retain that position. In the 1950s, General Motors was at its apex, yet it too experienced decline. Other once-great corporations that have experienced organizational decline include National Lead, International Harvester, Chrysler Corporation, Levi Strauss, and Bank of America. For some, decline led the firm to the brink of bankruptcy, while for others it merely led to stunted growth. For still others, it led to their demise.

The phenomenon of decline in organizations has been increasingly recognized by scholars.[53] This same phenomenon that occurs in organizations has also been identified in nations.[54]

Organizational decline is typically a product of many complex factors. Some of the most common factors include increasing competition in a firm's markets, loss of competitive skills from an erosion of leadership, a sense of complacency that inhibits organizational change, and, as described throughout this book, the inability of management to build an organizational infrastructure sufficient to keep pace with the demands of organizational growth.

The most common causes of decline—competition and the related phenomenon of market saturation—tend to increase throughout an organization's life. During the early stages of growth after a new market has been identified, an organization will typically grow and prosper simply as a "reward" for having found the market for that given product or service. For example, Apple Computer "found" the market for "personal computers" and grew to approximately $1 billion in annual revenues. During this period, IBM—potentially a major competitor for Apple—kept telling its customers that there was no need for personal computers. Once the market was developed to the point where it was sufficiently large enough to attract IBM's interest, IBM brought out its own version of a PC and "took" 30 to 35 percent of the total market, squeezing Apple Computer's sales and profitability. Eventually, a number of "IBM clones" were introduced, and the market for PCs became even more competitive. When Apple had the market virtually to itself, it earned premium profitability. Once competition increased, Apple no longer had the profit cushion that would mask its underlying organizational problems.

Another major cause of organizational decline is an erosion of leadership and entrepreneurial management skills. Unfortunately, the longer organizations exist and the larger they grow in size, the greater the likelihood that they will "outgrow" their founder's capabilities. Similarly, as people age, they must inevitably step down from leadership. For example, the Watsons inevitably retired from IBM, Seymour Cray left Cray Research, and Loraine Mecca left

Micro D; they were replaced by others who were "grown" or hired to assume positions of leadership. However, as organizations increase in size they are less likely to attract or "grow" people who are true entrepreneurs, and they may become more political. As organizations become increasingly political, decisions tend to become compromises. It is only when the organization is in a crisis that it allows a single individual to forcefully articulate a strategic vision. This was the case with Lee Iacocca at Chrysler. Iacocca was accepted as a "savior," and brought about a strategic vision for Chrysler's revitalization.

A third contributing cause to organizational decline is an increasing sense of complacency. When an organization is successful, people reasonably expect to be rewarded. Sometimes the rewards are too great for the organization to sustain. Moreover, the very fact that success has persisted over time may lead people to come to expect rewards as an entitlement. This form of managerial hubris can create a self-congratulatory atmosphere that produces a resistance to change and ultimately leads to decline. In many firms, this is reflected in a lack of concern about whether or not there are new products in the pipeline. It may also be reflected in an attitude of "We know best what the customer wants," without actually listening to customers. This attitude can be disastrous when a firm competes in markets where others have systems in place to both monitor and respond to customer needs. The classic symptom of this problem is a "country club" atmosphere.

A final major contributing factor to organizational decline is the inability of management to develop an organizational infrastructure sufficient for the organization's stage of growth. This problem has been one of the key themes throughout this book. Indeed, the problem is the crucial issue of stages II through IV, and when management is unsuccessful in meeting these developmental challenges, organizational decline is an inevitability. Lack of infrastructure can be a problem to support not only internal growth but growth through acquisitions as well, as illustrated by Maxicare.

The key challenge, then, for a stage VII firm is revitalization. The organization must rebuild itself almost from the ground up. This, in turn, requires that the firm become entrepreneurial in nature once again. Some firms try to achieve revitalization by acquiring other companies that are more entrepreneurial than the purchaser. For example, in a bid to revitalize, General Motors has acquired Electronic Data Systems (EDS), founded by entrepreneur H. Ross Perot, as well as Hughes Aircraft.

We should also note that a firm does not have to reach the multibillion-dollar level before it experiences decline. Decline may occur much sooner. Companies such as Osborne Computer, People Express, and Victor Technologies are all examples of premature corporate decline. By the time a firm has reached the multibillion-dollar level, however, it is sure to have the seeds of future potential decline within—even though it appears to outsiders to be at the apex of its success and power.

Managing Transitions at Stages V Through VII

We have examined the nature of stages V through VII, and the managerial challenges that occur at each of these stages. This section deals with the issues involved in managing the transitions required at each of these stages.

Managing Transitions at Stage V. The transition to stage V requires a redeployment of entrepreneurial skills. The entrepreneurship that was the basis of founding the firm in stage I has not been needed again to the same degree until the firm reaches stage V. Because the original product vehicle was sufficient to carry the firm along in its chosen market, the managerial problems involved building the operational and management infrastructure. However, the need to diversify translates into the need to be entrepreneurial again.

Unfortunately, it may not be possible for the firm to simply go back to its original entrepreneur and have that person repeat the entire process that began some time ago in stage I. In some cases, the entrepreneur is no longer with the firm. There are many examples in business where the original entrepreneur has not been available to grow with the firm as it developed from one stage to the next. For example, Steven Jobs and Steven Wozniak are no longer with Apple Computer, Nolan Bushnell is only with Atari in an advisory capacity, Mitchell Kapour is no longer with Lotus Corporation, the

Watsons are long gone from IBM, the founders of Ashton-Tate are no longer with the firm, and Seymour Cray has left Cray Research.

Even if the entrepreneur is still with the firm, a significant amount of time usually has elapsed as the firm passed from stage I through stage IV, and at this point the entrepreneur is now burdened by a significant number of organizational activities. This means that the entrepreneur may not have the time or mindset available for thinking "entrepreneurially" about new products and markets.

It is often, then, extremely difficult for entrepreneurs to repeat their earlier success. There are many examples of firms where there was a brilliant entrepreneurial success, but a failure to repeat that success at any significant level. Accordingly, what is needed is to reestablish entrepreneurship in the organization, but it must be done in a different way. Rather than looking to a single entrepreneur, firms at stage V must develop a cadre of "entrepreneurial managers."

An entrepreneurial manager is different from a pure entrepreneur. Adam Osborne, Steven Jobs, or Ross Perot are relatively "pure" entrepreneurial types very different from professional managers. An entrepreneur is typically someone who is above average in intelligence, and has a very strong sense of the way he or she wants things to be done in the organization. This means they have a very high need for control. Some people might even consider the entrepreneur to be a workaholic, or to have an obsessive personality. Nevertheless, these are the very personality traits that are both necessary and useful to a firm during its early stages of growth. While a stage V firm needs to develop a cadre of entrepreneurial managers, it is not necessary for these managers to have the same personality as an entrepreneur; rather, what is necessary is to train the entrepreneurial manager to "mimic" or simulate some of the behavioral patterns of the entrepreneur.

During the past few years, a number of organizations have been experimenting with the reintroduction of entrepreneurship and the training of entrepreneurial managers. A new term has arisen to distinguish this process of reintroducing entrepreneurship through entrepreneurial managers from the entrepreneurs required to start a new company. The term is the *intrapreneur*. The entrepreneur is someone who can create a new business where none existed previously. In contrast to the entrepreneur, the corporate "intrapreneur" or "entrepreneurial manager" is someone who can create a new business venture within an established organization.[55] The challenge, then, is to create development programs that will help people make the transition to "intrapreneur." Further, the firm must develop systems and a way of thinking (a culture) that supports "intrapreneurship," the creation of a business within a business.

Managing Transitions at Stage VI. An organization that has completed stage V has both a multiple product line and a multiple set of businesses to manage. This is typically accomplished through the divisional form of organizational structure, which has been described in Chapter Eight.

The central problem facing corporations in stage VI is how to integrate a set of diverse divisions into one unified business entity. It is at this point in the firm's development that a new managerial system must be designed. The new management system at the corporate level must be designed to manage a set of businesses, rather than just one business.

Stated differently, from stages I through V the firm has been developing a management system that is appropriate for a single business entity. By the time it reaches stage VI it will have developed a number of these individual business entities, and now needs to develop a comprehensive management system for managing each of these individual units as part of an integrated whole.

There are a variety of issues that must be addressed during this stage of organizational growth. One such issue involves questions of managing the corporate culture. Specifically, each of the separate divisions within a company may have somewhat varying cultures. Another such issue involves the process of strategic planning, both at the corporate level and within each division, and the problems involved with integrating both. Similarly, there are also issues involving the proper organizational structure of each division. Finally, there are issues involving the specific control systems that need to be developed within each of the business entities. The systems and culture of each division may need to be, in some cases, blended so as to promote the cooperation needed to achieve goals, while in other cases the company needs to promote the belief that differences in systems and culture between divisions will be maintained in the service of meeting the firm's long-term goals.

A critical issue underlying the design of a management system for a stage VI organization involves the degree of centralization or decentralization of authority accorded to each division. Companies vary widely in the amount of decentralization that they grant to their operating divisions. This issue can be viewed as points on a continuum. At one end of the continuum are firms that attempt to control virtually everything their operating divisions do. This is the centralized form of management as typified by ITT under Harold Geneen.[56] At the other end of the continuum, a corporation essentially operates as a passive investor with a "portfolio" containing various companies. The strategy here defers strategic decisions and daily operations to the divisional general managers, while requiring a specified performance in terms of return on investment or amount of profit. This type of managerial philosophy has been used for many years at Beatrice and at Teledyne.

At Beatrice, for example, divisions may be required to achieve an 18 percent pretax return on investment. The methods of achieving this target return are left to divisional managers. If a division fails to meet this corporate mandated target rate of return, it may initially find itself inundated with "advisers" from the corporate office. If these advisers are unsuccessful in "helping" the division achieve its target rate of return, the division is sold. The key challenge at this stage, then, involves deciding how best to integrate the systems and corporate culture of the various units created in stage V into an effective "system."

Managing Transitions at Stage VII.   The final stage in the organizational life cycle is stage VII. This stage has been labeled that of organizational decline and revitalization. The key issue facing management at stage VII involves revitalization of the entire organization.

In contrast to most of the other stages, which constitute a sequential hierarchy as an organization grows in size, an organization can "jump to" stage VII from almost any other stage. While it is typically the larger organizations that are most in need of revitalization, there are examples of organizations at $30 million, $100 million, $1 billion, $10 billion, and even $100 billion dollars that have reached stage VII and are in need of revitalization.

The stage of organizational revitalization seems to be inevitable. The problems that underlie the need for organizational revitalization appear to result from an organization's own success. With organizational success come increases in the organization's size. Increases in an organization's size seem to create a certain degree of resistance to change, with respect to both those occurring in its external environment and those affecting its internal systems. This can result from the vested interests of people who control the organization, or it can be that the organization's size has made it very ponderous, creating lengthy delays between the time the organization identifies a trend or problem and the time it takes action. For example, Kodak, which has long been a successful company, missed major new markets (such as instant photography, videotape recorders, and 35 mm cameras) because its size, structure, and culture all made it move too slowly. Accordingly, very successful organizations—even those at the apparent height of their success—are already headed toward decline.

Organizational size does not seem to protect against decline; indeed, size itself may be one of the major factors creating the need for revitalization. A wide variety of organizations—including Chrysler, Wickes Corporation, International Harvester, Pan Am, General Motors, and Bank of America—have all recently faced the need for organizational revitalization despite their multibillion dollars in assets and revenues. Even such an outstanding organization as IBM has faced the need for a revitalization effort.

In addition, it is becoming increasingly recognized that, beyond a certain point, size may not be a strategic advantage. For example, T. J. Rodgers, founder of Cypress Semiconductor, has stated: "I would rather see our billion dollar company of the 1990s be ten $100 million companies, all strong, growing healthy, and aggressive as hell. The alternative is an aging billion-dollar company that spends more time defending its turf than growing."[57]

Although there are a number of issues involved in any example of organizational decline and revitalization, the basic problem that makes revitalization so difficult is that an organization at this stage must focus on all six of the key organizational development areas. The organization must now simultaneously rethink its markets, its products and services, its resources, its operational systems, its management systems, and its corporate culture. While organizations at every stage must give some attention to all six key areas, stages I through VI have only required that an organization concentrate on one or two key areas. In stage VII, it is critical that an organization simultaneously concentrate on all six areas, and this makes revitalization so difficult.

The Special Challenge of Revitalization

Stage VII presents the firm with special problems, the most significant being the fact that all six levels of the pyramid of organizational development must be simultaneously focused on and changed. This is the stage where the corporation must "reinvent itself." The demands on the leadership and individual members of the organization can be enormous. An organization that has been accustomed to success now faces the real possibility of failure. Moreover, the organization is encumbered by a variety of people with perceived entitlement. The sheer size of the organization requires a great deal of investment in political effort to achieve some kind of a workable consensus among the players, whereas in smaller organizations the decision authority may be concentrated in a smaller number of individuals, obviating the need for such politics. Each of these issues will be examined below.

Revitalizing Markets. During stage I the firm was able to establish itself because it was successful in identifying a single market. In stage V, the diversification efforts lead to the development of new markets. One of the fundamental reasons a stage VII firm experiences difficulty is that the organization's size has gotten out of sync with its ability to derive revenue from its traditional market segments. Instead of being able to focus its attention on a single market segment, the organization is now typically involved in a number of "mature" markets, meaning that the rate of growth in these markets is decreasing, with profit margins being squeezed.

The firm is trapped in a "scissors effect," facing decreasing revenues from its markets on the one hand, and rising operating costs caused by its increasing size and related inefficiencies on the other. With both blades of the scissors simultaneously closing in on the organization, management is busy doing its best to hold them apart.

The primary task now facing management is to identify a new set of markets for the organization. These will be markets offering higher potential rates of growth and higher profit margins. A good example of the successful search for new markets is Kodak. Kodak's traditional market has been photography, but in 1984 under Colby Chandler, Kodak began a process of redirection and revitalization that led it to identify new potential markets. Kodak entered into markets ranging from biomedical products, to information management, to chemicals and health care.

Each of Kodak's separate business units—which numbered about thirty in the late 1980s—has its roots in three underlying scientific disciplines (chemistry, optics, and electronics), all of which Kodak entered via its expertise in photography.

Revitalizing Products. Another typical problem of organizations in decline is the need to develop a whole new set of products and services. A firm that has reached stage VII has been the beneficiary of a product or set of products that have been well entrenched for a long period of time. Unfortunately, these products have reached the mature stage, and may even have been made obsolete by new competition from different companies. The critical problem in this situation is that the moment a firm becomes aware that its products are no longer competitive in the marketplace, it has already lost a sufficient amount of lead time needed to react. Thus, the organization is forced into a crisis: At a time when it needs additional revenues to invest in new directions, it finds that its revenues are declining for competitive reasons.

Revitalizing Resources. One of the relative advantages of established organizations is that they should have had the opportunity to accumulate resources over a period of time. These resources need to be invested in both product research and development and in corporate acquisitions for the purpose of acquiring new technologies. Since this is a relatively lengthy process, companies cannot expect any quick fix.

At stage VII, a company's resource situation will typically be somewhat inconsistent. The firm probably has a significant amount of resources at its disposal, but some of these resources will be redundant. Some of its inventory, its plant and equipment, and even its people, will not be appropriate for the new challenges it faces. The firm may also find itself with the need to redeploy some of its assets from one market segment to another. At this stage the firm will have to make major investments to revitalize the organization. Unfortunately, the firm may not be accustomed to making these types of investments, and will encounter internal resistance to investing in the resources needed to revitalize itself. When it comes to the issue of resources in organizational revitalization, the process is essentially one of building an almost entirely new organization on the foundation of the existing organization. In a sense, it is analogous to creating a totally new entrepreneurial effort, but at a much larger scale. It has been termed a process of "reinventing in the corporation."[58]

Revitalizing Operational Systems. The firm's operational systems are typically quite well established. This can simultaneously be both a blessing and a burden. It will be a blessing because the firm will not have to create some of the basic systems needed to operate a new enterprise. However, if the firm's systems have become too entrenched and are bureaucratic in nature, the firm may well need a "scorched earth" policy, requiring it to literally abandon some of its traditional systems. While abandonment is a drastic option, it may be the only effective catalyst for instituting new operating systems. Unfortunately, until the new systems are instituted, abandonment often has the adverse effect of choking the development of the new enterprise that needs to be created.

An effective strategy is to conduct an organizational assessment to determine which of the firm's systems are in need of revitalization. This assessment can be conducted by external consultants, by convening an internal task force, or a combination of both. If an internal task force is used, care must be taken to prevent members from protecting their vested interests in preserving certain systems, which may be beneficial to that member, but hurt the overall organization.

A traditional area for operational systems problems involves product development. Organizations needing revitalization usually possess a functional organization structure in which there is divided responsibility for product development. This responsibility is typically divided between production, sales, and engineering, which tends to create a very lengthy product development cycle. The revitalization period requires a unity of purpose within the organization. Accordingly, new products need to be developed with centralized coordination of engineering, manufacturing, and sales. The structure most appropriate for this is a divisional structure. In our judgment, it is not an accident that many of the revitalization efforts occur in organizations that have been using functional organizational structures.

Revitalizing Management Systems. The next area involved in the revitalization process is the firm's management systems. The firm's planning system may be well developed, but is probably not as entrepreneurially oriented as needed. What is usually needed is the institution of an entrepreneurially oriented strategic planning process that focuses on the kinds of questions that were previously articulated in Chapter Seven.

The firm's organization structure must be reevaluated. As noted above, the structure will probably have to be changed from either a functional or a matrix structure to a divisional structure which allows a considerable degree of autonomy.

Management development may need to be instituted in order to create a cadre of "entrepreneurial managers." An entrepreneurial manager is someone who thinks more like an entrepreneur than a professional manager. Professional managers are a valuable asset to the organization, and are critically needed during several of the earlier stages of development. However, when an organization reaches stage VII, it is in serious need of entrepreneurship, and some of the firm's core of managers need to rethink their orientation with respect to managing the business. Management development can assist this process, especially by using mind-stretching exercises that are designed to create new patterns of thought and open up lines of creativity.

This is a period of a firm's development when the firm will face a paradox in its need for control; it will need simultaneously both more and less control. On the one hand, as profit margins decrease, it will be very necessary for a firm to control its expenses. On the other hand, there are times when a firm must invest money, regardless of the rate of return, merely to stay in business. This means that some of the traditional accounting measures used in control systems may not be very relevant.

One of the critical dimensions of a revitalization effort is, of course, leadership. If existing management is unable to mount a successful turnaround, companies are likely to seek new leadership, sometimes known as "crisis management teams." One of the most famous is that led by Sanford Sigoloff, who has a history of successful rescue missions, including Republic Corporation, Daylin, and Wickes. In 1989, Sigoloff took over the U.S. retail operation of the Australia-based L. J. Hooker Corporation, which included Bonwit Teller and B. Altman, and began another revitalization project.

Revitalizing Corporate Culture. Finally, the culture of the firm will have to be modified. All established companies have complex cultures. Sometimes, they may have several subcultures. One of the typical problems of established companies is that, unintentionally, the culture begins to emphasize politics and avoidance of conflict and risk more than performance, quality, customer service, and profitability. Many people will have well-entrenched positions and some are likely to resist the required changes even though they are needed by the organization.

If a revitalization effort is undertaken without attention to the cultural dimensions, it is not likely to be effective. Many of the lessons of Chapter Twelve are appropriate here.

Successful Revitalization: Case Study. One reasonably successful revitalization effort was that accomplished at Navistar (formerly International Harvester). International Harvester had operated in a wide variety of businesses, including agricultural equipment, which was its historical foundation, and trucks. The company's strategy was to divest itself of unprofitable operations and focus on a single core business: trucks. Navistar now specializes in the manufacture and distribution of medium and heavy trucks.

One of the key assets of the business is its network of dealers. Each dealership is a separate business. Many of the dealers are former employees of International Harvester. Navistar has provided a variety of programs to help the dealers become more professionally managed. One resource for dealers is a management development program to help the dealerships make the transition from an entrepreneurship to a professionally managed firm.[59] This program was designed to assist the dealers in developing the skills required to help their firms make the successful transitions required at different growth stages, as well as to develop the skills required by the CEO to lead the firm throughout these transitions.

The situation at Navistar is significant not only because of the revitalization of the company, but because of the existence of many entrepreneurial subunits (the dealerships). The dealerships must professionalize while the parent company strives to rekindle its entrepreneurial spirit. Although the company has continued to face difficulties, it survived a period of great trauma. That is in itself a reasonable definition of successful revitalization.

Summary

Once a firm has completed the development challenges required to take it through stages I through IV, it has become a professionally managed organization. However, its life cycle is not completed, and the firm must now deal with the problems and challenges posed by the advanced stages of growth—stages V through VII.

Stage V involves efforts to diversify the firm because it can no longer rely on its initial product for continued profitability. The firm's success has attracted competitors, and its products are now competing in a saturated market. The firm must develop new products or services to "restart" another cycle of success. A prudent firm has not waited until this stage to begin the process of diversification, and has been investing a portion of its profits into the development of new products. Because the original entrepreneur is often no longer available, many firms are training managers to mimic the behavior of entrepreneurs, thereby creating "intrapreneurs" who will serve as catalysts for diversification.

Stage VI involves integrating the new businesses that were created around the new products developed in stage V. These businesses may be only partially related. The challenge is to coordinate these entities while allowing each sufficient independence to derive the benefits of acting in an entrepreneurial manner. Such issues as the amount of centralized control over differing divisions, integrating the separate planning activities, and managing the overall corporate culture must be addressed.

Finally, stage VII requires that a company overcome the pressures leading to decline, whether they are caused by market saturation, an erosion of management's entrepreneurial skills, the inability to develop an organizational infrastructure to support the growth realized from previous stages, or a feeling of complacency. The organization must "revitalize" itself, but the difficulty in doing so is that management must give its full attention to all six levels of the pyramid of organizational development simultaneously.

14. The Transition CEOs Must Make to Survive Beyond the Entrepreneurial Stage

Most of this book has dealt with the organizational and managerial issues that arise when entrepreneurial firms make the transition from one stage of growth to another. This chapter, in contrast, is more personal. It is directed primarily to the CEO of an entrepreneurial company, because this person will have the major responsibility to direct and guide the transition process of the whole organization. However, the ideas included here should also be of interest to senior managers, corporate advisers, venture capitalists, and others who are concerned about the welfare of business enterprises.

The chapter will focus on two kinds of issues facing the CEO: (1) personal issues—such as the nature of the CEO's role, behavioral and attitudinal changes required, and changes required in managerial style during organizational transitions; and (2) strategic issues involved in designing and implementing the changes required for healthy organizational development.

Personal Issues

To understand transitions that CEOs must make as their firms grow, it is useful to first consider who they are as people and how they got to be CEOs. Unlike the CEOs of large, Fortune 500–type organizations, who are typically promoted through the ranks over a period of many years, the CEO of an entrepreneurial company is typically someone who either founded the company, was part of a founding group, or is the spouse or child of the founder.

Characteristics of Entrepreneurs. Although there are no precise demographic and psychological profiles available, our experience has shown that CEOs of entrepreneurial companies tend to have certain things in common. About 90 percent of these people have one of three types of background: (1) a marketing background; (2) a background in some technical area, such as engineering or computers; or (3) a background in a particular industry. For example, an individual may have sold computers for a large company before deciding to start his or her own company. Alternatively, a person may have been an engineer or other technical specialist and become skilled at product development before deciding to establish a new business. Finally, someone may have worked in a particular industry such as travel, executive search, construction, real estate, or garment manufacturing.

Most CEOs of entrepreneurial firms are enthusiastic about markets and products but are not very interested in management or the "nuts and bolts" of day-to-day operations. Many of them find accounting boring. They have no more interest in their own accounting system than the typical homeowner has in the household's plumbing: They want it to work, but they do not care to understand how it works. Many tend to look at financial statements only to determine "the bottom line."

Entrepreneurs are typically above average in intelligence, willing to take risks, uncomfortable in environments in which they are told what to do, and fond of seeing things done their way. Most, but not all, do not have good listening skills. They are used to being the dominant person in business situations. Most of these CEOs have made open-ended commitments to their business, which means that business does not merely consume a great deal of their life; in most instances, their business is their life. The pejorative term *workaholic,* however, would be a misleading description of such people; rather, they view the business as a rather complex game. It is a source of profound personal pleasure. Above all, entrepreneurs possess a strong desire to be independent of others' ability to control their behavior. They like to feel "in control."

The Personal Control Bind. The most important of all these characteristics, from the standpoint of making organizational transitions, is the entrepreneurial CEO's desire for things to be done his or her way—the desire for control. The typical CEO of an entrepreneurial company either consciously or unconsciously values control both as an end in itself and as a means to other ends. This personal preference has most likely been reinforced in a variety of ways for a relatively long time.

During the first two stages of organizational growth, the typical attributes of an entrepreneurial CEO are beneficial and necessary for the company. Fledgling enterprises need strong direction and open-ended commitment to make everything work properly. At this time, a compulsive CEO who knows about everything that is going on and pays attention to the smallest detail will have a tremendous positive impact on operations.

Many consequences of an entrepeneurial CEO's desire for control, however, are less favorable during the later stages of a company's development. Specifically, both the CEO and the organization's staff may have become used to the idea that almost every issue, whether major or not, will be brought to the CEO's attention for decisions or final approval. More insidiously, if the CEO has not been extremely careful, an entire organization inadvertently may have been built on people weaker than the CEO. In other words, the CEO may have become an unwitting bottleneck in the organization. Even though the firm has grown in size and added many managers and professional specialists, the CEO may remain the most skilled person in the company in most, if not all, areas. This means that the CEO has not been able to increase the company's capabilities beyond his or her own admittedly considerable personal skills. Such a situation puts limits on the organization's capacity to grow and develop.

The CEO's desire for personal control over everything done in the organization, which was a considerable strength during stages I and II, thus becomes a limitation or bind on the company during stage III. Some CEOs consciously want to retain control and therefore do not want to hire people who are better than they are at any particular task. Others are afraid that if they hire someone to perform a task that they cannot do themselves, they will become too dependent on that person. For example, the CEO of one service firm with $5 million in annual revenues was doing most of the company's computer programming work himself. When asked why he was spending his time in this way, he replied, "If I had someone else do it, I would be vulnerable if he left me."

Some CEOs are able to recognize their own limitations relative to their companies' changing needs. As one founder and CEO of an entrepreneurial firm stated: "I'm an entrepreneur. I'm very good at controlling things—making a decision and seeing it accomplished by sheer willpower alone, if necessary. But our company has grown beyond that style. I'm not uncomfortable with the company, but I'm not as effective." Such CEOs realize that, for the good of the firm, they need to make the transition from a manager who is used to controlling everything and being the center of all that happens to someone who is still important but is not an omnipresent, omnipotent figure.

Even when the need for it is recognized, however, this type of change can be stressful. For some CEOs, whose identities are closely bound up with their companies, it represents a threat—a potential loss of potency. Many CEOs are simply not able to give up control to any significant degree and end up strangling their organizations.

Some CEOs go through the motions of giving up some degree of control because intellectually they know that this is essential but emotionally they cannot really bring themselves to do it. For example, one entrepreneur built an organization that achieved a billion dollars in revenues in less than one decade. Recognizing that the size of the enterprise now made it impossible for him to manage in the old way, he brought in two "heavyweights": experienced, professional managers whom he had to pay high salaries to attract. One was a marketing manager, and the other was a finance-oriented manager who would be responsible for day-to-day operations. The entrepreneur himself moved up to chairperson. Unfortunately, he then proceeded to turn the professional managers into "managerial eunuchs." When the organization began to do poorly, he announced that he had experimented with professional managers but, reluctantly, he had to reassume personal control himself.

Alternatives for the CEO. Four basic alternatives are available to the CEO of an entrepreneurial organization who recognizes that the organization can no longer be run in the old way. They are (1) do nothing, (2) sell the business and start over, (3) move up to chairperson and bring in a professional manager to run the organization, or (4) make a systematic effort to change personal behavior to fit the needs of the company at its new stage of development. Let us look more closely at each of these alternatives.

First, the CEO can do nothing—or, rather, do "business as usual"—and hope for the best. This could be called the "ostrich strategy." The strongest argument for this course of action is that the company has been successful with its current style to date, and "If it's not broken, don't fix it." Unfortunately, corporate graveyards are littered with companies that had promising starts but, because of this strategy, did not continue to develop.

The second strategy is for the CEO to become chairperson and bring in a professional manager to run the business. This is the approach Steven Jobs tried at Apple Computer. After Apple reached a billion dollars in revenue, Jobs recruited John Sculley of Pepsico, who had the track record of a successful professional manager. The pitfall of this strategy is that if it is to be effective, the founder must give up considerable control to the new manager. The strategy also may not work out politically. It certainly did not for Jobs, who left Apple Computer in 1985. A variation on this theme is for the company's board of directors to replace the original CEO with another who has a different leadership style, as Commodore did with Jack Tramiel.

A third strategy is for the entrepreneurial CEO to sell the company when it gets too big to continue with an entrepreneurial style, then set about building a new company. A variation on this theme is merging with another company to bring in new senior managers. This was the strategy of the founder of Conductron, who sold that company to McDonnel Douglas and then went on to found KMS Industries. Similarly, Steven Jobs began to develop a new company Next, after leaving Apple.

Finally, a CEO may choose to make the personal and managerial style changes necessary to be able to take the organization to its next growth stage successfully. A critical ingredient in the success of such an attempt is the CEO's willingness to live with less control over the organization and its activities.

The CEO as "Organizational Glue."   The CEO who elects to stay with the company and delegate authority to managers now faces another problem. As more than one such person has asked us, "What do I do now? What is my role?" It is likely to be more than a little discomforting for a person who has been hyperactive and involved in virtually all phases of an organization's activities to find that all tangible roles have been delegated and the only thing left is to be a catalyst—a kind of "organizational glue."

The entrepreneurial CEO has been used to being the most versatile person in the orchestra: the individual who could play violin, bass, trombone, drums, or harp. He or she could even be a one-person band. Now, however, the CEO's job is more like that of an orchestra leader. The CEO may not be at all sure that he or she likes or values this new and unfamiliar role. It does not seem to be productive in a concrete way.

In fact, this role is indispensable. Yet the CEO may not be equipped to handle it because of lack of a concept of the role or the skills to perform it or both. Moreover, many CEOs cannot admit weakness by letting anyone guess that they know neither what to do next nor how to do it. Some try to bluff their way through by acting "in an executive manner" and issuing peremptory edicts. Others try to cope by becoming hyperactive, burying themselves in their work. Often, however, this is merely make-work or busy work, an attempt to fool themselves into believing that they are still doing something valuable. A CEO who does not know what to do next but is afraid to admit it and seek help is setting the stage for future organizational crises.

At this stage of the company's development, the CEO's proper role is to be concerned with the future direction of the enterprise and its long-term objectives. It is to be a strategic leader and a role model for others. Finally, it is to focus on the culture of the enterprise. Each of these aspects of the CEO's new role requires the ability to think abstractly or conceptually about the business rather than merely in terms of concrete products. Unfortunately, many entrepreneurial CEOs either do not have the ability to think conceptually or do not feel comfortable in thinking in this way.

Organizational Issues

In addition to making personal changes, CEOs and other senior managers of entrepreneurial firms must face the challenge of helping their organizations make the transition to professionally managed firms. This section describes some steps they can take to meet that challenge. It recapitulates several themes we have developed throughout this book. There are two broad areas that the CEO must focus on: (1) understanding the "target" of change for the organizational development process, and (2) managing the steps in the organization development process.

The "Target" Of Organizational Development

To help his or her firm make the transition from an entrepreneurship to a professionally managed firm, the CEO must understand how to manage the key components of the pyramid of organizational development at each stage of growth. This has been the subject of this book, with Chapters Four through Six focusing on stages I through IV individually. In this section, we summarize the key organizational development changes, or "targets" for change, that need to occur from stages I through IV. This is summarized in Table 14.1.

Table 14.2 shows what management's overall focus or "target" should be during each of the first four stages of growth. It also summarizes what each of the key aspects of the pyramid of organizational development will look like at each stage of growth. In brief, management's overall focus should be to make and sell the basic product and service in stage I, to expand resources and develop operational systems during stage II, to build the management infrastructure during stage III, and to consolidate the culture in stage IV.

In stage I the key challenge for management is to identify a market and if possible to establish a market niche. During stage I the firm must also develop its core products and services. During this stage of development its resources will be stretched thin and its

Table 14.1. Management Systems at Different Stages of Growth.

Growth Stages	Strategic Planning	Organizational Structure	Management Development	Control Systems
I	• Very informal "In entrepreneur's head"	• Prefunctional structure	• On-the-job training	• Control through "personal observation"
II	• Basic corporate strategic plan • Annual retreat	• Functional structure	• Basic management development program: First-line supervisors Fundamentals of management	• Personal management control system • Responsibility accounting • Basic reporting and meeting system
III (A)	• Corporate strategic planning	• Functional structure	• Basic management development program for all levels	• Basic "MBO" System
(B)	• Departmental strategic plans	• Divisionalizing	• Advanced management development	• Cost and profit center control system • Performance appraisal system
(C)	• Strategic planning is "a way of life" • Divisional strategic plan	• Divisional structure	• Leadership development	• Comprehensive control systems
IV	• Same as above	• COO • Complex structures	• Same as above	• Control systems for decentralized management

Table 14.2. Organizational Characteristics During Each Stage of Growth.

Key Organizational Development Areas	Stages of Organizational Growth			
	I	II	III	IV
Overall management focus during each stage	Make and sell	Expand resources and products	Build the management infrastructure	Spread the culture
Corporate culture	Informal but understood	Attenuating	Tenuous	Explicitly defined
Management systems	Informal	Informal	Formalizing	Formal
Operational systems	Basic	Developing	Well-developed	Well-developed
Resources	Thin	Stretched thin	Increasing surplus	Strong
Products	Develop core products	New products	Established products	Established products
Markets	Define markets and niche	Market	Well-defined market	Well-defined market

351

operational systems will be relatively basic. Management systems will be relatively informal and its corporate culture will also be informal but will be understood. The culture will be transmitted primarily through the day-to-day interactions with various people.

By the time the firm reaches stage II its markets, and its products and services will be relatively well established. It will now be going through a period of rapid growth with its resources being stretched thin. The firm will be in the process of developing its operational systems but there will probably be a great deal of problems in this area. Its management systems will still be relatively informal and its corporate culture will begin to be attenuated as increasing numbers of people enter the organization. Management's overall focus will be to expand its resources and develop the operational systems needed to support further growth.

By the time the firm reaches stage III it has a well-defined market, and perhaps even a niche. It will also have relatively established products. During stage III, as the firm is professionalizing, it may well be developing an increasing surplus of resources. Its operational systems should be relatively well developed. The key issue during stage III is to develop and begin formalizing its management systems. Corporate culture, however, will become more tenuous as increased numbers of people join the firm but have not yet adopted all of its values. The overall focus of management during this stage will be to build the overall management infrastructure.

By the time the firm is in stage IV, its markets and products will still be the same as stage III, which are relatively well developed and established. Its resources will be relatively strong and its operational systems should be developed. By this time the firms management systems should also be well developed and the key issue will be to work on management of the corporate culture. At this point the firm will have at least 500 people, and the people who have joined the firm will have entered in various waves. The critical issue will be to help all the people who have joined the firm develop and support the same set of values, beliefs, and norms, which constitute core aspects of corporate culture.

Steps in the Organizational Development Process

There are four key steps in the process of beginning the transition from an entrepreneurship to a professionally managed organization: (1) conduct an organizational audit, (2) formulate an organizational development plan, (3) implement the plan, and (4) periodically monitor progress. Although the steps are relatively straightforward to explain, in practice they can be quite complex to perform, as illustrated by the case studies in Chapters Four through Six.

Organizational Audit. The first step in planning for the transition from an entrepreneurship to a professionally managed organization is to do an "organizational audit." As you recall from Chapter Two, an organizational audit is a systematic assessment of the strengths, limitations, and developmental needs of an organization's performance in six areas: markets, products and services, resources, operational systems, management systems, corporate culture. The purpose of the audit is to gather data about the organization and its functioning and to use those data to make judgments about the organization's effectiveness and requirements for future development.

Many methods of data collection and analysis may be used in an organizational audit. One effective method is the "focus interview." A focus interview involves meetings between a trained interviewer and selected members of the organization. The interviewer asks a variety of questions dealing with critical aspects of organizational performance. The process of the interview and the sequence of the questions is often as important as their content. (Exhibit 14.1 gives an illustrative sample of types of questions used in an organizational audit.) A number of interviewers may be used, and the information they derive may be pooled in an analysis session.

An organization can do its organizational audit internally. If this is done, an employee trained in organizational development, with a degree from a reputable university and several years of experience, ought to be used. Alternatively, the organization may have an independent consultant perform the audit. Such a person may

Exhibit 14.1. Sample Questions for Organizational Audit.

1. Market and Market Niche
   1.1 What are the firm's present market segments?
       a. Have the market segments been clearly identified and
          defined?
       b. Has a strategic market analysis been conducted to answer the
          following questions:
          (1) Who are our customers?
          (2) What are their needs?
          (3) Through what channels do they buy?
          (4) What is value for them?
       c. What are the key factors that will determine success in satis-
          fying the market's needs?
       d. What is the firm's strategy for competing in its chosen
          markets?
          (1) Who are the firm's major competitors?
          (2) What are their strengths and limitations?
          (3) What are their comparative advantages?
          (4) What are our comparative advantages?
       e. Is there a good (satisfactory, better than satisfactory, optimal)
          fit between the market's needs and the firm's strategy?
   1.2 Does the firm have a present or potential market niche (a place
       where it possesses a comparative advantage)?
       a. If it has a niche, is that niche relatively permanent or
          perishable?
       b. If it does not have a niche, can one be developed?
2. Products and "Productization"
   2.1 Have the firm's present products been adequately geared (produc-
       tized) to meet the needs of its present markets?
       a. If not, why not?
       b. If so, what can be done to improve the fit?
   2.2 Are there any present or potential market segments for which ex-
       isting products (ours or competitors') are unsatisfactory?
       a. In what respects?
       b. Can we develop products to capture such markets?
   2.3 How effective is the firm's process (skills) at "productization"
       (tailoring products to meet market needs)?
3. Resources
   3.1 How adequate are the firm's present resources to implement its
       strategy?
   3.2 What additional resources are required to implement the firm's
       market strategy and productization plans?
       a. People
       b. Financial resources
       c. Facilities
       d. Equipment
       e. Other

have a greater degree of objectivity and more experience in conducting such audits than any organization employee.

An organizational audit often includes a special study of the firm's management capabilities and developmental needs. This sub-audit may be termed a "Management Development Audit."

Organizational Development Plan. Once the organizational audit has been completed, the next step is to prepare an organizational development plan. As you may recall, this is a plan for the systematic development of an organization in each of the six key areas: markets, products, and so forth. The plan must list the specific objectives and goals that the organization wants to achieve in each key area.

Later Steps. The third step in making the transition is to implement the organizational development plan, and the fourth step is to monitor and revise the plan. Many organizations use an organizational development task force to serve as a planning and advisory group.

Chapters Four through Six describes how specific organizations underwent the transitions from one growth stage to the next. As we noted there, organizational development is a lengthy process. It may require time ranging from several months to many years. During this period it is often useful to repeat the audit process to assess what progress, if any, has been made.

Managing Organizational Transitions: A Capstone Case

To help tie together the concepts and approaches presented in this book and to illustrate how one CEO faced the transitions discussed in this chapter, we will examine the case of Bob Mason. We shall discuss both the personal and organizational transitions which had to be made by Mason's company, Medco.

Medco's Early History

Bob Mason, the founder of Medco, began his career as a salesman for a major medical products manufacturing and marketing firm. Bob worked hard to learn all he could about the industry, and discovered that the company for which he was working was not adequately meeting all of its customers' needs, and that there was an untapped market for disposable medical products. So, in 1978, he decided to start his own company. Apparently Bob's belief about the demand for his products was accurate, because within a few years his firm began to experience rapid growth.

By the beginning of 1985, the company had reached more than $20 million in annual revenues, and it was estimated that by 1990 it would achieve $50 million in yearly sales. Medco's personnel increased from 25 in 1975 to 200 in 1986.

Growing Pains

As early as 1983, Medco was beginning to experience certain organizational problems, symptoms of growing pains. Some symptoms were more serious than others, but they all signaled that there were some deeper problems which eventually could lead to Medco's failure. These symptoms are described below.

Many People Were Not Aware of What Others Were Doing. A significant number of people did not understand what their jobs were, what others' jobs were, or what the relationships were between their jobs and the jobs of others. This problem resulted, in part, from a tendency to add personnel without developing formal descriptions of roles and responsibilities. Since employees were added on an *ad hoc* basis whenever a staff shortage seemed imminent, there was often little time to orient them to the organization's operations or to train them adequately in what their own responsibilities would be. Indeed, there was no formal training program.

Some people were given job descriptions, but did not adhere to their specified roles. Others were given a title, but no explicit responsibilities. Surprisingly, many individuals often did not know to whom they were to report, and managers did not know for which employees and activities they would be held accountable. People learned what they were supposed to do on a daily basis; long-range planning was nonexistent.

Interactions Between Departments Was Also a Problem. Managers often did not understand what their responsibilities were and how what they were doing fit in with the firm's overall operations. New departments were created to meet Medco's product and marketing needs, but many managers were not aware of how these departments fit in with the rest of the organization. One manager complained, "People sit outside my door, but I don't even know what they do." Another new manager described his introduction to Medco as follows: "I was walked to an area and was told: 'It's your department. Run it.'"

This lack of formal roles and responsibilities made it easy for personnel to avoid responsibility whenever a task was not completed or was completed unsatisfactorily. This also led to duplication of effort between departments. Since no one knew precisely whose responsibility a particular task was, two or more departments or people often would complete a task, only to find that it had already been accomplished by someone else.

People Felt There Were Not Enough Hours in the Day. Most employees felt "overloaded." They commonly stayed after hours to complete their work. Department managers, in particular, felt that their workload was too great and that deadlines were unrealistic.

This situation resulted, in part, from the lack of adequately developed operational systems to support Medco employees' work. The accounting, operational planning, and communication systems were adequate for a small company, but quite inadequate for one as large as Medco had become. Systems for purchasing, inventory control, and even small distribution were either poorly developed or nonexistent.

People Spent Too Much Time Putting Out Fires. Perhaps the best indication that Medco was beginning to choke on its growth was that employees spent an increasing amount of time dealing with short-term problems resulting from the lack of long-range planning. This was particularly evident in the constant lack of space within the company's headquarters. It appeared to most employees that as soon as the company increased its office space, the space already was filled, and it was time to begin planning for another move. It seemed that there was never enough space or equipment to support the company's staff adequately. When they worked at the firm's headquarters, salespeople usually arrived early to ensure they would be able to find a vacant desk from which to make their calls. Employees who did not go out into the field attempted to handle the cramped space by creating "schedules" for using phones, computer terminals, and even desks.

Employees Began to Feel That Medco Never Planned, It Simply Reacted.   (An informal joke around the company was: "At Medco, long-range planning means what I am going to do after lunch.") This was caused partly by the changes in the marketplace and the new demands placed upon the company. It also resulted from the tendency of entrepreneurial companies like Medco to spend most of their time simply staying afloat without keeping an eye on the future.

Employees began to think that, simply because "crisis is the norm" at the company, that is the way they should operate. They began to call themselves "the fire fighters," and even took pride in their ability to deal with crises.

There Were Not Enough Good Managers.   Most managers at Medco were promoted to their positions in recognition of service. Some were good managers, but most were described by their subordinates as "good technicians who lack people skills." Further, they were seen as clones: Many employees believed that management had one and only one way of doing things, and that to deviate from the norm would result in adverse consequences.

Plenty of people had the title "manager," but relatively few really behaved as managers. After promotion, many people simply kept doing the things they had done in their former roles. They were poor delegators, often doing the work themselves rather than assigning it to others. As a result, employees came to believe that their managers did not trust them.

Bob Mason was a strong individual who wanted things done his way, and he wanted to control almost everything. Bob recognized this, referring to himself as "someone who sticks his nose into everything." Few decisions were made without Bob's approval or review. As a consequence, one of two things tended to happen concerning managers: (1) the stronger managers tended to "butt heads" with Bob and ultimately left; and (2) the remaining managers were slowly marginalized. Those managers who decided not to leave Medco tended not to take Bob on, at least directly, and they had little real authority and certainly no power. Inadvertently, Bob had created an organization of "managerial pygmies." In effect, Bob was a victim of his own need for control. This phenomenon is part of what has been termed the *entrepreneur's syndrome.*[60]

When Business Plans Were Made, There Was Very Little Follow-Up, and Things Did Not Get Done. As is true of many small and growing firms, Medco had traditionally operated on an ad hoc basis. No formal strategic planning system was needed, since Bob had provided all of the firm's direction. Further, the informal structure had allowed Medco's employees the freedom to generate new product and marketing ideas.

As the company grew, however, Bob and his senior management team began to realize the firm needed to monitor its operations. Unfortunately, Medco had not developed the systems necessary to have accountability.

There Was a Lack of Understanding About Where the Firm Was Going. Many Medco employees complained that not only did they not know what was expected of them; they could not understand where the company was headed in the long term. This resulted from the inability of Medco's management to communicate its vision for the future to the company's personnel. Employees were aware that changes were being made, but were not always sure how these changes would affect them or their departments. Consequently, employees experienced high levels of anxiety. When this anxiety became too great, many left the firm.

Most People Felt Meetings Were a Waste of Time. Employees complained that too many meetings were held among top managers and not enough among the lower levels of the organization. In addition, those meetings that were held were often inefficient and did not result in resolutions to problems. It was because few meetings had written agendas or minutes—many of those attending described them as "free-for-alls." They were at best discussions, and at worst fights between departments or individuals. Worst of all, they went on interminably.

Moreover, people complained that most meetings were called on an ad hoc basis. Since these meetings were unscheduled, people typically came to them without any sense of their purpose and certainly with no preparation. Thus, they tended to have the atmosphere of "bull sessions" in which people shot from the hip. In addition, people felt that they could not plan their work because they were constantly interrupted for "crisis" meetings.

Some People Began to Feel Insecure About Their Places at the Firm. This problem grew out of the many changes taking place and the large number of problems the firm was encountering as it grew. Some original "founding members" were terminated and replaced. This caused people to wonder who was next. Although many recognized that some employees had not grown as the company grew, they worried about their jobs and their places within the firm. This, in turn, led people to spend an increasing amount of their time "covering their 'vested interests.'"

The Company Grew in Sales But Not in Profits. Medco, like many entrepreneurial firms, traditionally had been most concerned with increasing sales. It adopted the philosophy of many growing firms: "If we're selling more, we must be making more profits." Unfortunately, this is not often the case. The other side of the profit equation, costs, often increases along with sales, and if costs are not contained, the firm soon may find itself in a position of losing, rather than making, money. Thus, although Medco sales were increasing at a rapid rate, profits were remaining relatively constant.

Medco's problems certainly are not unique. Indeed, they are the classic symptoms of organizational growing pains. It should be noted that while these "symptoms" represent problems in and of themselves, they also suggest a deeper, more systemic organizational problem. Specifically, they signal that the organization is coming precariously close to choking on its own growth. This, in turn, indicates that the organization must change its very nature; it must make a transition to a different kind of organization, a more professionally managed firm.

The Need for a Transition

During 1984, Bob Mason recognized that his firm was experiencing problems. He began a program to help his company successfully make the transition from an entrepreneurship to a more professionally managed firm and, in turn, overcome the problems associated with growth. The four specific steps in the program were as follows:

> STEP I: Perform an organizational audit.
> STEP II: Formulate an organizational development plan.
> STEP III: Implement the organizational development plan.
> STEP IV: Monitor progress.

Step I: Conduct an Organizational Audit. An organizational audit was performed to assess Medco's current state of development and future needs. The audit involved collecting information from employees about their perceptions of Medco and its operations. One tool used in this process was the "Organizational Growing Pains Questionnaire" presented in Chapter Three. This questionnaire measures the extent to which an organization is experiencing the ten classic symptoms of growing pains and is in danger of choking on its own growth.

At Medco the scores on this questionnaire ranged from 30 to 34, with an average score of 32. This indicated that the company was experiencing some very significant problems which required immediate attention. Specifically, the audit revealed that the company needed to

- Better define organizational roles and responsibilities and linkages between roles.
- Help employees plan and budget their time.

- Develop a long-range business plan and a system for monitoring it.
- Increase the number of qualified present and potential managers.
- Identify the direction the company should take in the future.
- Reduce employee and departmental feelings that they always "need to do it themselves" if a job is to get done.
- Make meetings more efficient by developing written agendas and taking and distributing meeting minutes.
- Become profit oriented rather than strictly sales oriented.

Steps II–IV: Formulate and Implement an Organizational Development Plan and Monitor Progress. Having identified its organizational problems and developmental needs, Medco proceeded to the next step: designing and implementing a program that would resolve problems and help the company develop the infrastructure necessary to accommodate its rapid growth. Management met at a retreat to design a plan for the firm. The plan included specific action steps to overcome its problems.

Some of these steps were (1) acquisition of human resources and development of operational systems needed to make the transition to professional management; (2) implementation of a strategic plan which defined the company's business, mission, key result areas, goals, and action plans; (3) implementation of control systems to motivate people to achieve the company's goals; (4) design of a management development program to help people become better managers and overcome the "doer syndrome"; (5) development of a system to explicitly manage the corporate culture. In addition, Bob began to focus on making some important changes in his own role, behavior, and attitudes.

Acquisition of Resources and Development of Operational Systems. As the company grew, so did its need for greater skills and sophistication in certain functional areas. A controller was recruited to replace the firm's bookkeeper. A national sales manager was appointed. Medco also hired a personnel director and a marketing manager. Moreover, the firm engaged a consultant to serve as its "adjunct" management development and organizational development adviser. In brief, the firm made a significant investment in its human resources. These people, in turn, were responsible for developing the operational systems required to manage growth in various areas. The most significant of these were systems for job descriptions and performance appraisals.

Implementing Strategic Planning. One of the first steps Medco took to manage its growth was to begin developing a strategic plan. The major goal of this process was to motivate the company's managers to begin to take a longer-range view than "what's happening after lunch." A related goal was to affect the corporate culture at Medco and make planning a way of life.

The process began with a two-day strategic planning retreat which focused on some fundamental issues necessary to guide the future development of the company, including:

1. What business is Medco in?
2. What are our competitive strengths and limitations?
3. Do we have a market niche?
4. What are the key factors responsible for our past success, and to what extent will they be accountable for our future requirements for success?
5. What should our objectives be for developing Medco as an organization?
6. What should our action plans be, and who is responsible for each action plan to implement our specific objectives?

In addition to these generic strategic planning issues, which are relevant to all organizations, the company also examined certain specific strategic issues peculiar to its operations.

After the strategic planning retreat, a draft of a corporate strategic plan was prepared. This plan specified the firm's business definition, mission, key result areas, objectives and goals, and action plans. The plan was circulated among the firm's senior managers for their comments and input. It was revised and approved by Bob, and then distributed to all senior managers. The plan provided a "blueprint" for future development, including specific objectives focused upon eliminating the problems leading to the company's growing pains.

The firm then held quarterly meetings to review the company's results, compare them with the plan, and make required adjustments. This signaled that the plan was more than merely a "paper plan"—it was a real management tool.

A key decision by management was to be more selective in accepting new business until the firm had digested its present growth by building the required infrastructure.

Control Systems.   As part of Medco's effort to develop its overall management systems, a new system of management control was put into place. As an output of the firm's strategic planning, Medco had identified its key result areas. These areas were seen as the vital areas for managing the business.

The next step was to develop measurements which could be used to monitor performance in each one of the key result areas. These measurements were developed as part of an organizational development team meeting in which all of Medco's senior management participated. Once the measurements which were to be used to monitor each key result area had been decided upon, the next step was for Medco to revise its information system so that the data required could be obtained. Some of the data came directly from the firm's accounting information system. For example, information about sales, gross margins, and net profitability came from this source. Other information had to be obtained separately. The firm felt that one of the vital aspects of the business concerned the percentage of merchandise which was being shipped to dealers as opposed to end users. This information began to be monitored on a regular basis.

Management Development.   Bob and Medco's other senior managers realized that people were Medco's true asset. The firm's technology, products, and equipment were really not proprietary; the true differentiating factor was the motivation and skills of its people.

Recognizing this, Medco believed the company had to make an investment in building its managerial capabilities for two reasons. First, there simply was not a sufficient number of effective managers. Although many people had managerial titles and could recite the right "buzzwords," relatively few were really behaving as managers. They were spending too much time as doers rather than managers; there was little true delegation; and insufficient effort was given to planning, organizing people, performance appraisal, and control, which are the essence of management. Another need for management development was more symbolic. Bob recognized that some of the people who had helped build Medco to its current size were in jeopardy of becoming victims of the "Peter Principle": They had been promoted to their level of incompetence. Bob felt that the company owed its people a chance to grow with it, and he saw management development as a chance to provide them that opportunity. Quite frankly, he felt that if people had this opportunity and failed to grow, the firm could feel it had met its responsibilities to them.

To deal with these issues, Medco asked a consultant to design a management development program for its personnel. Two programs were developed: one for top managers and one for middle managers.

Corporate Culture. Although Bob Mason had been aware that his firm had a culture, he had never taken any serious steps to manage it. He had always wanted the firm to be sales oriented, aggressive, and profit oriented. He hadn't realized that there were also a great many other facets to the firm's culture which had been embedded since the earliest days of its operation.

As the firm began to change, Bob became increasingly aware that he needed to manage the firm's corporate culture in order to reinforce the change. One of the unintended aspects of the firm's culture that had developed was that people felt that if they worked hard they should be rewarded regardless of the results. Bob felt that people needed to learn that hard work was simply not enough and that they had to be oriented toward bottom line results. Another aspect of the firm's culture had been that decisions would be pushed up to Bob. Since Bob was acknowledged to be an "entrepreneurial genius" and since his personality had tended to lead to nuclear explosions whenever someone made a mistake, people naturally pushed decisions to his desk. Bob now wanted to reverse the culture, and push the decisions down to the lowest level of responsibility in the firm where they could be meaningfully made. The firm also tried to emphasize that under the new culture mistakes would be examined, and corrected, but that people would not feel the brunt of a nuclear explosion if a mistake was made. Another aspect of the Medco culture had been that "we're good crisis managers." This meant that Medco managers had to learn to turn on a dime and solve whatever crises came up. Mason now wanted Medco to revise its culture to emphasize the importance of long-range planning. He wanted the culture to become one of "planning is a way of life at Medco." Another aspect of the Medco culture had been "we're hands-on managers." This needed to be revised so that managers stayed in touch with operations, but delegated responsibility to the lowest level capable of performing the required tasks.

One of the most important aspects of this change was that Bob, together with the senior managers, now realized that the management of the corporate culture was an important part of the strategic leadership function that they had to perform.

Changes in the CEO. Bob Mason realized that just as Medco had to change so did he. Bob realized that his basic skills were as a salesman and as an entrepreneur. He had worked hard and he had built a successful company. He had the title of president but he realized he was not acting like a president.

In spite of the fact that he was the CEO of the company, Bob continued to spend too much time dealing with the technical and marketing aspects of the business. This is what he knew how to do and this is what he enjoyed. He knew he was not devoting a sufficient amount of time to the broader aspects of organizational development.

Bob also understood that there were certain other problems with his management style and capabilities. In spite of the fact that his organization had grown substantially, he still wanted to control too many details of the business. He knew he still "poked his nose" into too many areas of the business. He began to understand that this was not only a problem that he was facing, but his behavior was seen as a role model by other managers in the organization who, in turn, were doing the same things at their level of responsibility.

The first change that Bob made was to decide to change. He

then proceeded to redefine his concept of his role. He decided to spend more time on the planning and organizational development aspects of the business and less time in many of the technical areas. He made a decision to give up control over the marketing area by delegating more responsibility than he had in the past. He decided to change his leadership style from one where most of the decisions were benevolent autocratic to one in which there was a great deal more participation. There were always going to be decisions where he would in effect have to decide what was best for the company and then announce it to the organization. However, he decided to get his senior managers more involved in planning not only the overall organizational changes but also in making day-to-day operational decisions.

Another aspect of Bob's behavior which needed to be changed was the way he was dealing with stress. Bob, like most entrepreneurs, was constantly under a great deal of pressure. Periodically he would "explode" or as one of his managers put it, "go nuclear." When Bob went nuclear everybody headed for the hills. If something went wrong, Bob might "nuke' em" in a meeting. This had led, over time, to people's avoiding Bob with "bad news." This, in turn, had created serious problems for the business because Bob was, at times, simply not in touch with information he and other senior managers needed to make effective decisions. As people began to see Bob dealing with conflict but not exploding, they became more open in discussing problems, and even disagreeing with the direction that Bob was proposing. His management team began to be a team in the true sense of the word.

Bob sent another signal to the organization about his willingness to change by participating in the organization's new management development program. As he stated: "If I want people to change, I've got to lead by example as well as by word."

Program Results. For eighteen months, Medco implemented its new program of organizational development. After this period, the organizational growing-pains score decreased from an average score of 32, which put the company in a "red flag" danger zone, to a score of 21, which indicated some problems but nothing of major concern. This improvement occurred despite the fact that the firm continued to grow. Moreover, the firm's profitability increased significantly during this period, as a wide variety of operational inefficiencies were eliminated.

In brief, Medco had made a fundamental transformation. It had gone from a firm about to choke on its own growth to one that was able to absorb growth and operate profitably and effectively. Medco had made the transition from an entrepreneurship to a professionally managed firm, and Bob Mason had made the transition from an entrepreneur to a true CEO.

Some Final Thoughts for the CEO

In this section, I would like to offer some final thoughts to present and potential CEOs of entrepreneurial organizations. These ideas are distilled from my research and consulting work with other CEOs who have gone through the same experience as you, and they may be of use in your own situation.

Understand Your Role. First, it is important to remember that regardless of the number of people working for you, the final responsibility for the development of your organization is not merely yours in the formal sense; it is yours emotionally as well. Your people will look to you as "the Rock." They will expect you to provide support to them, but they will not acknowledge your own needs. There is nothing personal in this. You are simply an object to them. You have all the power, and they perceive you as having the greatest skills. They may even think of you as Superman or Superwoman.

Think Out Loud—Carefully. You will also find that anything you say has enormous impact on the people around you. You may make an offhand comment and find that people have scurried around to do what they thought you sent them a signal to do, even though you were merely thinking out loud. If you do think out loud, you may be viewed as indecisive because people feel that you change your mind too often. Similarly, a hint of a negative comment about one of your employees is likely to echo through the grapevine and reverberate to a much greater extent than you ever intended or believed possible.

Consequently, you may not have anyone to talk to about your own problems in the organization. You may not be able to think out loud. Many CEOs take on confidential advisers for this reason. Doing so is not a sign of weakness or an indication that you can't perform your job; it is simply a functional necessity. You will probably find that you do need to talk things out, and it helps to have someone you trust serving as a sounding board.

Do Not Forget the Organizational Plumbing. One of the key tasks in making the successful transition from an entrepreneurial to a professionally managed firm is not to forget the "organizational plumbing," the unglamorous day-to-day systems that are necessary for your organization to operate efficiently and effectively. The organizational plumbing includes the accounting system, the personnel recruitment and training system, credit and collection, advertising, manufacturing, shipping, and operations planning and control. One CEO of a major company going through a rapid growth spurt ignored the company's organizational plumbing and later found that there was a mess in the firm's accounting system that required more than a year to fix. Bank reconciliations had not been done for more than a year, even though the firm's revenues exceeded $300 million.

View Your Organization as a Fine Machine. You should view your company as a machine. It has a variety of parts, and all these parts must be properly connected if the machine is to function. Your managers are key connecting rods in your organizational machine. A major part of their role is to serve as a mechanism of transmission between different parts of the organization.

View Your People as Assets. Your people are a valuable asset. They are just as costly as your furnishings, computers, or other equipment. If you purchase a Mercedes for more than $40,000, you would undoubtedly be willing to spend the necessary $500 to $1500 per year on maintenance. Many of your employees cost you many thousands of dollars. You are more likely to derive a positive

return on your investment in them if you provide training and
development for your human assets.

Overcome the "Poverty Syndrome."   Even if your business
did not begin in a garage, you may still be bringing a poverty
mentality to the way you operate. One area in which you can no
longer afford the "poverty syndrome" is the area of employees and
advisers. Hire only the best, and expect to compensate accordingly.
Hire fewer people, if necessary, and motivate them to do the work
of more. A few highly motivated, well-trained people can often
outperform a large number of less qualified people, exerting mere
"brute force."

Remember the Omelette.   Every chef knows that if you want
to make an omelette, you must break some eggs. If you are aware
of your firm's growing pains and understand the need for change,
you must be prepared to face the negative side of change as well.
You will not be able to continue to operate exactly as you have in
the past. Both things and people will have to change. Some people
will resist change because it is uncomfortable or because change is
not in their personal interests. Others will be unable to change.
Some people will leave the organization, voluntarily or not. Thus,
my final word of advice for CEOs is "Remember the omelette."

Some Thoughts for the Associates of a CEO

Throughout this chapter we have examined the issues facing
the CEO during organizational changes and transitions. This section is intended to offer some guidance to the associates of a CEO
who is confronting the need for personal, professional, and organizational transitions. Specifically it is intended for senior and middle managers as well as others who may be in the position of
needing to motivate a CEO to make some changes or to assist the
CEO in the change process.

In my experience, not all CEOs are aware of the need to make
the personal and professional changes that have been described
throughout this book. Especially if the CEO has been the founding
entrepreneur of a business he or she may simply feel that since the

company has been able to operate for a very long time without changes, changes may not be needed. This attitude reminds me of an individual who jumped off a thirty-story building in the downtown area of a major metropolitan city. He got down to the fifteenth floor, looked around and said, "No problem yet!" Unfortunately, he was in for a very unpleasant surprise.

The "no problem yet" phenomenon is often found in successful entrepreneurial businesses. A business may have experienced relatively uninterrupted success for a very long period of time, sometimes in excess of twenty years, before a wide variety of problems finally accelerate into a crisis. Others around the CEO may be quicker to see the emergence of difficulties. Yet they may be unable to convince the CEO to pay attention to the warning signs.

The central challenge facing the associates of a CEO who find themselves in this situation is to get that person's attention. In my experience one of the best ways to get the individual's attention is to provide information about the growing pains facing the business, together with the framework which has been described throughout this book so that the CEO can understand the significance of those growing pains. To accomplish this, the organizational growing pains questionnaire presented in Chapter Three can be administered to a number of members in the firm. Ideally, this should be done on a confidential basis so that the CEO cannot ask people to justify their particular scores. The scores on the organizational growing pains questionnaire will indicate the degree of seriousness of the problems facing the organization. In the case of many CEOs, this may be enough to get their attention. In certain other cases, it may be necessary to obtain the assistance of an independent consultant to perform an organizational audit, and provide confidential feedback to the CEO in order to get his or her attention.

Once management has the attention of the CEO and an acknowledgment that there are developmental problems facing the company, the next step is to formulate an organizational development plan. Since one of the problems typically facing entrepreneurial companies in need of transition is the need for the CEO to give up some measure of control, I strongly recommend that the organizational development process be a participative process which includes all of senior management. To assist in this process it is important that all members of the organizational development team share a common framework and perspective as to what needs to be done. For example, most of the firms that I am familiar with who have accomplished this have shared the framework and perspective that has been presented throughout this book so that each individual had a "common language" and common frame of reference for dealing with the organization's problems.

The next step will be a series of organizational development meetings. These meetings can be conducted over a period of time and are designed to focus in a systematic manner on all of the key issues facing the organization at its current stage of growth. By using the framework presented in the pyramid of organizational development, the organization can examine its markets, products, resources, operational systems, management systems, and corporate culture in order to identify the changes which are required to assist the firm in moving to the next stage of growth successfully. My experience in working as an adviser with organizations suggests that the best way to accomplish this is to hold these meetings on a regularly scheduled monthly basis. During this period of time the management team can expect to devote a day to a day and a half per month on the organizational development effort. In some cases depending upon its specific situation, a greater amount of effort will be required.

If the associates of the CEO have been successful in getting that individual's attention prior to the emergence of a crisis, then the organizational development process will have the advantage of being able to proceed in a thoughtful way without undue stress. If a CEO should wait for a crisis to precipitate an organizational development effort, then the management team will be faced with the dilemma of simultaneously trying to run the business on a day-to-day basis while finding time to engage in the total restructuring of the organization's infrastructure.

I would advise the associates of a CEO who are trying to convince that individual of the need for change that a great deal of patience will be required. Most CEOs of entrepreneurial companies have relatively strong opinions about the way their firm should be managed. Accordingly, one behavioral trait may well be a frequent use of the word *no*, regardless of the idea that is brought to their attention. If the CEO's associates are timid, they may feel frequently rebuffed by this initial reaction. The strategy that has to be undertaken here is to present the concepts and ideas to the CEO, let the initial reaction occur, and then re-present the ideas, perhaps even in a different form. Over time, the CEO will begin to become more comfortable with the thought that perhaps the organization requires some change.

It is important to remember that most of the organizations which will require the kinds of transitions we have been talking about in this book are very successful organizations. These organizations are not failures. Instead, their very success has caused them to outgrow their infrastructure and, in turn, created the need for change. Many CEOs will "hear" the criticism of growing pains as somehow being a criticism of what they have accomplished. Nothing could be further from the truth. It is, therefore, important for the associates of the CEO to present the need for change in the context of the organization's success and their desire to help this success continue. Otherwise, the CEO is likely to resist change simply because it is interpreted as a criticism.

Although nothing can guarantee the motivation of any individual to change, I have become increasingly optimistic that an awareness of the need for organizational transitions can be created in entrepreneurial CEOs if it is done in a skillful manner.

Summary

This chapter has examined the personal issues facing the CEO during organizational transitions. It focuses on the changes that the CEO needs to make as his or her organization grows. It also examines the alternatives available to CEOs who face such transitions. The chapter presents some action steps that may be taken by a CEO whose organization is in transition from one stage of growth to the next, and also examines a case study of Bob Mason, CEO of Medco, in making these changes. The chapter also presents some final advice for CEOs of entrepreneurial organizations, as well as the associates of those CEOs, to assist them in making the required transitions.

There is no one way to make a successful transition from an

entrepreneurship to a professionally managed organization. However, the key to making this change is for the entrepreneur to recognize that the company's former mode of operation will no longer be effective.

All change is accompanied by risk, and many of us feel uncomfortable during the process of change. Unfortunately, the need for organizational transitions and their accompanying personal changes is an inevitability.

Annotated References: Key Resources for Further Information

Part One: A Framework for Developing Successful Organizations

Baty, G. B. *Entrepreneurship for the 80's.* Reston, Va.: Reston, 1981. This book provides a catalogue of concerns for new entrepreneurial ventures. It is not a reference tool for problem solving; rather, it provides a quick overview of potential problems and suggests appropriate information sources.

Carland, J. W., and others. "Differentiating Entrepreneurs from Small Business Owners: A Conceptualization." *Academy of Management Review,* 1984, *9,* 354–359. This review of the literature describes the characteristics of both the entrepreneur and the entrepreneurial ventures and proposes two conceptualizations: one for differentiating entrepreneurial ventures from small businesses and another for differentiating entrepreneurs from small business owners/managers. The critical distinctions between the two involve the entrepreneurs' greater innovative abilities and such entrepreneurial traits as goal orientation, internal locus of control, and the need for independence, responsibility, and power. Risk-taking behavior is rejected as a distinguishing characteristic of entrepreneurship. The authors present definitions of small business venture, entrepreneurial venture, small business owner, and entrepreneur.

Dalton, D. R., and Kesner, I. F. "Organizational Growth: Big Is Beautiful." *Journal of Business Strategy,* 1985, *6* (1), 38–48. The observation that bigger is better for the business enterprise is a controversial one. An attempt is made to (1) review growth as an organizational phenomenon and a near-universal goal, (2) discuss the supposed association between size and organizational performance, and (3) develop an argument that growth and absolute size should be legitimate goals of an organization whether or not size can be meaningfully related to performance. While it is clear that the size of the organization is not related to performance—financial and otherwise—there are many nonfinancial advantages that accrue to the larger organization, such as (1) pure clout, (2) larger executive salaries, (3) recognition, and (4) ability to afford specialists in all fields. There is also a downside to bigness, though. For example, larger firms are subject to closer scrutiny, greater social responsibility is expected of them, and problems of coordination and allocation of resources become more complex.

Kennedy, A. "Every Employee an Entrepreneur." *Inc.*, April 1984, 108–117. In this interview, Allen Kennedy, coauthor of *Corporate Cultures*, explains its theory from an anthropological perspective, claiming that each company has its own policy and internal behavior that strongly affect its business practice. He predicts a trend away from major corporations and toward entrepreneurship and decentralization. Kennedy discusses his own entrepreneurial venture.

Kimberly, J. R., Miles, R. H., and Associates. *The Organizational Life Cycle: Issues in the Creation, Transformation, and Decline of Organizations.* San Francisco: Jossey-Bass, 1980. This is a collection of works on the nature of organizational birth, transformations, and decline, and the challenges organizations face at each stage of their life cycle. Many of the articles presented are empirical studies of how organizations or populations of organizations change and how they have or have not solved growth-related problems.

Moltz, R. "Entrepreneurial Managers in Large Organizations." *Business Horizons*, 1984, *27*, 54–58. This article highlights the importance of entrepreneurial managers in complex, well-established organizations. An entrepreneurial manager can constantly monitor and potentially redefine the organization's objectives as well as meet a changing environment full of new opportunities. How a company can adapt to the entrepreneurial personality is discussed, and strategies for producing innovation within a large company are presented.

Peters, T. J., and Waterman, R. H. *In Search of Excellence: Lessons from America's Best Run Companies.* New York: Harper & Row, 1982. Based on a study of large U.S. corporations, this book outlines eight basic practices that the authors argue are found consistently in excellent organizations. The authors selectively illustrate these practices in a variety of companies.

Powell, J. D., and Bimmerle, C. F. "A Model of Entrepreneurship Moving Toward Precision and Complexity." *Journal of Small Business Management,* 1980, *18,* 33-36. This article reviews the entrepreneurial process through the use of a model emphasizing the complexity of the venture initiation decision. The model outlines entrepreneurial descriptors, precipitating factors, and venture-specific factors, as steps leading to the final entrepreneurial venture. Previous, simplistic models are criticized as having limited predictive utility.

Tushman, M. L., and Nadler, D. "Organizing for Innovation." *California Management Review,* 1986, *28,* 74-92. This article provides a practical discussion of the steps management can take to develop an organization that facilitates innovation and creativity.

Tushman, M. L., and Romanelli, E. "Organizational Evolution: A Metamorphosis Model of Convergence and Reorientation." In B. Staw and L. L. Cummings (eds.), *Research in Organizational Behavior.* Vol. 7. Greenwich, Conn.: JAI Press. The authors present a model of organizational change that suggests that firms grow and change in a revolutionary rather than an evolutionary fashion. They also examine the impact of a succession of top-management teams on organizational success.

Part Two: Management Strategies for Each Stage of Organizational Growth

Ditlea, S., and Tanjorra, J. "The Birth of an Industry." *Inc.,* January 1982, 64-70. The development of the completely new personal computer software industry is described through examples of the growth of the seven original companies in the field. Case studies of the companies are presented, starting from their inception and working through to their current problems. These problems involve decisions on how to structure their organizations, what products to make, and how to sell those products.

Drucker, P. F. *Innovation and Entrepreneurship: Practice and Principles.* New York: Harper & Row, 1985. Drucker describes a new, dynamic, entrepreneurial economy in America. Through systematic management of organized activity, innovation is no longer left to chance. The author examines seven sources of innovative opportunities and explains the practice of entrepreneurship.

Gumpert, D. E., and Stevenson, H. E. "The Heart of Entrepreneurship." *Harvard Business Review,* 1985, *63,* 85-94. The steps of the entrepreneurial process are outlined along with the necessary structure and characteristics a firm should have to maintain an entrepreneurial environment. The administrative state of mind, whose focus involves guarding resources and reducing risk, is contrasted with that of the entrepreneur.

Harrigan, K. R. "Managing Declining Businesses." *Journal of Business Strategy,* 1984, *4* (3), 74-78. Corporations often face the problem of preventing strategic business unit (SBU) performance from flagging in a declining business. Success frequently depends on differences in attitude and infrastructure. This study addresses the aspects of managing declining demand that require special attention. There are a number of ways to reap profits within declining SBUs by managing the affected segment intelligently. If analysis in the horizon forecast indicates that the declining business's profitability potential is low because of inferior strategic posture or if the firm lacks the planning infrastructure and managerial skills to obtain high performance levels, then the firm should exit in a nondisruptive and timely fashion. Repositioning the SBU can be an untidy solution, while divestiture constitutes a clean break. Both industry and organizational factors can hinder the firm's progress in dealing with the declining SBU. Appointing a manager who has the skill to deal with the affected SBU is important, and the company must clearly communicate its policy for dealing with the problem.

Howy, F., and Vaught, B. C. "The Rural Entrepreneur: A Study in Frustration." *Journal of Small Business Management,* 1980, *18,* 18-24. This study of 150 rural Texas entrepreneurs lists the major problems faced by these businesses and shows that there are certain types of problems—such as personnel problems, government regulations, and economic conditions—that because of their external nature frustrate managerial attempts to overcome them. Entrepreneurs cite these issues as major problems inhibiting the successful operation of their businesses, yet they do not seek outside help. They do seek outside help for what they perceive as the most significant types of problems over which they feel they have control, such as marketing-related problems. The study concludes that more education is needed in the area of goal expectancy. Goal accomplishment, as opposed to the skills training, should be emphasized so that frustration will be minimized as awareness of control is gained by management.

Kidder, T. *The Soul of a New Machine.* New York: Avon, 1981. This narrative explores the development of a new computer at Data General Corporation. It illustrates the dynamics of new-product development within an entrepreneurial organization.

Mintzberg, H. "Power and Organizational Life Cycles." *Academy of Management Review,* 1984, *9,* 207-224. This article presents a life-cycle model based on organization power and describes how organizations move from one type to the next through the destruction of power. It also discusses the implications of this model for managers and organizations.

"Prophets of the New Age." *Inc.,* April 1984, 81-91. Case studies are presented that depict the beginnings and subsequent successes of six entrepreneurs who have formed highly profitable corporations. Included among the six are Steven Jobs of Apple Computer and Fred Smith of Federal Express.

Richman, T. "Going Their Way." *Inc.,* December 1982, 70-76. This article reviews the achievements of America's fastest-growing private companies, named in the "Inc. 500." Brief case studies of the top twenty-five entrepreneurial companies are presented, and characteristics shared by all the companies are described.

Sculley, J. *Odyssey.* New York: Harper & Row, 1987. The author, CEO of Apple Computer, Inc., describes the problems his firm faced and how they were overcome as Apple Computer made the transition from an entrepreneurship to a professionally managed firm.

Part Three: Mastering the Tools of Professional Management

Strategic Planning

Brandt, S. C. *Strategic Planning in Emerging Companies.* Reading, Mass.: Addison-Wesley, 1981. This book provides the basic perspective necessary for strategic planning and outlines its various dimensions. The author integrates comments on organizational units and corporate culture within the framework of strategic planning.

Eisenhardt, K. M. "Making Fast Strategic Decisions in High Velocity Environments." *Academy of Management Journal*, 1989, *32* (3), 543–576. Eisenhardt examines how executive teams make strategic decisions in the high-velocity environment of the microcomputer industry. She finds that fast decision makers use more, not less, information than do slower decision makers. They tend to develop more rather than fewer alternatives and use a two-tiered advice process. Conflict resolution and integration among strategic decisions and tactical plans are also critical to the pace of decision making. Most importantly, these faster decision processes lead to superior performance in the market.

Glueck, W. F., and Jauch, L. R. *Strategic Management and Business Policy.* New York: McGraw-Hill, 1984. This text walks the reader through the strategic management process, emphasizing the need for continuous planning. Focus is on the environment and internal competitive advantages. Choices and evaluation of strategy provide a firm understanding of the model.

Lorange, P. *Implementation of Strategic Planning.* Englewood Cliffs, N.J.: Prentice-Hall, 1982. Lorange provides an overview of the issues involved in implementing strategic plans. In addition, a considerable amount of discussion relating to planning systems provides a framework for evaluating a strategic planning system.

Porter, M. E. *Competitive Advantage: Creating and Sustaining Superior Performance.* New York: The Free Press, 1985. Porter develops an integrated framework for analyzing strategic problems. He helps the reader frame strategic problems and develop the appropriate analyses.

Steiner, G. A. *Top Management Planning.* New York: Macmillan, 1969. Steiner offers readers an important foundation in an overview of corporate planning terminology and concepts. A topmanagement perspective places the emphasis on overall results for the business while also discussing planning in many of the functional areas.

Tylee, W. J. "Strategic Planning at R. J. Reynolds Industries." *Journal of Business Strategy,* 1985, *6* (2), 22–28. Despite recent criticisms of strategic planning and its effectiveness, R. J. Reynolds Industries, Inc. (RJR) views strategic planning as a necessity for business success. Practical and visionary strategic planning is responsible for the firm's high level of profitability. At RJR, the emphasis of strategic planning is on the development of practical, relevant plans that are feasible to implement and contribute to the evolution of the firm. Planning is integrated into the operations of the firm at all levels of management. Through strategic planning, RJR has established its basic mission as a consumer products firm and identified product/market segments for strategic development. Both internal and external growth strategies are pursued, with internal strategies focused on spurring excellence in existing businesses and external strategies on solidifying market position through acquisitions.

Control Systems

Koenig, J., Flamholtz, D. T., and Flamholtz, E. G. *Organizational Control Systems.* New York: Touche Ross & Co., 1985. A monograph that outlines control and control systems, this book also addresses the role of accounting and organizational control. It considers the organization's need for control and how to evaluate this need.

Kotter, J. P., Schlesinger, L. A., and Sathe, V. *Organization.* Homewood, Ill.: Irwin, 1979. Texts, cases, and readings on the management of organizational design and change attempt to bridge the gap between social science research and practical management concerns. The authors emphasize that through design and control, organizational effort can be coordinated to accomplish objectives. Further, they discuss how to implement changes in control systems.

Newman, W. H. *Constructive Control.* Englewood Cliffs, N.J.: Prentice-Hall, 1975. This book describes how managerial control can obtain positive responses through ties to desired results. The structural and behavioral elements of control are explored along with their applications in a variety of operations. Finally, systems to coordinate controls are reviewed.

Management Development

Cox, C., and Beck, J. *Management Development.* New York: Wiley, 1984. Through a selection of articles, the book deals with many current issues of management development. Issues treated include women in management, managerial obsolescence, and responsibility for training.

Katz, R. L. "Skills of an Effective Administrator." In *People: Managing Your Most Important Asset,* a collection of *Harvard Business Review* classics. Boston: *Harvard Business Review,* 1988. Katz identifies and examines three basic skills—technical, human, and conceptual—that every successful manager must have. He suggests that these skills are required in varying degrees, according to the level of management at which the manager is operating.

London, M. *Developing Managers: A Guide to Motivating and Preparing People for Successful Managerial Careers.* San Francisco: Jossey-Bass, 1985. Throughout this study of career motivation, guidelines and issues are brought to the attention of management. In addition, it reviews types of training programs and their potentials and includes a description of strategies for coping with mid-career crises.

Lopez, F. E., Rockmore, B. W., and Kesselman, G. A. "The Development of an Integrated Career Planning Program at Gulf Power Company." In H. G. Heneman and D. T. Schwab (eds.), *Perspectives on Personnel/Human Resource Management.* Homewood, Ill.: Irwin, 1982. This article provides a model and case study for developing a career matrix for management development.

Whetten, D. A., and Cameron, K. S. *Developing Management Skills*. Glenview, Ill.: Scott, Foresman, 1984. Competence in interpersonal skills is a critical prerequisite for a successful career in management. Strong analytical and quantitative skills are important but not sufficient. This book can best be described as a management practicum that includes a combination of conceptual learning and behavioral practice, since both are necessary for effective skill development.

Leadership

Bennis, W. *On Becoming a Leader*. Reading, Mass.: Addison-Wesley, 1989. Using a series of interviews with people such as director Sydney Pollack, *Ms.* editor Gloria Steinem, and Apple CEO John Sculley, the author examines the nature of leadership. He also describes the differences between managers and leaders and provides suggestions for how organizations can help develop effective leaders.

Likert, R. *The Human Organization*. New York: McGraw-Hill, 1967. A classic, this book deals with leadership styles and their effects on the management and value of human resources. Likert postulates four different styles or systems of management, which parallel the first four styles of management described in Chapter Ten of the present book.

Maccoby, M. *The Leader*. New York: Simon & Schuster, 1981. Maccoby challenges the traditional concepts of management and proposes a picture of the leaders who will eventually prevail in the United States. Through descriptions of six types of leaders, both in business and government, the author documents leadership principles and then goes on to discuss the development of leadership.

Organizational Structure

Galbraith, J. R. *Designing Complex Organizations*. Reading, Mass.: Addison-Wesley, 1973. This book presents an analytical framework for the design of complex organizations. It focuses primarily on organizations with complex lateral relationships and matrix components. The ambiguous levels of authority and responsibility created in this type of organization warrant the special attention Galbraith provides.

Merrell, D. W. "The Impact of Restructuring on Employees." *Journal of Buyouts and Acquisitions*, 1986, *4* (1), 60–62. The impact of restructuring on employees is often overlooked. The organization will suffer during a restructuring as long as workers are uncertain about their future. The lack of information and failure to communicate with employees during this process intensify feelings of uncertainty. This results in insecurity and a loss of motivation as well as a desire to sabotage the restructuring effort. This article describes some steps that management can take to minimize these negative consequences.

Miner, J. B. *Theories of Organizational Structure and Process.* Chicago: Dryden Press, 1982. This book provides a survey of the major bodies of theoretical literature concerning organizational structure and processes. It includes a discussion of Likert's System 4, sociotechnical systems theory, technology, administrative behavior, organizational structure, and a variety of other major theories.

Robey, D. *Designing Organizations.* (2nd ed.) Homewood, Ill.: Irwin, 1986. Robey provides a useful conceptual bridge between the macro and micro views of organizational design. Thus, he balances the literature on organization theory and strategy with that of organizational behavior (which relies on the work group as the level of analysis). In the second edition, he includes extended materials on strategy, life cycles, power, culture, and information processing.

Corporate Culture

Dalziel, M. M., and Schoonover, S. C. *Changing Ways: A Practical Tool for Implementing Change Within Organizations.* New York: AMACOM, 1988. The authors present detailed strategies for managing change in organizations. They focus on three critical questions associated with the change effort: (1) How can I get my organization ready to change? (2) How do I ensure a smooth and successful implementation plan? and (3) What types of people do I need to make the implementation successful?

Deal, T. D., and Kennedy, A. A. *Corporate Cultures: The Rites and Rituals of Corporate Life.* Reading, Mass.: Addison-Wesley, 1982. In this book the authors suggest that long-term corporate success is dependent on company culture. Specifically, the company's culture must match its strategy. Moreover, a person's success within a company can be a direct result of how well he or she interprets that culture. Through numerous examples the book portrays aspects and types of culture.

Kilmann, R. H., Saxton, M. J., Serpa, R., and Associates. *Gaining Control of the Corporate Culture.* San Francisco: Jossey-Bass, 1985. The authors—who include leading scholars, managers, and consultants—present the state of the art on corporate culture today. Emphasizing an integrated approach to culture management, they focus on a number of actual case studies such as AT&T, NCR, Atari, and Levi Strauss to demonstrate their points.

Sathe, V. *Culture and Related Corporate Realities.* Homewood, Ill.: Irwin, 1985. Sathe provides a comprehensive text on the definition, implications, assessment, and management of organizational culture. The book includes text and cases to help understand the relevant problems and issues associated with the management of organizational culture.

Schein, E. H. *Organizational Culture and Leadership: A Dynamic View.* San Francisco: Jossey-Bass, 1985. Schein defines corporate culture and describes how it evolves over time in response to organizational changes. He also provides a framework for identifying and analyzing corporate culture.

Part Four: Role of the Entrepreneur in a Growing and Changing Company

Burgelman, R. A. "A Process Model of Internal Corporate Venturing in the Diversified Major Firm." *Administrative Science Quarterly,* 1983, *28,* 223–244. The focus of this field study is the process through which a diversified major firm transforms R&D activities into a new business through internal corporate venture (ICV). The article specifically examines the relationship between

project development and business development, as well as how
new organizational units developed around new businesses become integrated into the operating system of the corporation.
The components necessary for a successful ICV effort are
presented.

Cameron, K. S., Sutton, R. I., and Whetten, D. A. *Readings in
Organizational Decline.* Cambridge, Mass.: Ballinger, 1988. This
collection of readings presents both the theory of organizational
decline and empirical studies that examine the decline process
from a sociological as well as a psychological or behavioral perspective. It also includes articles that describe the steps organizations can take to prevent or overcome the problems
encountered at this stage of growth.

Grove, A. S. *High Output Management.* New York: Random
House, 1983. The president of Intel—who is also one of its
founders—describes his concept of Intel's management philosophy. The book stresses an output orientation and introduces the
concept of management leverage team management. Finally, an
analogy to sports is drawn to illustrate obtaining peak individual
performances among the business team.

Levinson, H., and Rosenthal, S. *CEO.* New York: Basic Books,
1984. This book outlines the practice of leadership by CEOs.
Through documented interviews at six well-known companies,
the authors provide a glimpse of what leadership involves in a
highly organized setting.

Steiner, G. A. *The New CEO.* New York: Macmillan, 1983. This
book reviews the changing social and political environment of
U.S. business and the extent to which the forces that shape it
compel the CEOs of large firms to get involved in external affairs. These new responsibilities, particularly in the public policy area, require CEOs to have a variety of talents and the ability
to balance constituent interests.

Family Business

Buchalter, G. "A Desert Fox." *Forbes,* Oct. 16, 1989, 244–250.
Twenty-five years ago, Laughlin, Nevada—located across the
Colorado River from Bullhead City, Arizona—did not exist.

There was just an unnamed strip of bleached-out desert with a few inhabitants and a rundown tavern with some slot machines. Today, town founder Donald Laughlin presides over a booming gambling town of 4,000 residents that attracted 2 million tourists in 1988. When Laughlin came to the area in 1964, he saw potential revenues in every direction. He opened Riverside Resort Hotel and Casino in 1966. In 1988, the Riverside Resort had revenues of $79 million and netted some $7 million. Laughlin had become the fourth largest gambling city in the United States. The town's growth attracted established gaming syndicates, such as Circus Circus Enterprises, Sahara, and Harrah's. Laughlin has had problems with Nevada's gaming laws. These include the placement of family members in key positions and the drug problems of family members. Laughlin owns the town's movie theaters and convention hall, its two banks, a local bus company, ferryboats, and other real estate in Nevada and Arizona.

Deveny, K. "How Leonard Lauder Is Making His Mom Proud." *Business Week* (Industrial/Technology edition), Sept. 4, 1989, 68–73. Leonard A. Lauder, son of Estee Lauder, has been the chief executive of Estee Lauder, Inc. (New York) for the past seven years. Long before then, he began transforming the mom-and-pop business into a comestics empire. Thanks to him, the firm now boasts top-notch training programs for employees and strict financial controls. He insists that he has an edge on his publicly held rivals, pointing out that the firm's net margin consistently tops the industry average. The push is on to polish the image of the company's flagship Estee Lauder brand. The company's basic formula is to sell in upscale department stores and avoid new brands that only steal sales from existing ones. The ability to develop consistent brand images gives the firm big advantages over its less focused rivals. Leonard Lauder supports the strategy by assiduously cultivating retailers. In part, that means giving them exclusive promotions. He has built an idiosyncratic corporate culture that marries the paternalism of a small family operation with the marketing power of a big company.

Goldwasser, T. *Family Pride: Profiles of Five of America's Best-Run Family Businesses*, New York: Dodd, Mead, 1986. The best-run family businesses have always upheld the principles of quality, serving the customer, and treating employees with respect. Business critics of American industry are now looking at these companies with renewed interest. This book examines five family businesses that are still run by the founder or members of his family: Hallmark, Noxell Corporation, Marriott Corporation, H&R Block, and S. C. Johnson & Son. Goldwasser examines each company's beginnings, growth, diversification, cultures, and strategies.

Shifting Control of the Firm

Albo, W. P., and Henderson, A. R. *Mergers and Acquisitions of Privately Held Businesses.* (2nd ed.) Toronto: Canadian Institute of Chartered Accountants, 1989. This book provides a comprehensive guide through all steps of corporate acquisitions of small to mid-size firms. It examines a variety of critical factors in significant depth, including acquisition planning, planning of the sale, pricing, tax considerations, negotiation, financing, and postacquisition integration.

Buono, A. F., and Bowditch, J. L. *The Human Side of Mergers and Acquisitions: Managing Collisions Between People, Cultures, and Organizations.* San Francisco: Jossey-Bass, 1989. This book analyzes the human factor in mergers and acquisitions. It describes the uncertainty involved in the change as well as the implications of individual manager's actions throughout the process. The authors examine the hidden costs of combining organizations in addition to the turmoil brought about by shifting values, beliefs, and norms.

Golden, W. J., and Little, A. D. "Leveraged Buyouts as a Corporate Development Tool." *Journal of Business Strategy,* 1985, *6* (1), 7–14. Large-scale divestitures, especially those involving businesses in mature industries, are difficult to implement. The leveraged buyout (LBO) has proved very useful for such divestitures because it gets around the major implementation obstacles. However, it has not been used much by corporations, partly because LBO planning is perceived as too costly and time consuming. The purchase of a firm in an LBO is largely financed by debt.

The technique makes the most sense when a corporation expects to be unable to sell a business unit on a timely basis at a fair price. The most common buyer group in an LBO is the management of the unit to be divested. In the next five years, there will be a dearth of divestiture candidates qualified for LBOs relative to the number of interested buyers and the available supply of financing. Thus, corporations will be in a good position to negotiate favorable terms of sale for qualified candidates using the LBO technique. Areas that must be reviewed prior to beginning LBO negotiation include (1) pension effect, (2) documentation of operating risks, (3) objectives, and (4) valuation technique.

Holmes, R. E. "How to Retain Work Forces When Firms are Acquired." *Mergers and Acquisitions,* March/April, 1988, 61–63. In the sale of a small or mid-sized business, one of the key elements is the workforce. Good communication is critical during the acquisition process, and attempts at secrecy may be detrimental to the internal selling process.

Rosen, C. "The Growing Appeal of the Leveraged ESOP." *Journal of Business Strategy,* January/February, 1989, 16–20. Rosen discusses how more and more companies are linking their leveraged buyouts to an employee stock ownership plan. Three of the primary reasons are (1) to create shareholder loyalty, (2) to encourage superior performance, and (3) to benefit from the significant tax incentives that reward this type of transaction.

Schweiger, D. M., Ivancevich, J. M., and Power, F. R. "Executive Actions for Managing Human Resources Before and After Acquisition." *Academy of Management Executives,* 1987, *1,* 127–138. The authors conducted extensive interviews in target firms, finding (1) a loss of identity, (2) anxiety and a lack of information, (3) an obsession with self-survival, (4) the loss of talent through the loss of co-workers, and (5) family repercussions. Effective managerial actions to soften these consequences included (1) maintaining commitment to employees, (2) being honest, (3) showing a sincere understanding of employee concerns, (4) refusing to permit political behavior, (5) handling terminations and outplacements in a dignified manner, and (6) actively managing the aftermath of the acquisition.

Endnotes

[1] Robert A. Mamis, " 'Face to Face' with Adam Osborne," *Inc.,* 1983, p. 22.

[2] "Starting Small and Growing Big: The Essentials of Managing Growth," *Dividend,* Winter 1983, p. 8.

[3] Steve Coll, "The Rise and Fall of Adam Osborne," *California Magazine,* Nov. 1983, p. 92.

[4] Jill Andresky, "The Mess at Maxicare," *Forbes,* June 27, 1988, p. 64.

[5] John R. Dorfman, "Batting .857." *Forbes,* Oct. 25, 1982, p. 142.

[6] Laura Sachar, "At the Threshold of Pain," *Financial World,* Feb. 24, 1987, p. 20.

[7] Sachar, "At the Threshold of Pain," p. 21.

[8] Gary McWilliams, "Pulling It All Together," *Datamation,* Mar. 1, 1987, p. 24.

[9] See Eric Flamholtz, *Human Resources Accounting: Advances in Concepts, Methods, and Applications,* 2nd ed. (San Francisco: Jossey-Bass, 1985) for discussion of how to quantify these costs.

[10] See, for example, Adam Osborne and John Dvorak, *Hypergrowth: The Rise and Fall of Osborne Computer* (Berkeley, Calif.: IDTHEKKETHAN, 1984).

[11] Michael B. Abelson, "Students Turn Hot Idea Into Successful Firm," *Los Angeles Times,* May 8, 1984, sec. 4.

[12] "Starting Small and Growing Big: The Essentials of Managing Growth," *Dividend,* Winter 1983, p. 8.

[13] Abelson, "Students Turn Hot Idea into Succesful Firm," p. 2.

[14] Robert A. Mamis, " 'Face to Face' with Adam Osborne," *Inc.,* Nov. 1983, p. 21.

[15] Mamis, " 'Face to Face' with Adam Osborne," p. 22.

[16] For Osborne's own account of his company's rise and fall, see Adam Osborne and John Dvorak, *Hypergrowth: The Rise and Fall of Osborne Computer* (Berkeley, Calif.: IDTHEKKETHAN, 1984).

[17]Simon Caulkin, "Compaq's Compact Fortunes," *Management Today,* May 1985, p. 92.

[18]John Merwin, "Anticipating the Evolution," *Forbes,* Nov. 4, 1984, p. 166.

[19]Henry Altman, "A Business Visionary Who Really Delivered," *Nation's Business,* Nov. 1981, p. 54.

[20]Altman, "A Business Visionary Who Really Delivered," p. 55.

[21]"TWST Names Award Winners, Air Freight Industry," *Wall Street Transcript,* Mar. 28, 1988, pp. 88, 863–888, 864, 879.

[22]John Sculley with John A. Byrne, *Odyssey: Pepsi to Apple, a Journey of Adventure, Ideas, and the Future* (New York: Harper & Row, 1987).

[23]Debbi Fields and Alan Furst, *One Smart Cookie: How a Housewife's Chocolate Chip Recipe Turned into a Multimillion-Dollar Business: The Story of Mrs. Fields' Cookies* (New York: Simon & Schuster, 1987).

[24]Brian O'Reilly, "Apple Finally Invades the Office," *Fortune,* Nov. 9, 1987, pp. 52–53+.

[25]Tom Richman, "Mrs. Field's Secret Ingredient," *Inc.,* Oct. 1987, p. 67.

[26]The actual numbers and certain other facts have been changed to preserve the company's confidentiality. I have also exercised editorial license to select those aspects of the history of this company that are most pertinent to the theme of this chapter.

[27]Dean Doust and Resa W. King, "Why Federal Express Has Overnight Anxiety," *Business Week,* Nov. 9, 1987, p. 66.

[28]Alfred P. Sloan, *My Years with General Motors* (New York: McFadden-Bartell, 1964).

[29]The contrast in staff size can be quite significant. For example, under Harold Geneen a corporate staff of approximately 1,200 was required to manage ITT when it had $8 billion in revenues, while William Karnes at Beatrice prided himself on having a corporate staff of fewer than 100 for a company also with $8 billion in revenues.

[30]The "Organizational Value Analysis" approach described in this section was developed by the professional staff of Management Systems Consulting Corporation under the direction of Eric Flamholtz.

[31]"A New Strategy for No. 2 in Computers," *Business Week*, May 2, 1983, pp. 66-70+.

[32]Seneker, Harold. "DEC's Mid-life Crisis," *Forbes*, May 21, 1984, pp. 32-34.

[33]See Flamholtz, *Human Resource Accounting: Advances in Concepts, Methods, and Applications*, 2nd ed.

[34]Dale Feuer, "Training for Fast Times," *Training*, July 1987, p. 26.

[35]For further discussion, see Eric G. Flamholtz and Yvonne Randle, *The Inner Game of Management* (New York: AMACOM, 1987).

[36]This section of the chapter was coauthored by H. Stephen Cranston, former president of Knapp Communications Corporation.

[37]This questionnaire is part of the Management Assessment Program developed by Management Systems Consulting Corporation, under the direction of Eric G. Flamholtz.

[38]For a discussion of the statistical effects of this program on the participants, see H. S. Cranston and E. G. Flamholtz, "The Role of Management Development in Making the Transition from Entrepreneurship to a Professionally Managed Firm," *Journal of Management Development*, 1986, 5, 38-51.

[39]Tom Richman, "Mrs. Fields' Secret Ingredient," *Inc.*, October, 1987, 65-72.

[40]It should be noted that there are other aspects of a firm's overall control system in addition to the core control system. These will be discussed briefly in Chapter Twelve.

[41]M. McLuhan, *Understanding Media: The Extensions of Man* (New York: McGraw-Hill, 1964).

[42]S. Kerr, "On the Folly of Rewarding A, While Hoping for B," *Academy of Management Journal*, 1975, *18*, 769-783.

[43]See, for example, the discussion of the difference management style can make in successful organizations in T. H. Peters and R. H. Waterman, *In Search of Excellence* (New York: Harper & Row, 1982).

[44]For discussions of a contingency theory see, for example, F. E. Fiedler, *A Theory of Leadership Effectiveness* (New York: McGraw-Hill, 1967). For a discussion of situational leadership, see P. Hersey and K. H. Blanchard, *Managing Organizational Behavior* (Englewood Cliffs, N.J.: Prentice-Hall, 1977), 159-186.

[45]The late Rensis Likert developed a classic typology of four basic

leadership styles (autocratic, benevolent autocratic, consultative, and participative) in his book *New Patterns of Management* (New York: McGraw-Hill, 1961), 222–236. This typology was subsequently retitled as "Systems I–IV" in Likert's *Human Organization: Its Management and Value* (New York: McGraw-Hill, 1967), 3–12. R. Tannenbaum and W. Schmidt independently developed the concept of a continuum of leadership styles in their article "How to Choose a Leadership Pattern," *Harvard Business Review*, Mar.-Apr. 1958, p. 36. The conceptualization in this chapter is related to both of these prior efforts. The labels for our first four styles of leadership are identical with Likert's, but the definition of behavior we use for each style differs to some degree. The other two styles we list, consensus and laissez-faire, represent somewhat different patterns from those previously conceptualized by others.

[46]This conceptualization is a slight modification of the four-factor theory of leadership proposed by D. Bowers and S. Seashore in "Predicting Organizational Effectiveness with a Four-Factor Theory of Leadership," *Administrative Science Quarterly*, 1966, *11*, 238–263. The four factors identified by Bowers and Seashore are goal emphasis, work facilitation, interaction facilitation, and support. In this chapter we have subdivided the factor originally labeled "support" into two dimensions: (1) supportive behavior and (2) personnel development.

[47]For further information about this case, see "The Erik Brandin Case," a Management Systems Video Production, Management Systems Consulting Corporation, 1989.

[48]Stages V to VII will be discussed in Chapter Thirteen.

[49]James Chposky and Ted Leonsis, *Blue Magic* (New York: Facts on File Publications, 1988).

[50]Chposky and Leonsis, *Blue Magic*.

[51]See David Halberstam, *The Reckoning* (New York: Morrow, 1986).

[52]Frank Rose, *West of Eden* (New York: Viking, 1989), p. 61.

[53]K. S. Cameron, R. Sutton, and D. Whetton (eds.). *Readings in Organizational Decline* (New York: Ballinger, 1988).

[54]Paul Kennedy, *The Rise and Fall of the Great Powers* (New York: Random House, 1987).

[55]For a discussion of Intrapreneurship, see Eric G. Flamholtz and Yvonne Randle, *How to Make Entrepreneurship Work in Established Companies,* Management Systems Working Paper (Los Angeles: Management Systems Consulting Corporation, May 1987).

[56]For a discussion of Harold Geneen's management style, see Robert J. Schoenberg, *Geneen* (New York: Norton, 1985).

[57]Brian Dumaina, "What the Leaders of Tomorrow See," *Fortune,* July 3, 1989, p. 58.

[58]See, for example, Joel Dreyfuss, "Reinventing IBM," *Fortune,* Aug. 14, 1989, pp. 30–29.--PAGE ORDER???

[59]This management development program was provided by the author's firm—Management Systems Consulting Corporation—for Navistar, based on concepts and approaches described in Chapter Nine.

[60]See Flamholtz and Randle, *The Inner Game of Management.*

Index

A

Accountability, 293–294
Accounting. *See* Budgets and accounting system
Action plans, 168, 176–178
Ad hoc planning, 44
Aerotek, 327
Altman, B., 340
Altschuler, Melvoin, and Glasser, 225
Apollo Travel, 166
Apple Computer, 14, 19, 40–41, 51, 55, 58, 59–60, 62, 75, 78, 79, 113–114, 115, 117, 158–159, 179, 205, 220, 266, 267, 292, 293, 296, 298, 300–301, 303–305, 310, 320, 323, 329, 331, 347
Architectural Digest, 20, 228
Arrow Electronics, 84
Ashton-Tate, 20, 37, 75–76, 83, 323–324, 332
Atari, 157, 331
Audit, 49, 164, 353–355, 361–362
Autocratic leadership style, 265, 266
Autonomy, potential for, 270–271, 272

B

Ballard, Bill, 52
Bank of America, 328, 335
Beatrice Company, 29, 190, 334
Behavior: dysfunctional, 252–253; supportive, 277
Behavioral reliability, 252
Benesch, Fritzi, 179

Benevolent autocratic leadership style, 265, 266, 283
Boeing, 46
Bon Appetit, 228
Bonwit Teller, 340
Booth, Mark, 187
Bowman, Charlie, 280–281
Brandin, Bob, 278
Brandin, Erik, 278–280
Brandin, Evie, 278
Bristol Meyers, 276
Brown, Dolores, 92
Brown, Harvey, 92
Budgets and accounting system: in entrepreneurial vs. professionally managed firm, 45, 46; in professionalization stage of organizational growth, 94–95, 106, 108–109; in strategic planning process, 168
Bullock's, 157
Bureaucracy, 298
Bushnell, Nolan, 331
Business plan, 164–168, 178

C

Campeau, Robert, 326
Campeau Corporation, 326
Canion, Rod, 87, 268
Cascade effect, 232–233
CEO. *See* Chief executive officer
Chandler, Colby, 337
Change: planned, 304–305; resistance to, 104–105; uncontrolled, 303–304

Chief executive officer (CEO), 343–374; alternatives for, 347–348; associates of, 370–373; changes in, 366–367; leadership style of, 264; and management development, 216, 226; management of organizational transitions by, 355–368; as organizational glue, 348–349; in organizational hierarchy, 196; organizational issues for, 349–355; personal issues for, 343–349; understanding role of, 368

Chief operating officer (COO), 196, 216, 226, 264

Chrysler Corporation, 264, 285, 328, 330, 335

Claiborne, Liz, Inc., 78, 79

Coll, Steve, 38–39

Commodore International, 14, 62, 157, 266, 347

Communication: in consolidation stage of organizational growth, 140–141; lack of, 130–131; in professionalization stage of organizational growth, 96, 107, 110; top-down, 125–126

Compaq Computer, 9, 77, 78, 268, 293; comparison with Osborne Computer, 86–89; professionalization of, 114, 115, 117

Compensation: and control systems, 256–257; in professionalization stage of organizational growth, 97, 107, 111

Competition analysis, 163

Competitive advantage, 158–159

Conductron, 14, 347

Conflict, confronting, 142

Consensus leadership style, 265, 268–269, 283

Consolidation stage of organizational growth, 33, 41–43, 119–145; case study of, 121–143; and control systems, 261; issues in, 120; leadership in, 287–288; and management development, 236–237; management systems in, 350; organizational characteristics in, 351; and organizational culture,

316; and organizational structure, 210; strategic planning in, 182

Consultants, in strategic planning process, 182

Consultative leadership style, 265, 266–267, 283

Contingency theory, 265

Control, 240–262; of chief executive officer, 345–346; in entrepreneurial vs. professionally managed firm, 45; nature of, 241–242; personal, 345–346; postperformance, 247; preperformance, 247; span of, 194–195

Control systems: behavioral reliability of, 252; case studies of, 253–259, 364; in consolidation stage of organizational growth, 261; design of, 244–253; development of, 254–257; evaluating effectiveness of, 251–252; in expansion stage of organizational growth, 260; goals of, 247, 257; illustration of, 249–251; measurement and reporting in, 247–248, 257–258; in new venture stage of organizational growth, 259; objectives of, 245–247, 257; parts of, 245; performance evaluation and rewards in, 248–249, 256, 258–259; in professionalization stage of organizational growth, 95, 106–107, 109, 115–116, 260–261; tasks of, 242–244

Coordination, lack of, 56–57

Copyspot, 214, 278–280

Corbin, Jim, 213

Core management skills, 220

Cost-effectiveness analysis, 201–202

Cranston, H. Steven, 228, 232, 299

Cray, Seymour, 157, 205, 329, 332

Cray Research, 157, 205, 329, 332

Crisis management teams, 340

Cuisinarts, Inc., 325–326

Culture. See Organizational culture

Curtis, Cyrus, 161

Curtis Publishing Company, 161–162

Customer-client orientation, 290–291

Customer service, 29, 294–295
Custom Printing Corporation, 1–10, 20, 55, 56, 57, 58, 65, 242–243, 248
Cypress Semiconductor, 335

D

Daggs, Bob, 300
Daniel, Bob, 268
Data General, 164, 310
David's Cookies, 76, 79
Daylin Corporation, 340
dBASE, 20, 75, 323–324
DEC. See Digital Equipment Corporation
Decision making: in consolidation stage of organizational growth, 124–126, 138–139; in professionalization stage of organizational growth, 96, 107, 110; time available for, 272
Decline and revitalization, 323, 328–331, 334–341
De La Vega, Jerry, 74
Delta Airlines, 268
Design: criteria for, 194–197; organization, 8, 131–133, 194–197; of organizational control systems, 244–253
Design Corporation, 202–204
Developmental tasks, 18–26; acquiring resources, 22–23, 28, 84–85, 88; developing management systems, 24–25, 28–29, 90–118; developing operational systems, 23–24, 28, 85–86, 88; developing products and services, 21–22, 87–88; identifying and defining market niche, 18–21, 27–28, 87; managing corporate culture, 25–26, 29–30. See also Organizational development
Devon Industries, 162, 163
Digital Equipment Corporation (DEC), 56–57, 158, 164, 206–207
Disneyland, 298
Diversification, 323–326, 331–333
Divisional organizational structure, 189–192

Domino's Pizza, 21, 26, 36–37, 77–78, 115, 179, 213–214, 215, 298, 302
"Do your own thing" philosophy, 129–131, 142–143
Dreyer's, 19–20
Dysfunctional behavior, 252–253

E

Economy, national, 103–104
Electronic Data Systems (EDS), 331
Employees: as assets, 369–370; compensation of, 97, 107, 111, 256–257; confusion about roles and responsibilities of, 56–57, 59, 356, 357; insecurity of, 6, 61–62, 360; orientation of, 291–293; overloading, 4, 54–55, 357; recruitment of, 96–97, 107, 110; turnover of, 6, 54, 57, 61, 62, 102–103
Entrepreneurial management, vs. professional management, 44–47, 306
Entrepreneurial manager, 332–333, 339
Entrepreneurs: characteristics of, 344; vs. entrepreneurial managers, 332–333
Entrepreneurship: challenges of, 11–15; and leadership styles, 269; performance of key leadership tasks in, 278; transition to professionally managed firm, 7–10, 15–16, 97–105
Entry level of organizational hierarchy, 195, 216
Environmental scan, 159–163
Estridge, Philip D. ("Don"), 267, 269, 292, 299
Evaluation: of control systems, 251–252; criteria for, 194–197; organizational, 49, 164, 194–197, 353–355, 361–362. See also Performance appraisal
Excellence, emphasis on, 126, 139–140
Expansion stage of organizational growth, 33, 37–39, 79–89; comparison with new venture stage,

86-89; and control systems, 260; keys to success of, 84-86; leadership in, 286-287; and management development, 235; management systems in, 350; organizational characteristics in, 351; organizational culture in, 314-315; and organizational structure, 208; and Osborne syndrome, 81-82, 84; problems of, 81-84; strategic planning in, 179-181

F

Falsification, 253
Family atmosphere, 122-124, 137-138
Famous Amos Cookies, 37
Federal Express, 37, 76, 85, 112-113, 115, 116, 117, 161-162
Feedback, 248
Ferris, Richard, 166, 274-275, 284
Fields, Debbi, 76, 79, 114, 120, 243, 244
Fields, Randy, 120, 243
Financial goals, 175
Financial objectives, 174
Flamholtz, Eric G., 222
Follow-up, 60-61, 359
Ford Motor Company, 267
Frazer, George, 280-281
Functional organizational structure, 186-189
Future business situation, assessment of, 171-174

G

Geneen, Harold, 190, 266, 334
General Motors, 157, 189, 327, 328, 331, 335
General Products Corporation, 215
General Ribbon, 300
Goal displacement, 252
Goals: and control, 241-242, 247, 257; and operational leadership, 276; organizational, 168, 174, 175-176
Gray, Harry, 268
Gribi, John, 88

Growth. *See* Organizational growth
Growth rates, 67-70

H

Haagen-Dazs, 20
Harrison, Catherine Forest, 135-137, 142, 145
Harrison, Ronald, 121-132, 134-136, 145
Helbling, Bob, 276
Helix, Inc., 280-282
Hertz, 166, 284
Hewlett-Packard, 26, 212, 301
Hierarchy, organizational, 195-196, 215-216
Hilton International, 166, 284
Hitek Manufacturing Company, 206
Holistic perspective, 202
Hooker, L. J., Corporation, 340
Hot Rock, Inc., 74, 80-81, 179
Hughes Aircraft, 157, 327, 331
Humana Hospitals, 51-52, 162
Human relations school, 274
Hypergrowth, 68-70

I

Iacocca, Lee, 47, 264, 285, 330
IBM. *See* International Business Machines Corporation
Industrial Abrasives, Inc., 165-166
Industry, and growing pains, 65-67
Infotec, 269
Inner Game of Management (Flamholtz and Randle), 222
Innovation, in entrepreneurial vs. professionally managed firm, 45, 46
Instrumental objectives, 245-247
Integration, 323, 326-328, 333-334
International Business Machines Corporation (IBM), 26, 78, 157-159, 179, 212, 213, 215, 266, 267, 269, 327, 329, 332; corporate culture at, 291-294, 299, 309-310, 313; pyramid of organizational development at, 27-30
International Harvester, 328, 335, 340-341

Intrapreneur, 332-333
Ishag, David, 74
ITT, 190, 266, 334

J

Jacoby & Meyers, 156
Jobs, Steven, 14, 58, 75, 114, 205, 304, 320, 331, 332, 347

K

Kapor, Mitchell, 76, 78, 331
Kawasaki Motors, 245
KCC. *See* Knapp Communications Corporation
Key result areas, 167, 174, 196-197
Kierulff Electronics, 84
Kinder Care Day Care Centers, 37
KMS Industries, 14, 347
Knapp, C. T., 227-228
Knapp, Cleon ("Bud"), 20, 232
Knapp Communications Corporation (KCC), 20, 212, 299, 301-302, 313-314; background of, 228; growing pains of, 228-230; management development at, 227-234, 237, 238-239
Kodak, 189, 335, 337
Korman, Roger, 68
Kuppin, Larry, 68

L

Ladies Home Journal, 161
Laissez-faire leadership style, 265, 269
Language, and corporate culture, 298-299
Lashley, Hal, 75
Leadership, 263-288; case studies of, 278-285; in consolidation stage of organizational growth, 287-288; defined, 264; in entrepreneurial vs. professionally managed firm, 45, 46-47; in expansion stage of organizational growth, 286-287; and management development, 215; nature of, 264; in new venture stage of organizational growth, 286; operational, 132, 264, 275-278; in professionalization stage of organizational growth, 96, 107, 110, 287; situational, 265; strategic, 131, 264, 274-275; tasks of, 274-278; theories of, 273-274
Leadership styles, 265-273; autocratic, 265, 266; benevolent autocratic, 265, 266, 283; consensus, 265, 268-269, 283; consultative, 265, 266-267, 283; in entrepreneurial organizations, 269; factors influencing choice of, 270-273; laissez-faire, 265, 269; participative, 265, 267-268, 283; of peers and associates, 271-272; of supervisors, 271
Levi Strauss, 328
Liederman, David, 76, 79
Likert, Rensis, 276
Lion's Gate Studios, 68
Long-term planning, 4-6
Lotus Development Corporation, 76, 331
Lundy, Todd, 225

M

McBride, Joe, 1-2, 4, 6, 8, 9-10, 65
McDonnell Douglas, 14, 347
McLuhan, Marshall, 248
McNamara, Robert, 267
Macy's, 157
Management: entrepreneurial, 332-333; entrepreneurial vs. professional, 44-47; informal, 127-128; middle, 196, 216, 226; problems with, 5, 57-59, 127-131, 358-359; and rewards, 215; roles and responsibilities of, 94, 106, 108; senior, 196, 216, 226; top-down, 95, 106, 109, 125-126. *See also* Chief executive officer (CEO)
Management development, 212-239; case studies of, 227-234, 364-365; and changes in individual's psychology, 222-225, 226; and

changes in role concept, 217–219, 226; and changes in skills, 219–222, 226; in consolidation stage of organizational growth, 134–135, 236–237; critical dimensions of, 216–227; at different organizational levels, 215–216; in entrepreneurial vs. professionally managed firm, 45, 46; in expansion stage of organizational growth, 83, 325; functions of, 214–215; investment in, 237–238; nature of, 212–214; in new venture stage of organizational growth, 234–235; and operational leadership, 277–278; in professionalization stage of organizational growth, 99–101, 116, 235–236; program for, 9, 25; pyramid of, 220–222

Management review, 169

Management systems: chart of, 150; developing, 24–25, 28–29, 90–118; at different stages of growth, 350; revitalized, 339–340

Managerial psychology, 222–225

Manager-in-training (MIT) program, 213–214

Market, revitalized, 336–337

Market analysis, 159–163

Market need, defining, 78–79

Market niche, identifying and defining, 18–21, 27–28, 87, 157–158

Market segment, 157–158

Marvel Publications, 68

Mason, Bob, 355–361, 364–367

Matrix organizational structure, 192–194

Mature markets, 336–337

Maxicare, 41, 51, 55, 62, 68, 84, 86, 326, 327, 330

Measurement: in control systems, 247–248, 257–258; of growing pains, 62–67

Measurementship, 253

Mecca, Loraine, 14, 329–330

Medco Enterprises, 197, 355–368

Medical Engineering Corporation, 214

Meetings, 6, 59–60, 359–360, 372

Melvin Simon & Associates, 214, 275

Metro Realty, 55, 56, 59, 60, 61, 90, 91, 120, 243; growing pains at, 92–97; organizational development program of, 98–105; professionalization stage of growth at, 92–112, 115–116, 117; strategic planning at, 153, 169–178; transition to professionally managed firm, 97–105

Micro D, 14, 330

Middle-management level of organizational hierarchy, 196, 216, 226

Mileage Plus, 166, 284

Mission statement, 165–167, 174

Mitchell, Bob, 92

Monaghan, Thomas S., 36–37, 77–78, 79, 179, 302

Mortenson, John, 282, 283

Motorola, 21, 212, 215, 267

MPI, 166, 284

Mrs. Fields' Cookies, 76, 79, 85, 114, 116, 117, 120, 243–244

N

National Lead, 328

Navistar, 340–341

NCR, 189

Need, market, 78–79

Neiman-Marcus, 157

Neoscientific management, 273

New venture stage of organizational growth, 33, 35–37, 73–79; comparison with expansion stage, 86–89; and control systems, 259; issues of, 73–78; keys to success of, 78–79; leadership in, 286; and management development, 234–235; management systems in, 350; organizational characteristics in, 351; organizational culture in, 314; and organizational structure, 208; strategic planning in, 179

New World Entertainment (NWE), 68–70

NeXt, 347

Niche, identifying and defining, 18–21, 27–28, 87, 157–158

Niebla, Fernando, 269

Nominal corporate culture, 296–297

"No problem yet!" phenomenon, 371

Nordstrom, 295

NWE (New World Entertainment), 68–70

O

Objectives: and control systems, 245–247, 257; instrumental, 245–247; organizational, 168, 174–175; ultimate, 245–247

Olsen, Kenneth H., 207

O'Melveny & Meyers, 156

Operational leadership, 132, 264, 275–278

Operational management skills, 220

Operational systems: developing, 23–24, 28, 85–86, 88, 362–363; revitalized, 338–339

Organization: in entrepreneurial vs. professionally managed firm, 44, 45; layers of, 195–196; in professionalization stage of organizational growth, 106–107

Organizational assessment, 164

Organizational characteristics, at each stage of growth, 351

Organizational cost-effectiveness analysis, 201–202

Organizational culture: analysis of, 306–309; appropriate, identification of, 309–310; case studies of, 122–143, 365–366; changes in, 302–305; in consolidation stage of organizational growth, 42, 119–145, 316; in entrepreneurial vs. professionally managed firm, 45, 47, 305–306; in expansion stage of organizational growth, 314–315; and family atmosphere, 122–124, 137–138; implementing changes in, 137–143; and language, 298–299; and leadership styles, 272–273, 275; maintenance of, 310–

314; and management development, 215; management of, 25–26, 29–30, 305–314; manifestations of, 298–302; nature of, 290–295; in new venture stage of organizational growth, 314; and organizational success, 295–296; problems with, 122–131; in professionalization stage of organizational growth, 93–94, 105, 106, 108, 315–316; real vs. nominal, 296–297; redefining, 131–137; revitalized, 340; and rewards, 301–302; and rituals, 299–301; and symbols, 299; transformation of, 310–314

Organizational design, 8, 131–133

Organizational development, 17–31; and chief executive officer, 349–355; organizational growth vs., 47–48; plan for, 49–51, 355, 362; pyramid of, 19, 26–30; steps in process of, 353–355; and strategic leadership, 275; tasks in, 18–26

Organizational development skills, 222

Organizational evaluation, 49, 164, 194–197, 353–355, 361–362

Organizational growing pains, 12, 53–70; case studies of, 92–97, 356–361; causes of, 48; and growth rates, 67–70; and infrastructure, 67–70; measuring, 62–67; most common, 53–62; questionnaire on, 62–67

Organizational growth, 32–52; advanced stages of, 321–342; organizational development vs., 47–48; stages of, 32–43. *See also* Consolidation stage; Expansion stage; New venture stage; Professionalization stage

Organizational hierarchy, 195–196, 215–216

Organizational management skills, 220

Organizational role analysis, 200–201

Organizational structure, 184–211;

alternative forms of, 186–194; analysis of, 198–202; case studies of, 202–207; in consolidation stage of organizational growth, 210; criteria for design and evaluation of, 194–197; divisional, 189–192; in expansion stage of organizational growth, 208; functional, 186–189; matrix, 192–194; nature of, 185–186; in new venture stage of organizational growth, 208; in professionalization stage of organizational growth, 208–210

Organization size, and growing pains, 65, 66

Osborne, Adam, 38, 75, 78, 81–82, 332

Osborne Computer, 38–39, 48, 62, 68, 75, 78, 331; comparison with Compaq Computer, 86–88; problems at, 81–82, 86–88

Osborne syndrome, 81–82, 84

P

Page, Stewart, 132–136, 141, 145

Pan Am, 335

Participative leadership style, 265, 267–268, 283

People Express, 68, 85, 86, 295, 331

Pepsico, 220, 267, 293, 347

Performance appraisal: and control systems, 248–249, 256; in professionalization stage of organizational growth, 95–96, 107, 109

Perot, H. Ross, 331, 332

Perry, Doug, 103

Peter Principle, 46, 238

Pic 'N' Save, 20, 75, 157

Planning: action plan, 168, 176–178; ad hoc, 44; business plan, 164–168, 178; in entrepreneurial vs. professionally managed firm, 44, 45; follow-up in, 60–61; lack of, 4–5; long-range, 4–6; of organizational development, 49–51, 355; in professionalization stage of organizational growth, 94, 106, 108. See also Strategic planning

Plastic Molding Corporation, 187–189

"Playing it by ear," 127–128, 140–141

Postperformance control, 247

Poverty syndrome, 370

Preperformance control, 247

Process function, 248

Productization, 21–22

Products: ability to provide, 79; developing, 21–22, 79, 87–88; revitalized, 337

Professionalization stage of organizational growth, 33, 40–41, 90–118; case study of, 92–112; and control systems, 260–261; issues in, 91; keys to success of, 114–116; leadership in, 287; and management development, 235–236; management systems in, 350; organizational characteristics in, 351; and organizational culture, 315–316; and organizational structure, 208–210; other examples of, 112–114; strategic planning in, 181–182

Professional management: entrepreneurial management vs., 44–47, 306; transition from entrepreneurship to, 7–10, 15–16, 97–105

Profit: in entrepreneurial vs. professionally managed firm, 44, 45; goals for, 175; objectives for, 174

Profit orientation, vs. sales orientation, 3–4, 62, 360–361

Psychology, managerial, 222–225, 226

Putz, Rodney, 275

Pyramid: of management development, 220–222; of organizational development, 19, 26–30

Q

Questionnaire, on organizational growing pains, 62–67

R

Randle, Yvonne, 222
Reagan, Ronald, 269
Real corporate culture, 296-297
Recruiting, 96-97, 107, 110
Reporting, 248
Republic Corporation, 340
Resources: acquiring, 22-23, 28, 84-85, 88, 362-363; revitalized, 337-338
Revitalization: case study of, 340-341; challenge of, 336-341; and decline, 323, 328-331; management systems, 339-340; markets, 336-337; operational systems, 338-339; organizational culture, 340; products, 337; resources, 337-338
Rewards: and control systems, 248-249, 258-259; and corporate culture, 301-302; and management development, 215
Rituals, 299-301
Robbin, David, 224
Rodgers, T. J., 335
Roles and responsibilities: changes in concept of, 217-219, 226; of chief executive officer, 368; confusion about, 56-57, 59, 356, 357; defined, 185; and management development, 217-219, 226; organizational role analysis, 200-201; and organizational structure, 185-186; in professionalization stage of organizational growth, 94, 106, 108
Rollwaggen, John, 205
Ryan, Mary, 136

S

Safeway stores, 311, 327
Saks Fifth Avenue, 157
Sales orientation, vs. profit orientation, 3-4, 62, 360-361
Sandel, Dan, 163
Saturday Evening Post, 161
Scheib, Earl, 35-36
Scissors effect, 337

"Scorched earth" policy, 338
Scott, Mike, 303
Sculley, John, 58, 59-60, 113-114, 205, 267, 293, 303, 304, 310, 320, 347
Selective attention to organizational goals, 252
Senior-management level of organizational hierarchy, 196, 216, 226
Separate islands syndrome, 130, 133
Services: ability to provide, 79; developing, 21-22, 79
Short-term crises, 4-5, 55-56, 357-358
Siegel, K. M., 14
Sigoloff, Sanford, 340
Simon Institute, 214, 275
Situational leadership, 265
Skills: core management, 220; and management development, 219-222, 226; operational management, 220; organizational development, 222; organizational management, 220; transition management skills, 222
Sloan, Alfred P., 189
Sloan, Harry, 68
Smith, Frederick W., 76, 79, 112, 113, 116
Smoothing, 253
Span of control, 194-195
Stories, and corporate culture, 307-309
Stowers, Jim, Jr., 268-269
Strategic leadership, 131, 264, 274-275
Strategic planning: case studies of, 169-178, 363-364; in consolidation stage of organizational growth, 133-134, 139, 182; in expansion stage of organizational growth, 179-181; implementing, 363-364; issues in, 154-159; nature of, 154; in new venture stage of organizational growth, 179; ongoing functions of, 178; and organizational development program, 8-9; in professionalization stage of organizational growth,

115, 181–182; and transition between growth stages, 49–50
Strategic planning departments, 182
Strategic planning process, 159–169; budgeting, 168; business plan, 164–168, 178; environmental scan, 159–163; management review, 169; organizational assessment, 164
Strategic positioning, 155–157
Strategic vision, 274–275
Suboptimization, 252
Sun Microsystems, 292
Superior Alarm Systems, 253–259
Supervisors, leadership style of, 271
Supervisory level of organizational hierarchy, 195–196, 216, 226
Supportive behavior, 277
Surgitek, 214, 276
Symbols, 299

T

Tape streaming, 21
Tate, George, 75
Team leadership style, 265, 268–269, 283
Technology Systems Corporation, 282–284
Teledyne, 190, 327, 334
Televideo computer, 28
Tempo Products Unlimited (TPU), 55, 56, 57, 58, 59, 60, 61–62, 242, 243, 264, 303; background of, 121; consolidation stage of organizational growth at, 121–145; culture management at, 135–137; implementing changes in organizational culture at, 137–143; management development at, 134–135; organizational design at, 131–133; problems of organizational culture at, 122–131; redefining organizational culture at, 131–137; strategic planning at, 133–134
Texas Instruments, 295
Top-down management, 95, 106, 109, 125–126

TPU. *See* Tempo Products Unlimited
Training and development, 97, 107, 110–111
Trait theory of leadership, 273
Tramiel, Jack, 14, 62, 266, 347
Transition management skills, 222
Transitions: case study of, 355–368; from entrepreneurship to professionally managed firm, 7–10, 15–16, 97–105; between growth stages, 49–52, 331–336; need for, 361–368
Trend analysis, 163–164
Twentieth Century Investors, 214, 268–269

U

UAL Corporation, 166–167, 274–275, 284
Ultimate objectives, 245–247
United Airlines, 284
U.S. Steel, 22, 328
United Technologies Corporation (UTC), 268

V

Value added concept, 34–35
Victor Technologies, 331
Vons Grocery Store, 311, 327

W

Walker, Ken, 282–283
Wang, An, 57, 311–312
Wang, Frederick, 57
Wang Laboratories, 57, 62, 164, 311–312
Watson, Thomas, 29, 266, 329, 332
Westec Security, 214
Westin Hotels, 166, 284
Whittaker Corporation, 327
Wickes Corporation, 335
Wigley, Michael, 74, 80
Windham Hill Productions, 214
Wooden, John, 180
Workaholics, 344
Wozniak, Steven, 75, 301, 320, 331

X

Xerox Corporation, 22

Z

Zimmerman, William, 75